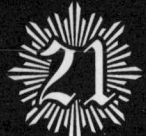

THE SEVEN DEADLY SINS

nakaba suzuki presents

21

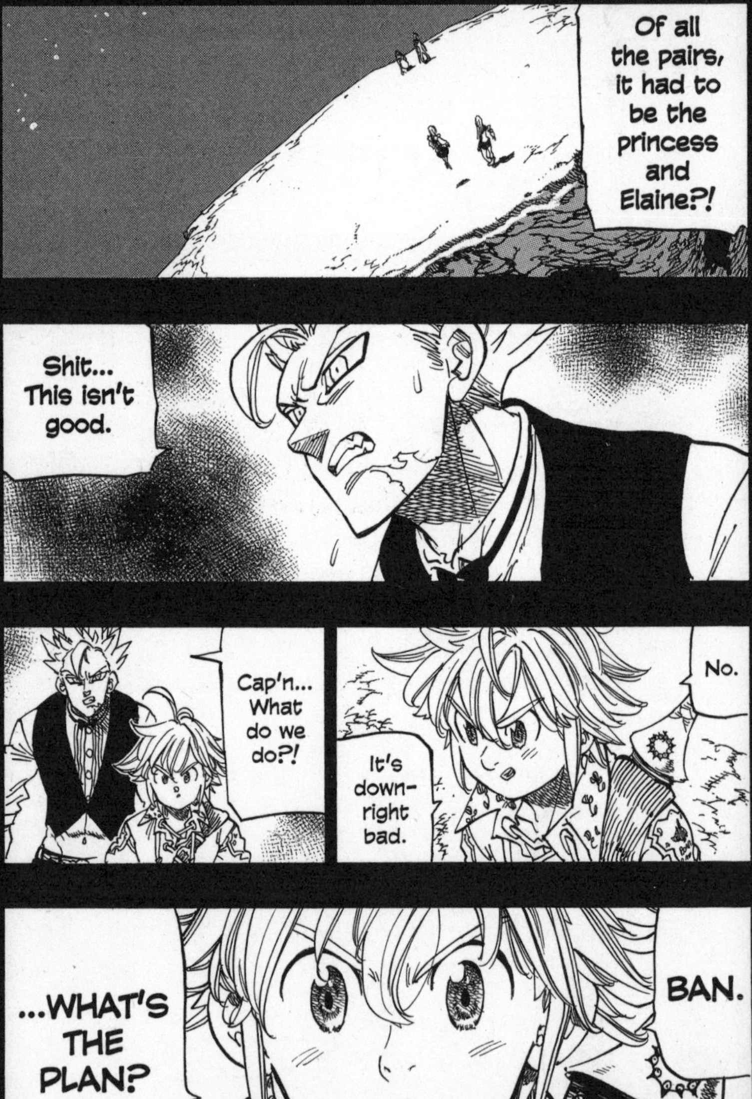
Of all the pairs, it had to be the princess and Elaine?!
Shit... This isn't good.
No.
It's downright bad.
Cap'n... What do we do?!
BAN.
...WHAT'S THE PLAN?

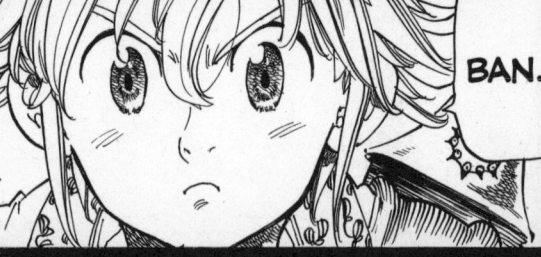

CONTENTS

BOAR HAT
The Seven Deadly Sins

Chapter 163 - The Princess & The Saint

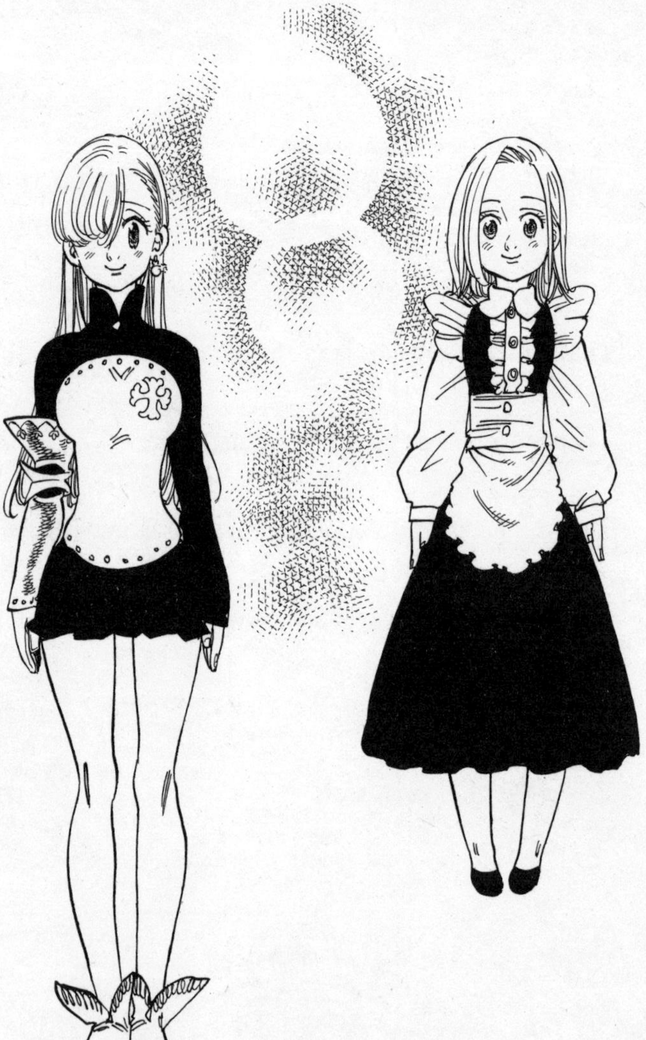

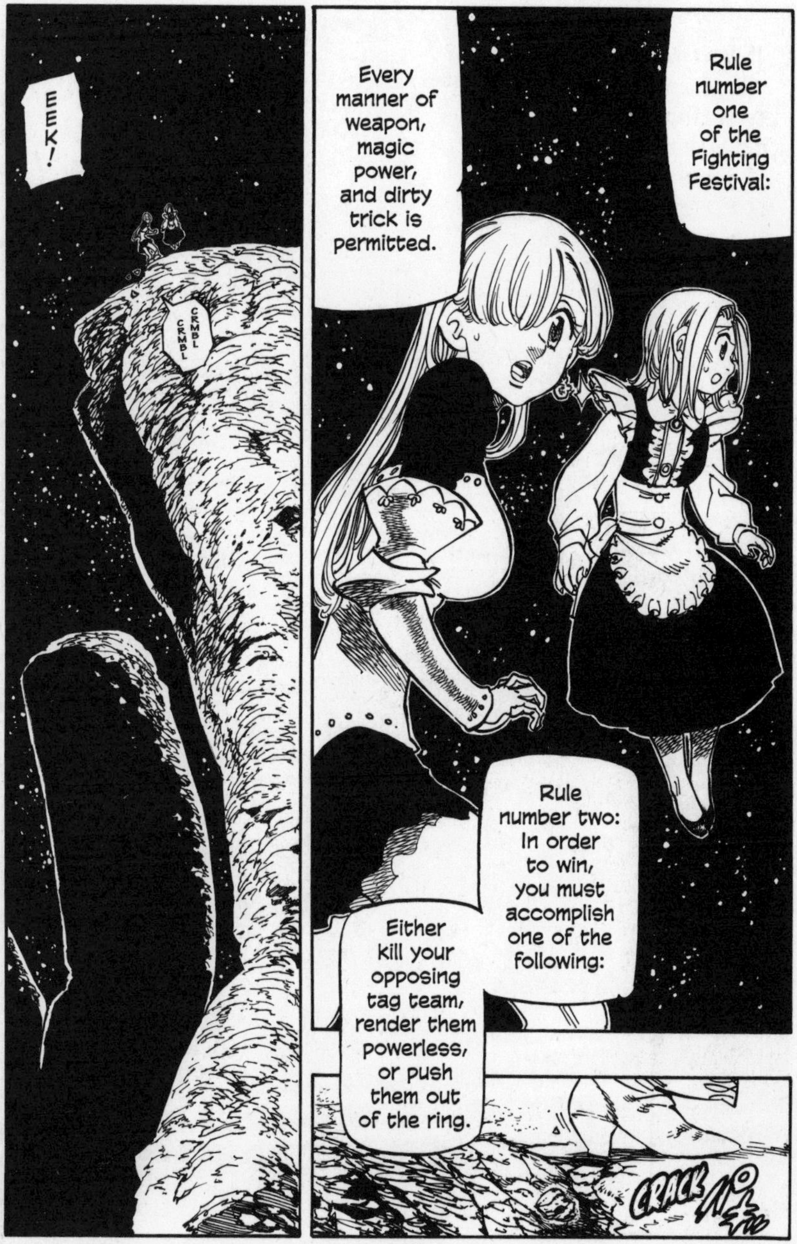

Rule number one of the Fighting Festival:
Every manner of weapon, magic power, and dirty trick is permitted.
Rule number two: In order to win, you must accomplish one of the following:
Either kill your opposing tag team, render them powerless, or push them out of the ring.
CRACK
CRMBL CRMBL
EEK!

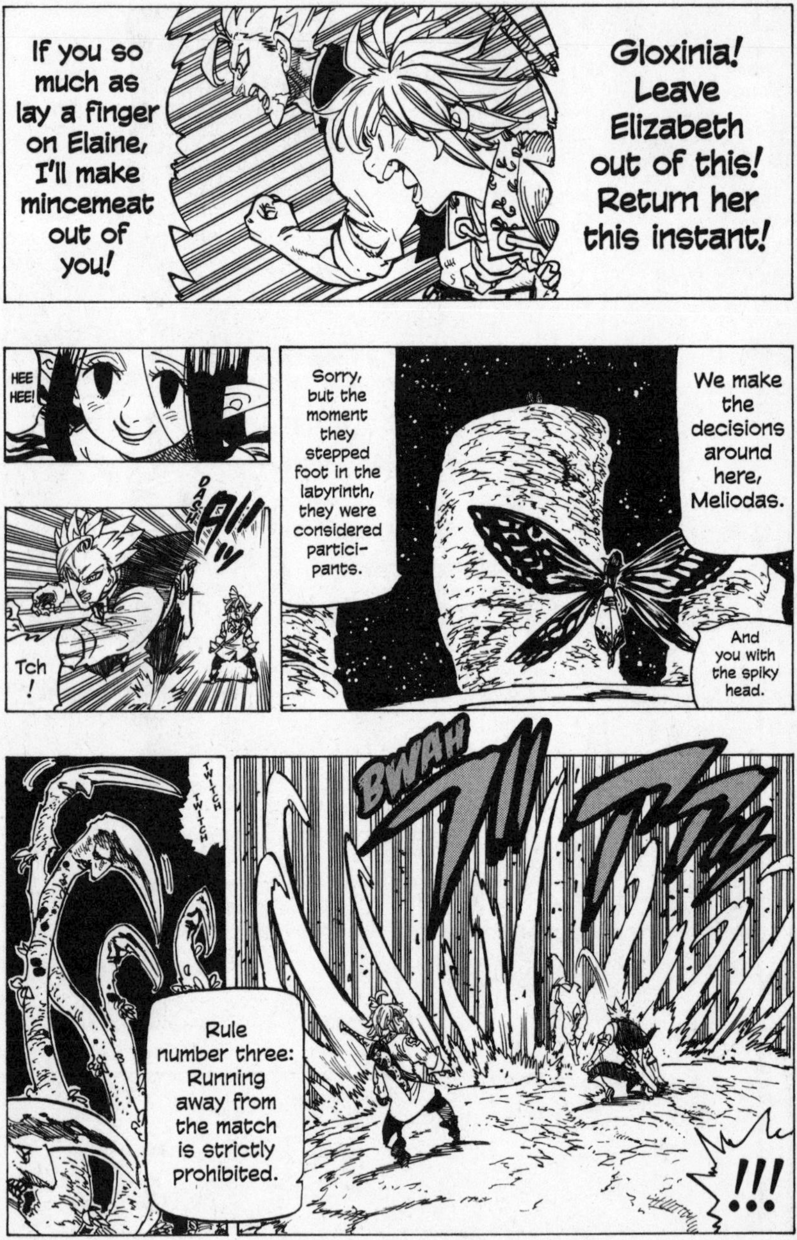
Gloxinia! Leave Elizabeth out of this! Return her this instant!
If you so much as lay a finger on Elaine, I'll make mincemeat out of you!
We make the decisions around here, Meliodas.
Sorry, but the moment they stepped foot in the labyrinth, they were considered partici-pants.
And you with the spiky head.
HEE HEE!
DASH
Tch!
BWAH
!!!
TWITCH TWITCH
Rule number three: Running away from the match is strictly prohibited.

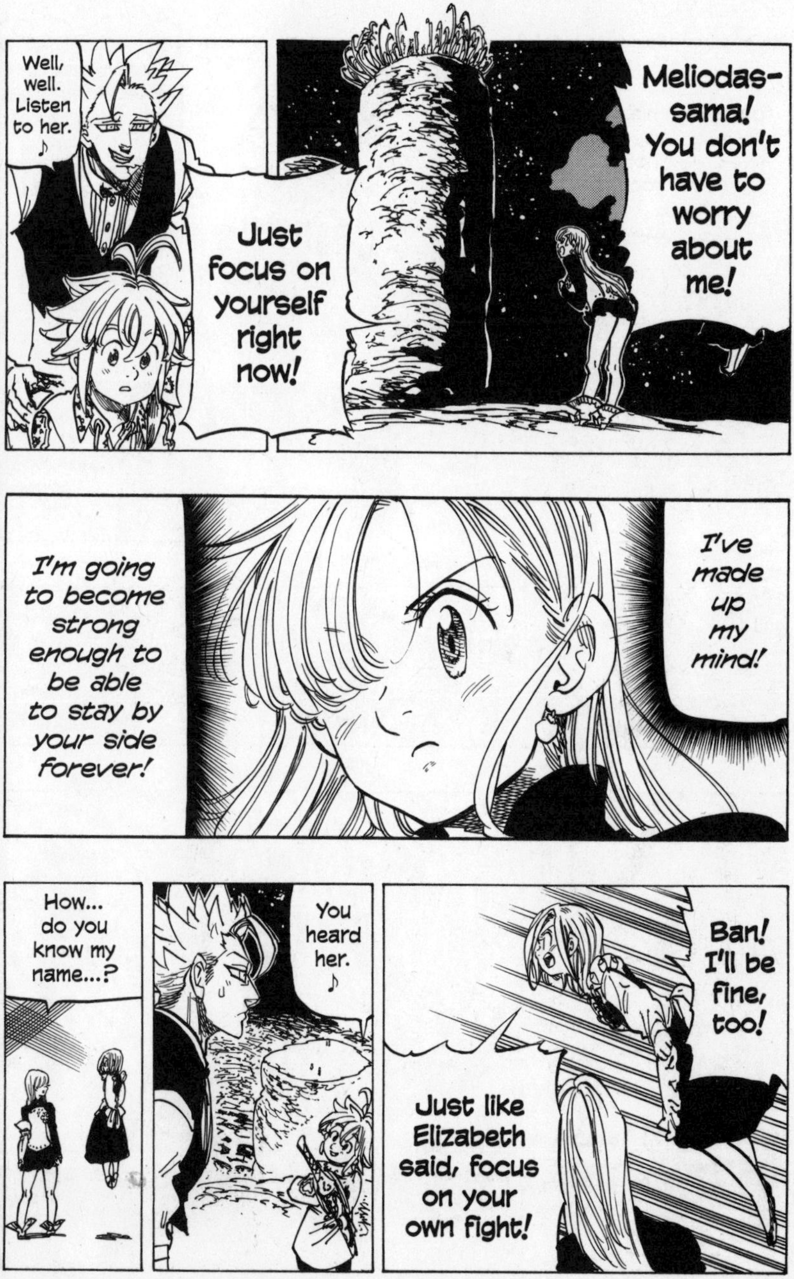
Meliodas-sama! You don't have to worry about me!
Just focus on yourself right now!
Well, well. Listen to her. ♪
I've made up my mind!
I'm going to become strong enough to be able to stay by your side forever!
Ban! I'll be fine, too!
Just like Elizabeth said, focus on your own fight!
You heard her. ♪
How... do you know my name...?

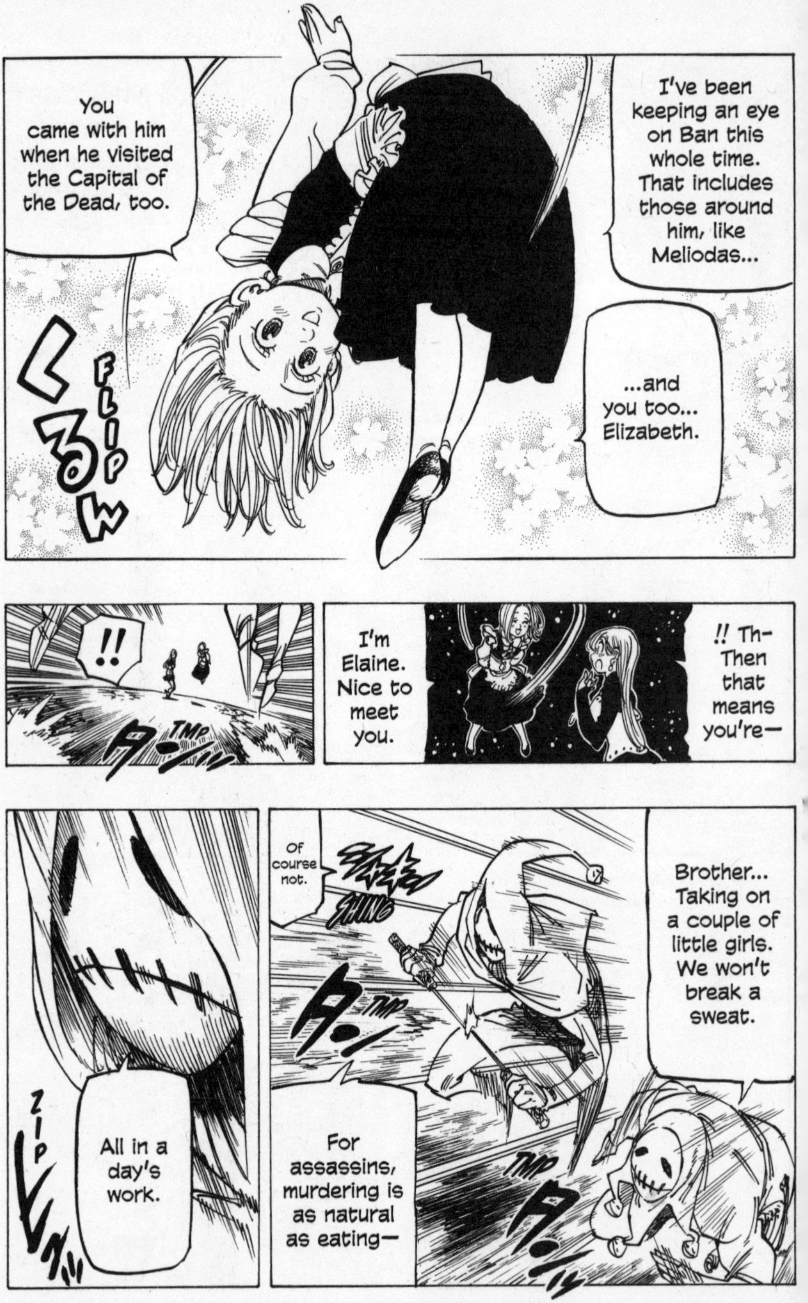

I've been keeping an eye on Ban this whole time. That includes those around him, like Meliodas...
...and you too... Elizabeth.
You came with him when he visited the Capital of the Dead, too.
FLIP
!! Th- Then that means you're—
I'm Elaine. Nice to meet you.
!!
TMP
Brother... Taking on a couple of little girls. We won't break a sweat.
Of course not.
SHING
TMP
TMP
For assassins, murdering is as natural as eating—
All in a day's work.
ZIP

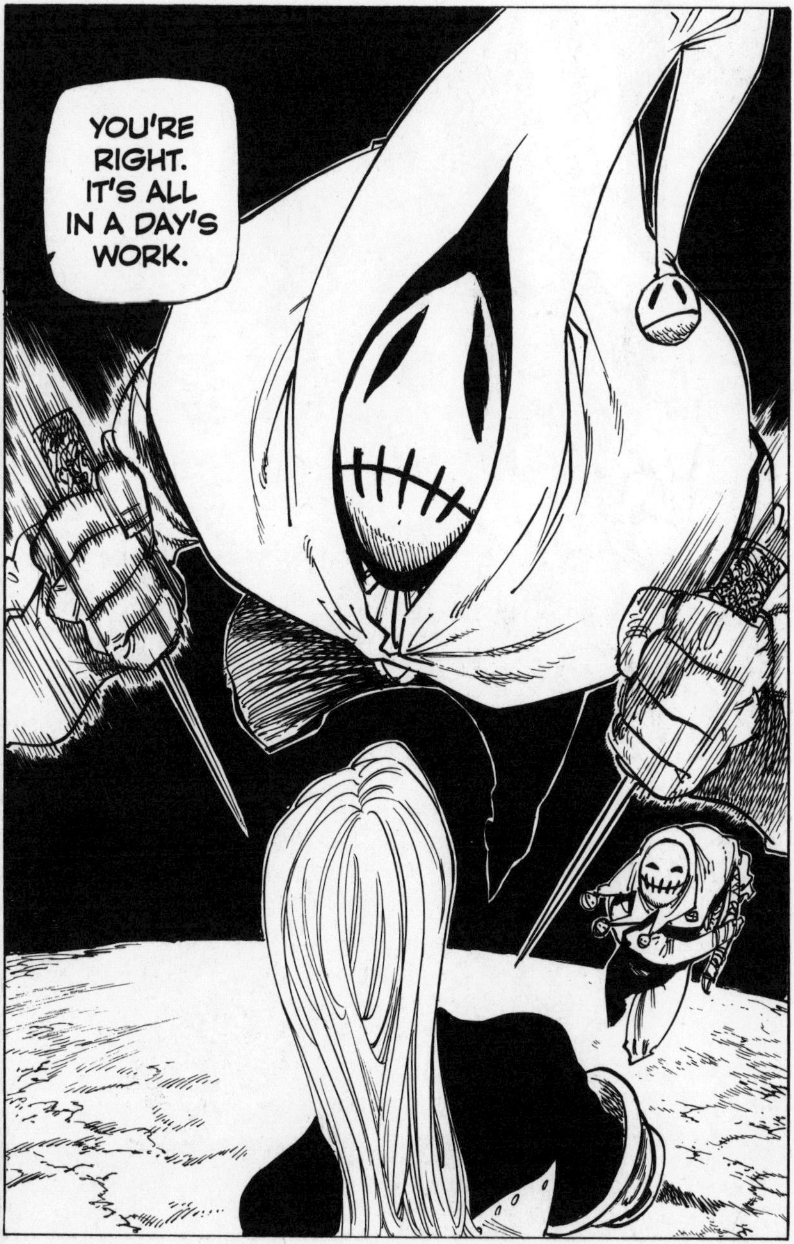
YOU'RE RIGHT. IT'S ALL IN A DAY'S WORK.

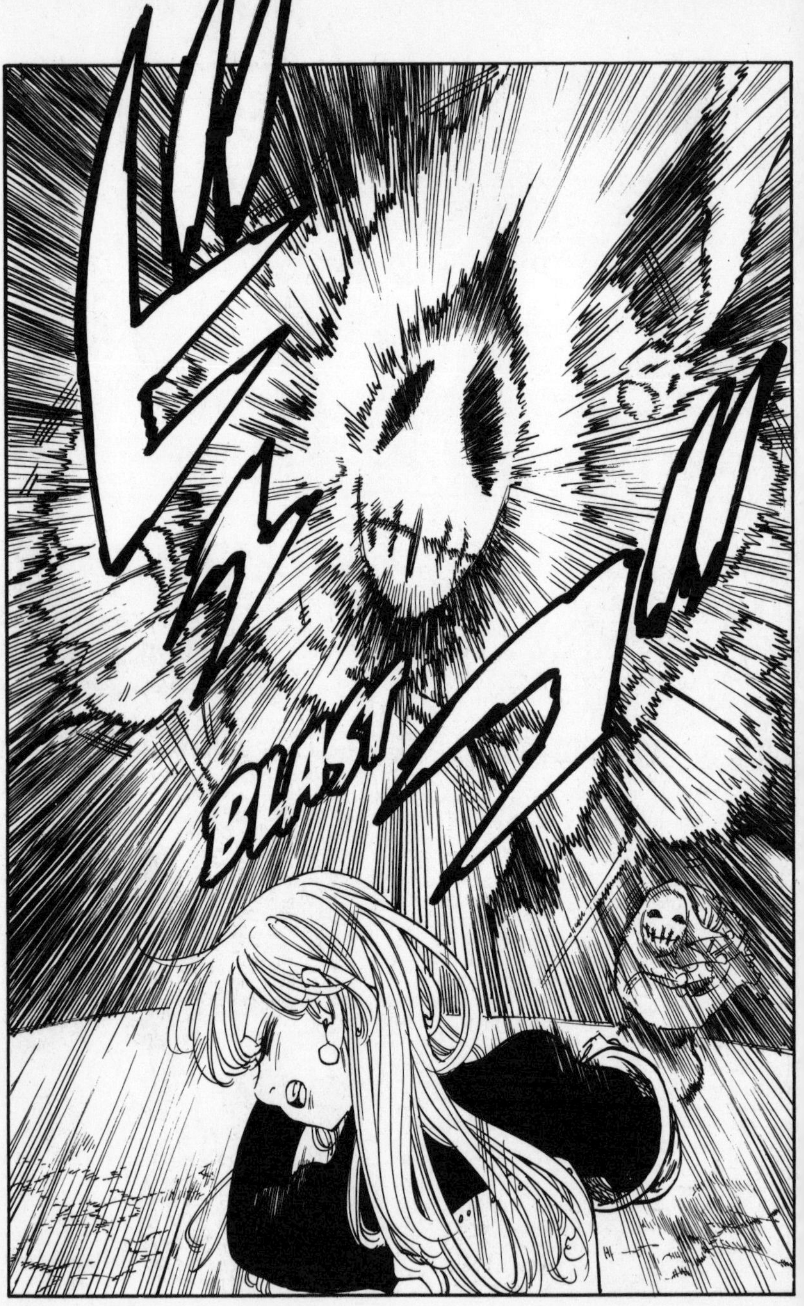
BLAST

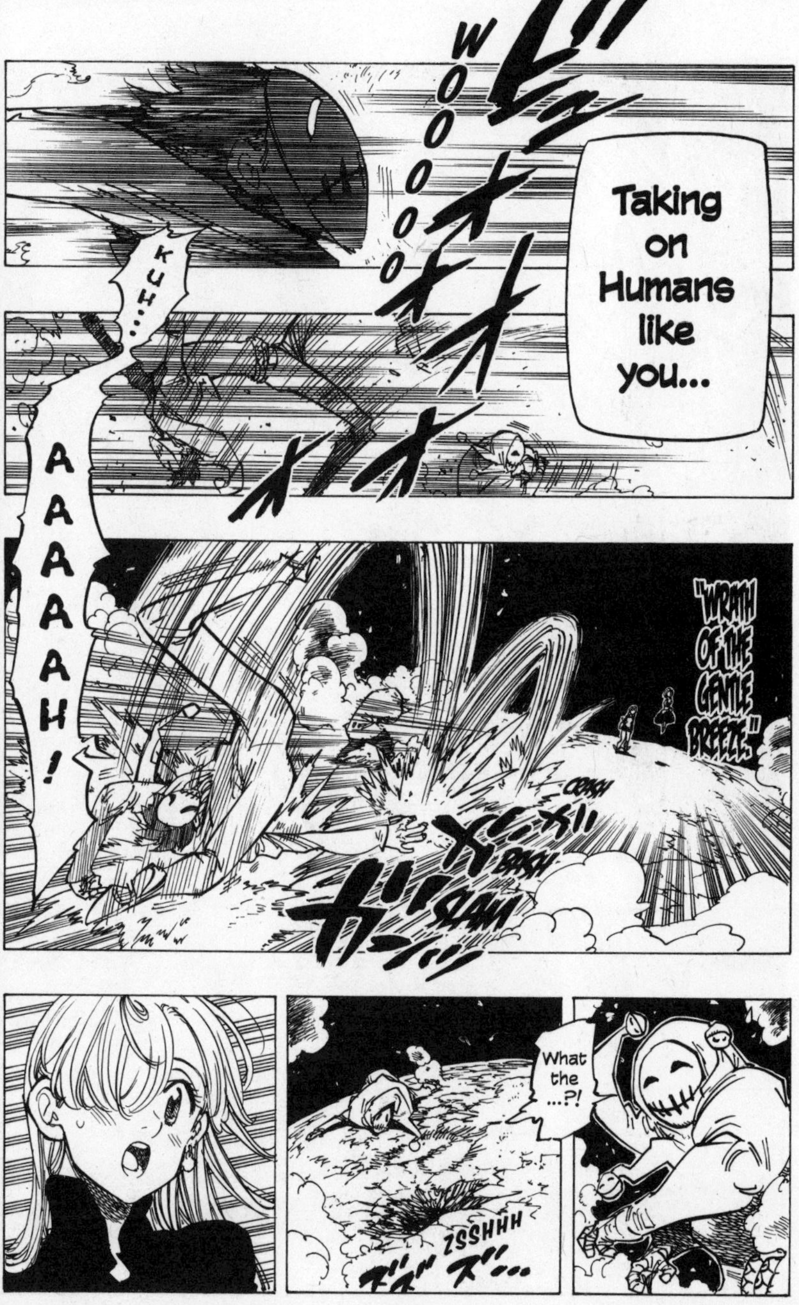
Taking on Humans like you...
WOOOOOOO
KUH...
AAAAAAH!
"WRATH OF THE GENTLE BREEZE."
CRASH
BASH
SLAM
What the ...?!
ZSSHHH

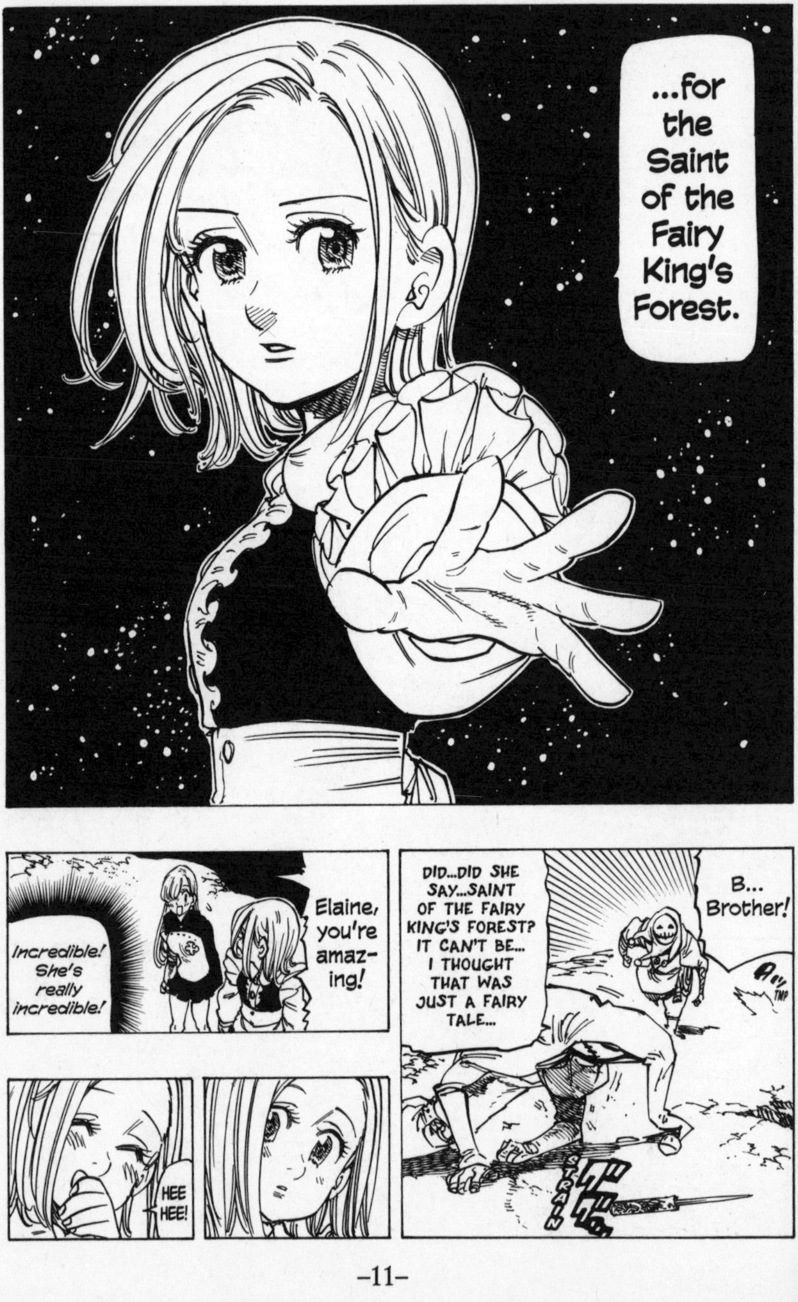
...for the Saint of the Fairy King's Forest.
B... Brother!
DID...DID SHE SAY...SAINT OF THE FAIRY KING'S FOREST? IT CAN'T BE... I THOUGHT THAT WAS JUST A FAIRY TALE...
TMP
STRAIN
Elaine, you're amaz-ing!
Incredible! She's really incredible!
HEE HEE!

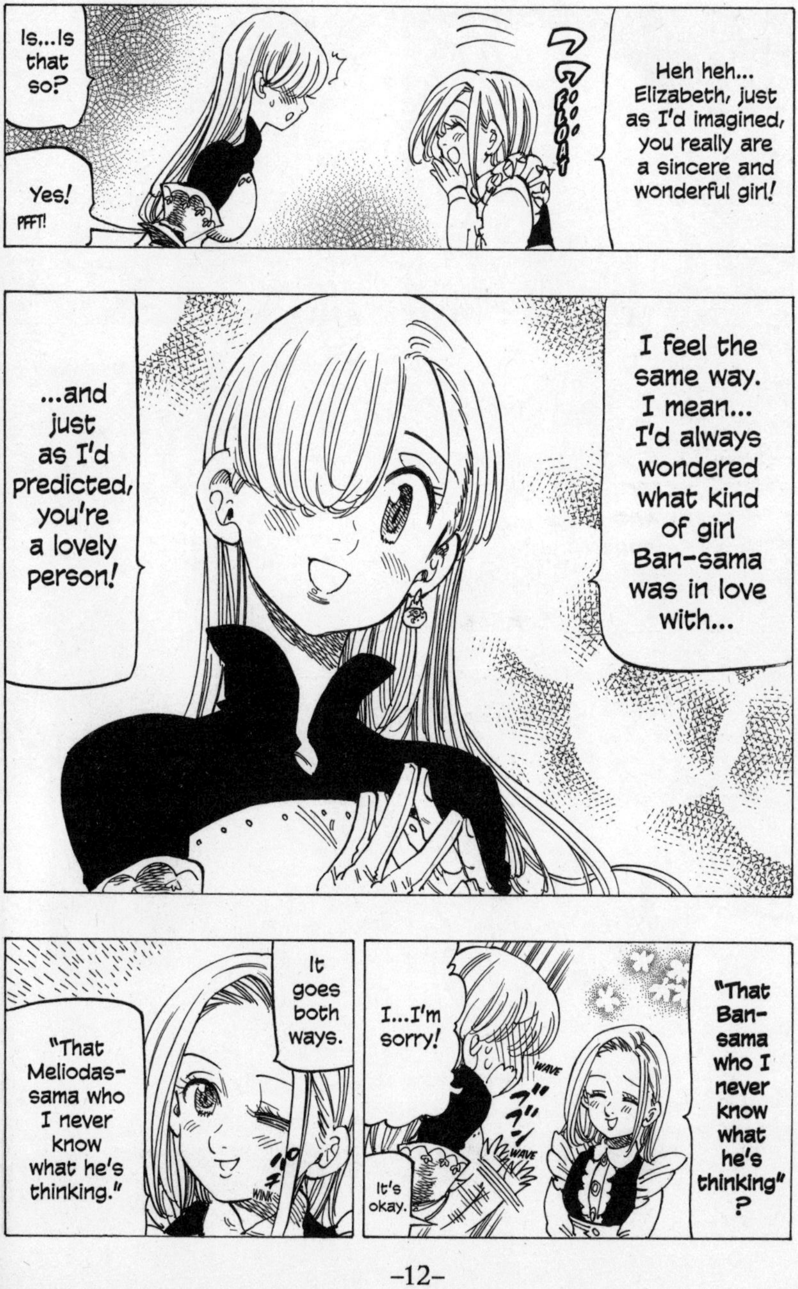
Heh heh... Elizabeth, just as I'd imagined, you really are a sincere and wonderful girl!
FLOAT
Is...Is that so?
Yes!
PFFT!
I feel the same way. I mean... I'd always wondered what kind of girl Ban-sama was in love with...
...and just as I'd predicted, you're a lovely person!
"That Ban-sama who I never know what he's thinking"?
I...I'm sorry!
WAVE
WAVE
It's okay.
It goes both ways.
"That Meliodas-sama who I never know what he's thinking."
WINK

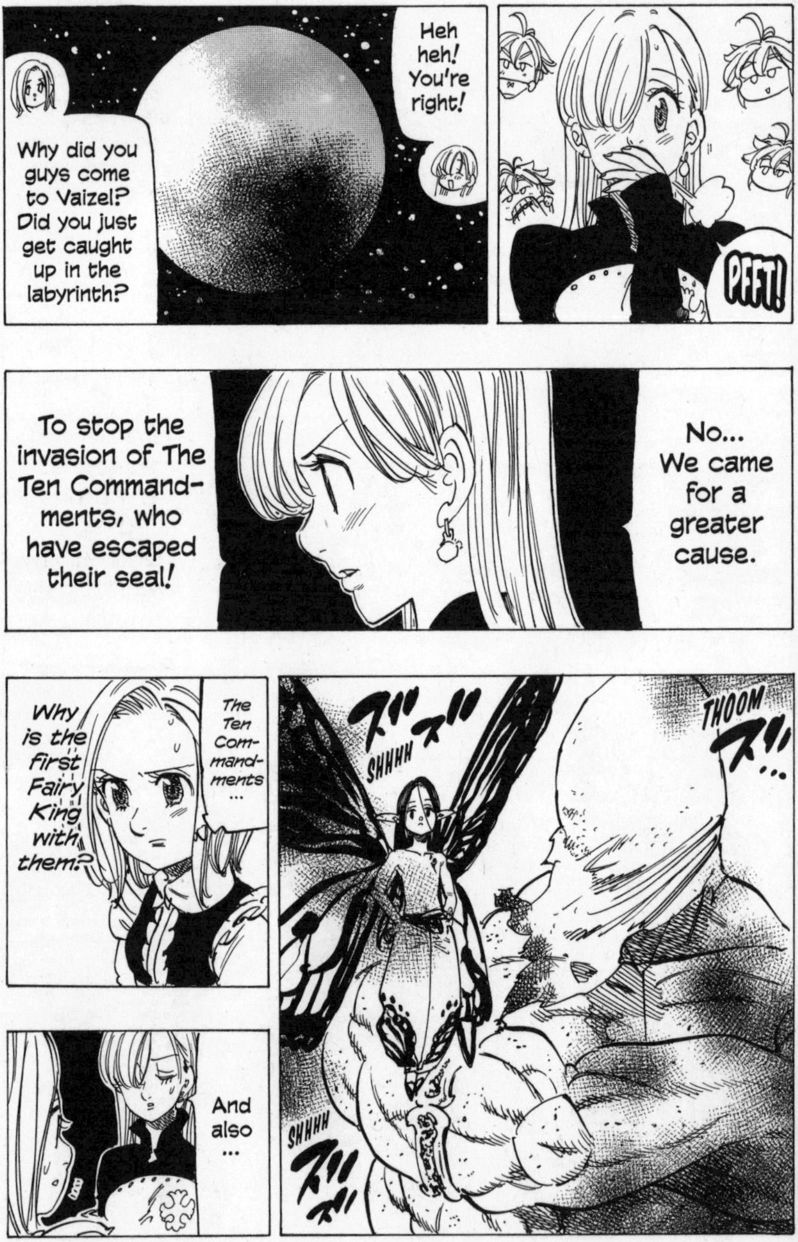
PFFT!
Heh heh! You're right!
Why did you guys come to Vaizel? Did you just get caught up in the labyrinth?
No... We came for a greater cause.
To stop the invasion of The Ten Command-ments, who have escaped their seal!
THOOM
SHHHH
SHHHH
The Ten Com-mand-ments ...
Why is the first Fairy King with them?
And also ...

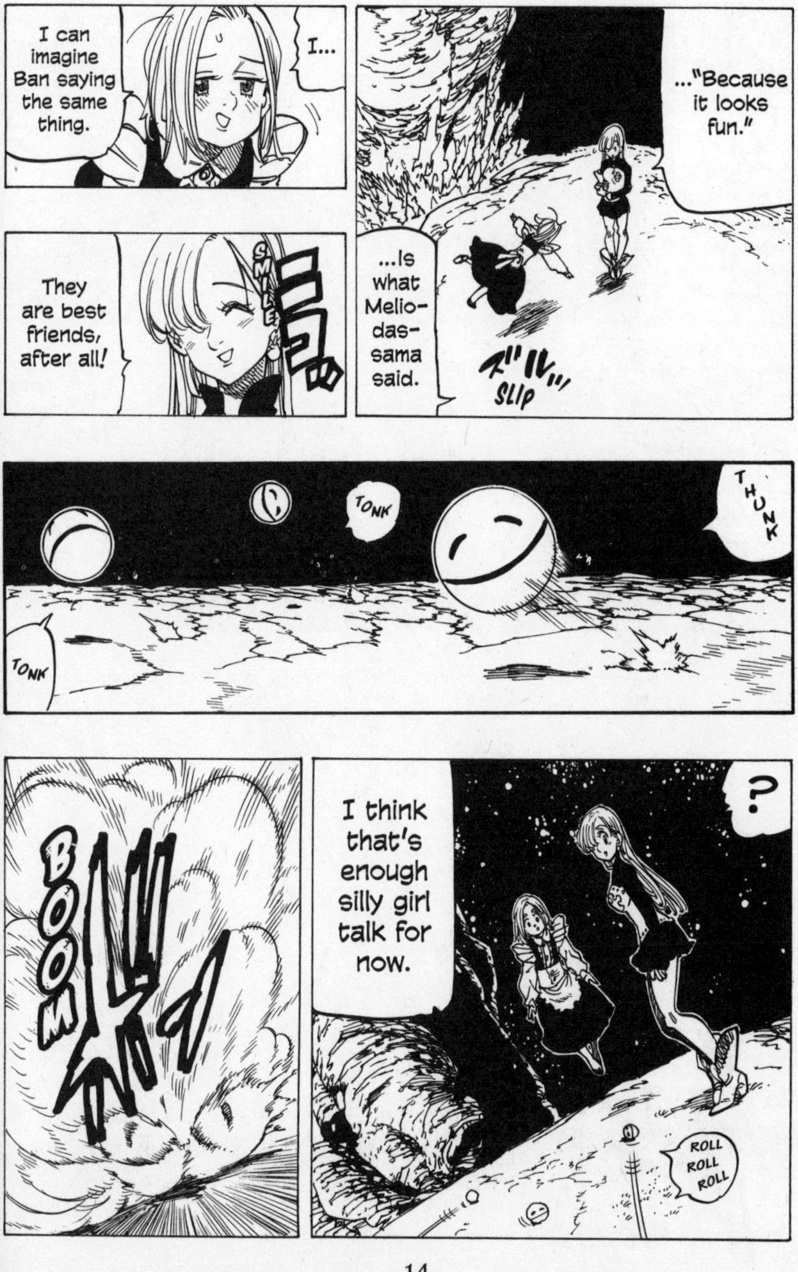

..."Because it looks fun."
...Is what Meliodas-sama said.
ズル
SLIP
I...
I can imagine Ban saying the same thing.
SMILE
They are best friends, after all!
THUNK
TONK
TONK
?
I think that's enough silly girl talk for now.
ROLL ROLL ROLL
BOOM

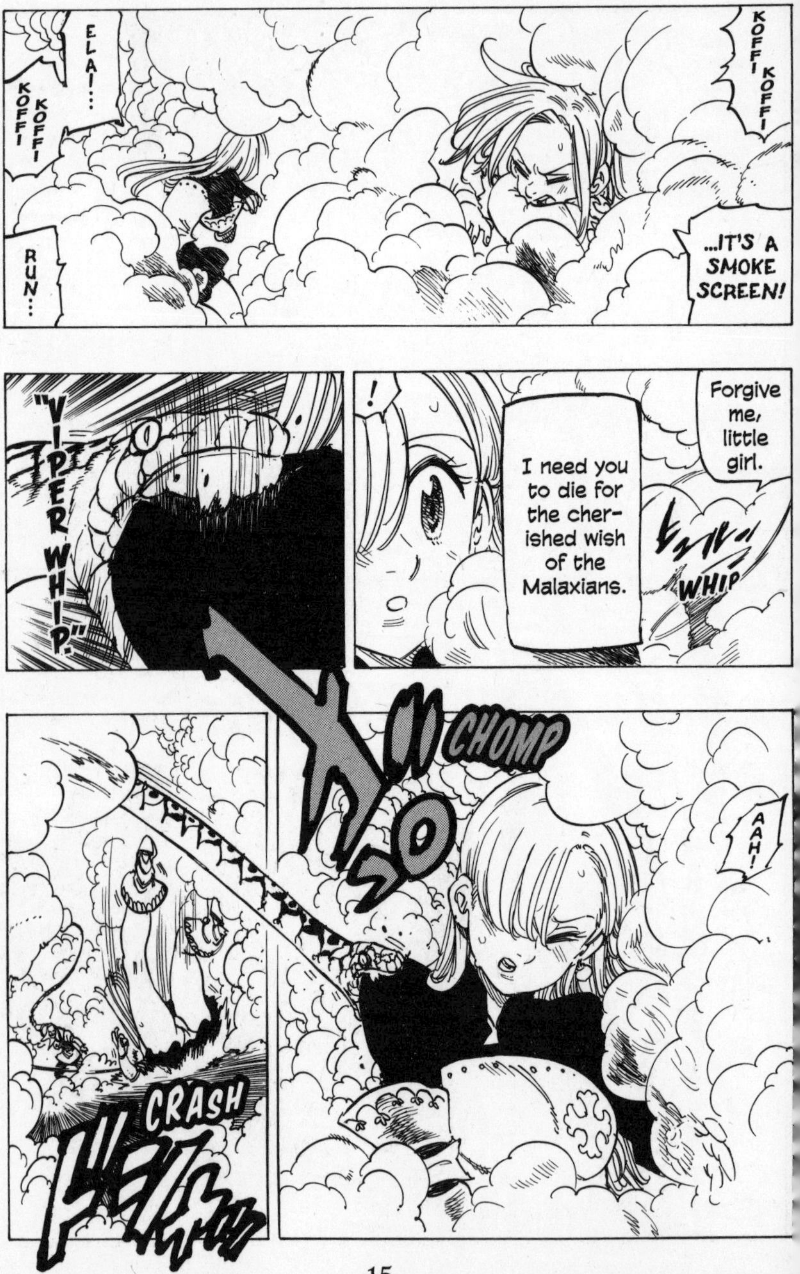
KOFFI KOFFI
...IT'S A SMOKE SCREEN!
ELAI...
KOFFI KOFFI
RUN...
Forgive me, little girl.
WHIP
I need you to die for the cher-ished wish of the Malaxians.
!
"VIPER WHIP."
CHOMP
AAH!
CRASH

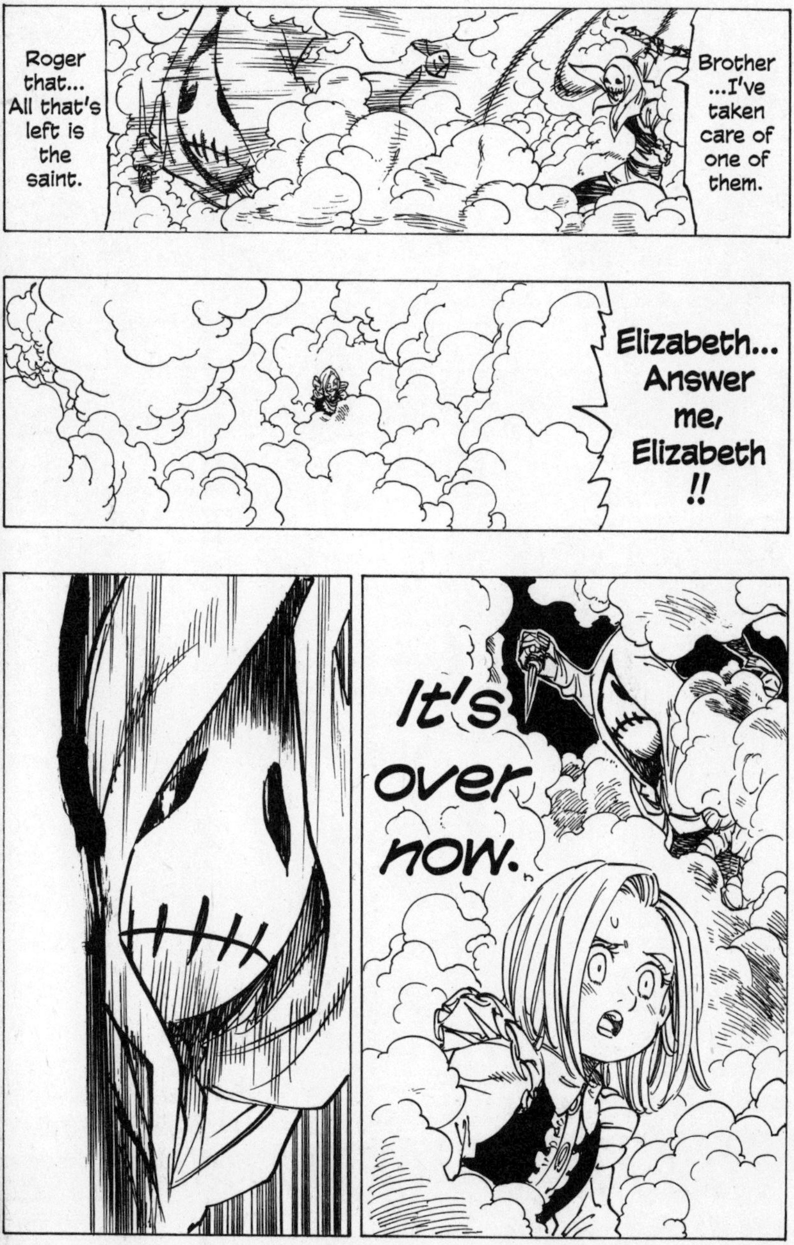
Brother ...I've taken care of one of them.
Roger that... All that's left is the saint.
Elizabeth... Answer me, Elizabeth!!
It's over now.

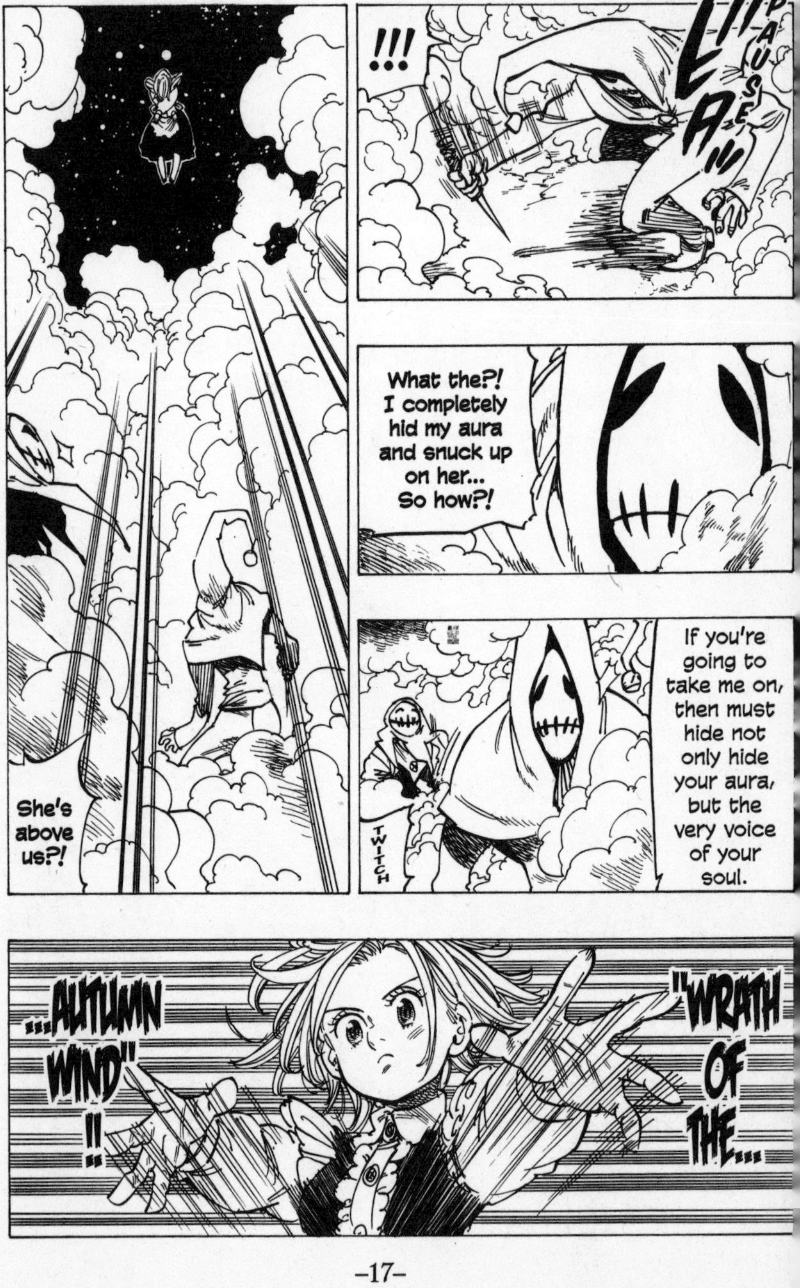
PAUSE
!!!
What the?! I completely hid my aura and snuck up on her... So how?!
If you're going to take me on, then must hide not only hide your aura, but the very voice of your soul.
TWITCH
She's above us?!
"WRATH OF THE...
...AUTUMN WIND"!!

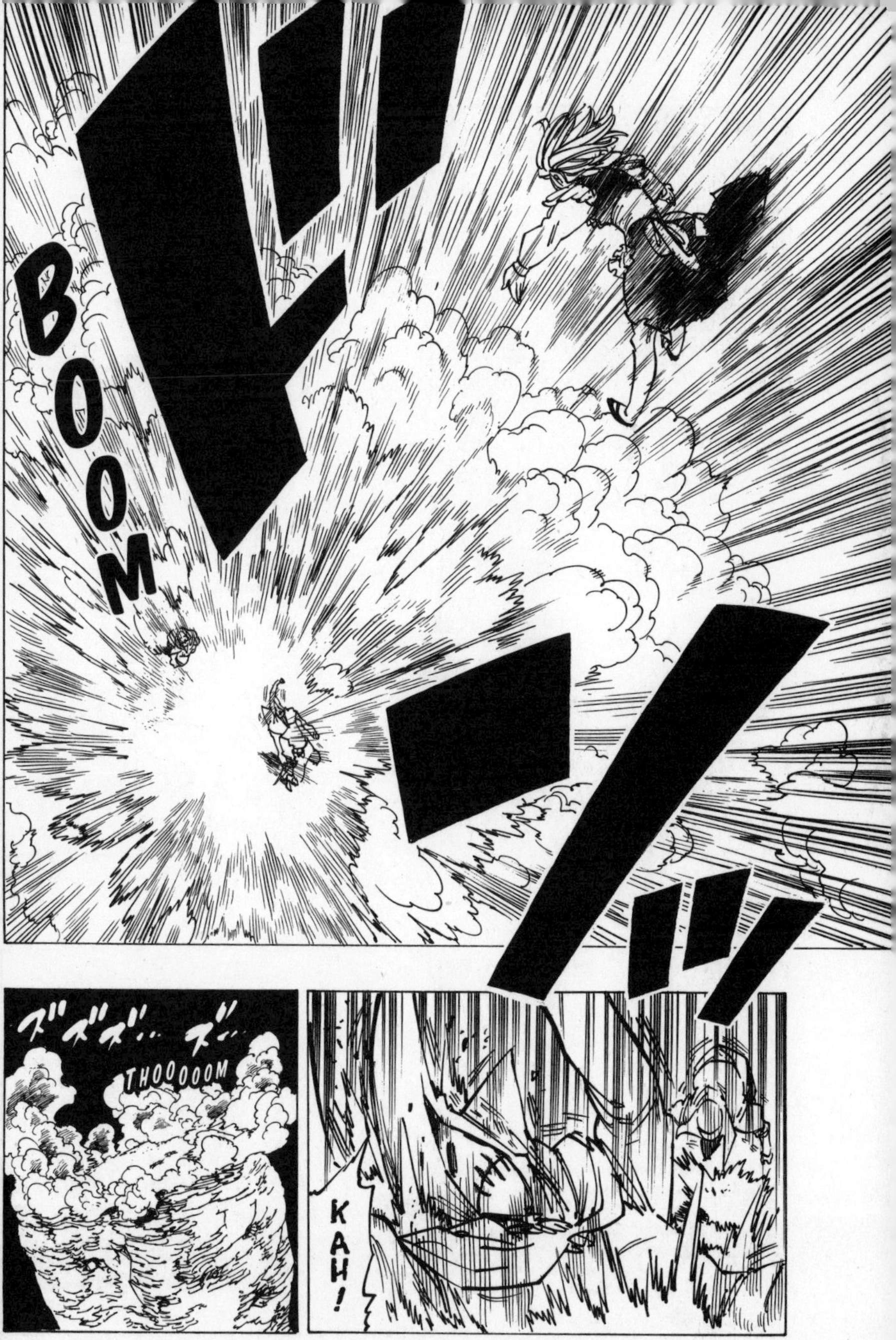
BOOM
KAH!
ズズズ… ズ…
THOOOOOM

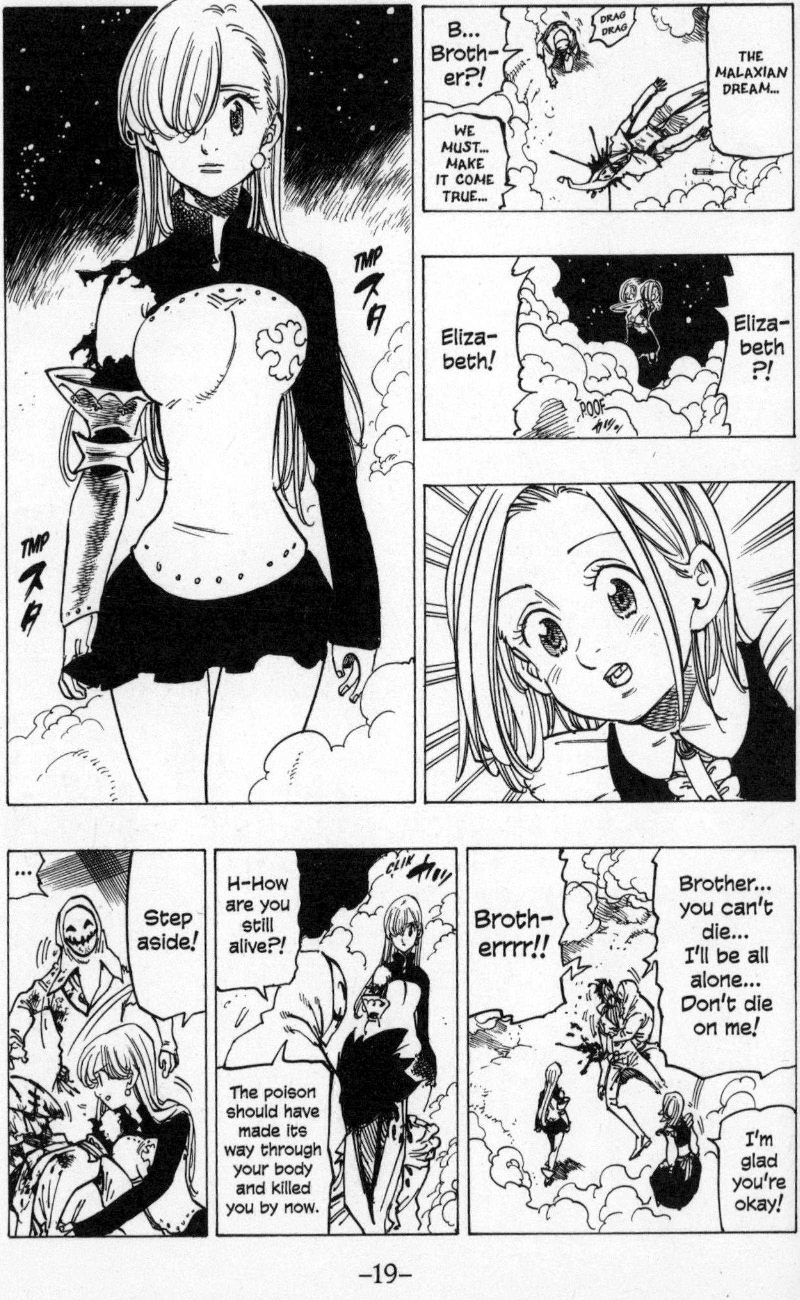
THE MALAXIAN DREAM...
DRAG DRAG
B... Brother?!
WE MUST... MAKE IT COME TRUE...
Elizabeth?!
POOF
Elizabeth!
TMP
TMP
Brother... you can't die... I'll be all alone... Don't die on me!
Broth-errrr!!
I'm glad you're okay!
CLIK
H-How are you still alive?!
The poison should have made its way through your body and killed you by now.
Step aside!
...

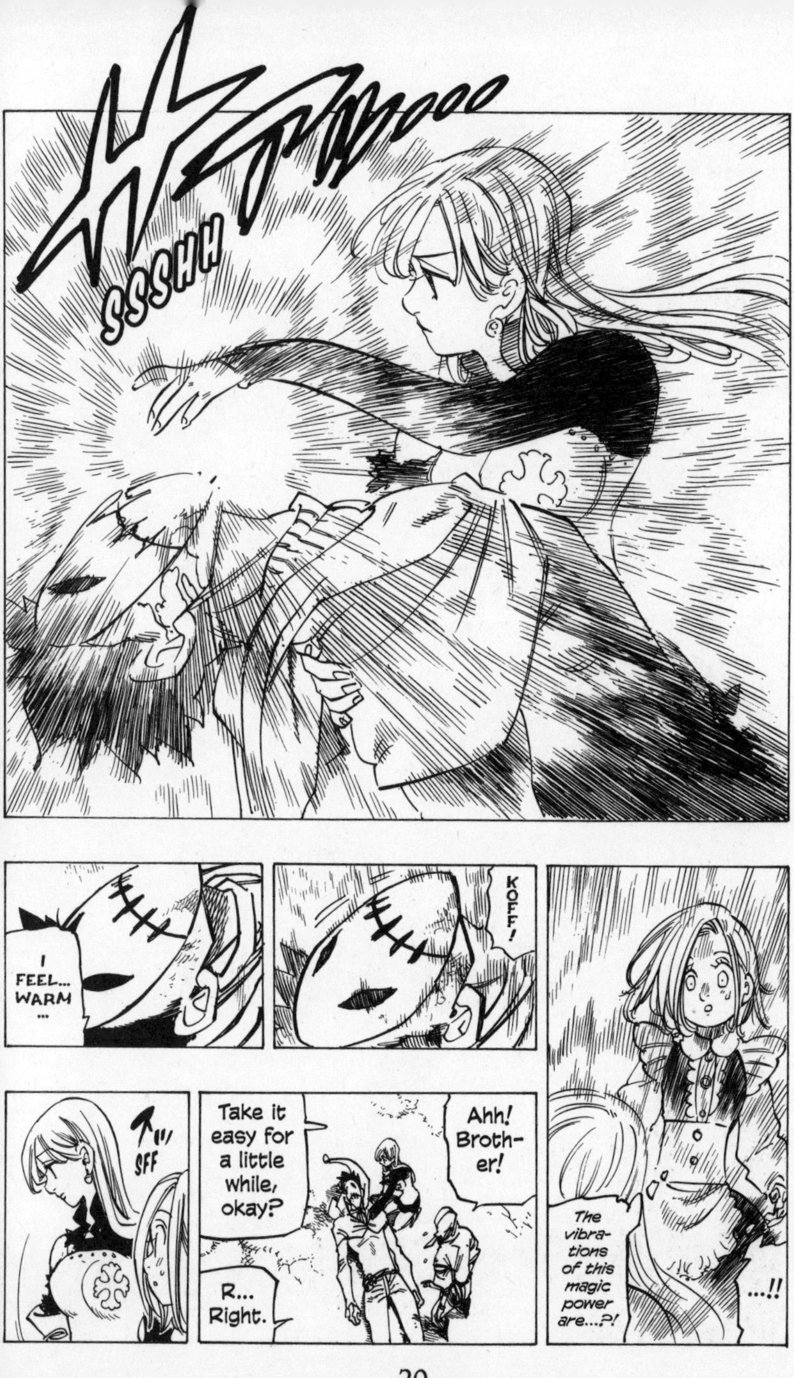
SSSHH
The vibrations of this magic power are...?!
...!!
KOFF!
I FEEL... WARM ...
Ahh! Brother!
Take it easy for a little while, okay?
R... Right.
SFF

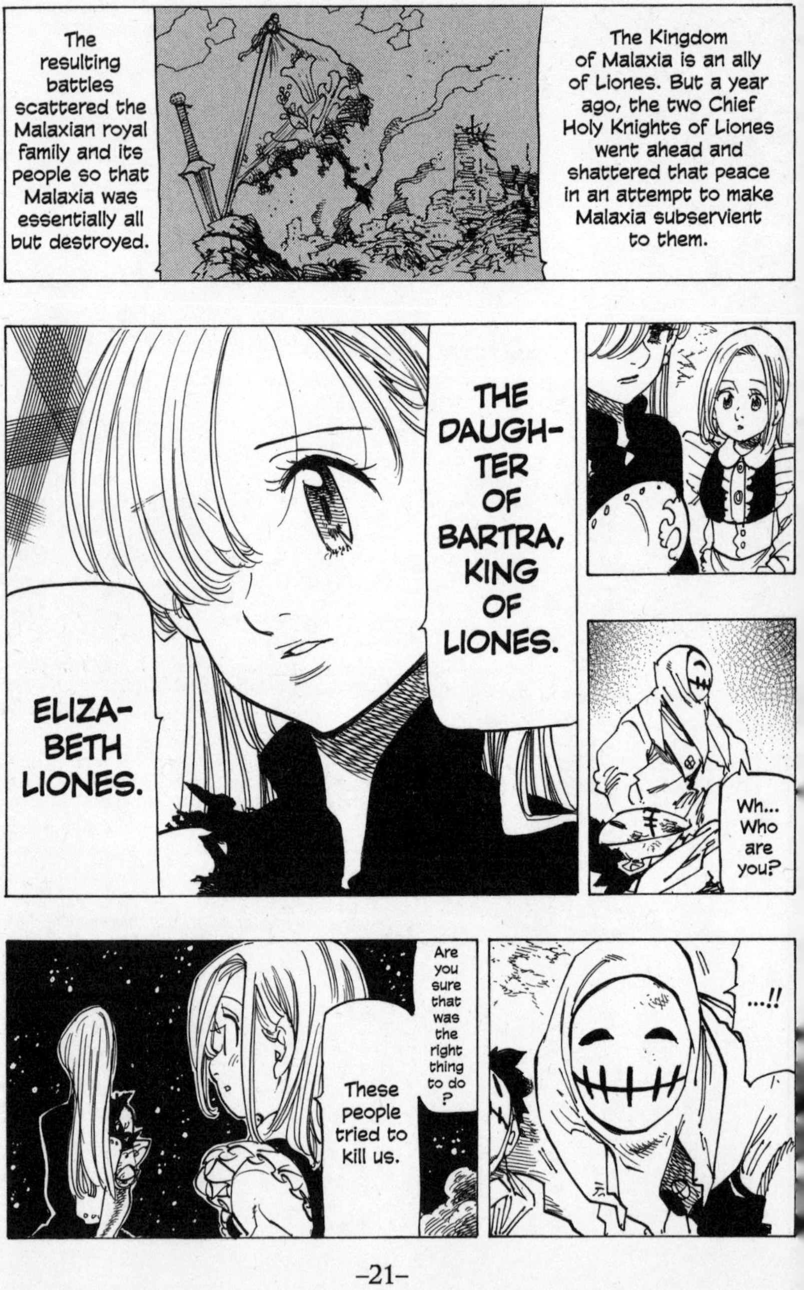
The Kingdom of Malaxia is an ally of Liones. But a year ago, the two Chief Holy Knights of Liones went ahead and shattered that peace in an attempt to make Malaxia subservient to them.
The resulting battles scattered the Malaxian royal family and its people so that Malaxia was essentially all but destroyed.
Wh... Who are you?
THE DAUGHTER OF BARTRA, KING OF LIONES.
ELIZABETH LIONES.
...!!
Are you sure that was the right thing to do?
These people tried to kill us.

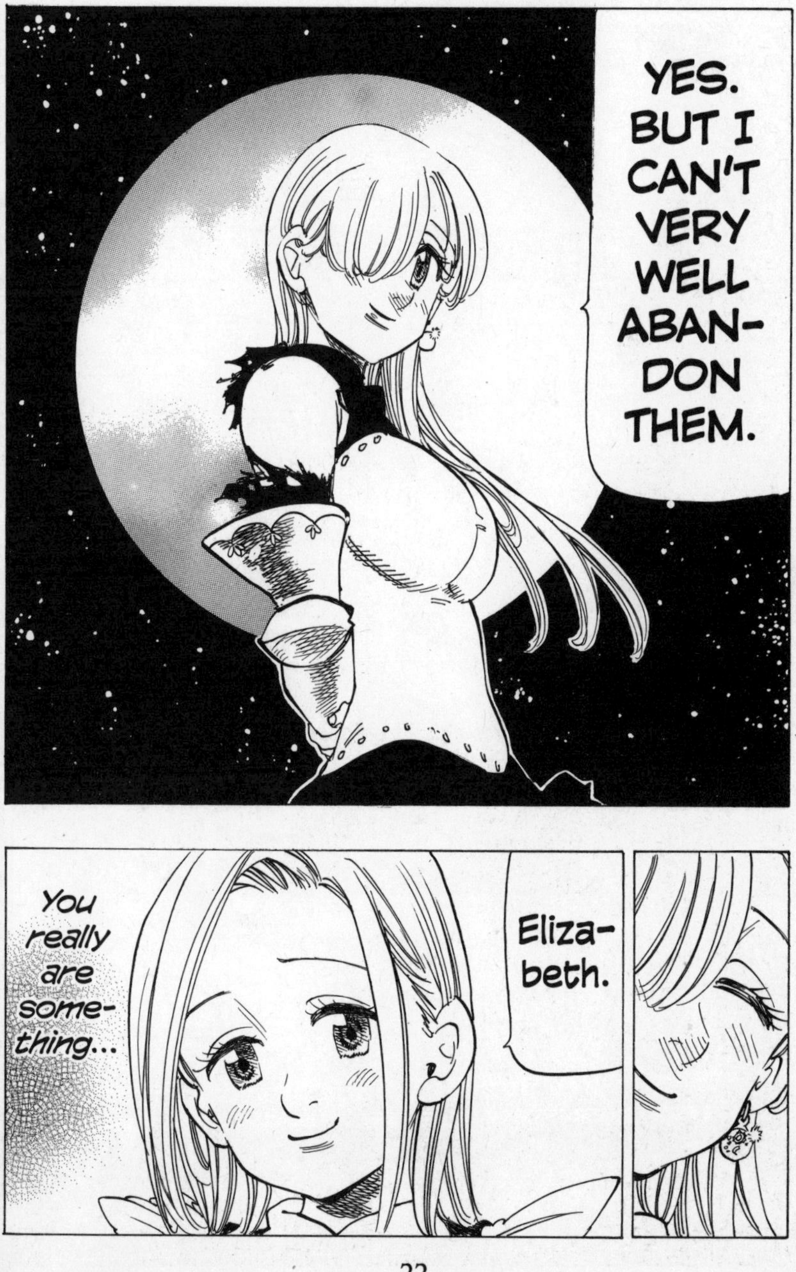
YES. BUT I CAN'T VERY WELL ABAN-DON THEM.
Eliza-beth.
You really are some-thing...

Chapter 164 - Those Who Won't Be Offered Up

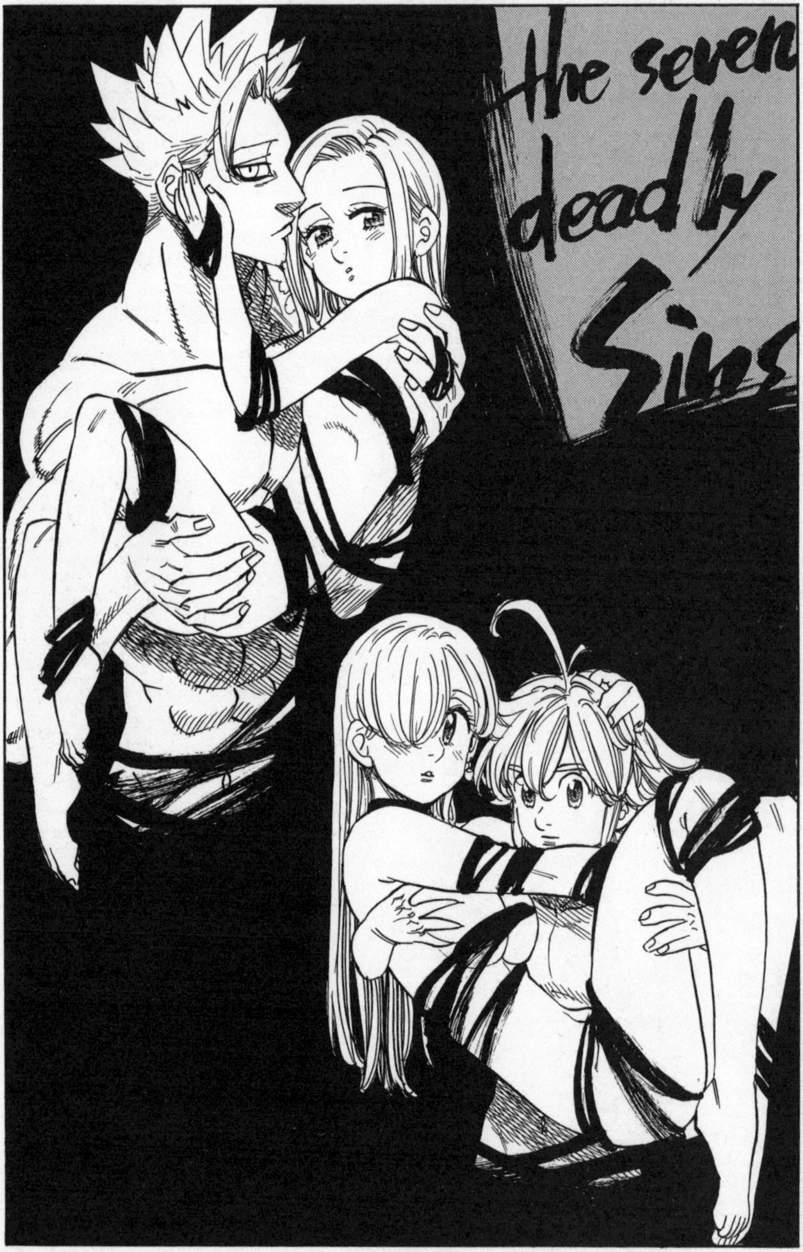
the seven deadly Sins

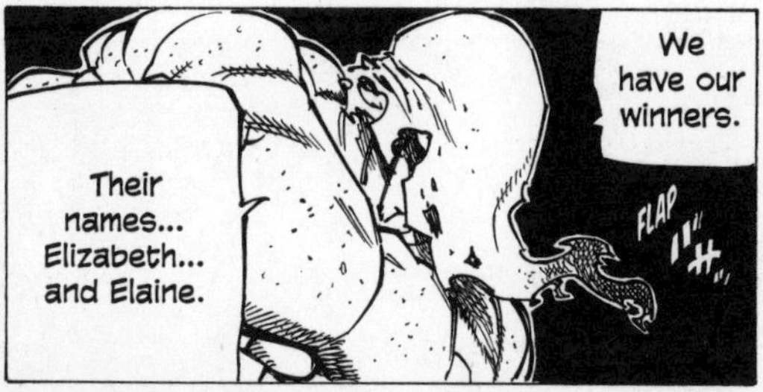
We have our winners.
Their names... Elizabeth... and Elaine.
FLAP
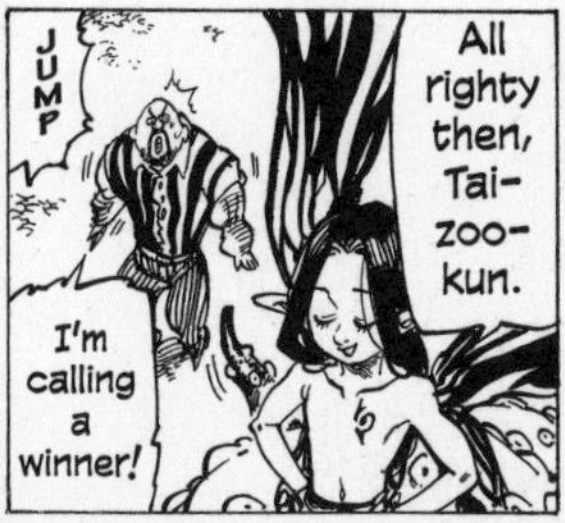
All righty then, Tai-zoo-kun.
I'm calling a winner!
JUMP
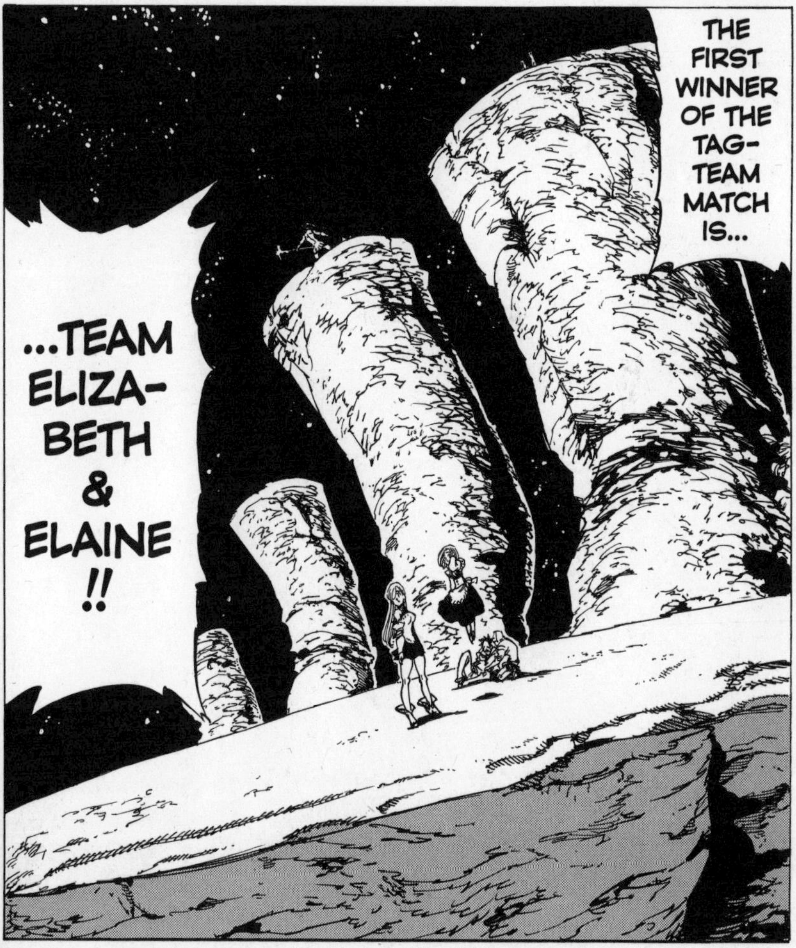
THE FIRST WINNER OF THE TAG-TEAM MATCH IS...
...TEAM ELIZA-BETH & ELAINE !!

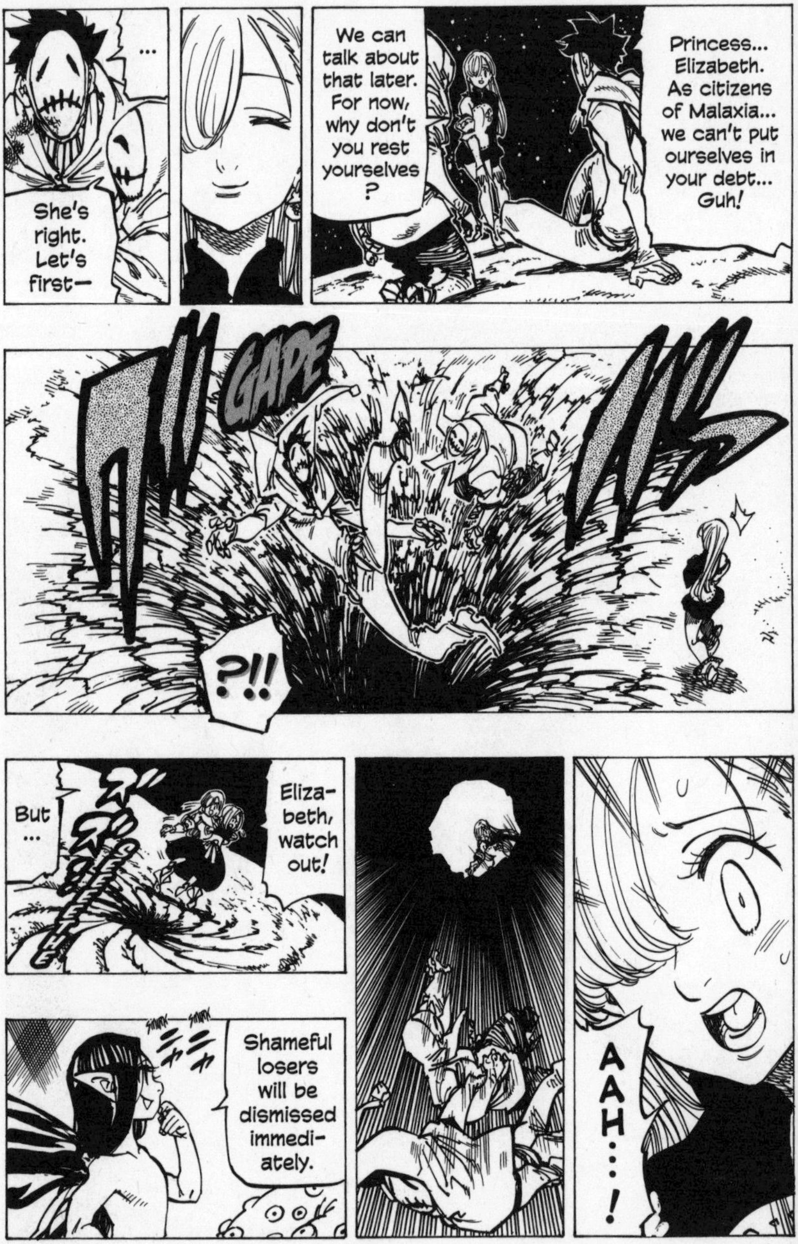
Princess... Elizabeth. As citizens of Malaxia... we can't put ourselves in your debt... Guh!
We can talk about that later. For now, why don't you rest yourselves?
...
She's right. Let's first—
GAPE
?!!
AAH...!
Eliza-beth, watch out!
But ...
Shameful losers will be dismissed immedi-ately.

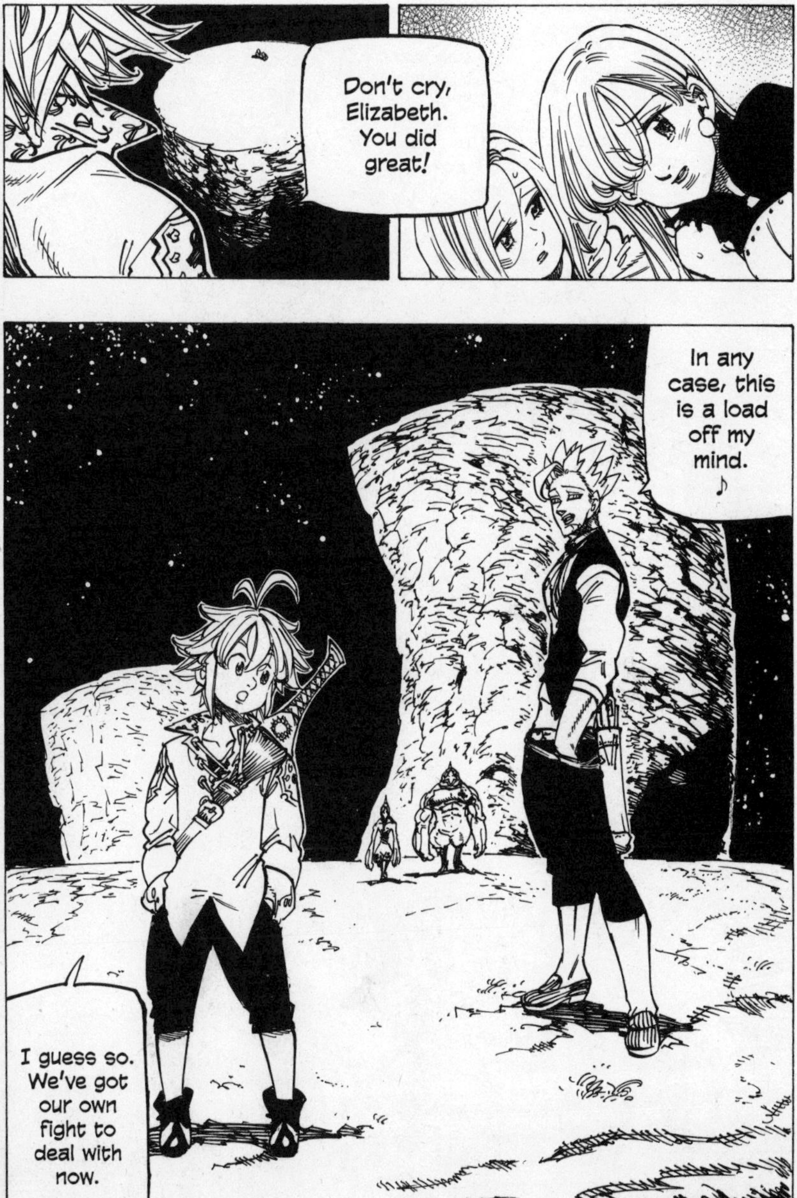
Don't cry, Elizabeth. You did great!
In any case, this is a load off my mind. ♪
I guess so. We've got our own fight to deal with now.

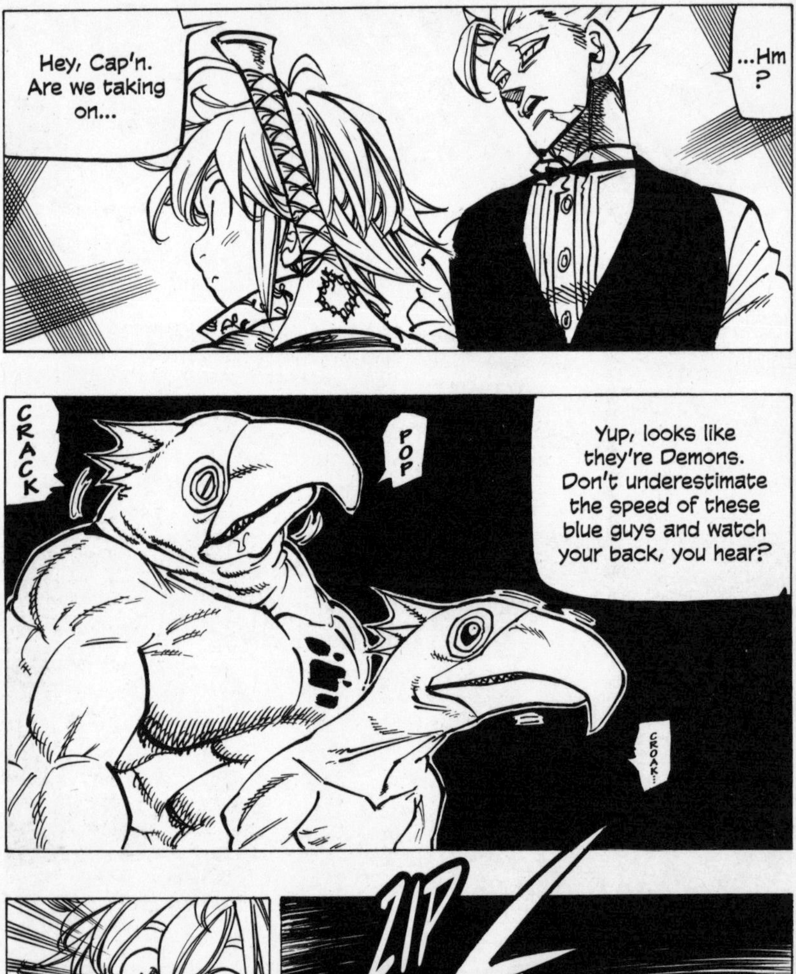
Hey, Cap'n. Are we taking on...
...Hm?
Yup, looks like they're Demons. Don't underestimate the speed of these blue guys and watch your back, you hear?
POP
CRACK
CROAK...
ZIP
Huh?

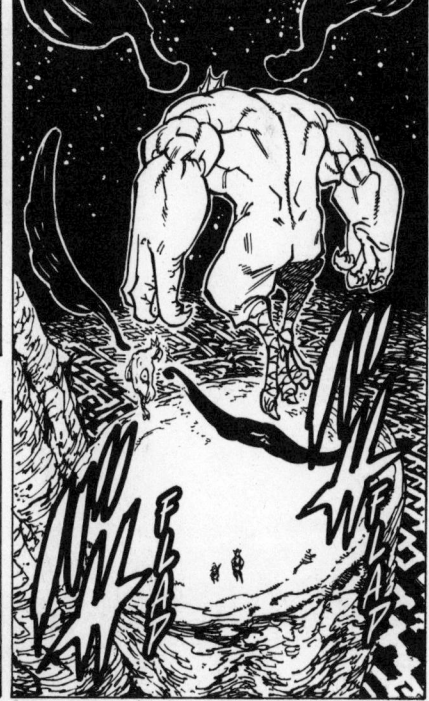

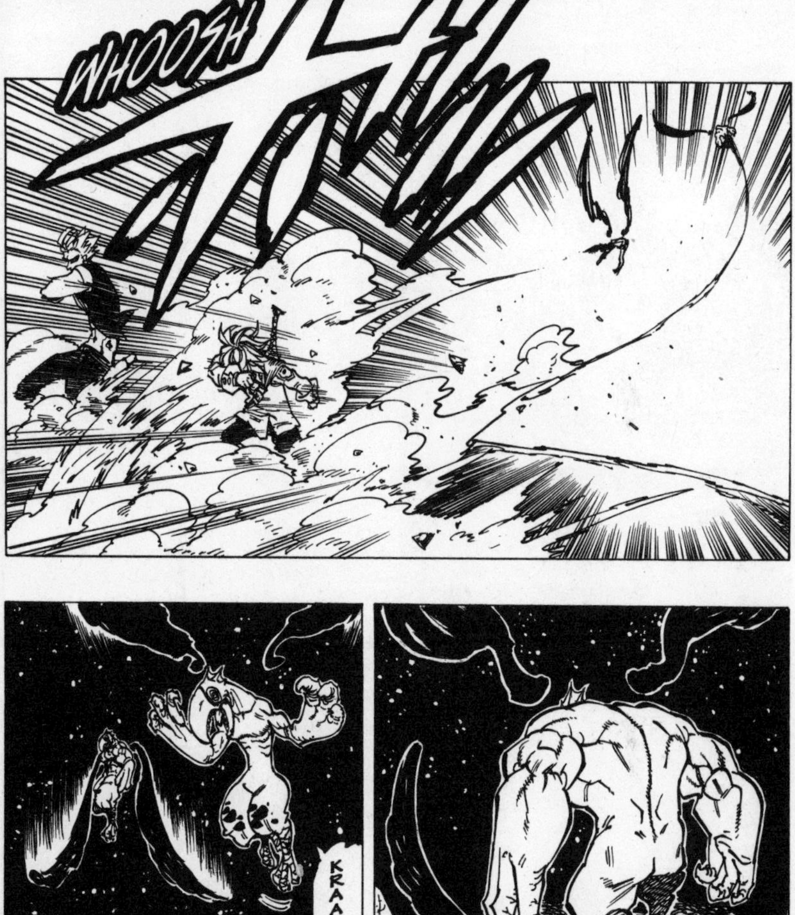
WHOOSH
FLAP
FLAP
KRAAAAW!
What gives? Flying's gotta be against the rules. ♪
It's going to be a pain catching these guys.

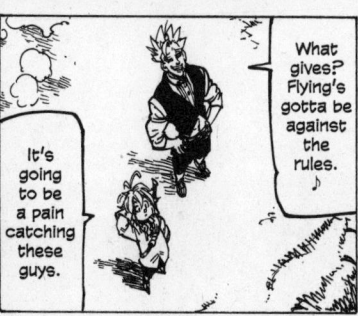

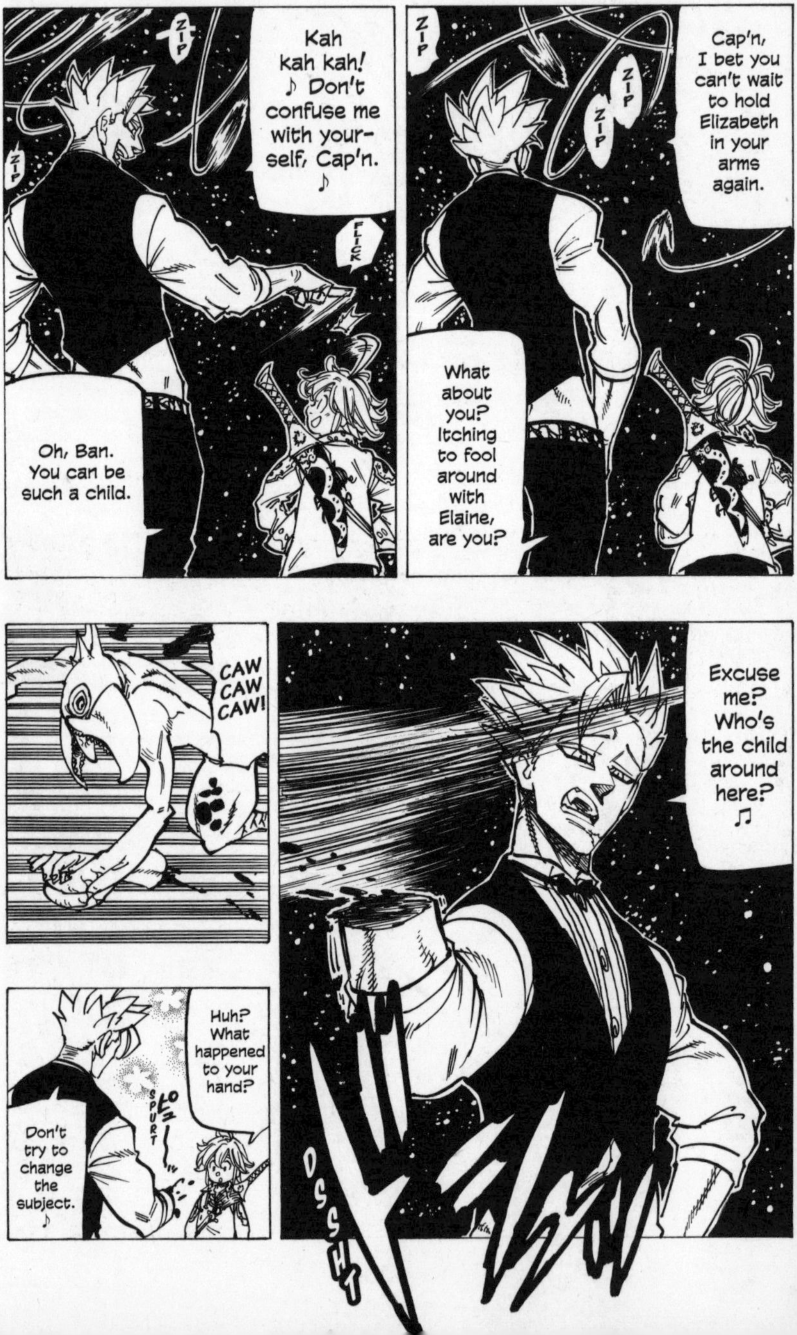
Cap'n, I bet you can't wait to hold Elizabeth in your arms again.
ZIP
ZIP
ZIP
What about you? Itching to fool around with Elaine, are you?
Kah kah kah! ♪ Don't confuse me with your-self, Cap'n. ♪
ZIP
ZIP
FLICK
Oh, Ban. You can be such a child.
Excuse me? Who's the child around here? ♫
DSSHT
CAW CAW CAW!
Huh? What happened to your hand?
SPURT
Don't try to change the subject. ♪

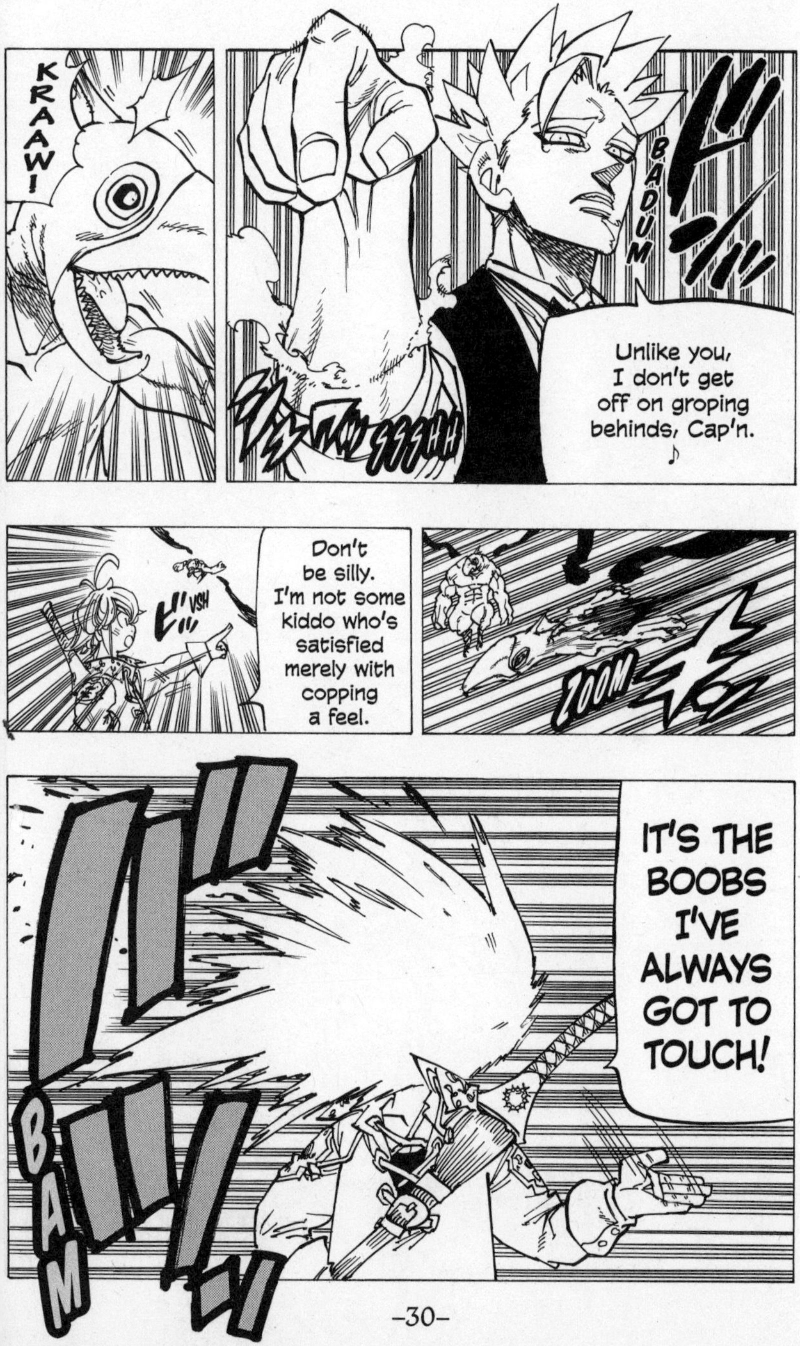

BADUM
SSSHH
Unlike you, I don't get off on groping behinds, Cap'n. ♪
KRAAWI!
ZOOM
VSH
Don't be silly. I'm not some kiddo who's satisfied merely with copping a feel.
IT'S THE BOOBS I'VE ALWAYS GOT TO TOUCH!
BAM

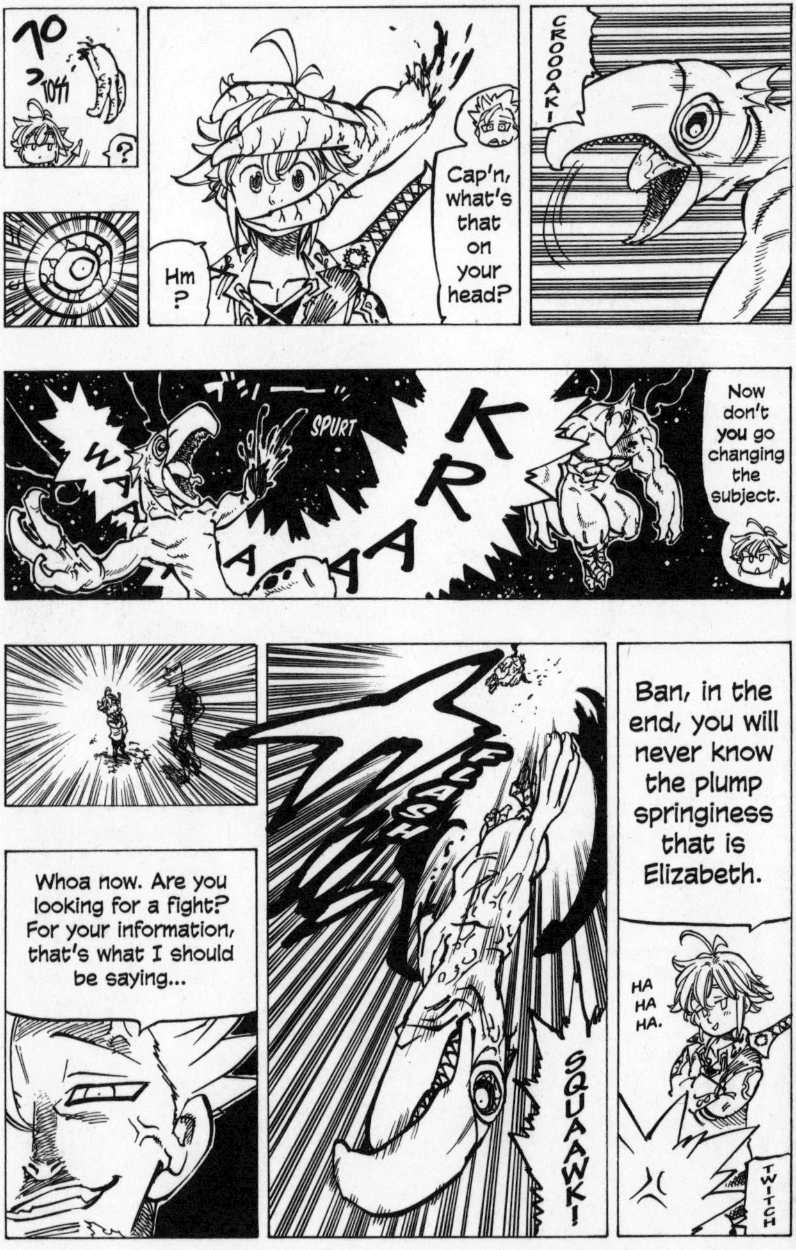
CROOOAK!
Cap'n, what's that on your head?
Hm?
TOSS
?
Now don't you go changing the subject.
KRAAA
SPURT
Ban, in the end, you will never know the plump springiness that is Elizabeth.
HA HA HA.
TWITCH
FLASH
SQUAAWK!
Whoa now. Are you looking for a fight? For your information, that's what I should be saying...

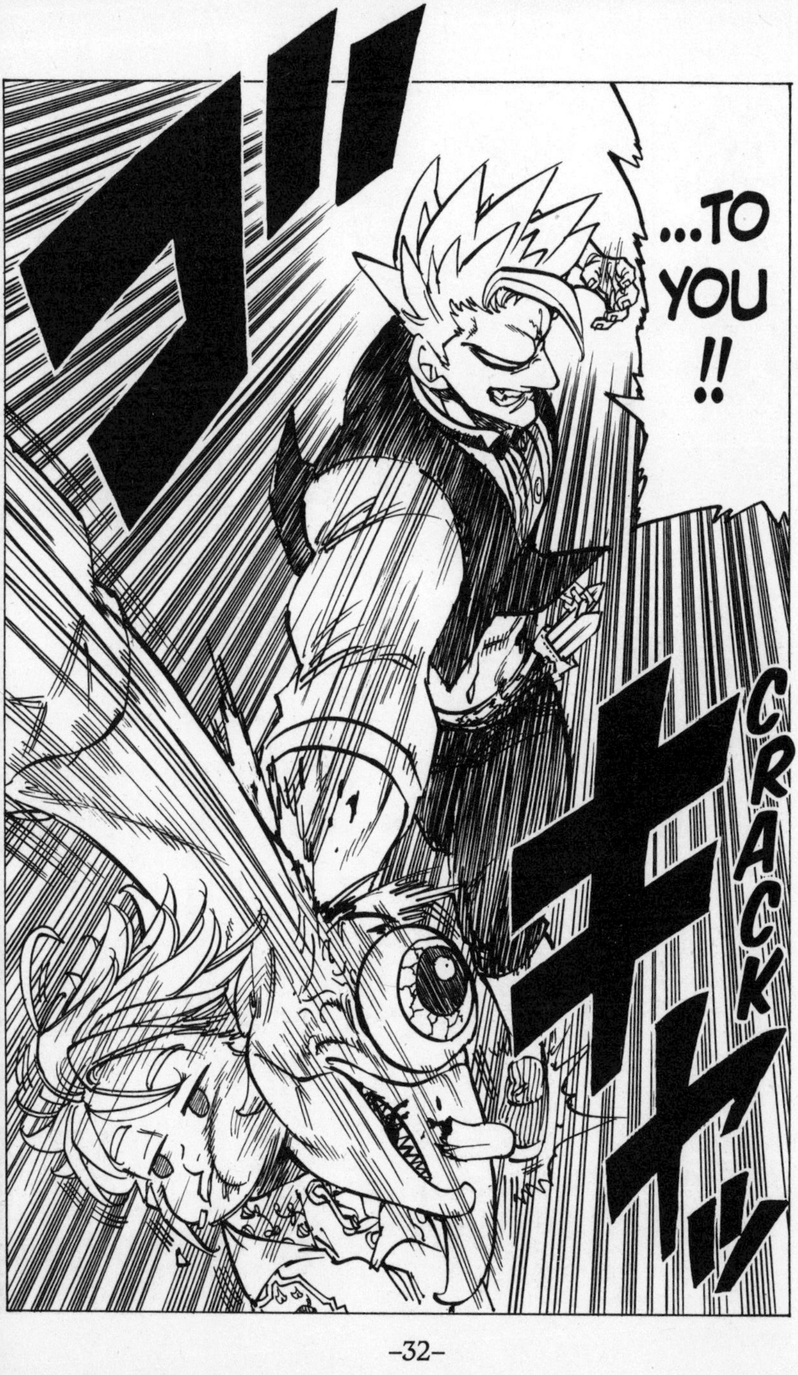
...TO YOU !!
CRACK

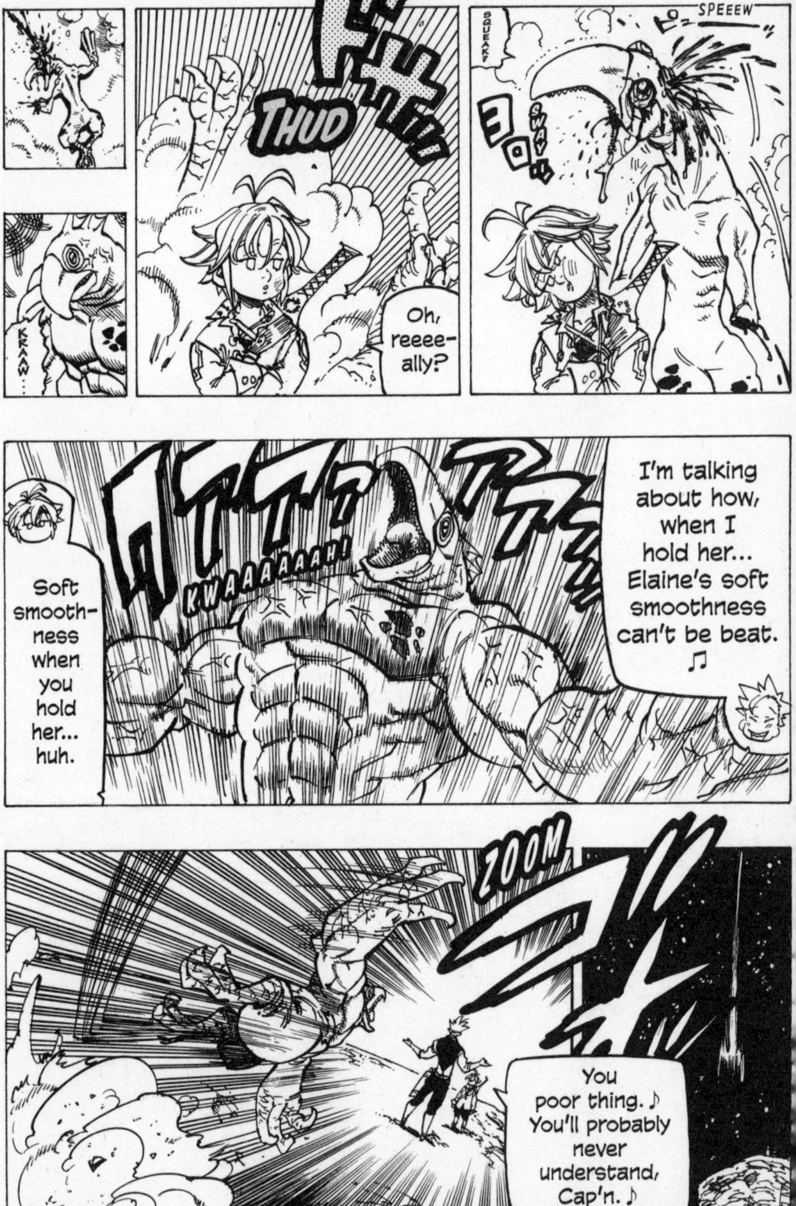
SPEEEW
SQUEAK
SWAY
THUD
Oh, reeee-ally?
KRAAW...
I'm talking about how, when I hold her... Elaine's soft smoothness can't be beat. ♫
KWAAAAAAAH!
Soft smoothness when you hold her... huh.
ZOOM
You poor thing. ♪ You'll probably never understand, Cap'n. ♪

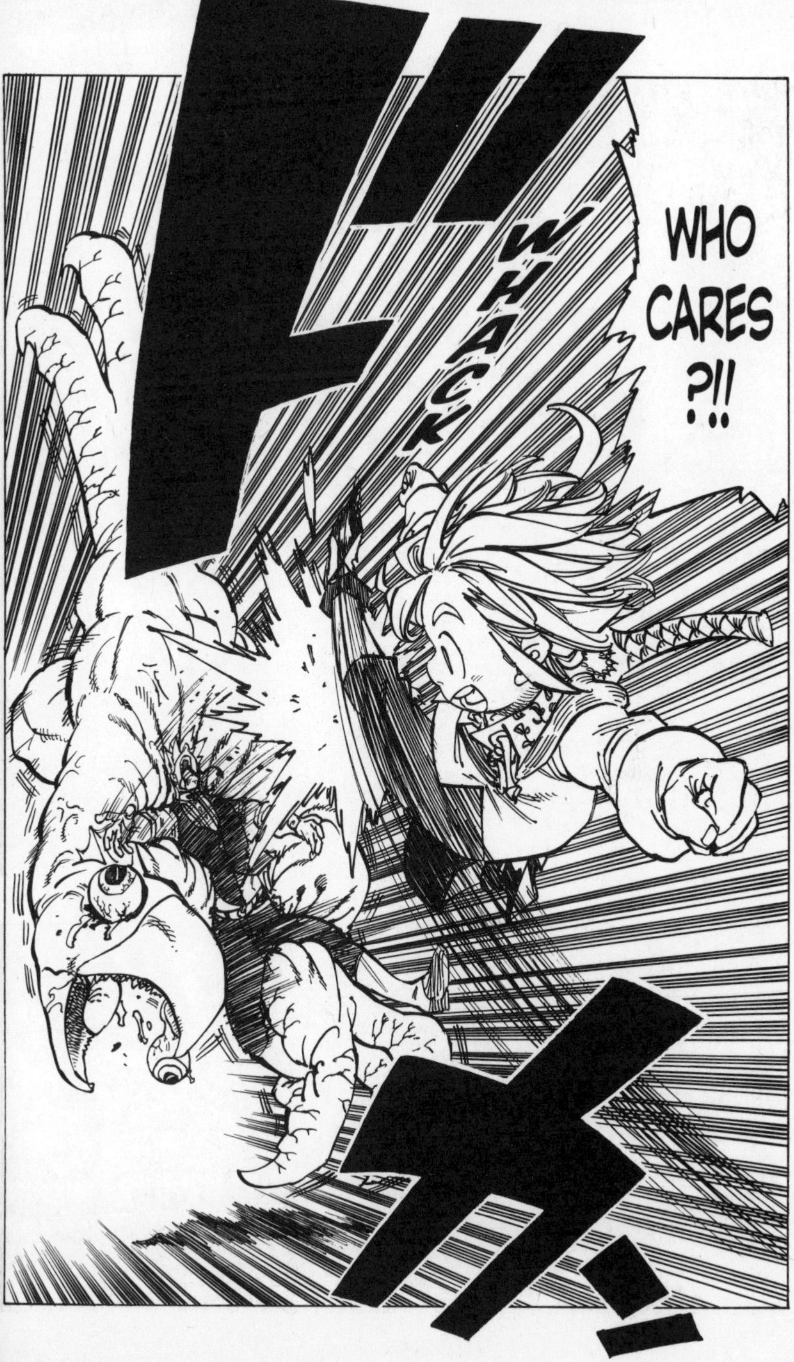
WHOCK
WHO CARES ?!!

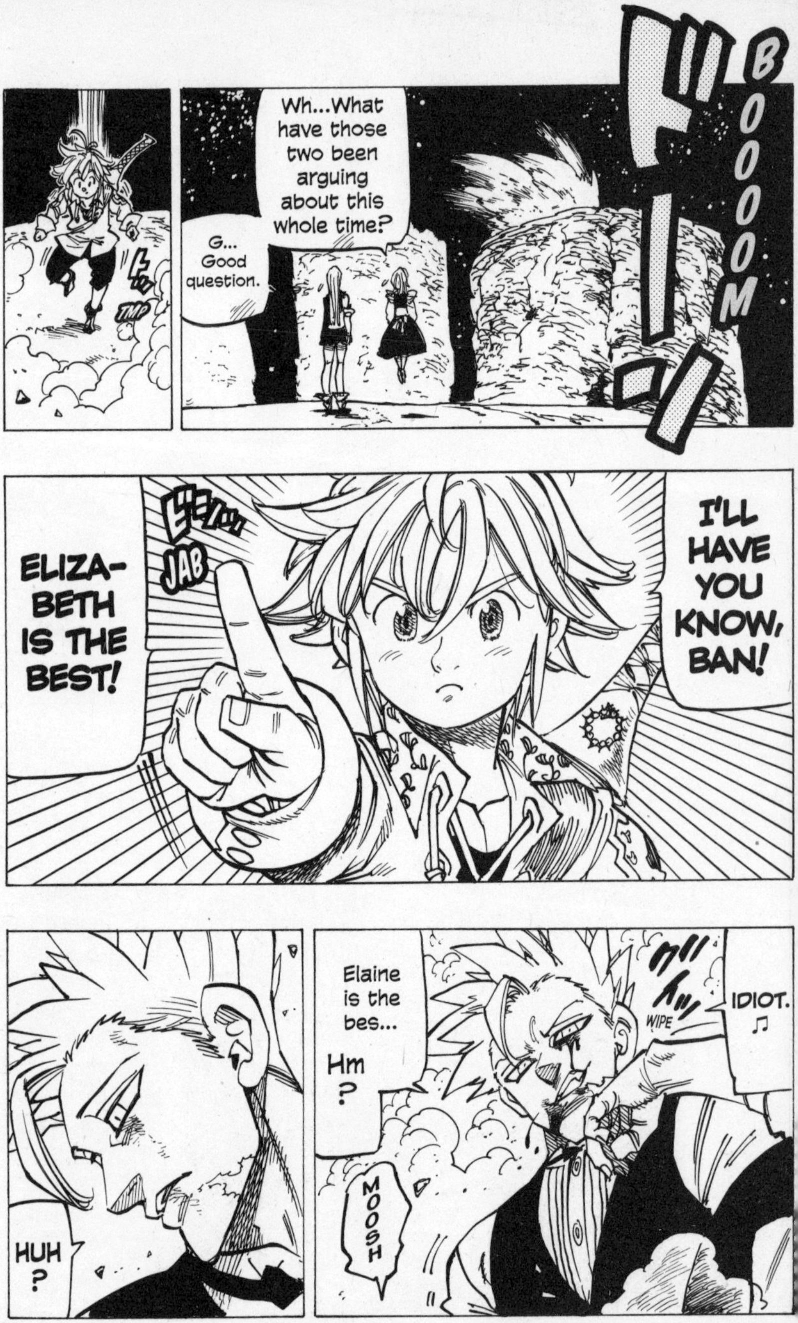
BOOOOOM
Wh...What have those two been arguing about this whole time?
G... Good question.
TMP
I'LL HAVE YOU KNOW, BAN!
JAB
ELIZA-BETH IS THE BEST!
IDIOT. ♫
WIPE
Elaine is the bes...
Hm ?
MOOSH
HUH ?

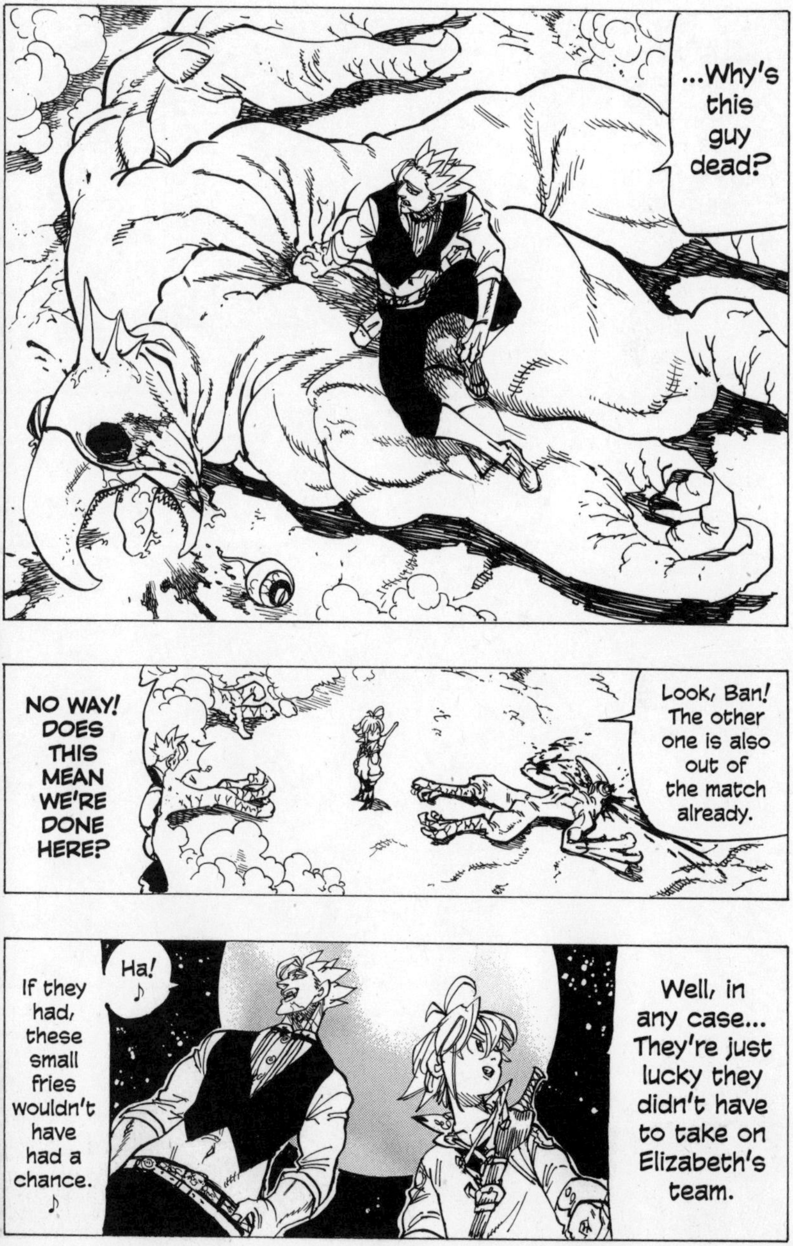
...Why's this guy dead?
Look, Ban! The other one is also out of the match already.
NO WAY! DOES THIS MEAN WE'RE DONE HERE?
Well, in any case... They're just lucky they didn't have to take on Elizabeth's team.
Ha! ♪
If they had, these small fries wouldn't have had a chance. ♪

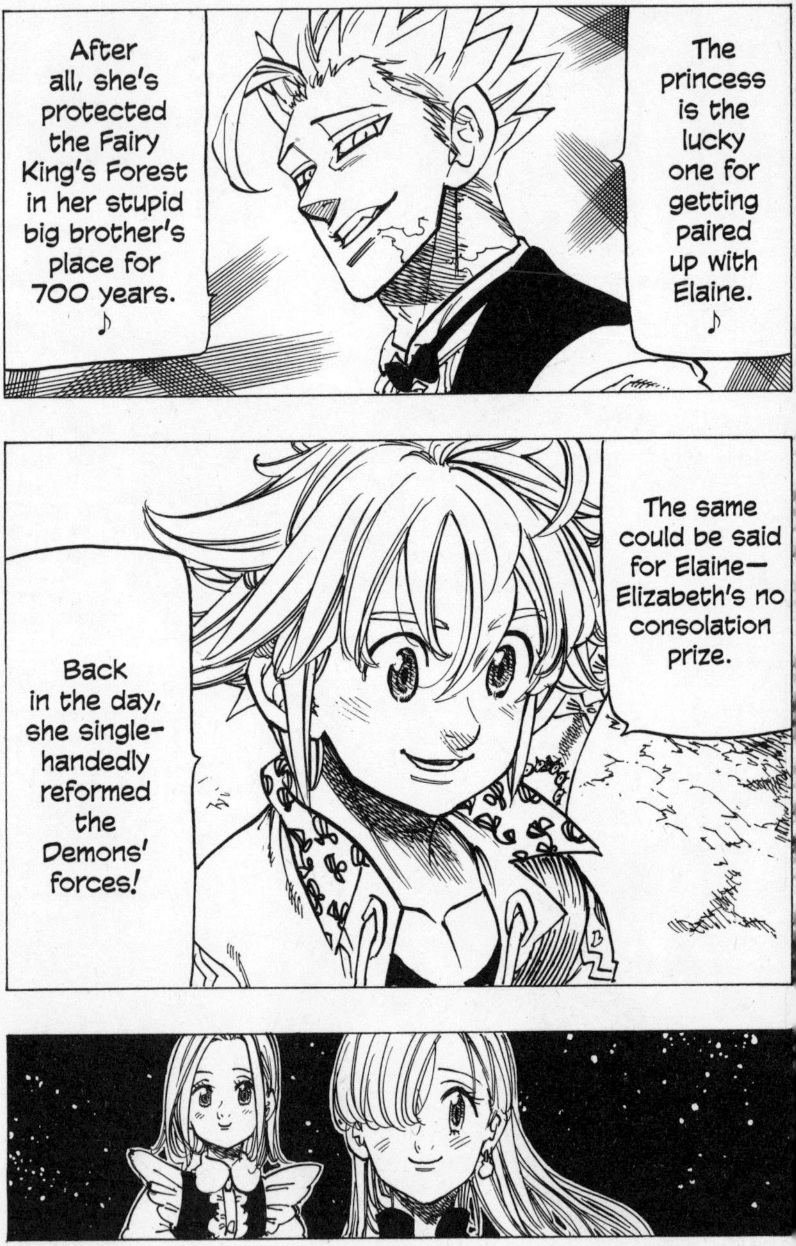
The princess is the lucky one for getting paired up with Elaine. ♪
After all, she's protected the Fairy King's Forest in her stupid big brother's place for 700 years. ♪
The same could be said for Elaine—Elizabeth's no consolation prize.
Back in the day, she single-handedly reformed the Demons' forces!

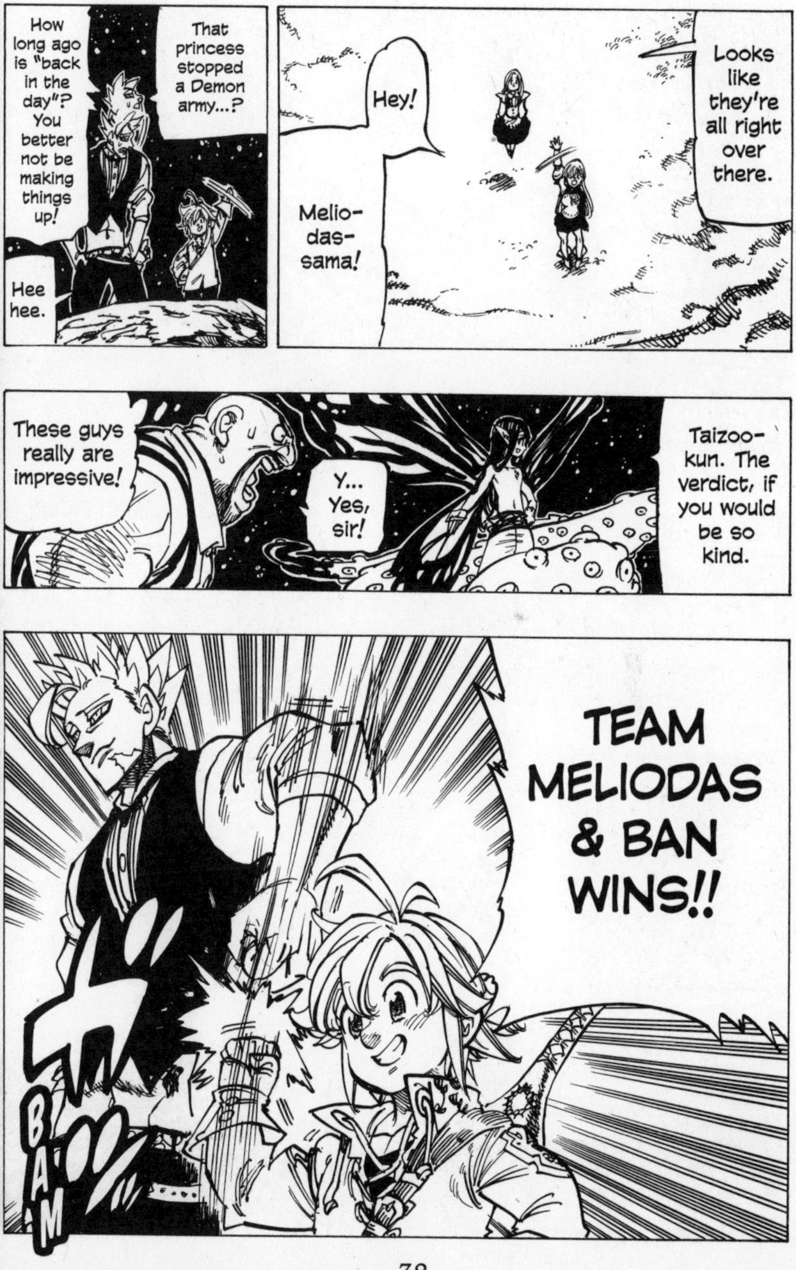

Looks like they're all right over there.
Hey!
Melio-das-sama!
That princess stopped a Demon army...?
How long ago is "back in the day"? You better not be making things up!
Hee hee.
Taizoo-kun. The verdict, if you would be so kind.
Y... Yes, sir!
These guys really are impressive!
TEAM MELIODAS & BAN WINS!!
BAM

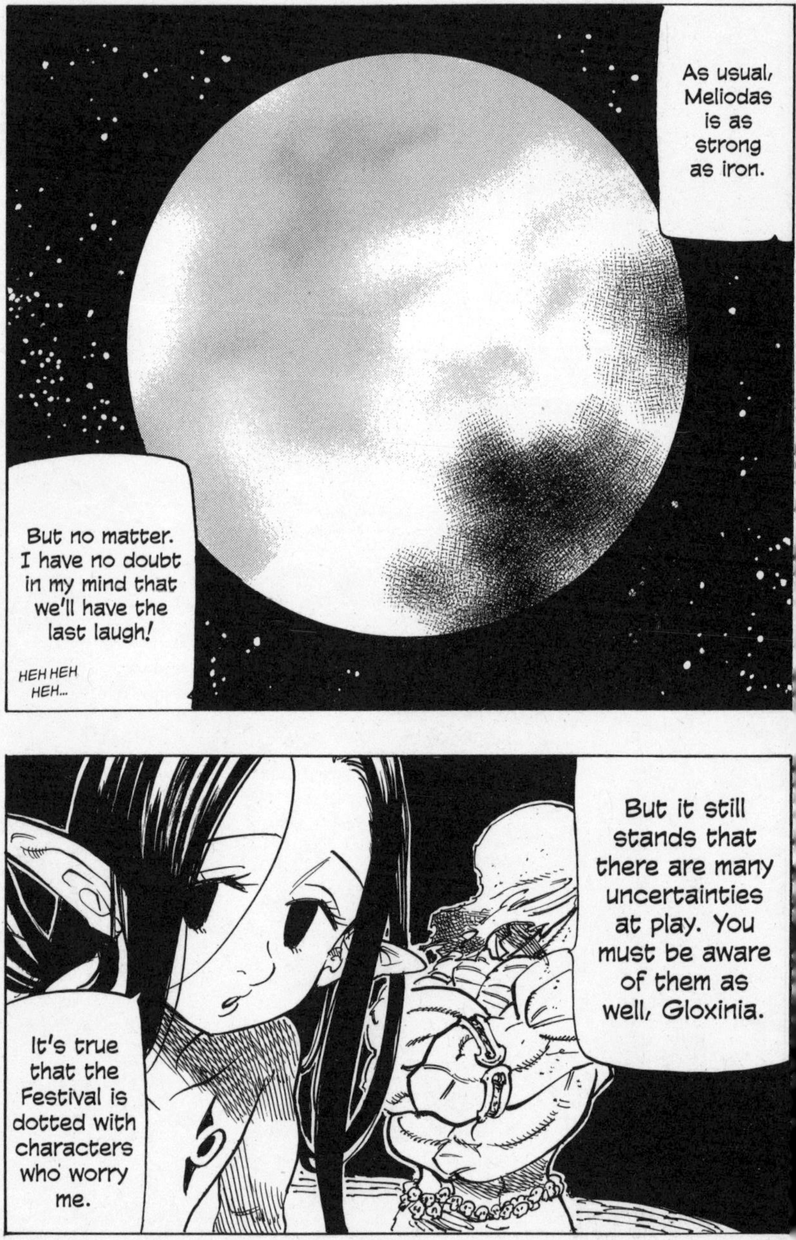
As usual, Meliodas is as strong as iron.
But no matter. I have no doubt in my mind that we'll have the last laugh!
HEH HEH HEH...
But it still stands that there are many uncertainties at play. You must be aware of them as well, Gloxinia.
It's true that the Festival is dotted with characters who worry me.

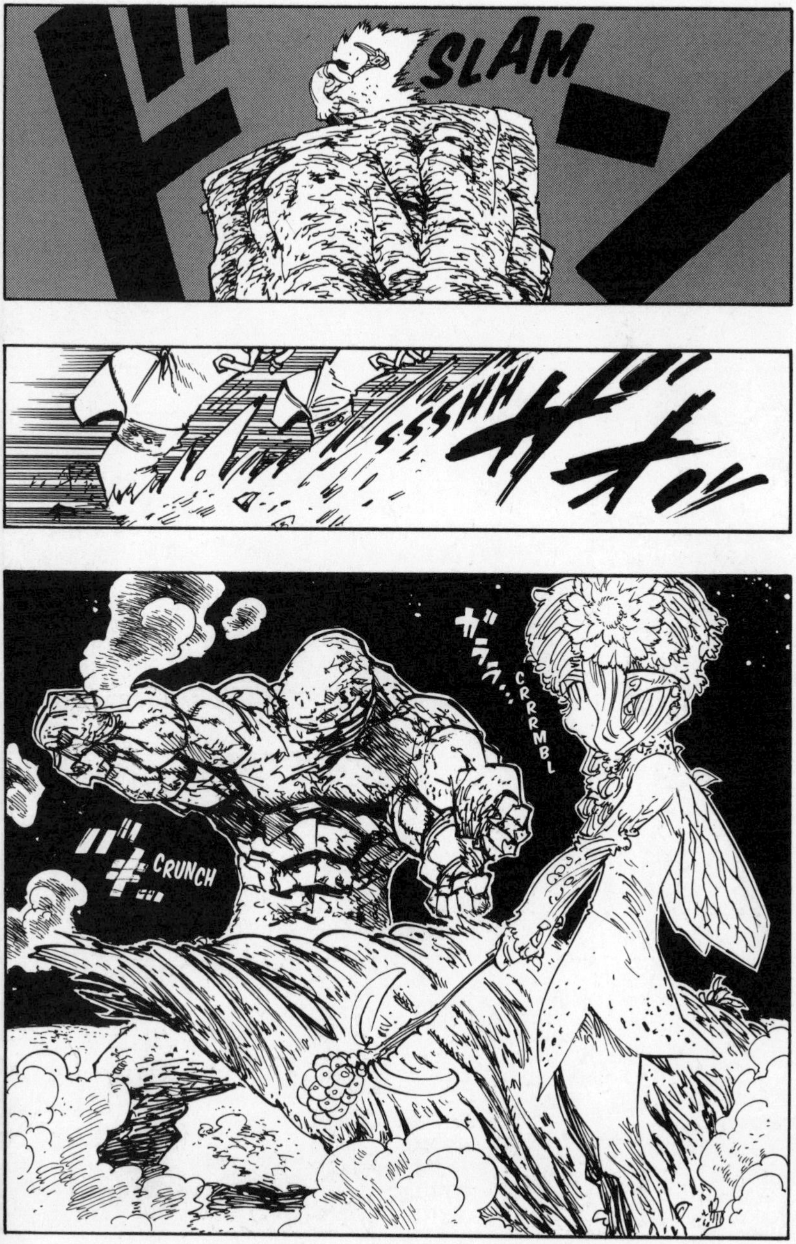
SLAM
SSSSHHH
CRRRMBL
CRUNCH

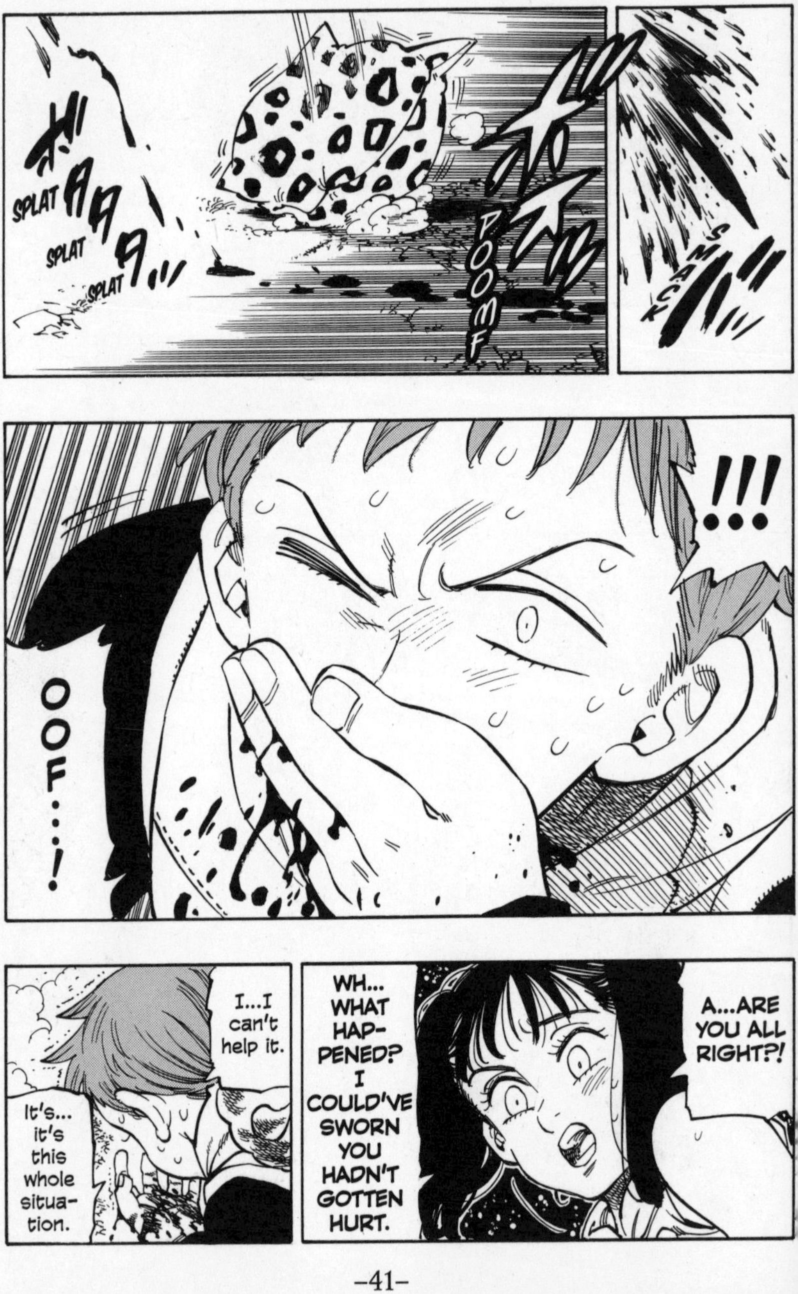
SMACK
POOMF
SPLAT
SPLAT
SPLAT
!!!
OOF...!
A...ARE YOU ALL RIGHT?!
WH... WHAT HAPPENED? I COULD'VE SWORN YOU HADN'T GOTTEN HURT.
I...I can't help it.
It's... it's this whole situation.

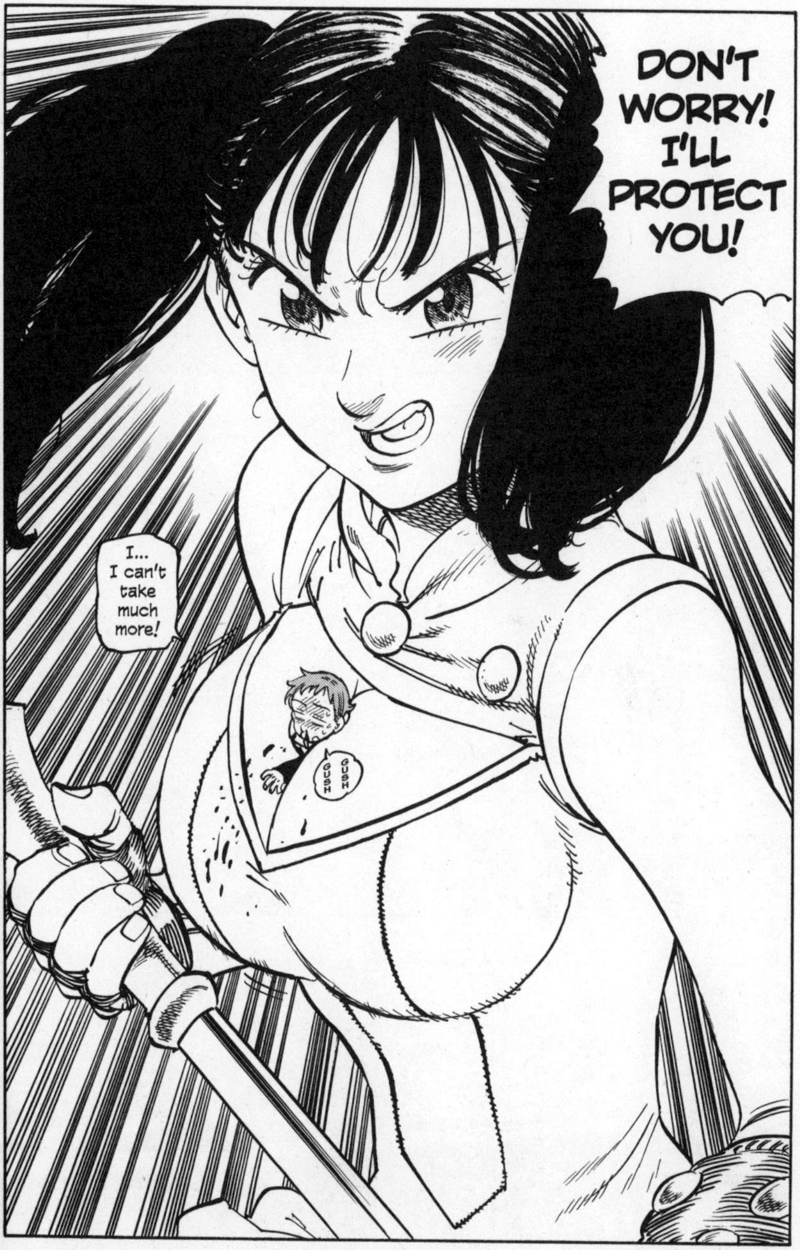
DON'T WORRY! I'LL PROTECT YOU!
GUSH GUSH
I... I can't take much more!

Chapter 165 - Incompatible Lovers

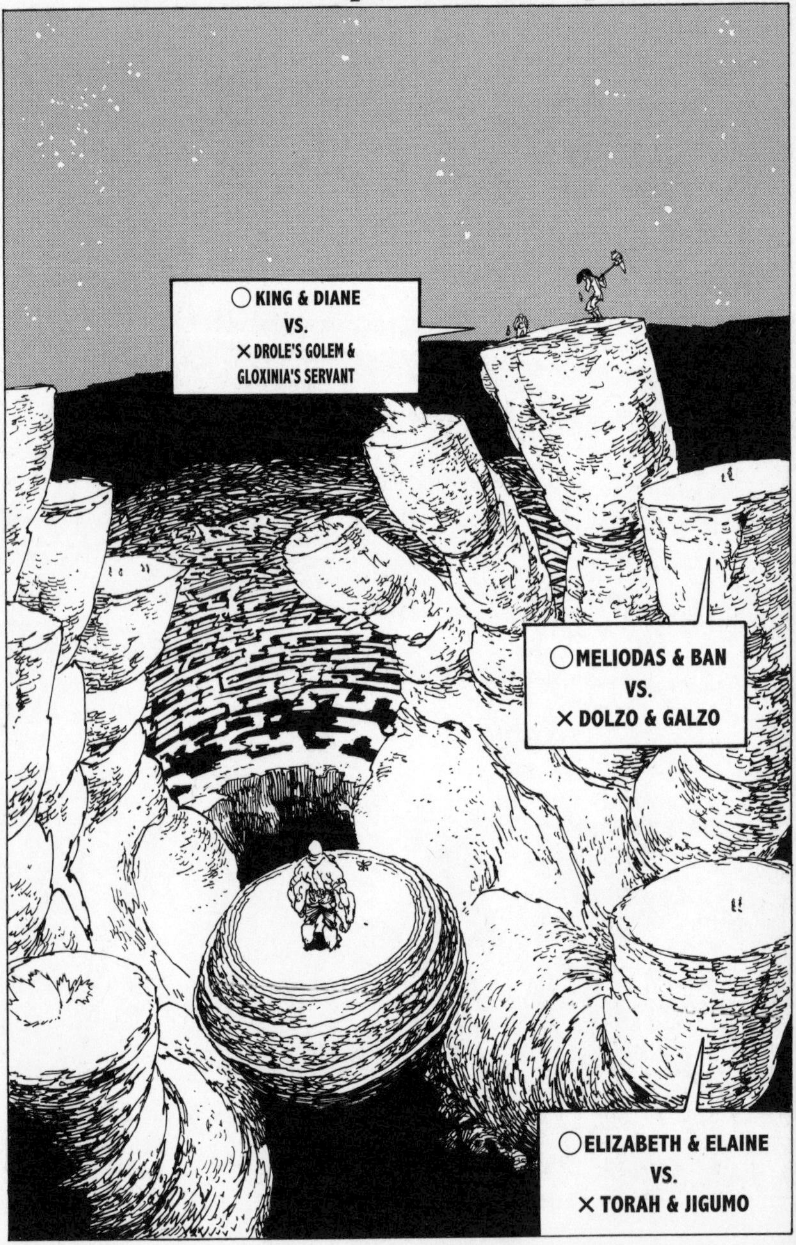
○KING & DIANE
VS.
×DROLE'S GOLEM & GLOXINIA'S SERVANT
○MELIODAS & BAN
VS.
×DOLZO & GALZO
○ELIZABETH & ELAINE
VS.
×TORAH & JIGUMO

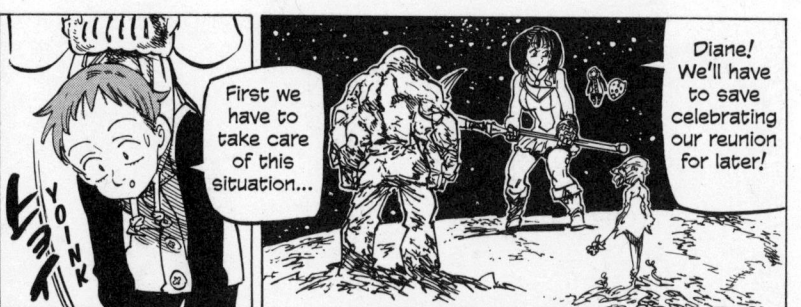

Diane! We'll have to save celebrating our reunion for later!
First we have to take care of this situation...
YOINK
We'll be taking on monsters, right?
So little kids have to hide in here!
POINK
STUFF
BLUSSSH
COME AND GET ME!
BAM
SPURT
Hm?

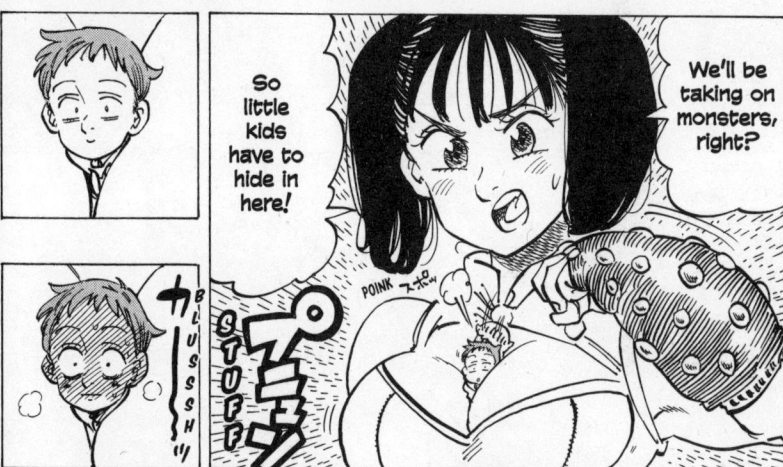

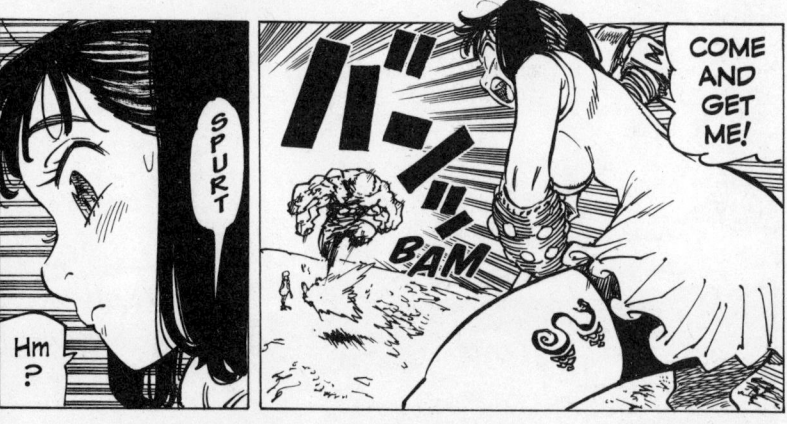

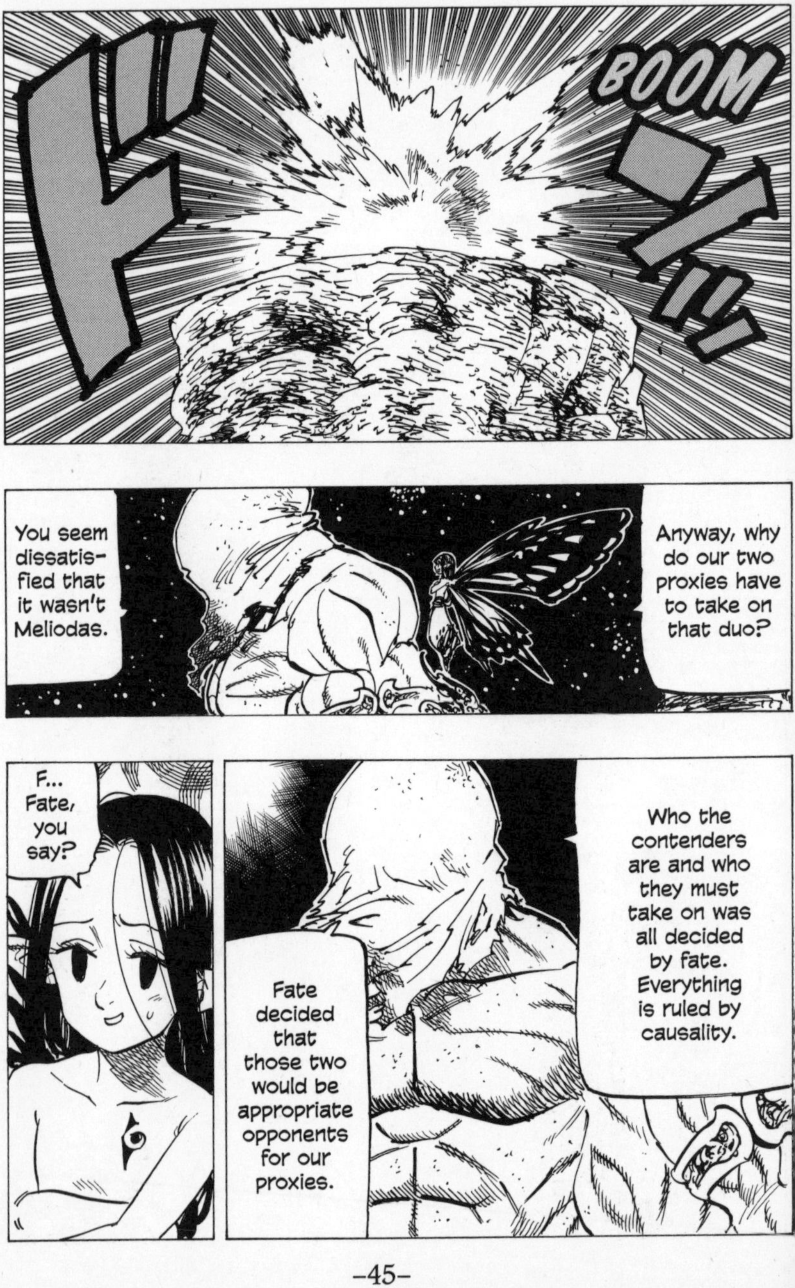
BOOM
Anyway, why do our two proxies have to take on that duo?
You seem dissatis-fied that it wasn't Meliodas.
Who the contenders are and who they must take on was all decided by fate. Everything is ruled by causality.
Fate decided that those two would be appropriate opponents for our proxies.
F... Fate, you say?

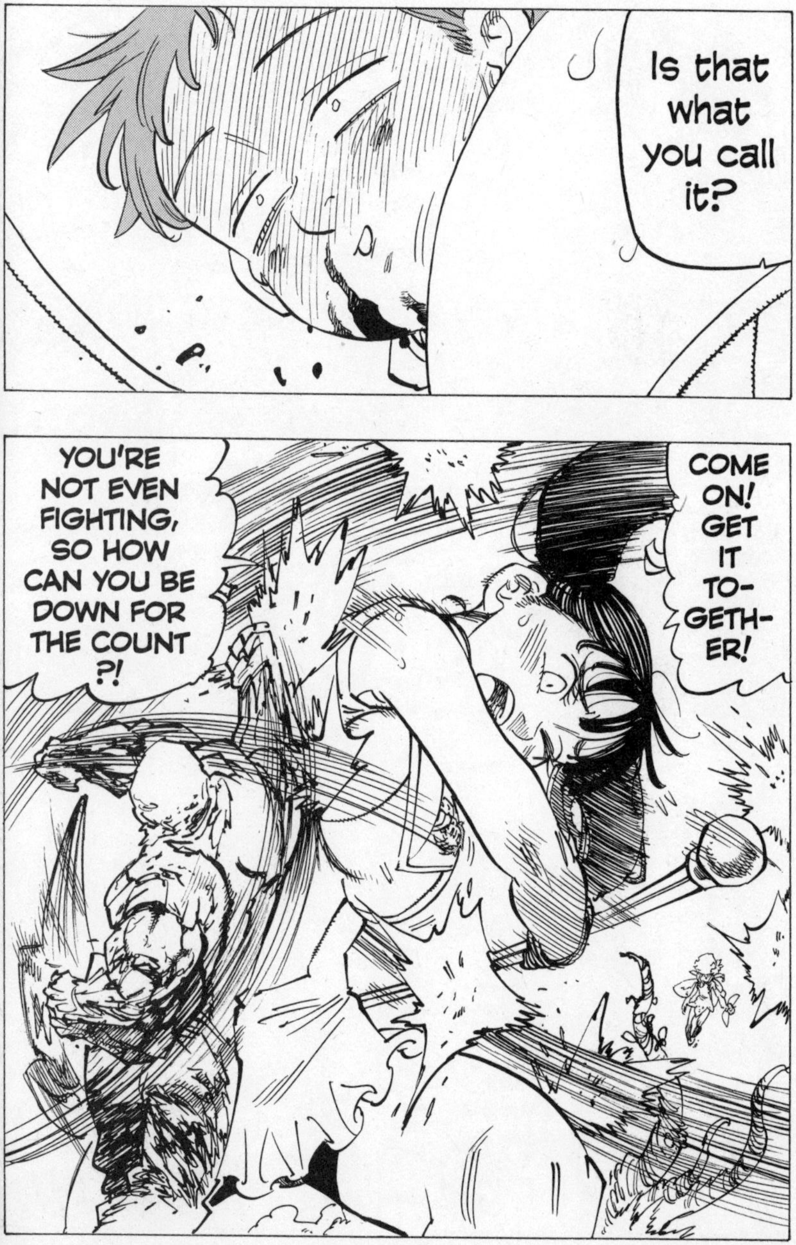
Is that what you call it?
COME ON! GET IT TO-GETH-ER!
YOU'RE NOT EVEN FIGHTING, SO HOW CAN YOU BE DOWN FOR THE COUNT?!

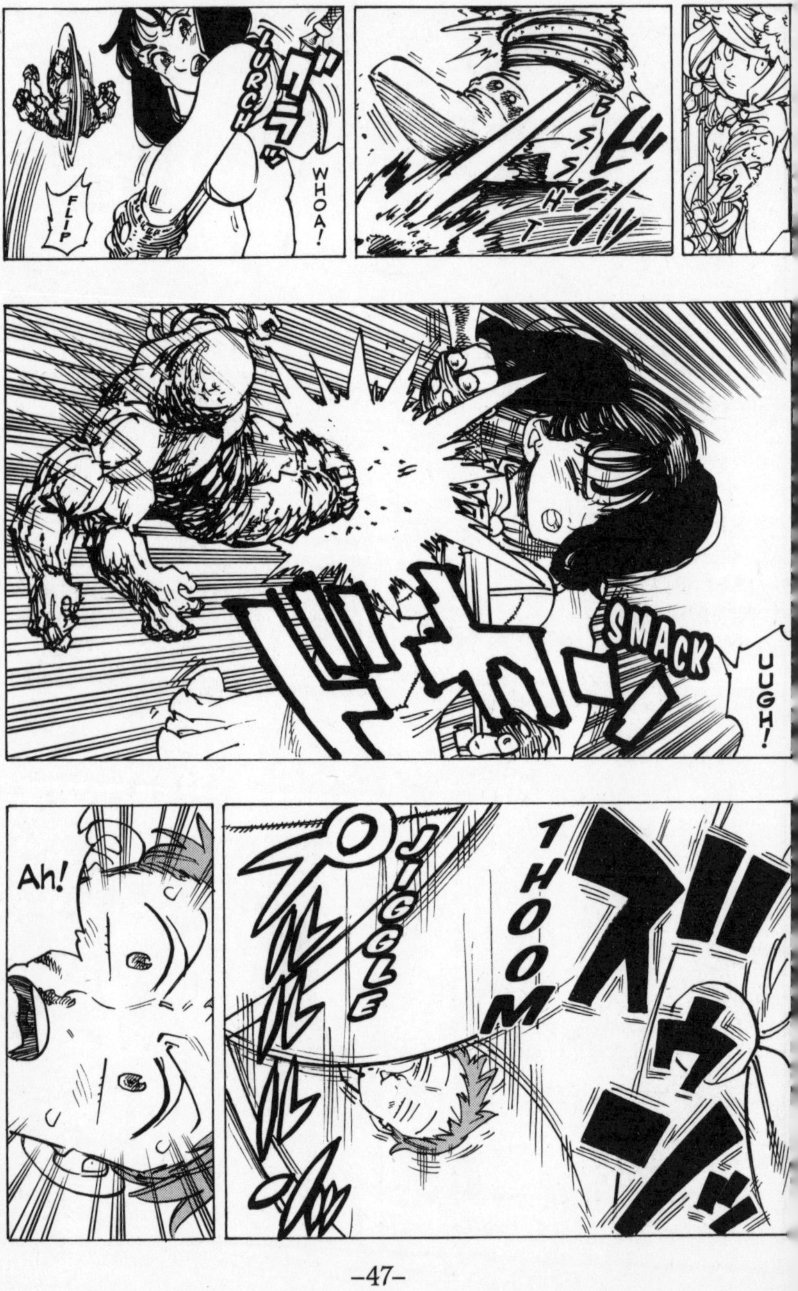
BSSHT
LURCH
WHOA!
FLIP
UUGH!
SMACK
THOOOM
JIGGLE
Ah!

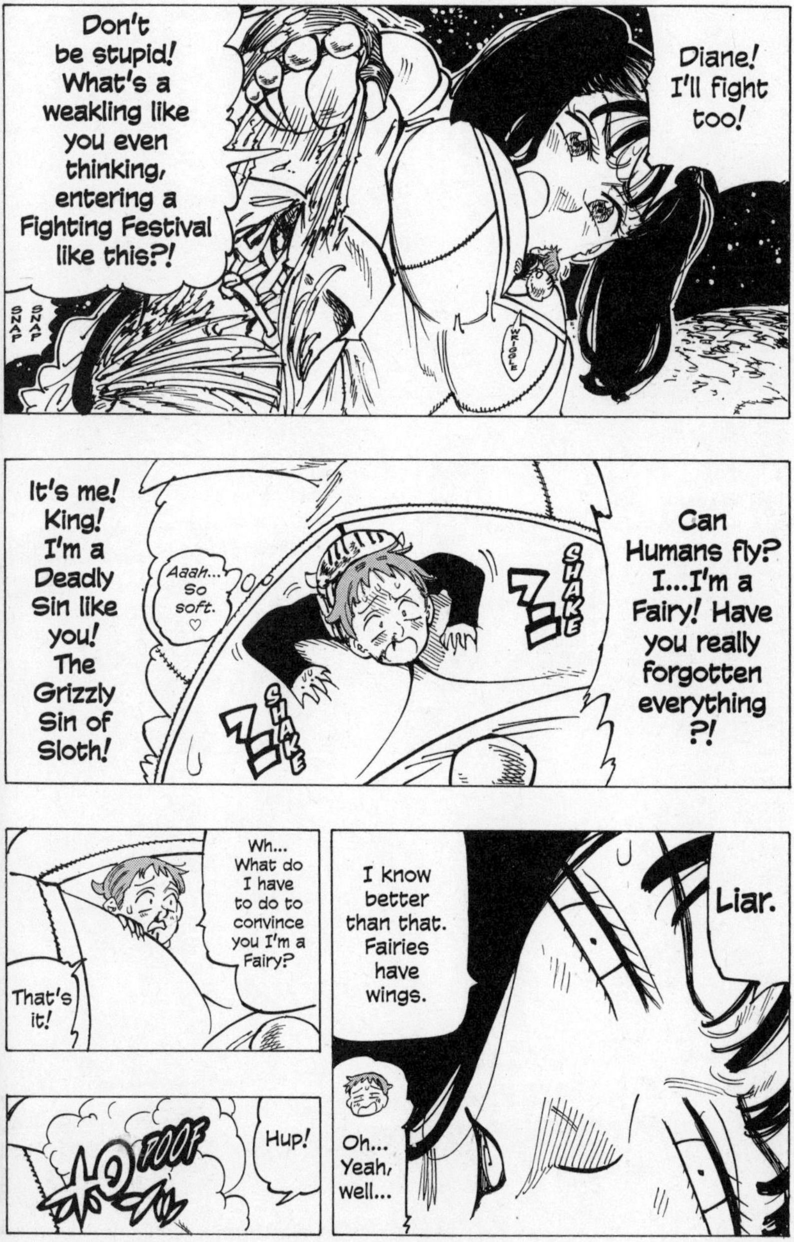
Diane! I'll fight too!
Don't be stupid! What's a weakling like you even thinking, entering a Fighting Festival like this?!
WRIGGLE
SNAP SNAP
Can Humans fly? I...I'm a Fairy! Have you really forgotten everything ?!
SHAKE
Aaah... So soft. ♡
SHAKE
It's me! King! I'm a Deadly Sin like you! The Grizzly Sin of Sloth!
Liar.
I know better than that. Fairies have wings.
Oh... Yeah, well...
Wh... What do I have to do to convince you I'm a Fairy?
That's it!
Hup!
POOF

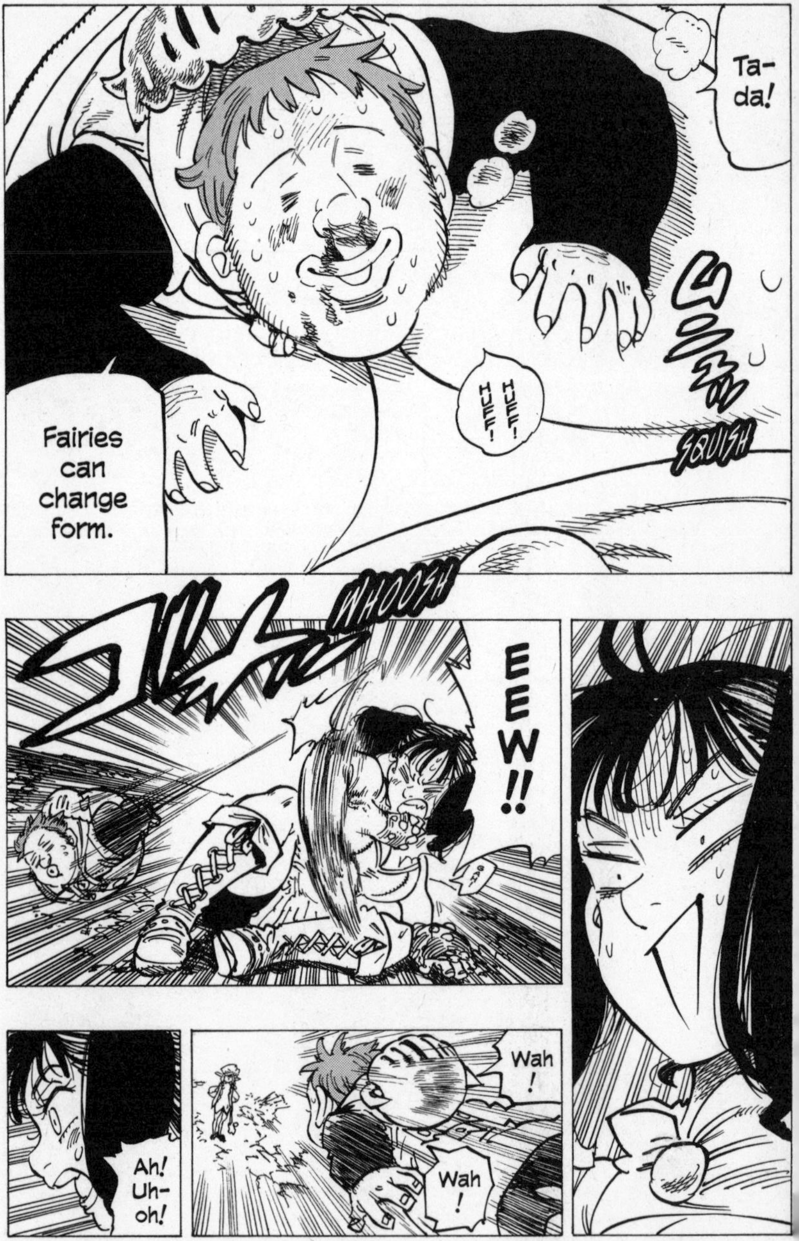
Ta-da!
SQUISH
HUFF! HUFF!
Fairies can change form.
WHOOSH
EEW!!
Wah!
Wah!
Ah! Uh-oh!

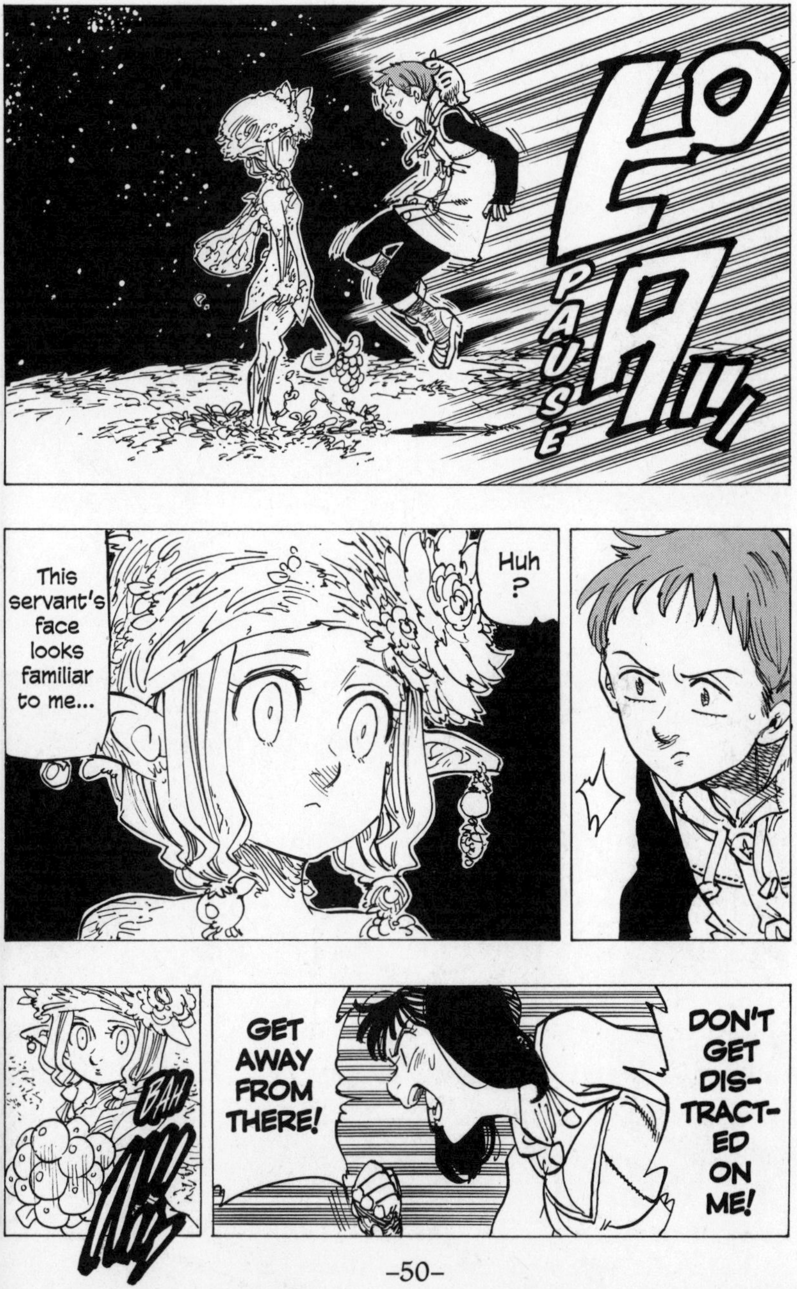
PAUSE
Huh?
This servant's face looks familiar to me...
DON'T GET DIS-TRACT-ED ON ME!
GET AWAY FROM THERE!

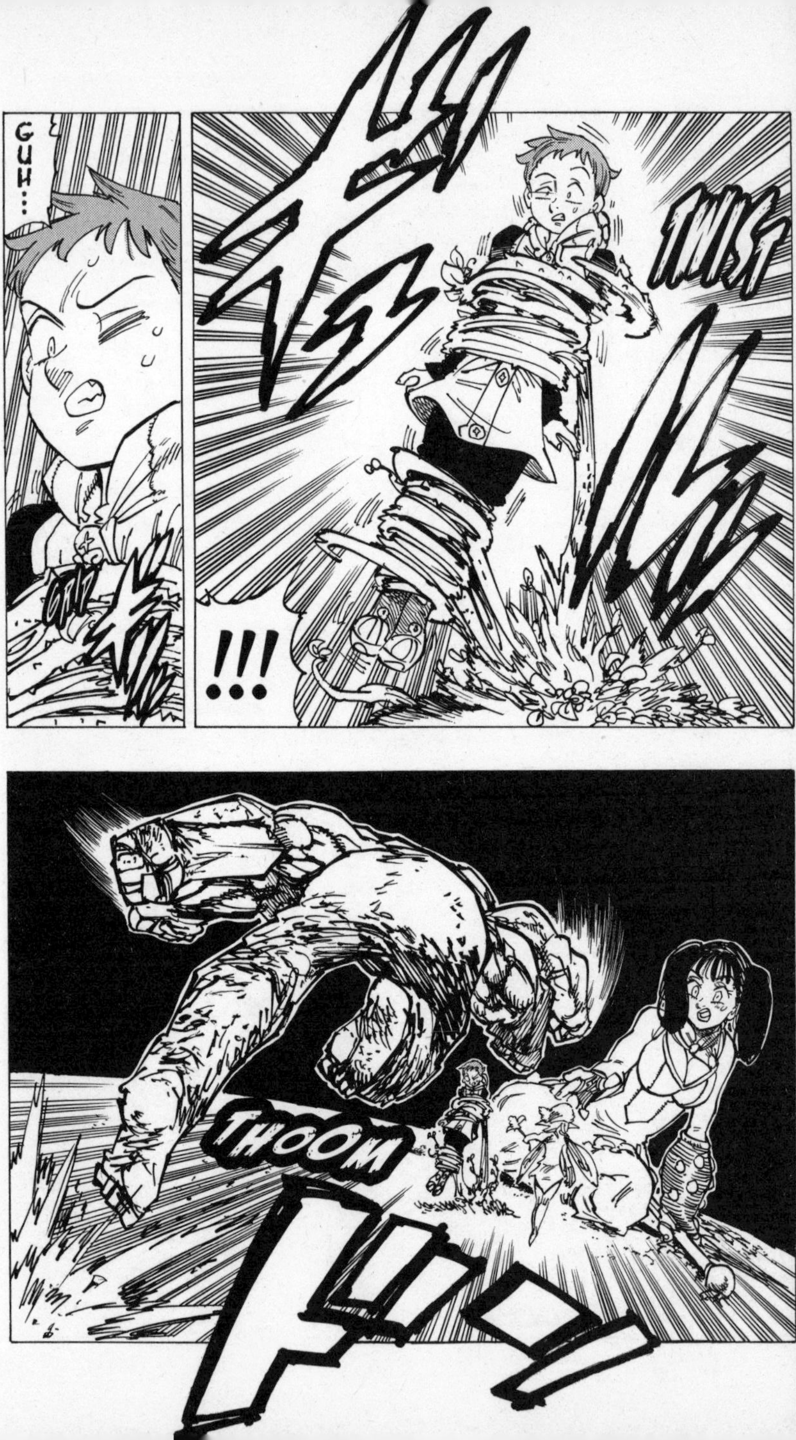

GUH...
GRIP
TWIST
!!!
THOOM

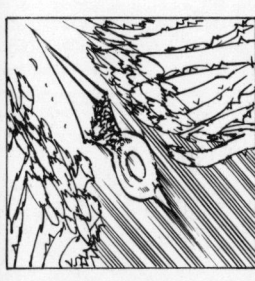

SHRED

SPIRIT SPEAR CHASTIEFOL...

FIFTH FORM! "INCREASE."

WHOOOOOM

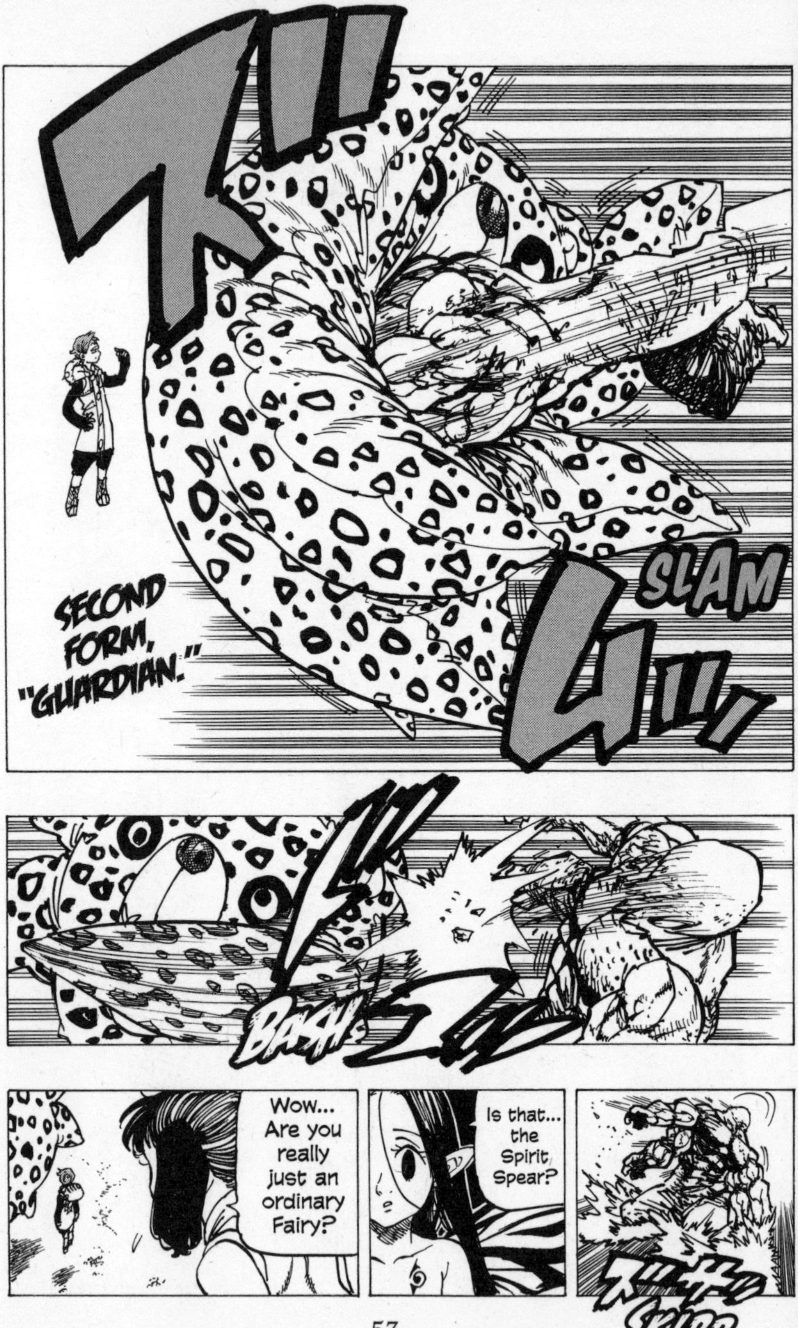
SECOND FORM, "GUARDIAN."
SLAM
BASH
SKIDD
Is that... the Spirit Spear?
Wow... Are you really just an ordinary Fairy?

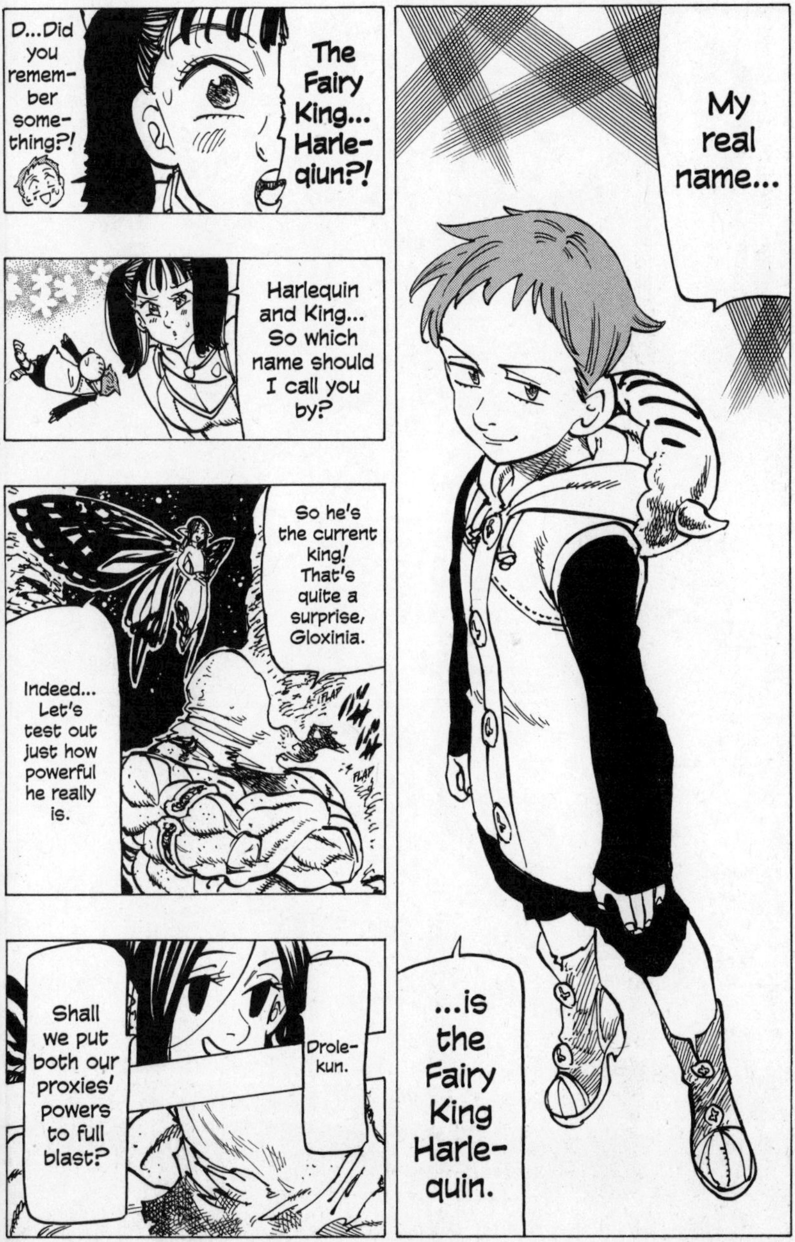
My real name...
...is the Fairy King Harlequin.
The Fairy King... Harlequin?!
D...Did you remember something?!
Harlequin and King... So which name should I call you by?
So he's the current king! That's quite a surprise, Gloxinia.
FLAP
FLAP
Indeed... Let's test out just how powerful he really is.
Drole-kun.
Shall we put both our proxies' powers to full blast?

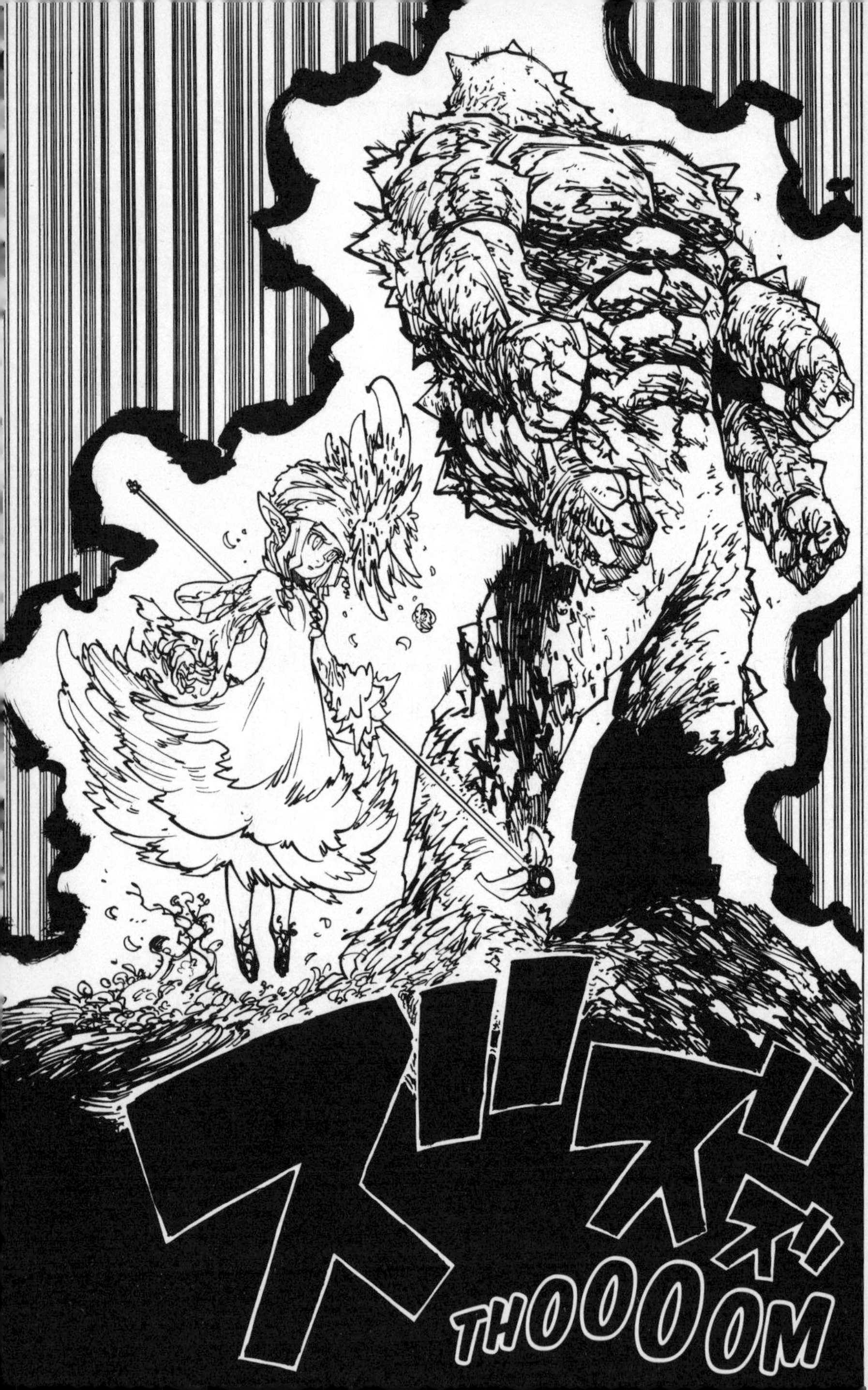
THOOOOM

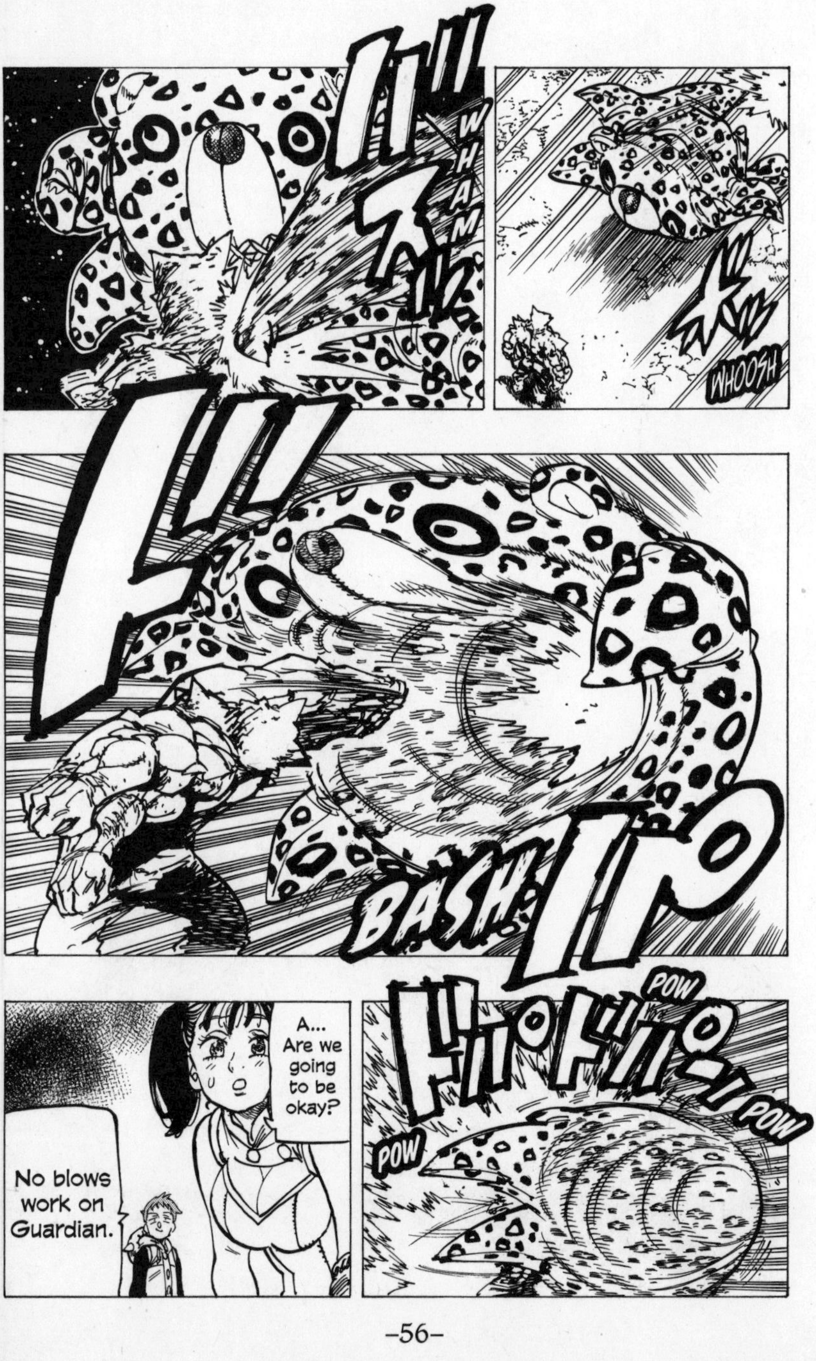
WHOOSH
WHAM
BASH
POW
POW
POW
A... Are we going to be okay?
No blows work on Guardian.

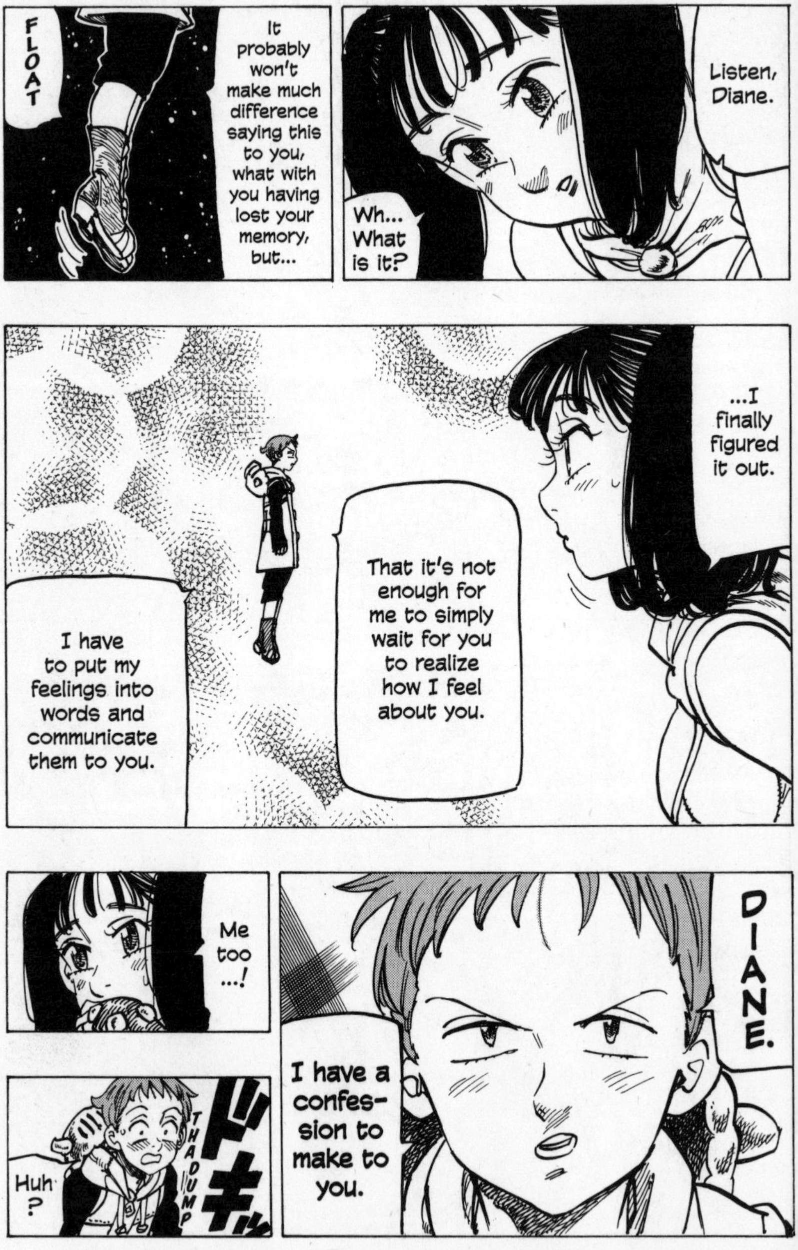
Listen, Diane.
Wh... What is it?
It probably won't make much difference saying this to you, what with you having lost your memory, but...
FLOAT
...I finally figured it out.
That it's not enough for me to simply wait for you to realize how I feel about you.
I have to put my feelings into words and communicate them to you.
DIANE.
I have a confession to make to you.
Me too ...!
THADUMP
Huh?

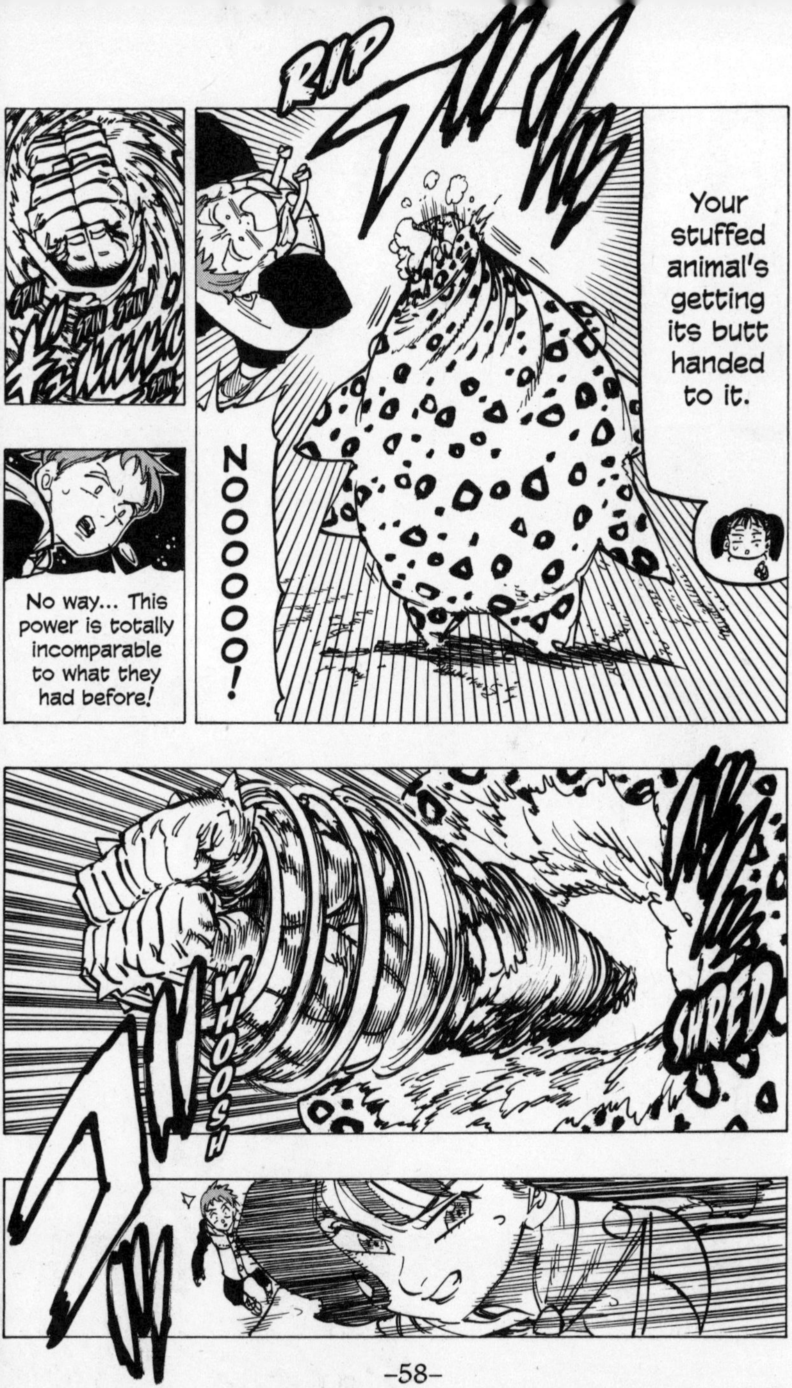
RIP
Your stuffed animal's getting its butt handed to it.
NOOOOOOO!
STIN STIN STIN STIN
No way... This power is totally incomparable to what they had before!
SHRED
WHOOSH

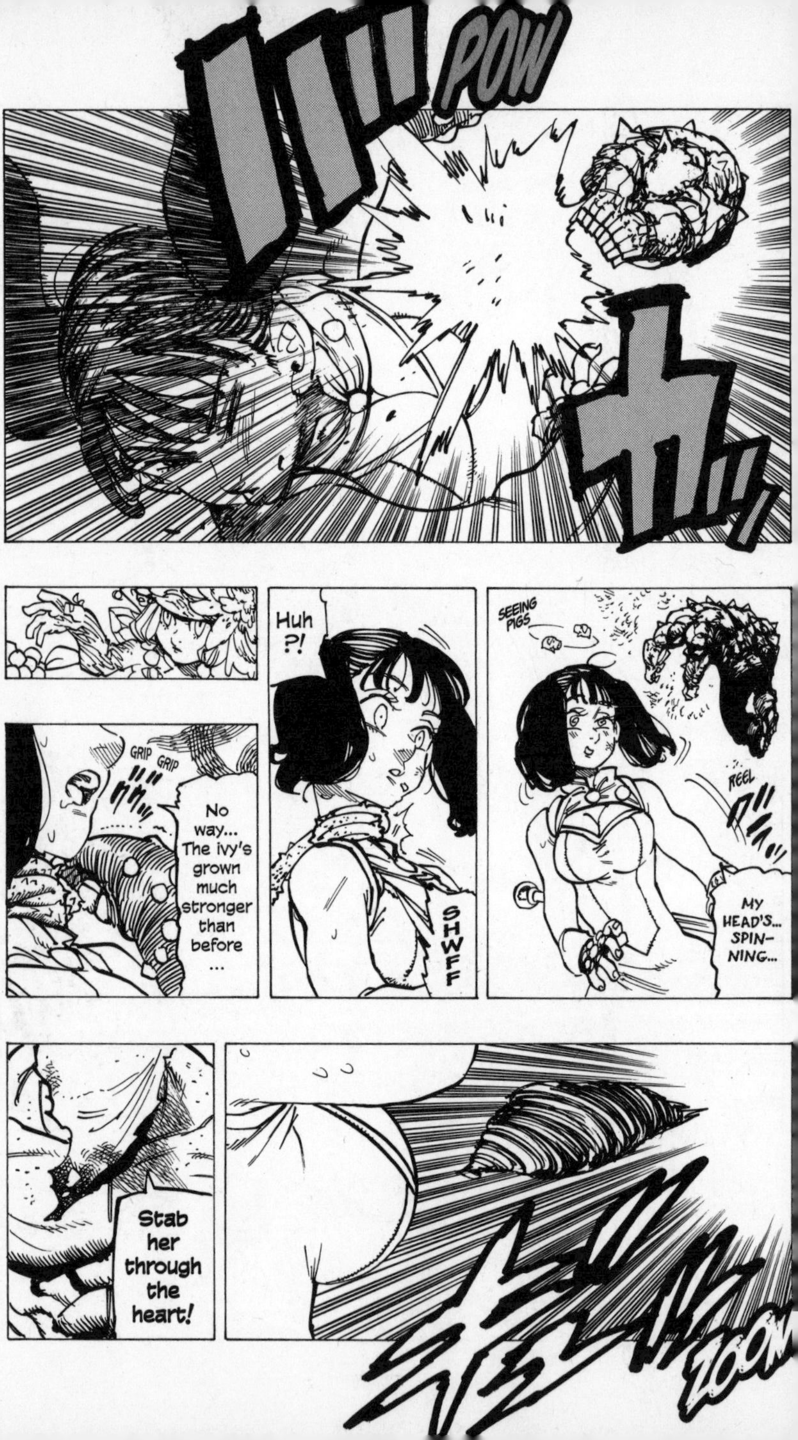
POW
SEEING PIGS
REEL
MY HEAD'S... SPINNING...
Huh ?!
SHWFF
GRIP GRIP
No way... The ivy's grown much stronger than before ...
ZOOM
Stab her through the heart!

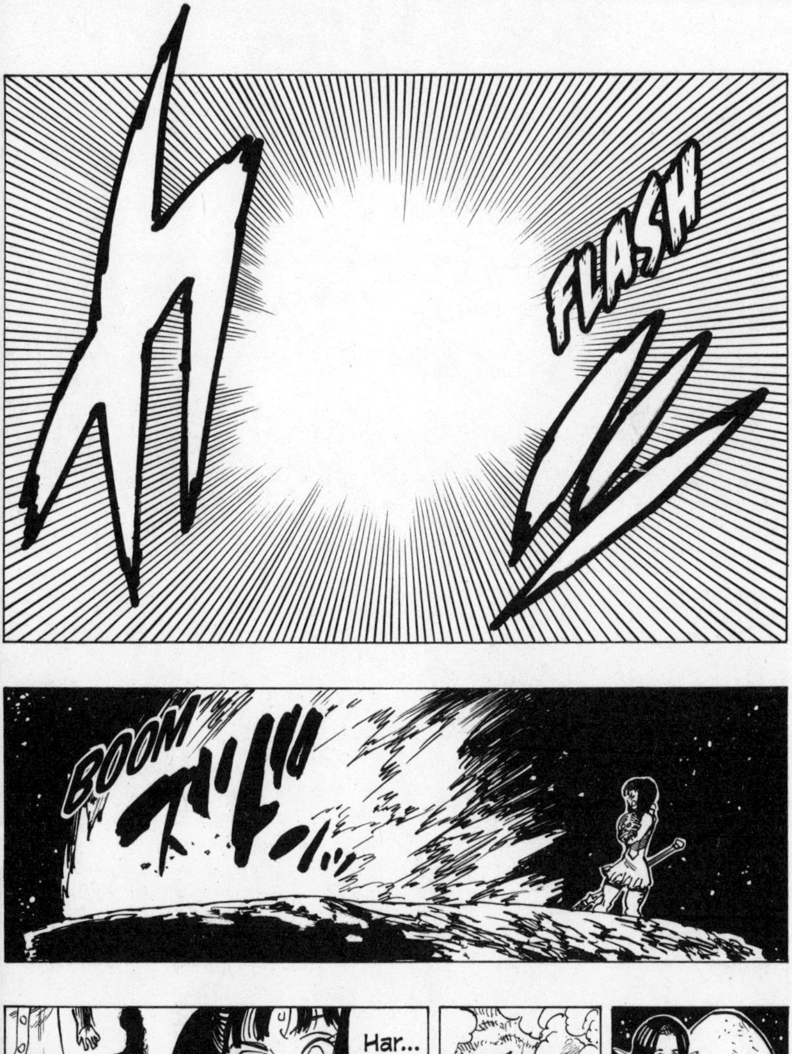
FLASH
BOOM
!!
Har... lequin?
DIANE.

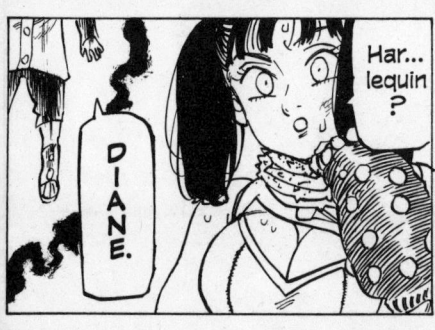

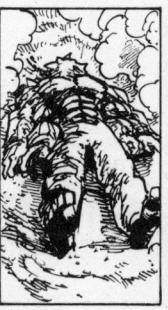

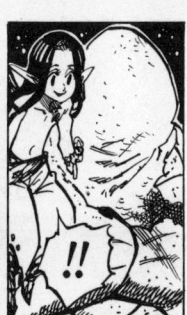

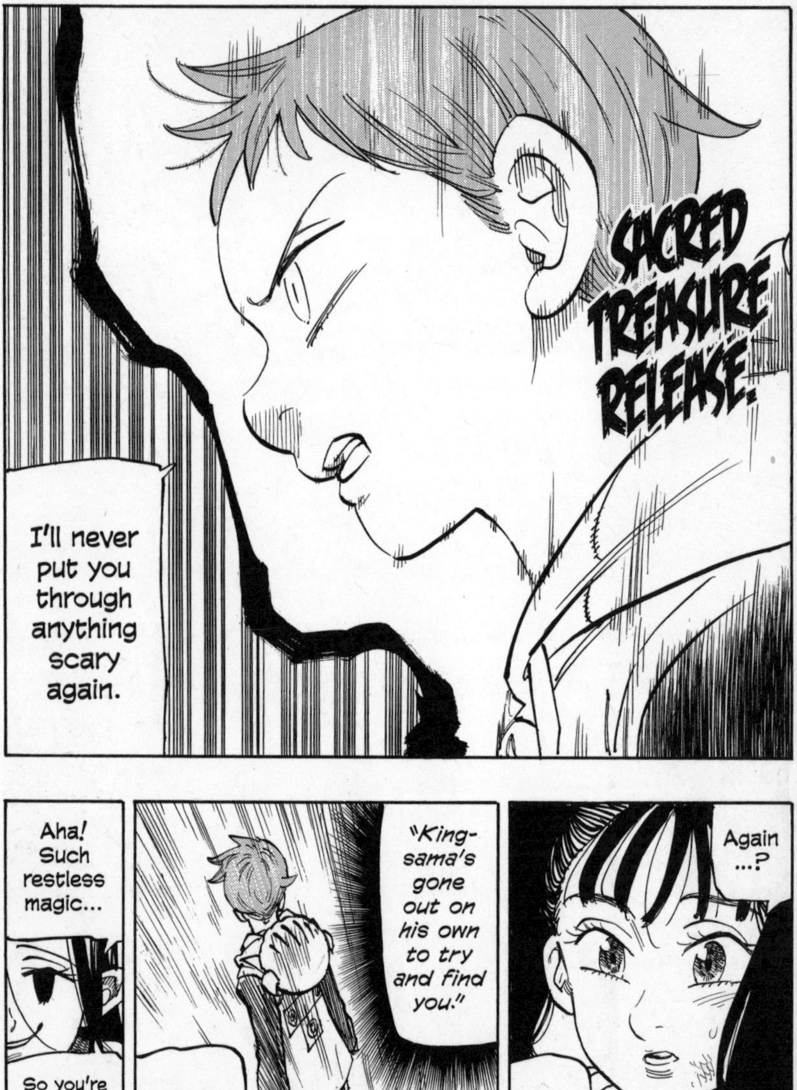
SACRED TREASURE RELEASE.
I'll never put you through anything scary again.
Again ...?
What have we been through ...?
"King-sama's gone out on his own to try and find you."
Elizabeth said the same thing...
Aha! Such restless magic...
So you're the one responsible for defeating the Albions!

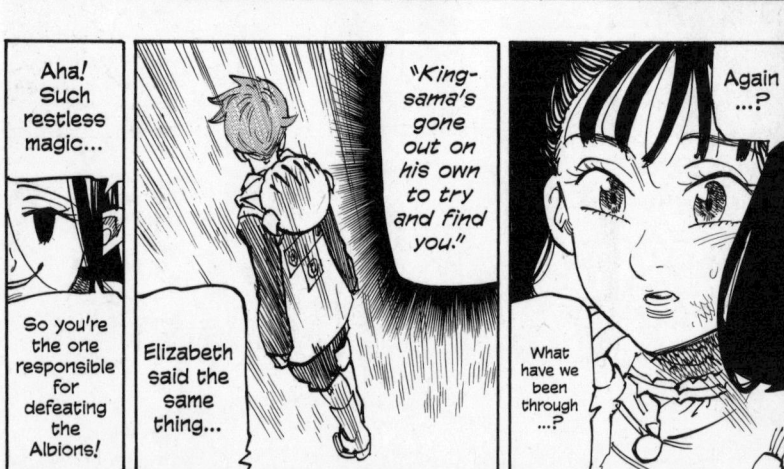

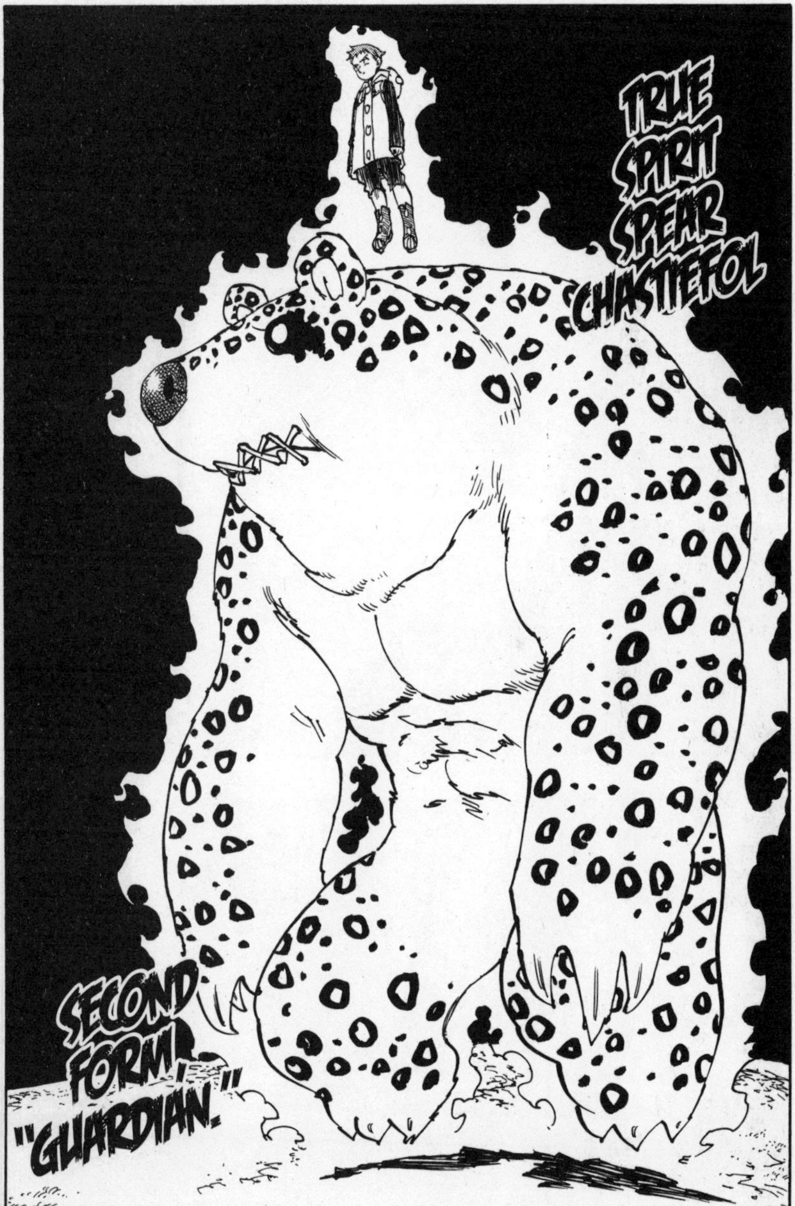
TRUE SPIRIT SPEAR CHASTIEFOL
SECOND FORM, "GUARDIAN."

Chapter 166 - What Sprouts There

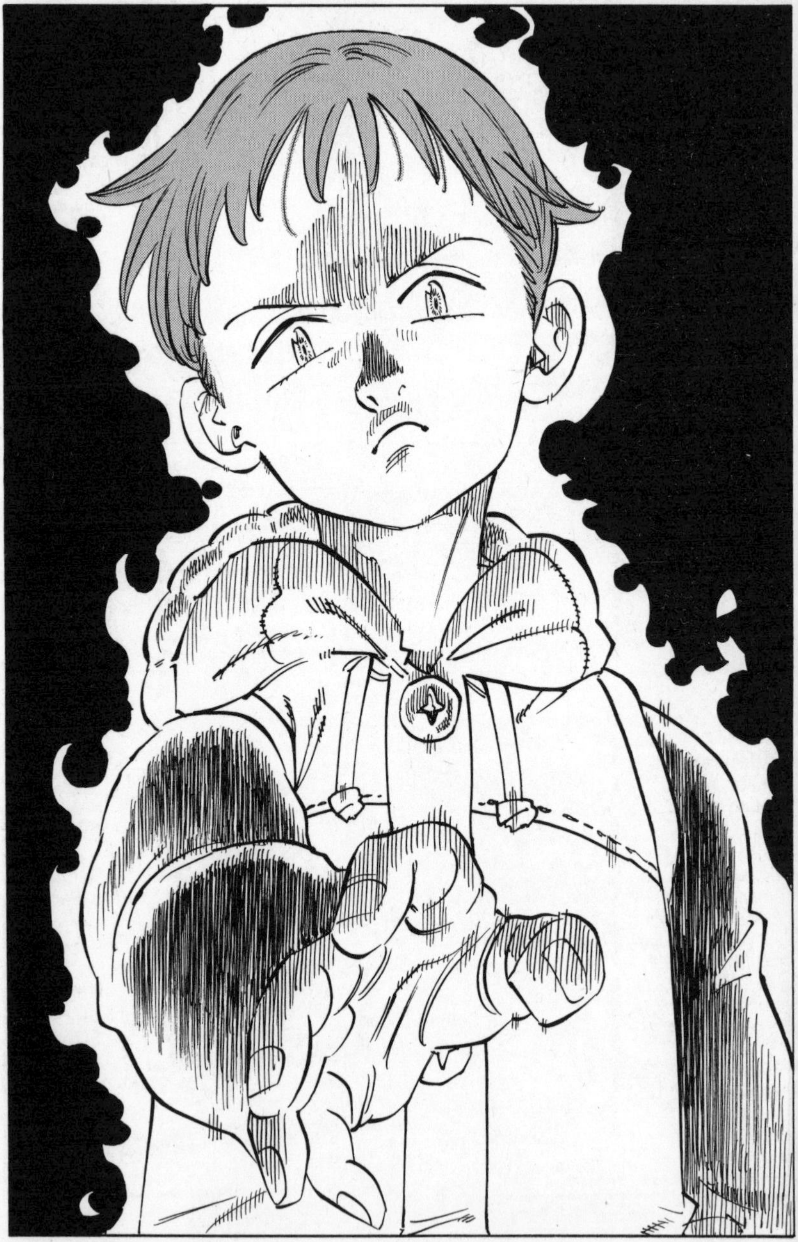

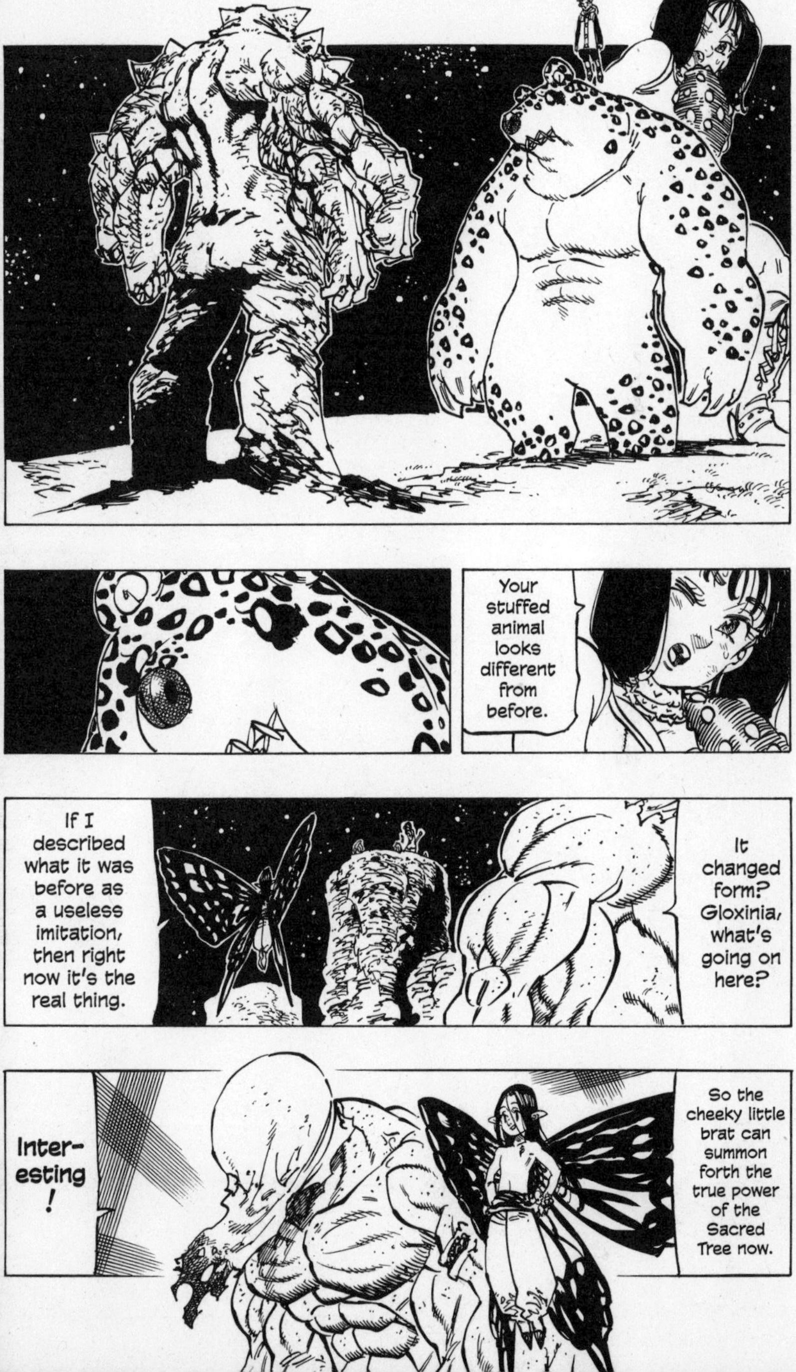
Your stuffed animal looks different from before.
It changed form? Gloxinia, what's going on here?
If I described what it was before as a useless imitation, then right now it's the real thing.
So the cheeky little brat can summon forth the true power of the Sacred Tree now.
Inter-esting!

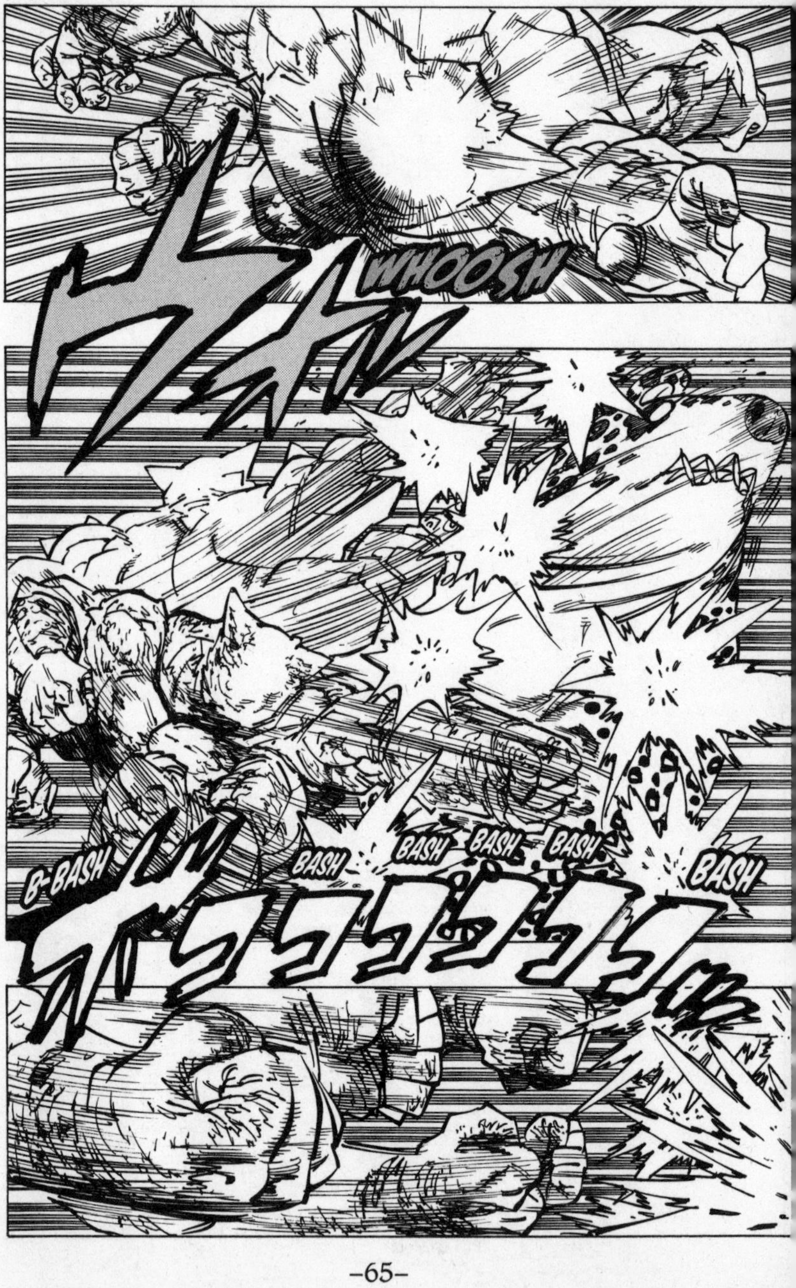
WHOOSH
BASH
BASH
BASH
BASH
BASH
B-BASH

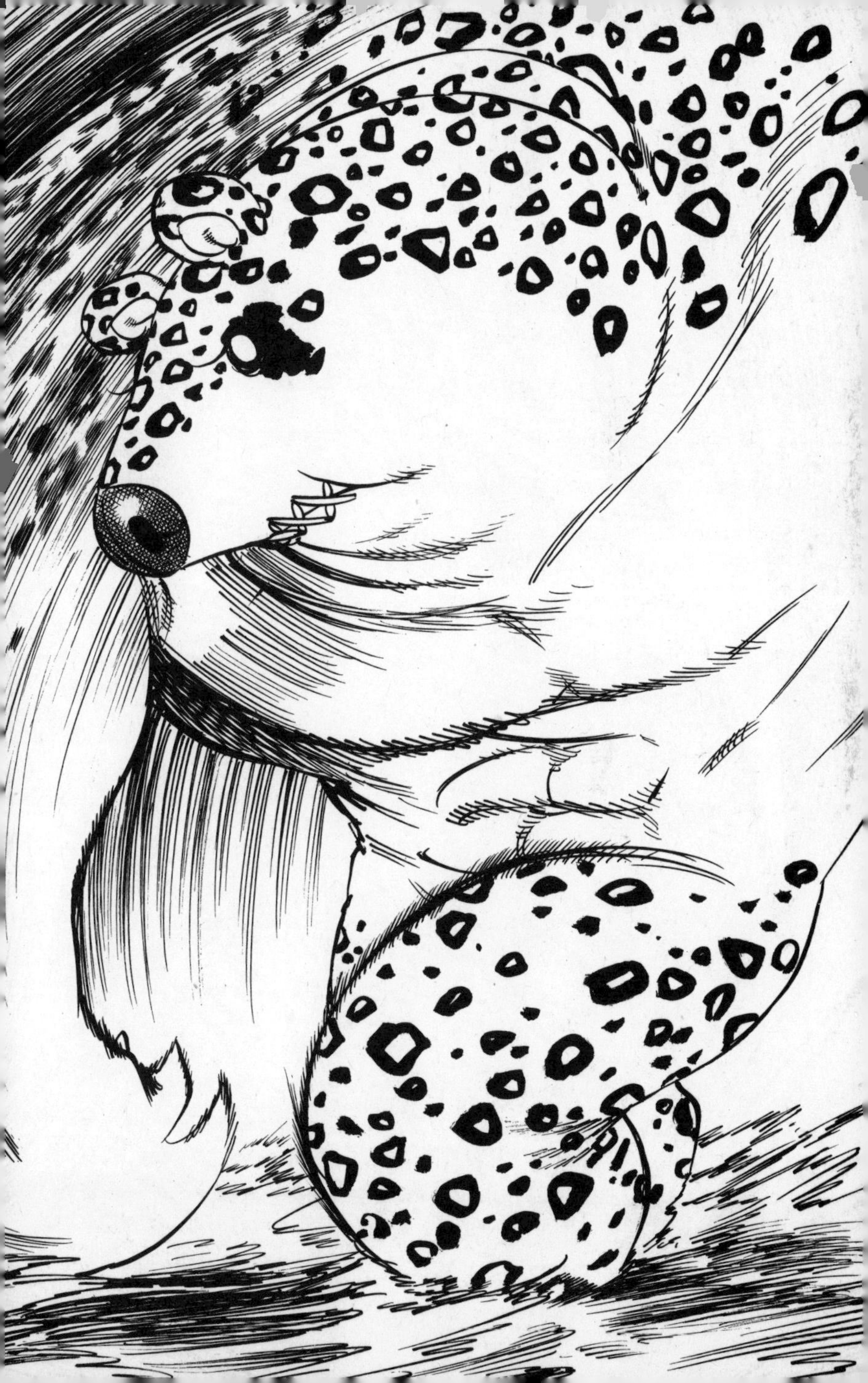

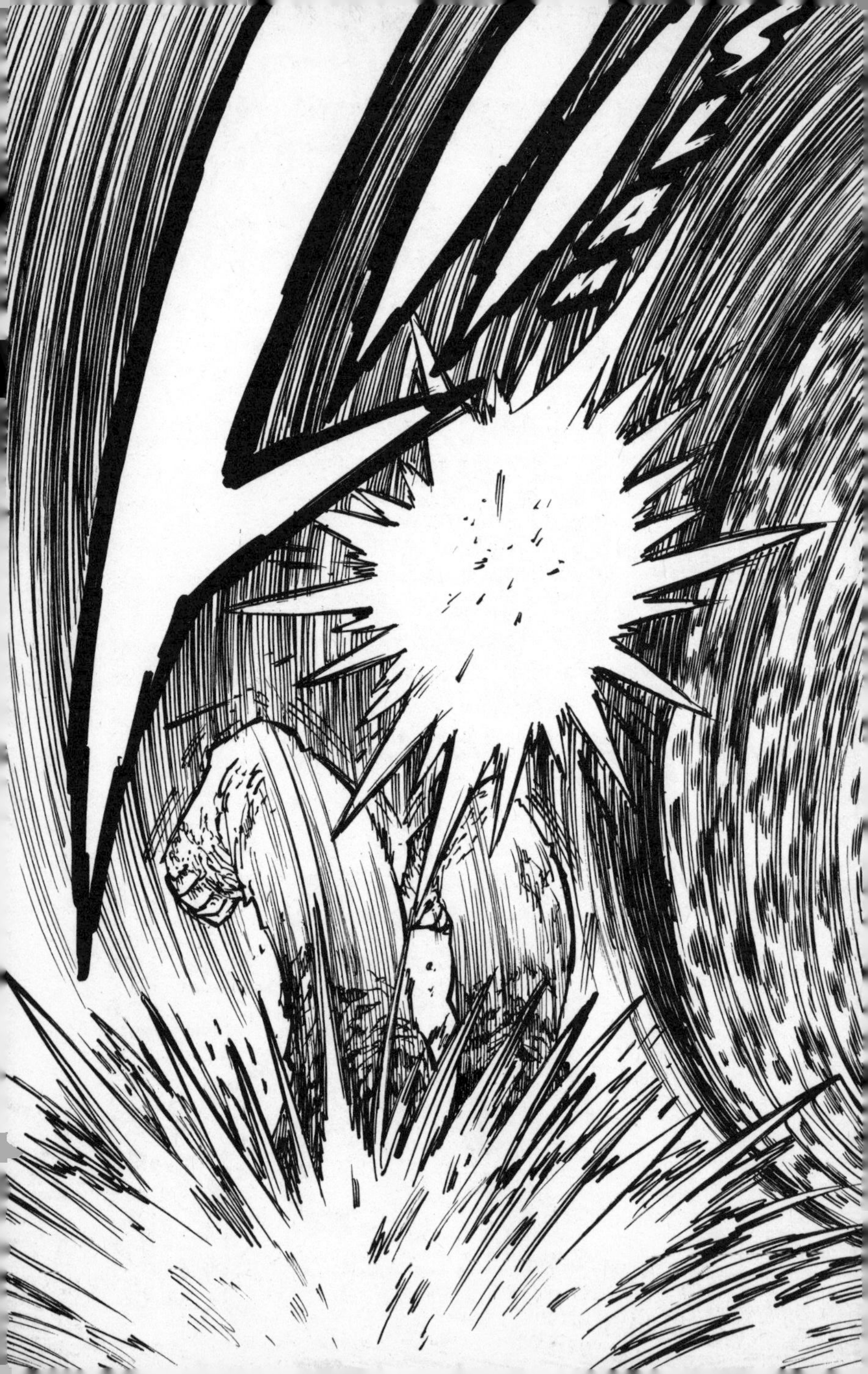
SLASH

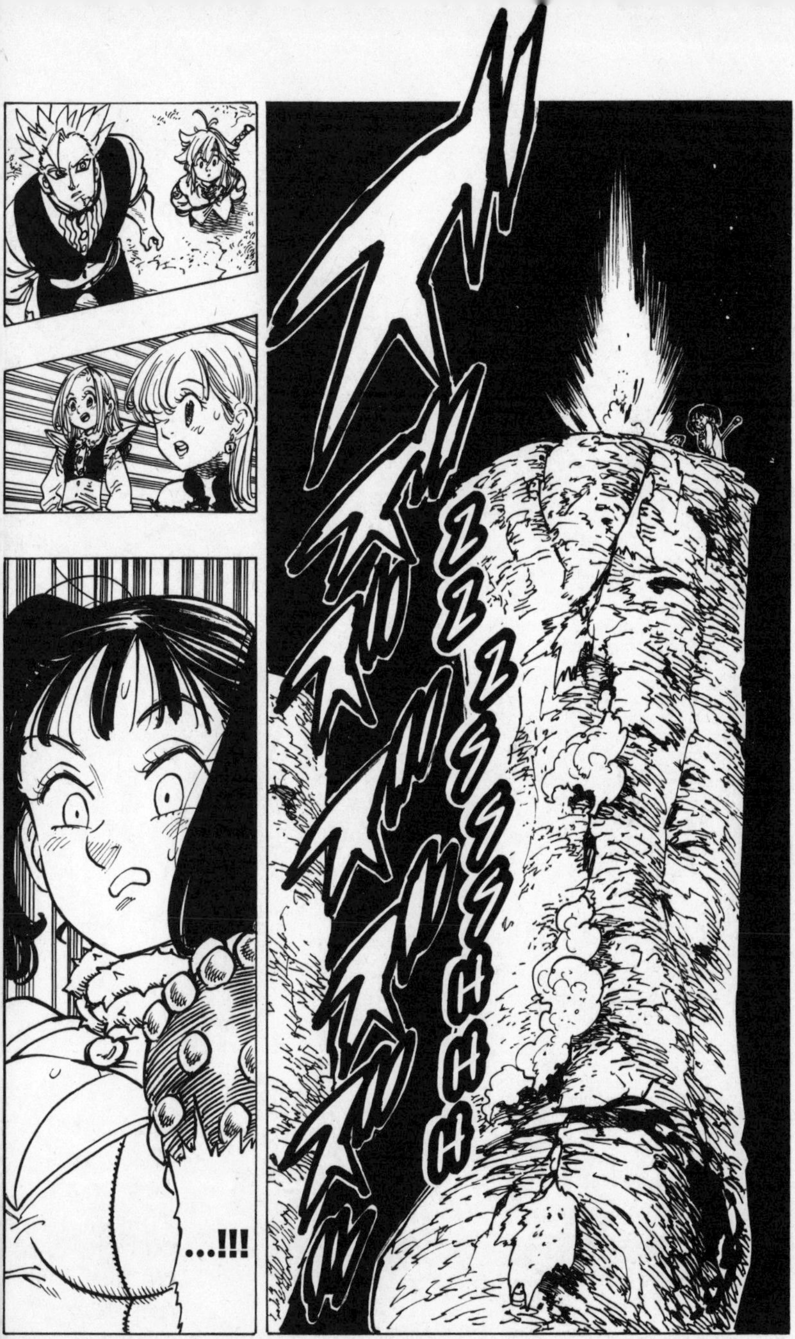
ZZZSSSSHHH
...!!!

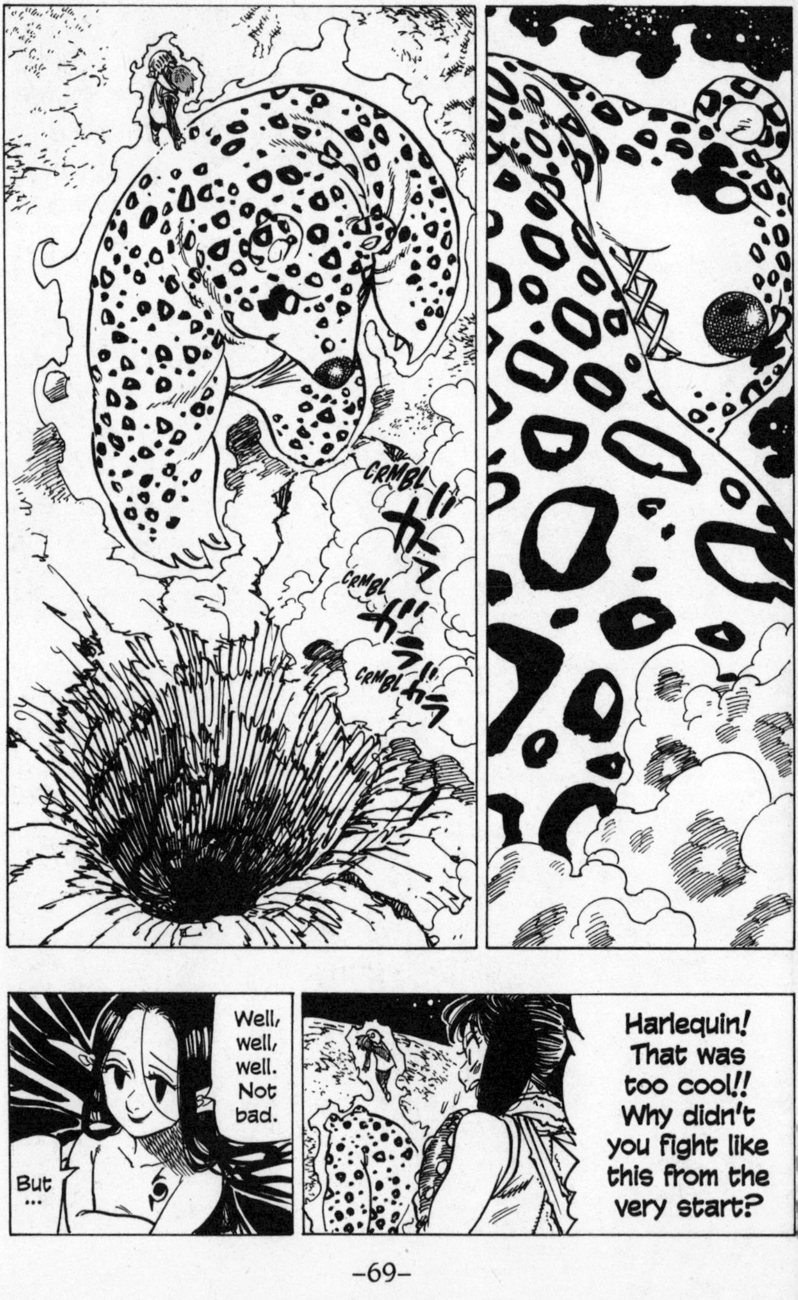
CRMBL
CRMBL
CRMBL
Harlequin! That was too cool!! Why didn't you fight like this from the very start?
Well, well, well. Not bad.
But ...

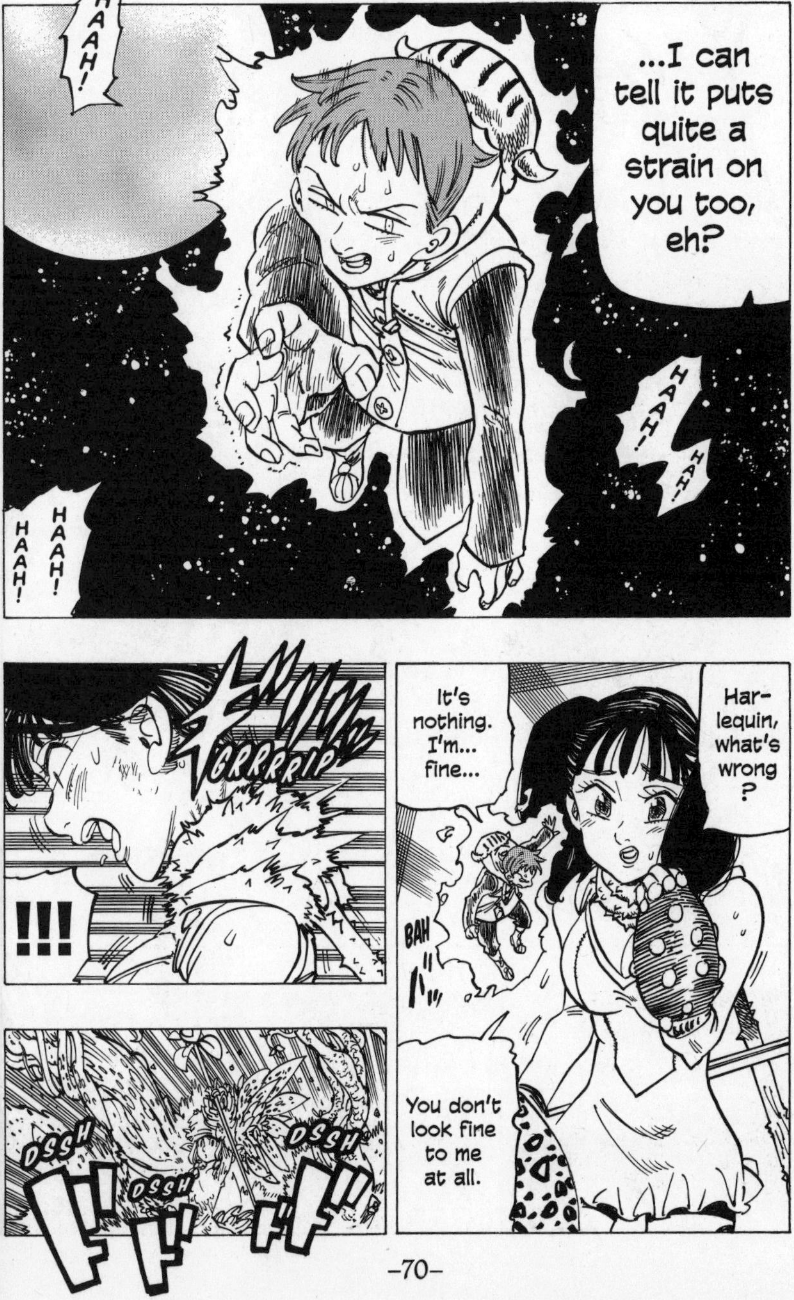
...I can tell it puts quite a strain on you too, eh?
HAAAH!
HAH!
HAAAH!
HAAAH!
HAAAH!
Har-lequin, what's wrong?
It's nothing. I'm... fine...
BAH
You don't look fine to me at all.
GRRRRIP
!!!
DSSH
DSSH
DSSH

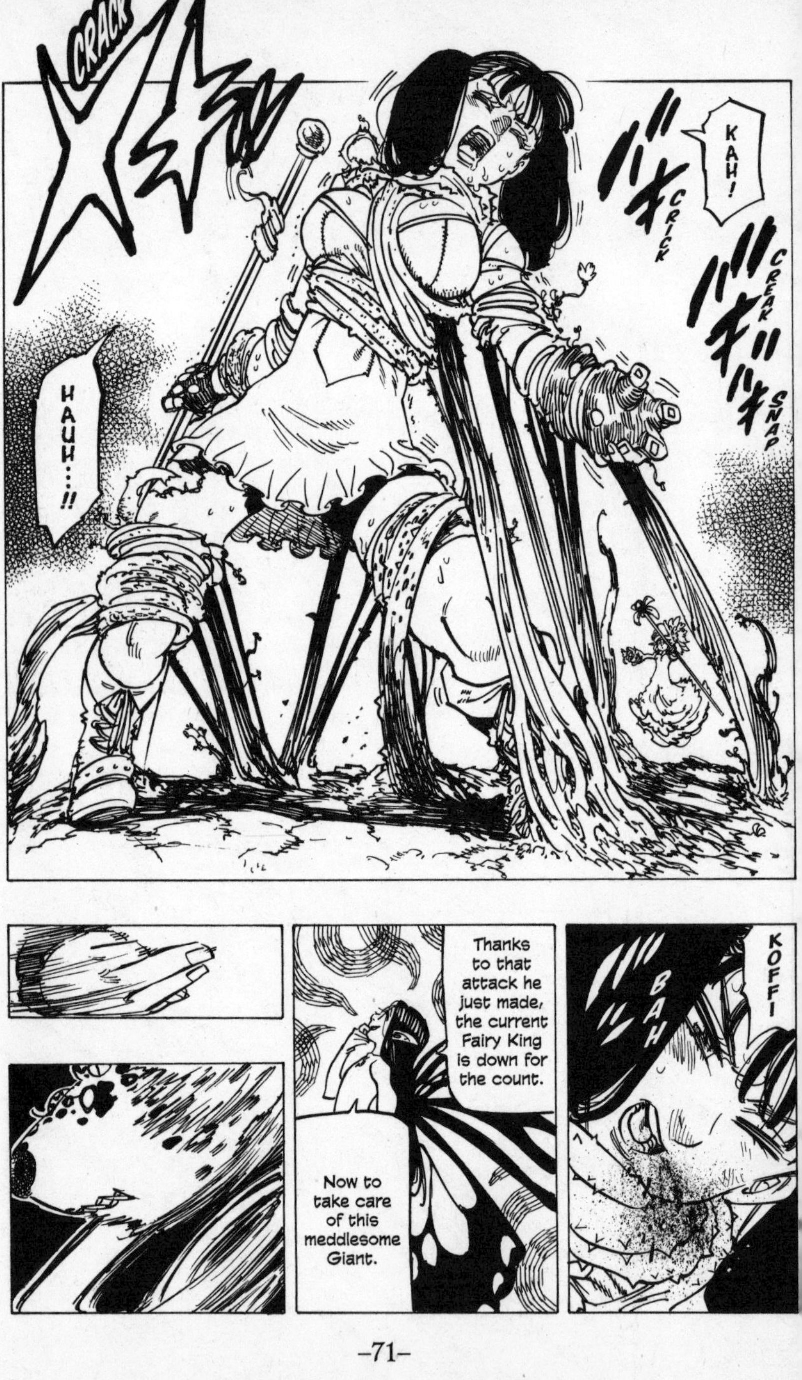
KAH!
CRICK
CREAK
SNAP
CRACK
HAUH...!!
KOFF!
BAH
Thanks to that attack he just made, the current Fairy King is down for the count.
Now to take care of this meddlesome Giant.

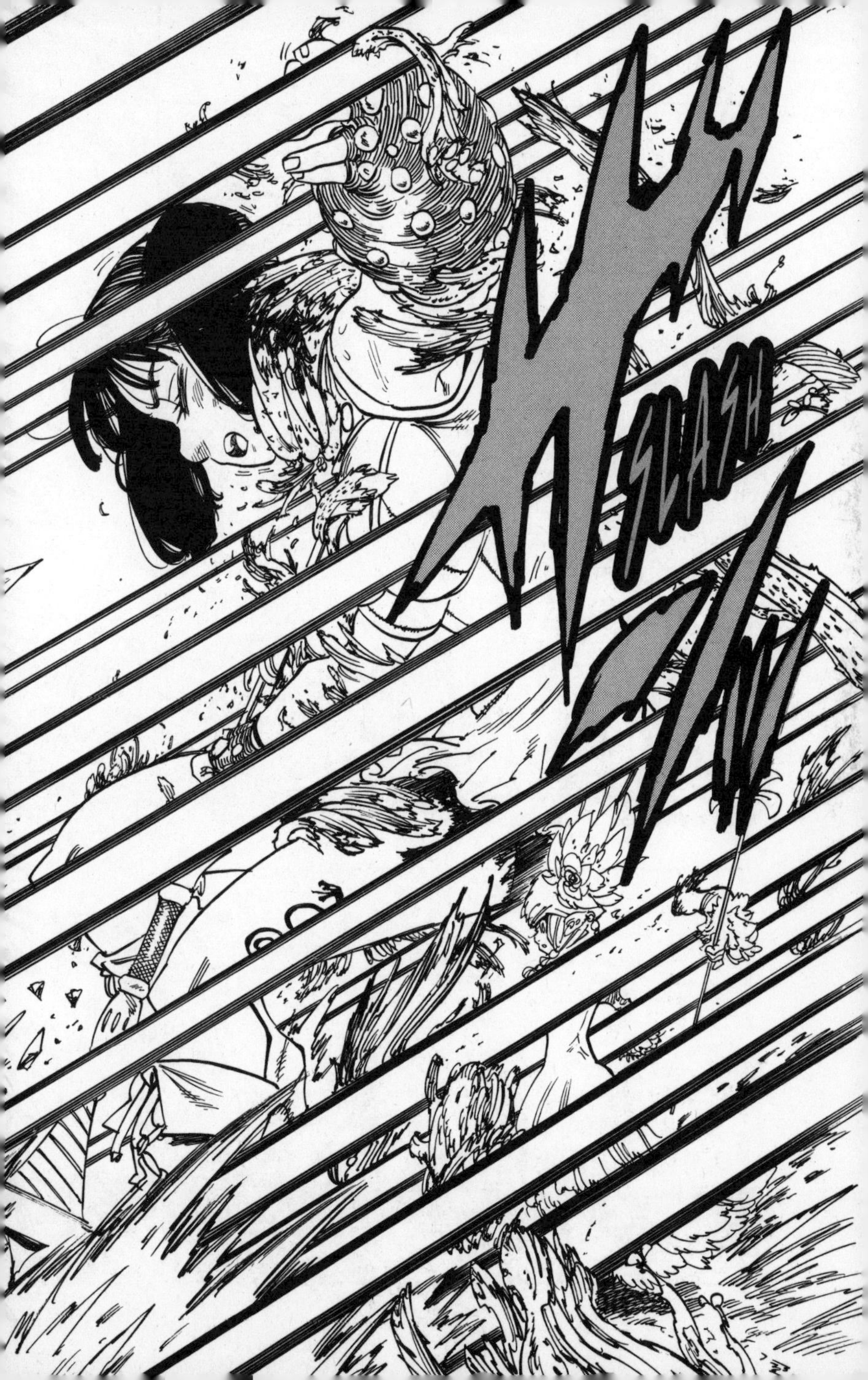
SLASH

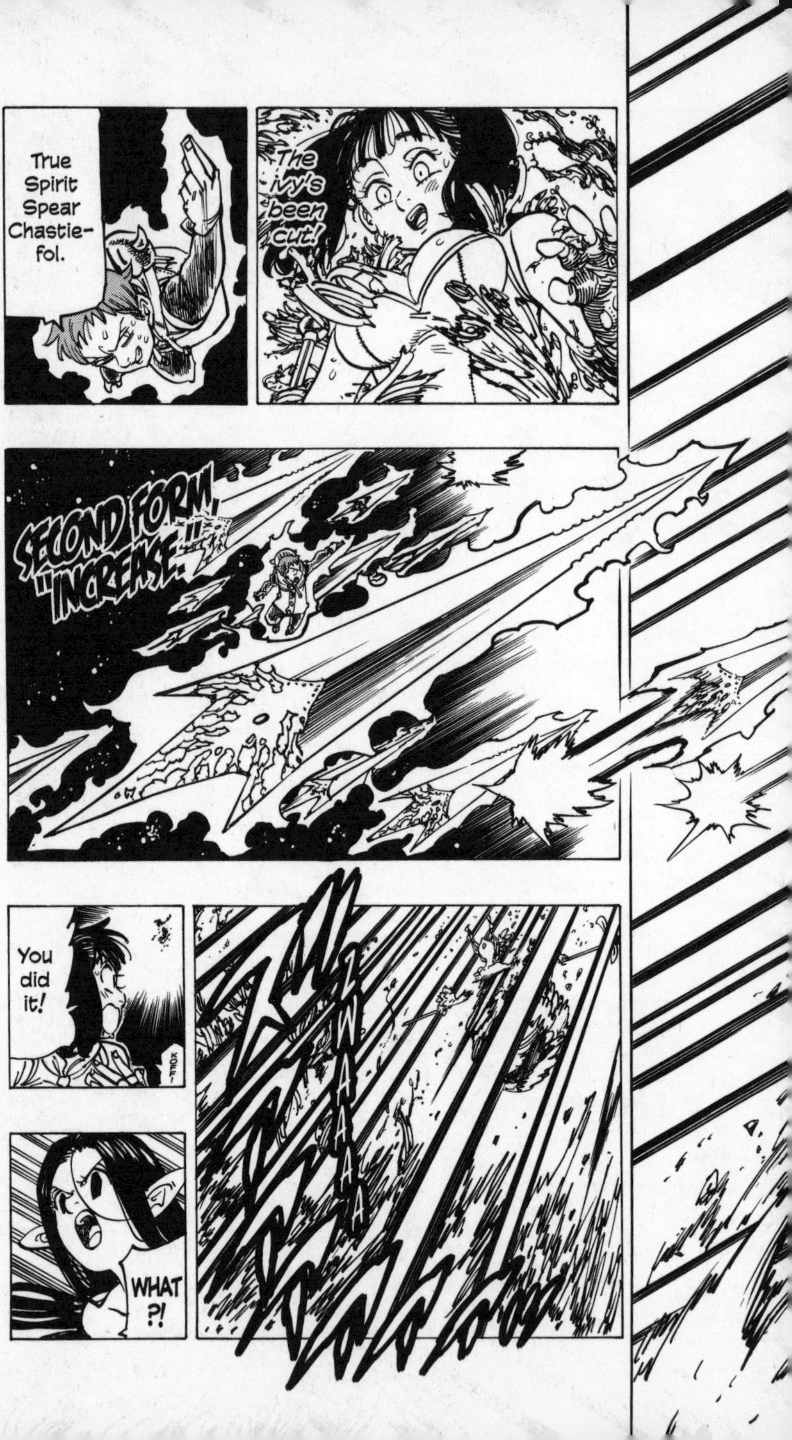
The ivy's been cut!
True Spirit Spear Chastiefol.
SECOND FORM, "INCREASE."
You did it!
KOFF!
WHAT?!

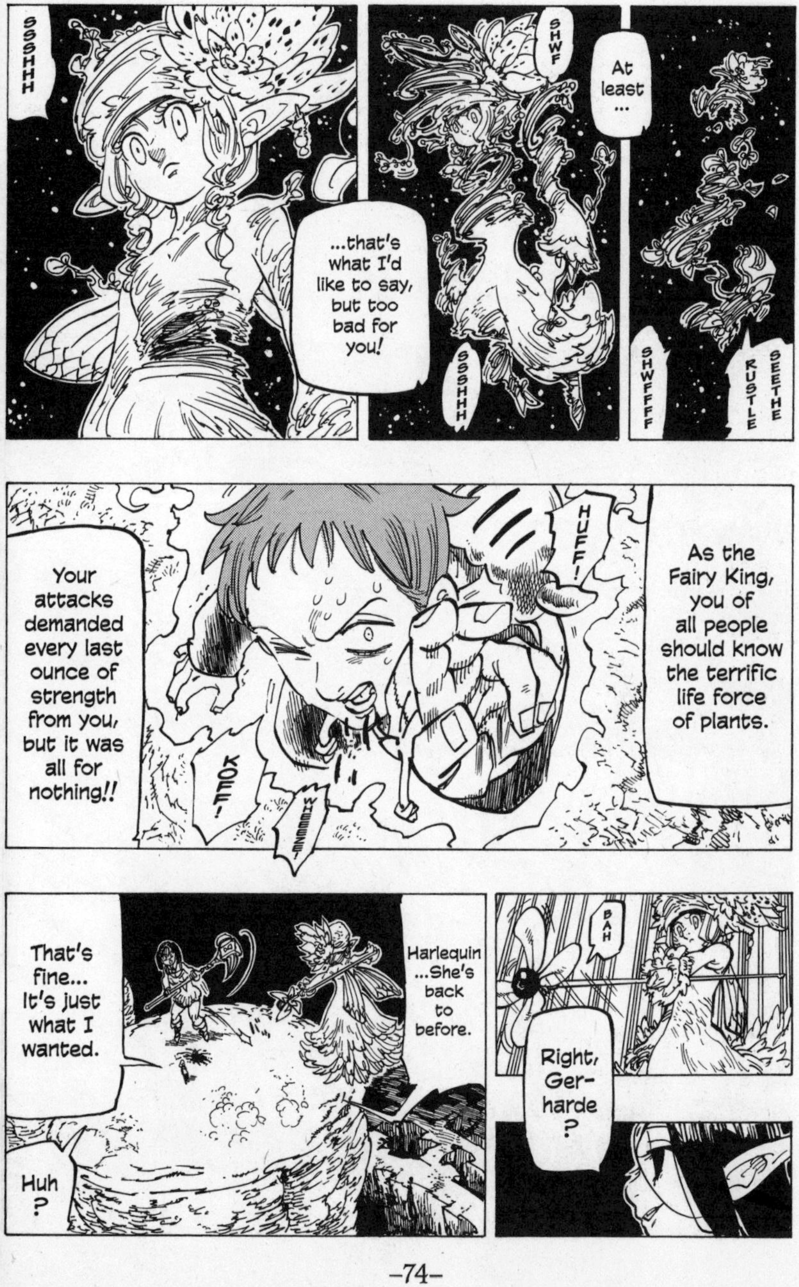
SEETHE
RUSTLE
SHWFFFF
SHWF
At least ...
SSSHHH
...that's what I'd like to say, but too bad for you!
SSSHHH
As the Fairy King, you of all people should know the terrific life force of plants.
HUFF!
KOFF!
WHEEZE!
Your attacks demanded every last ounce of strength from you, but it was all for nothing!!
BAH
Right, Gerharde ?
Harlequin ...She's back to before.
That's fine... It's just what I wanted.
Huh ?

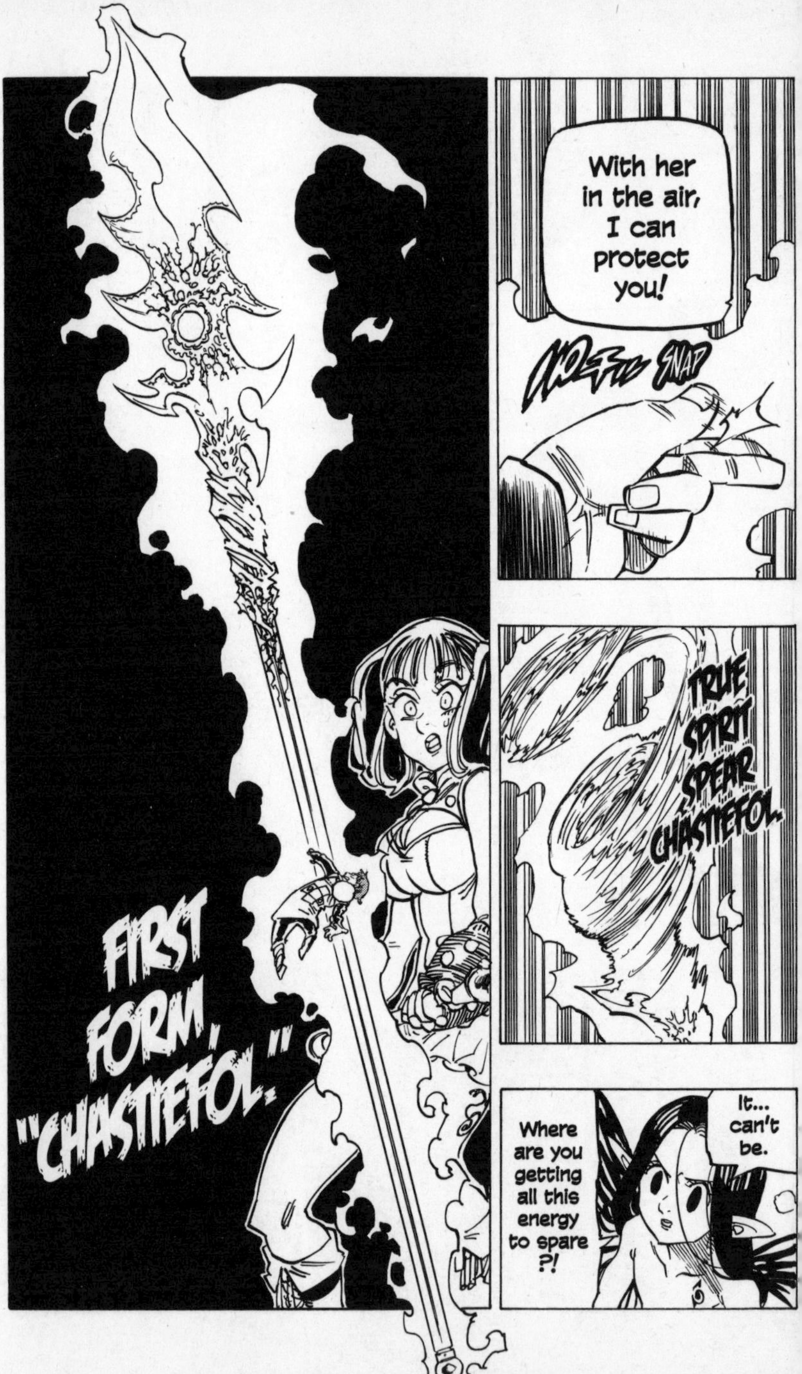
With her in the air, I can protect you!
SNAP
TRUE SPIRIT SPEAR CHASTIEFOL
It... can't be.
Where are you getting all this energy to spare ?!
FIRST FORM, "CHASTIEFOL."

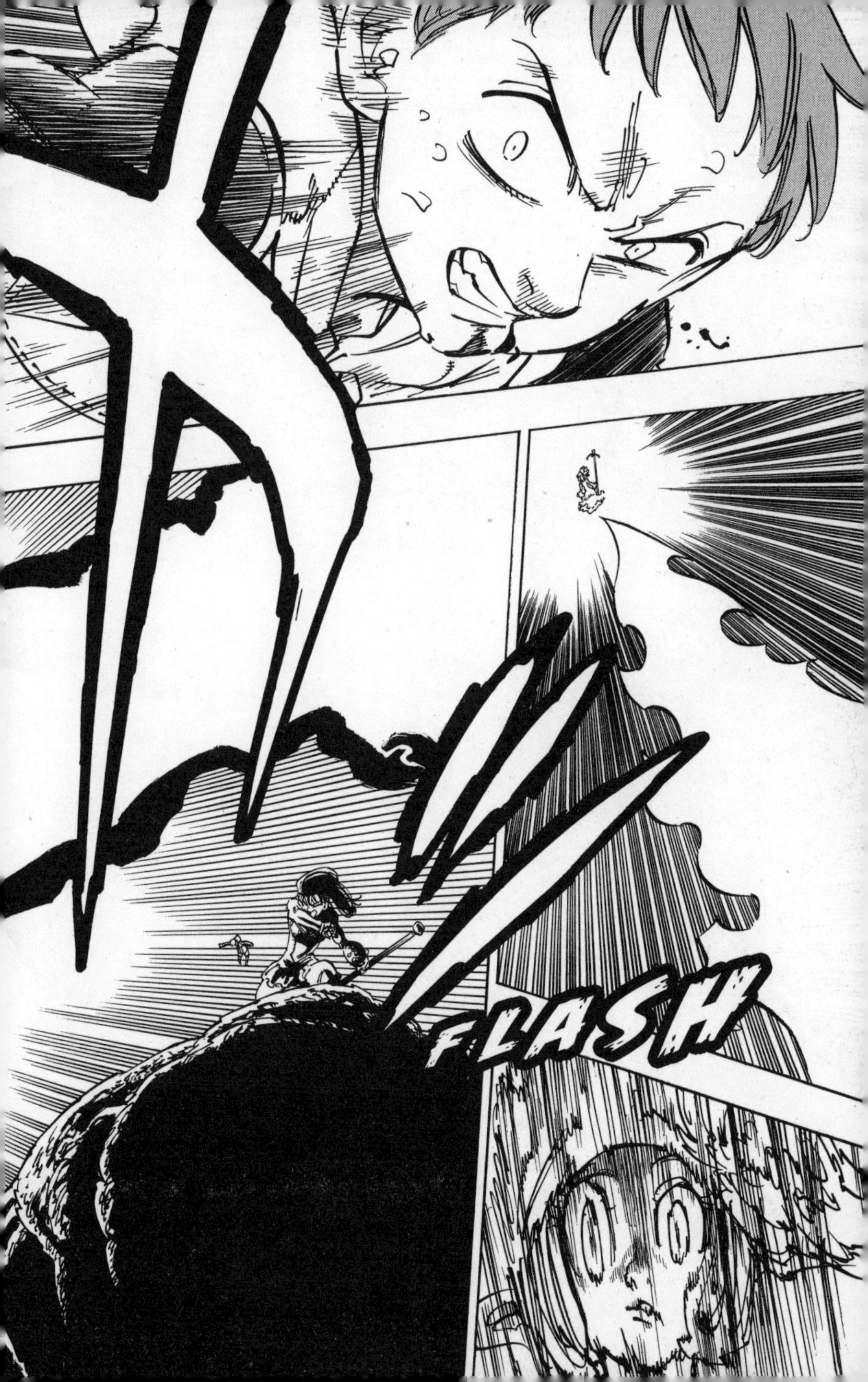
FLASH

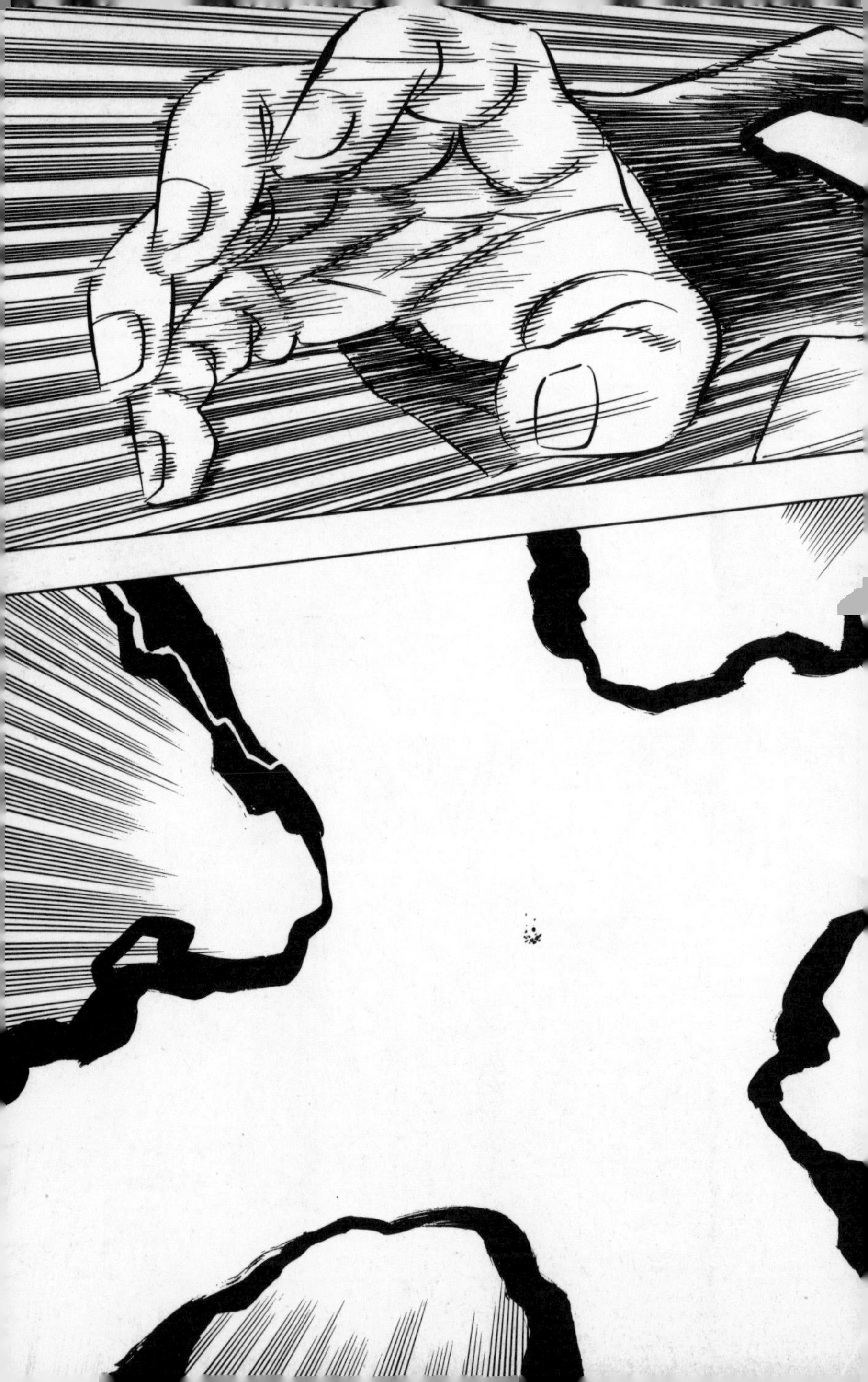

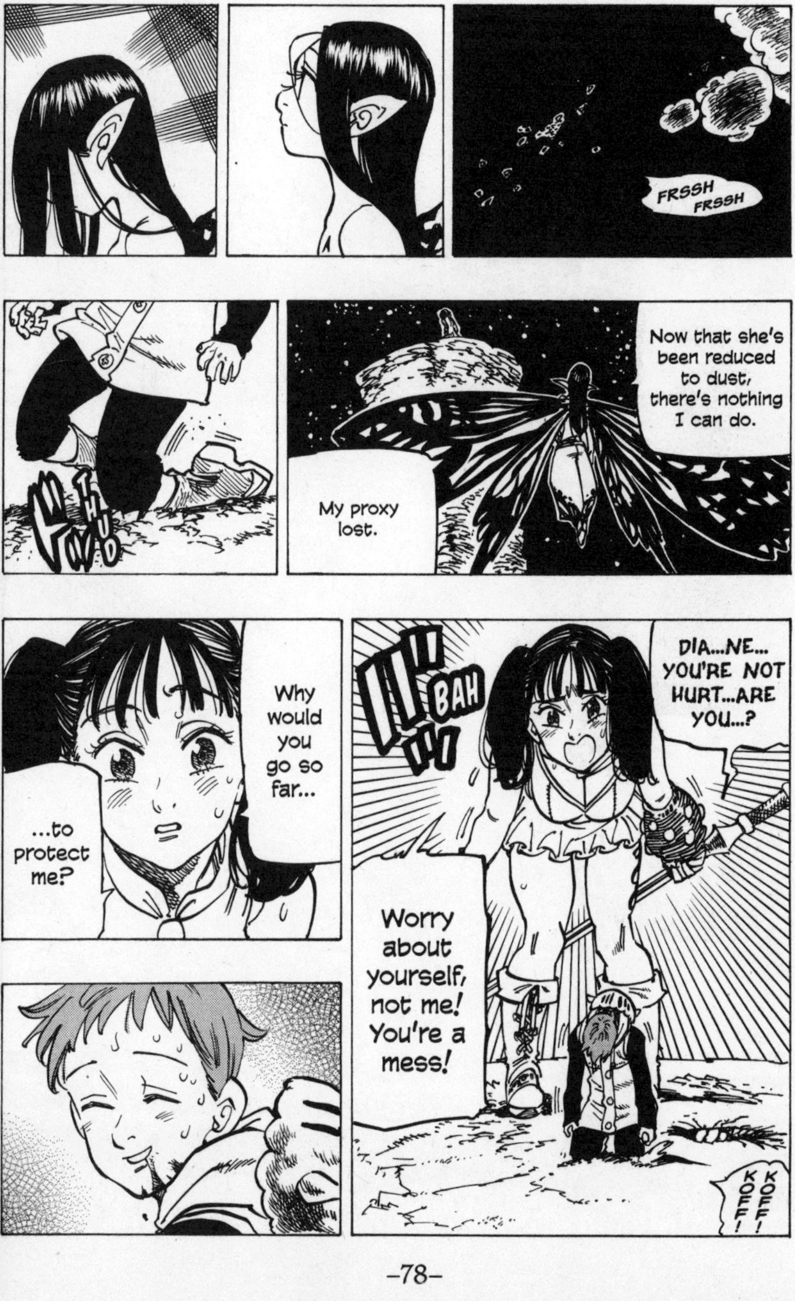
FRSSH
FRSSH
Now that she's been reduced to dust, there's nothing I can do.
My proxy lost.
THUD
DIA...NE... YOU'RE NOT HURT...ARE YOU...?
BAH
Worry about yourself, not me! You're a mess!
KOFF! KOFF!
Why would you go so far...
...to protect me?

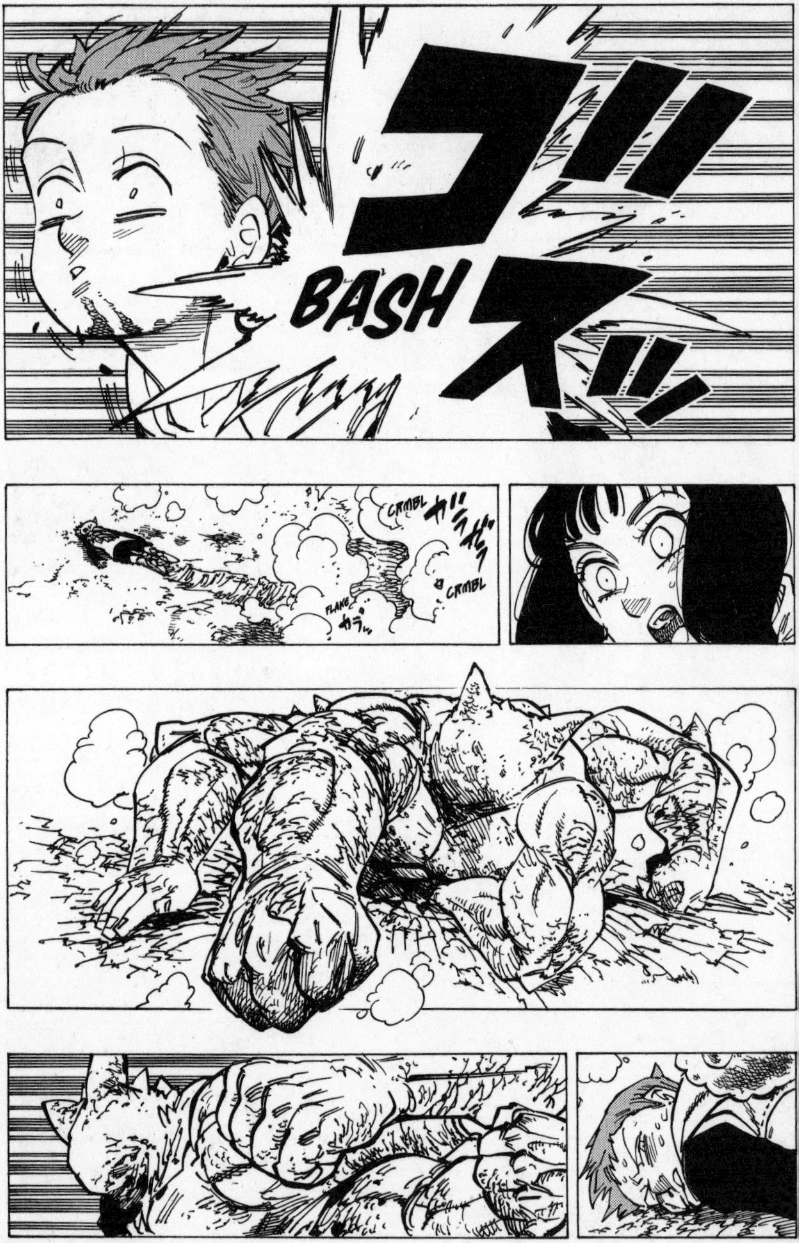
BASH
CRMBL
CRMBL
FLAKE

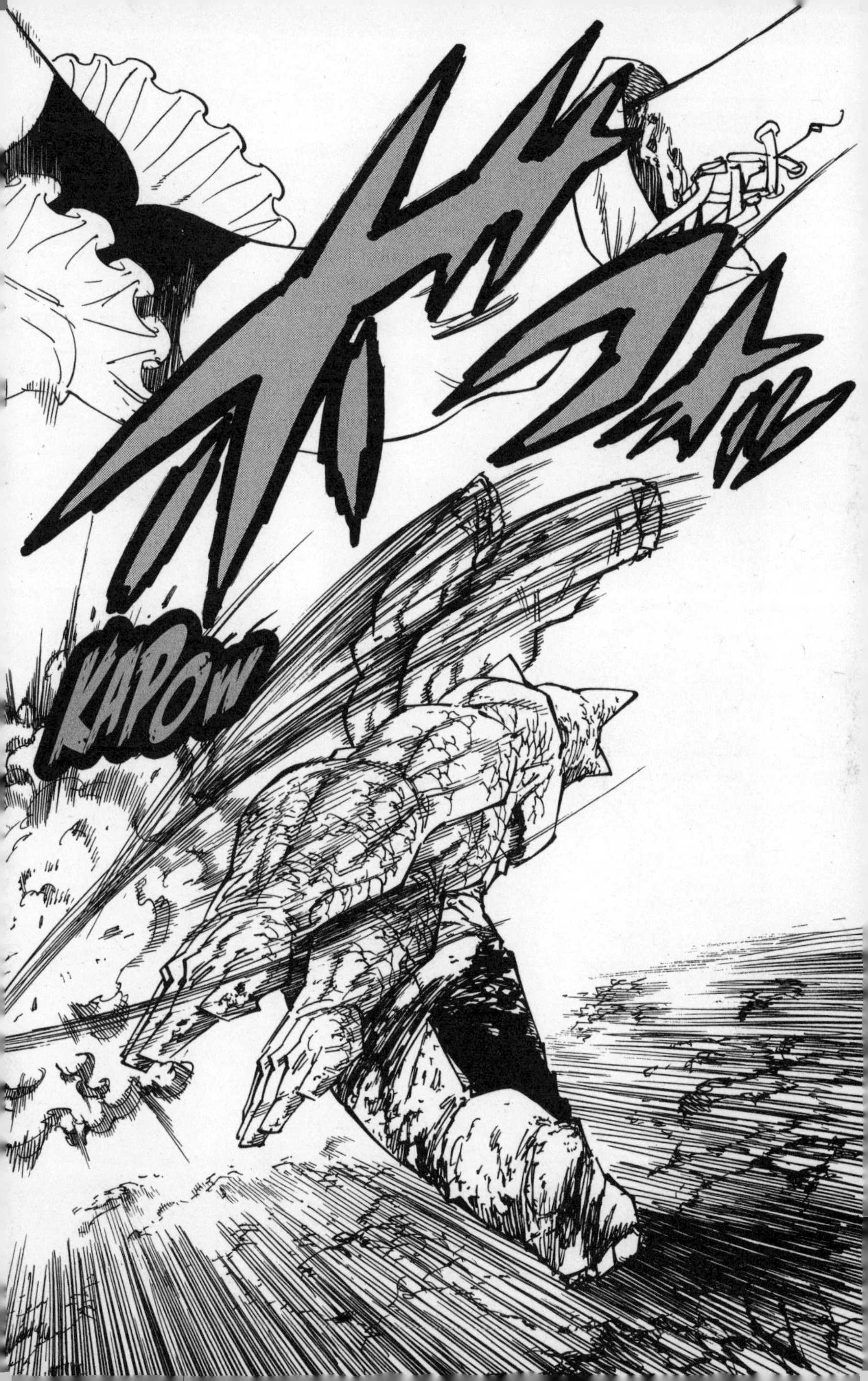
KAPOW
TICK

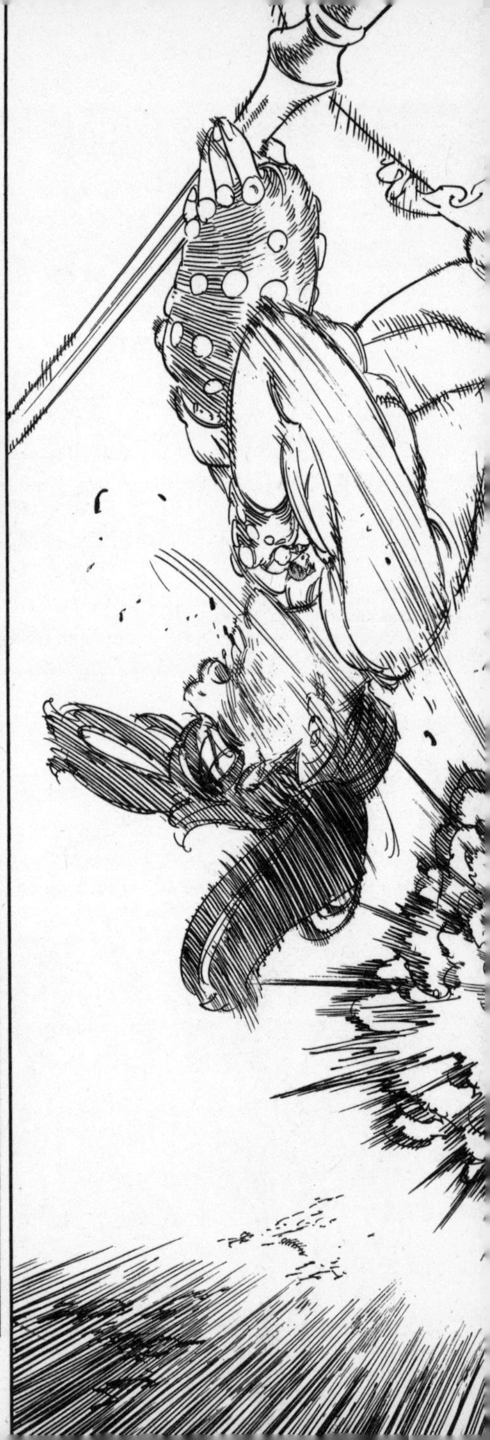
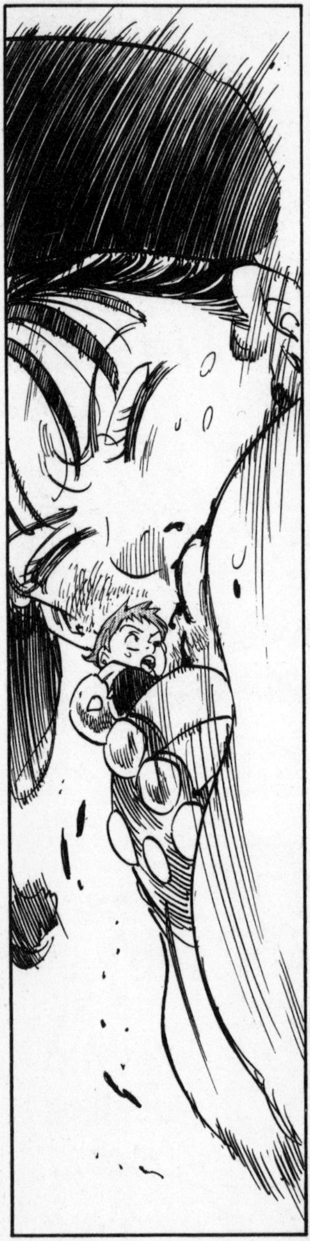

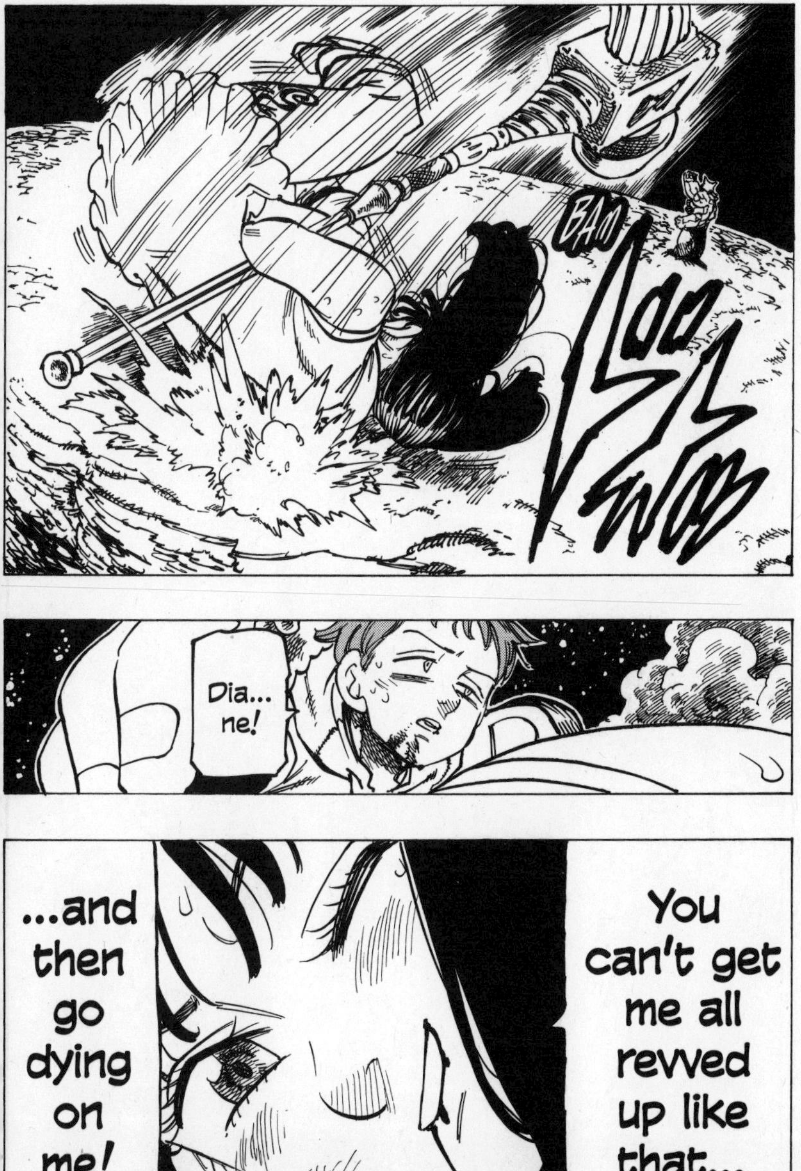
BAM
Dia... ne!
You can't get me all revved up like that...
...and then go dying on me!

Chapter 167 - The Special Thing Inside You

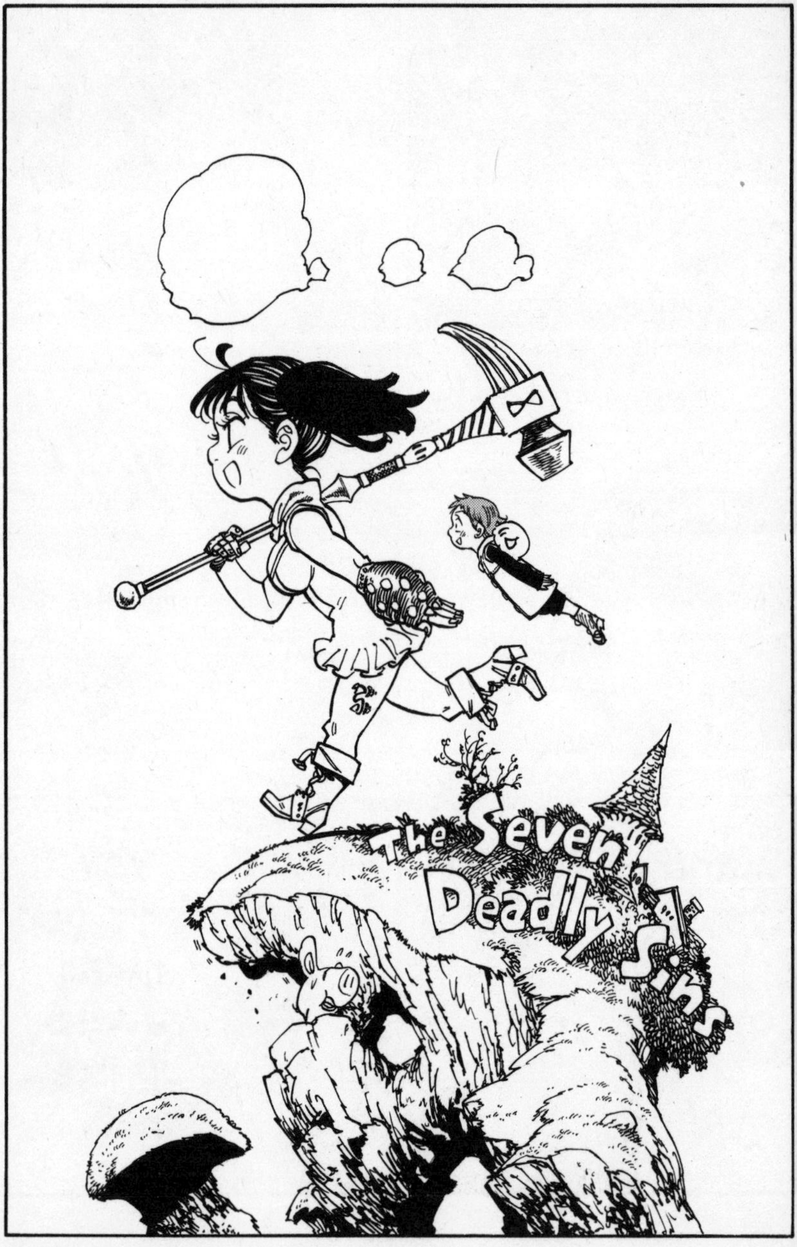

The Seven Deadly Sins

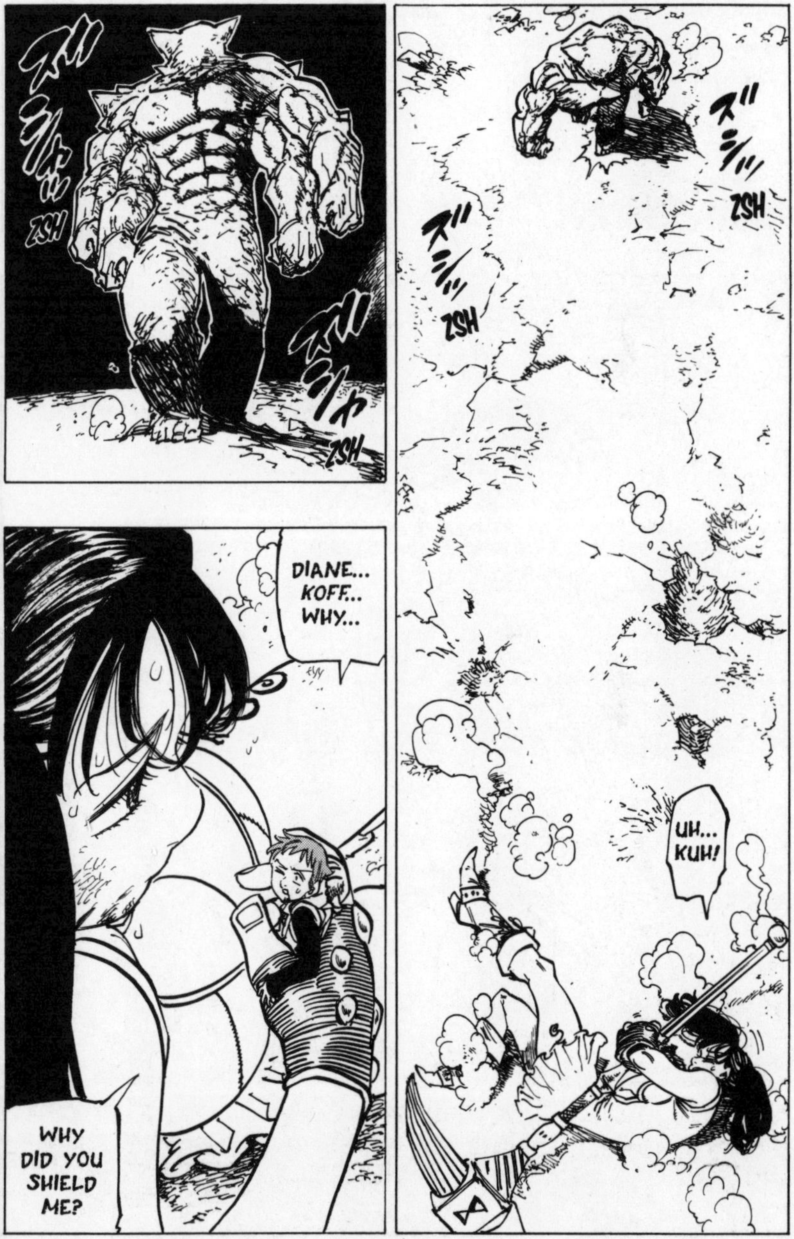
ZSH
ZSH
UH... KUH!
ZSH
ZSH
DIANE... KOFF... WHY...
WHY DID YOU SHIELD ME?

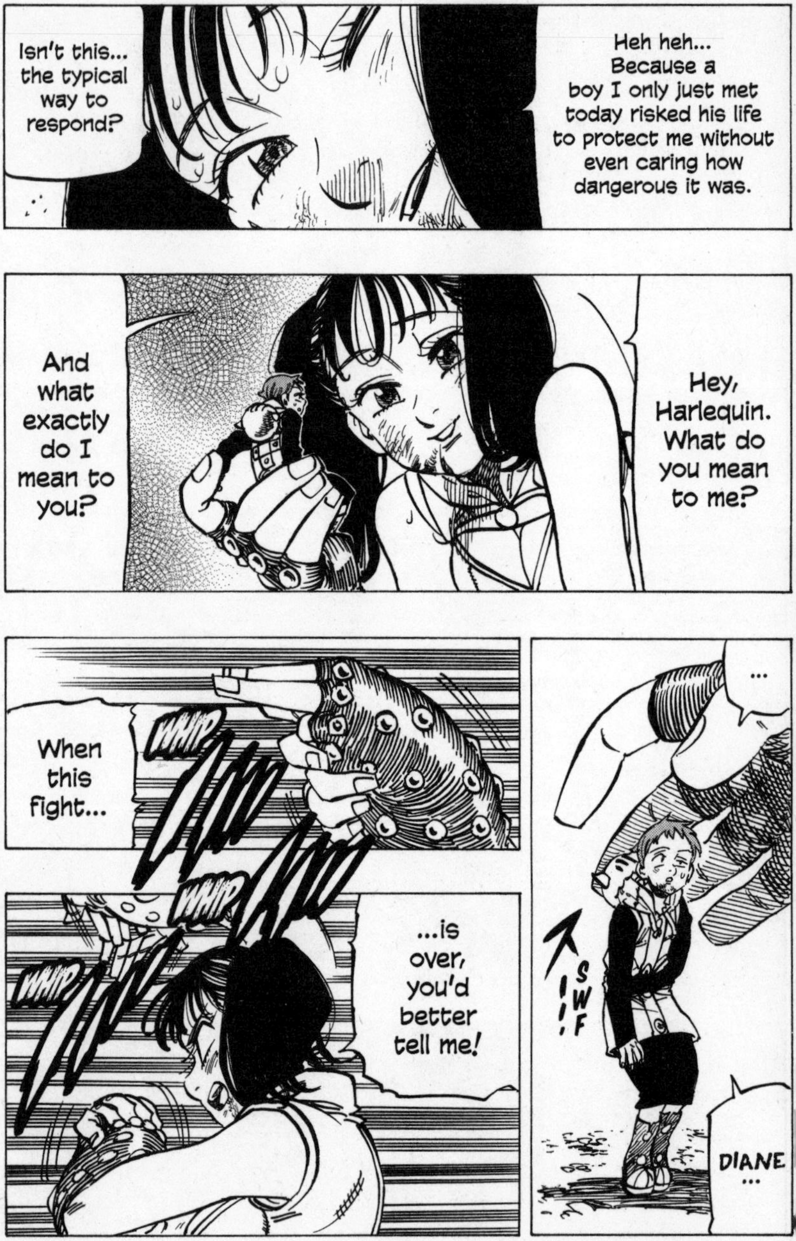
Heh heh... Because a boy I only just met today risked his life to protect me without even caring how dangerous it was.
Isn't this... the typical way to respond?
Hey, Harlequin. What do you mean to me?
And what exactly do I mean to you?
...
SWF
DIANE ...
When this fight...
WHIP
...is over, you'd better tell me!
WHIP
WHIP

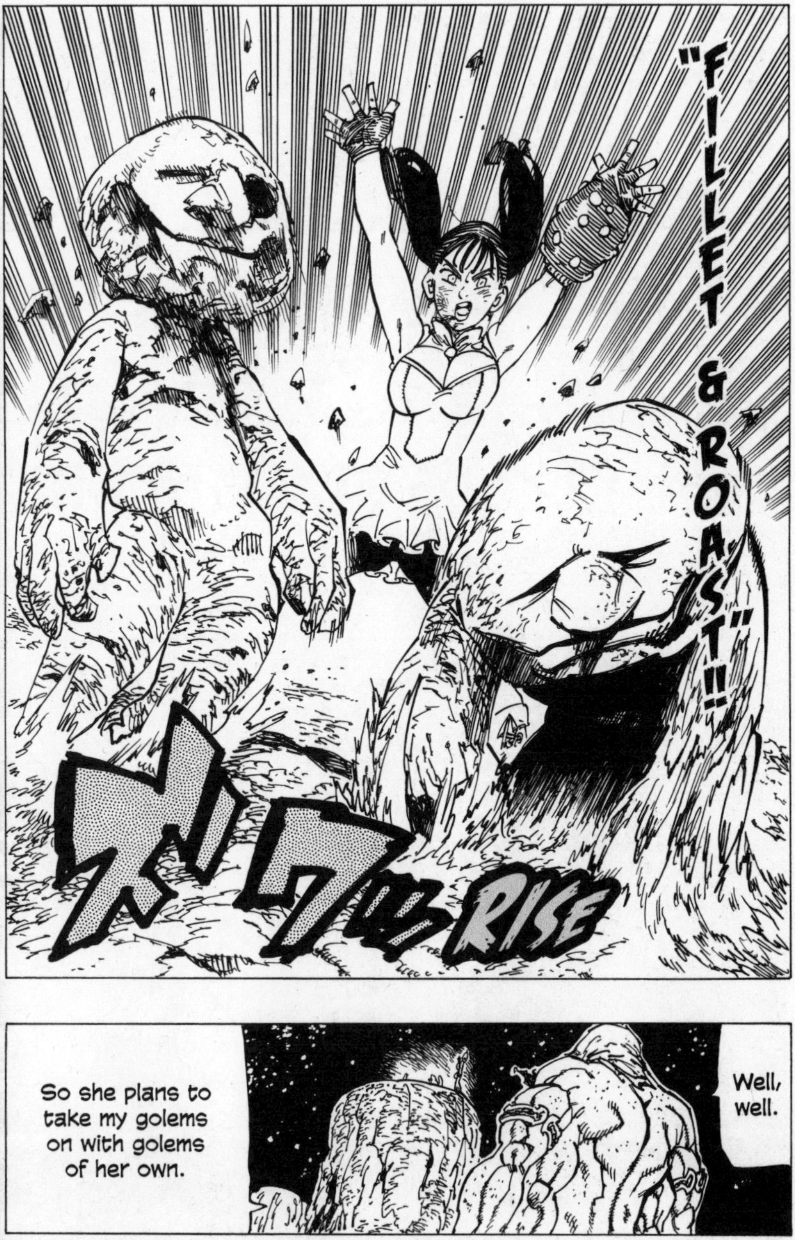
"FILLET & ROAST!!"
RISE
Well, well.
So she plans to take my golems on with golems of her own.

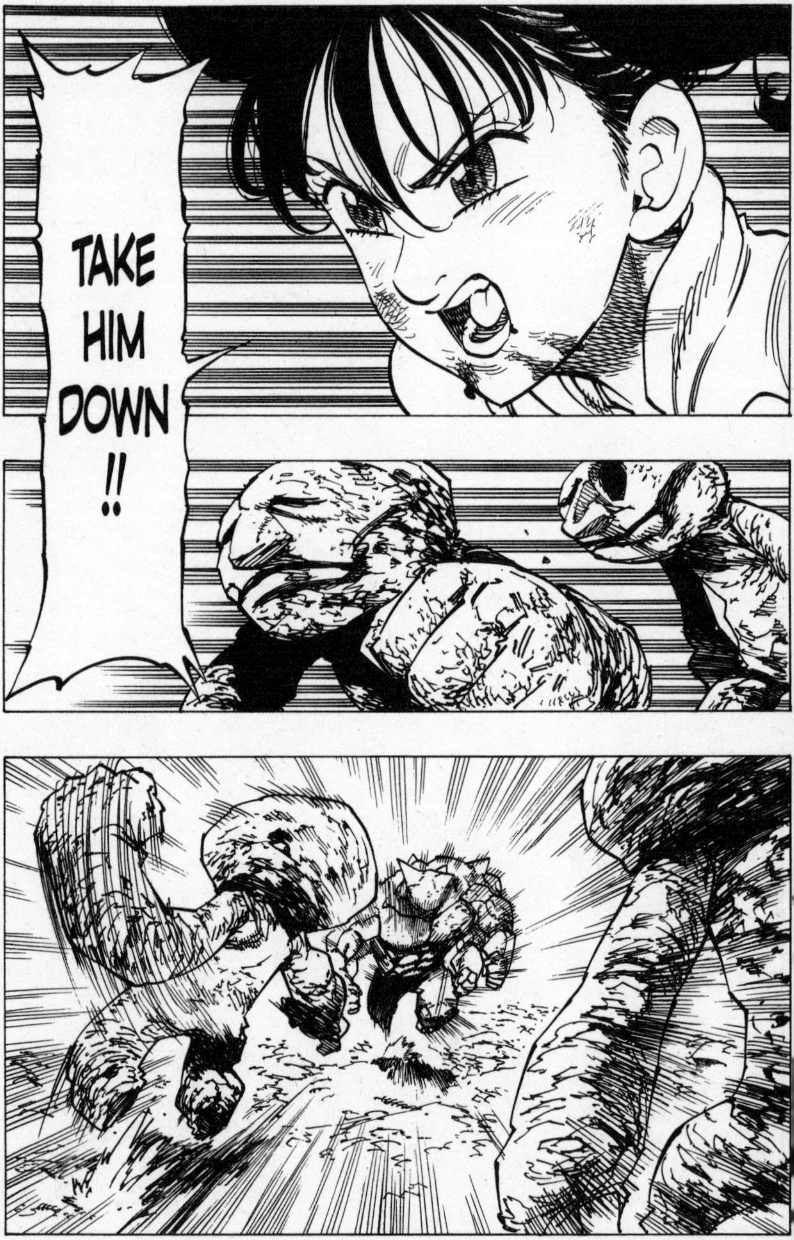
TAKE HIM DOWN!!

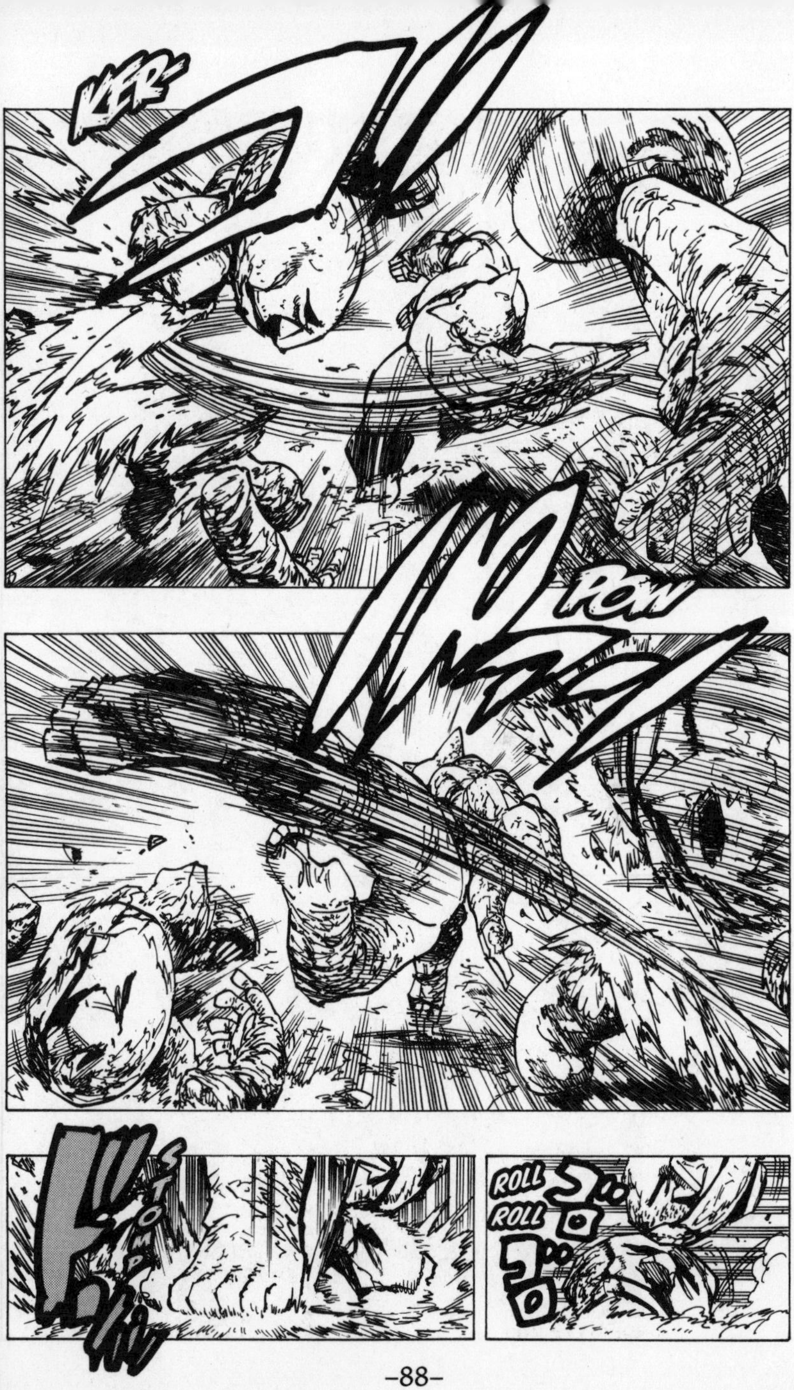
KER-
POW
ROLL
ROLL
STOMP

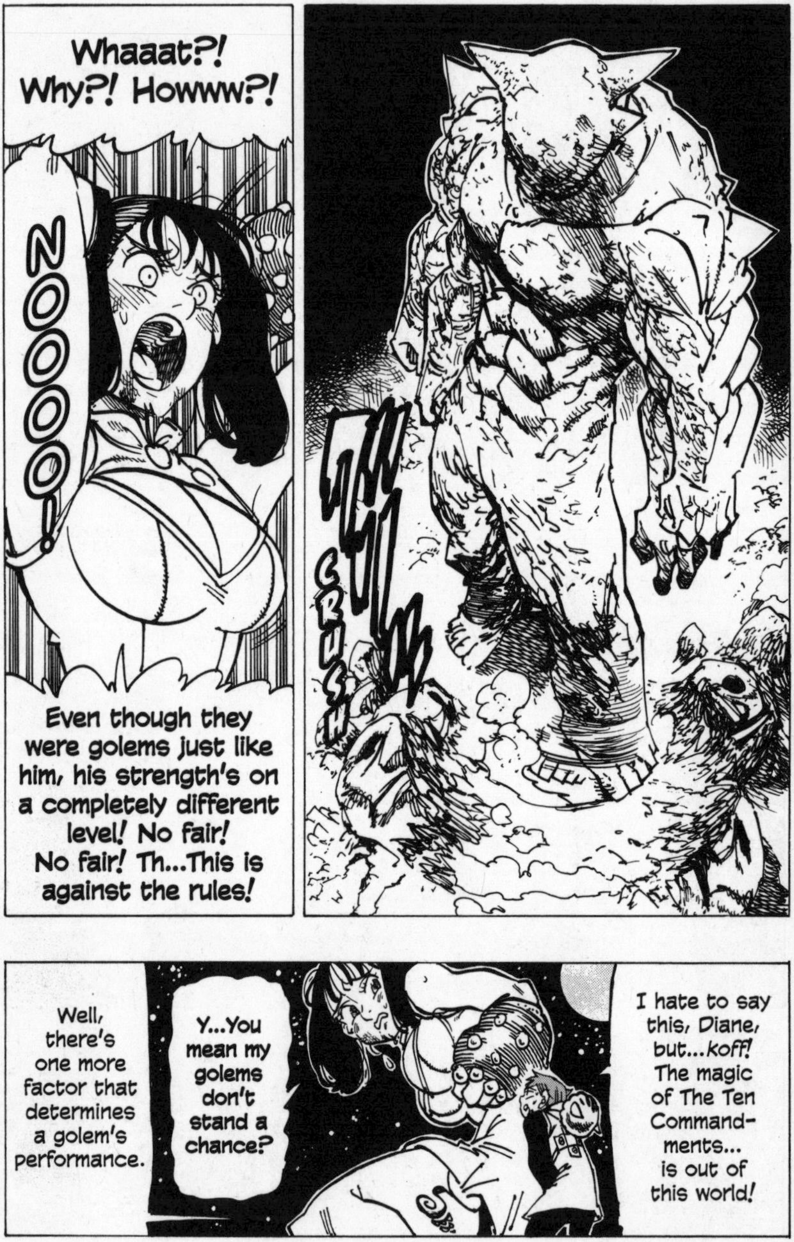
CRUSH
Whaaat?! Why?! Howww?!
NOOOOO!
Even though they were golems just like him, his strength's on a completely different level! No fair! No fair! Th...This is against the rules!
I hate to say this, Diane, but...*koff!* The magic of The Ten Command-ments... is out of this world!
Y...You mean my golems don't stand a chance?
Well, there's one more factor that determines a golem's performance.

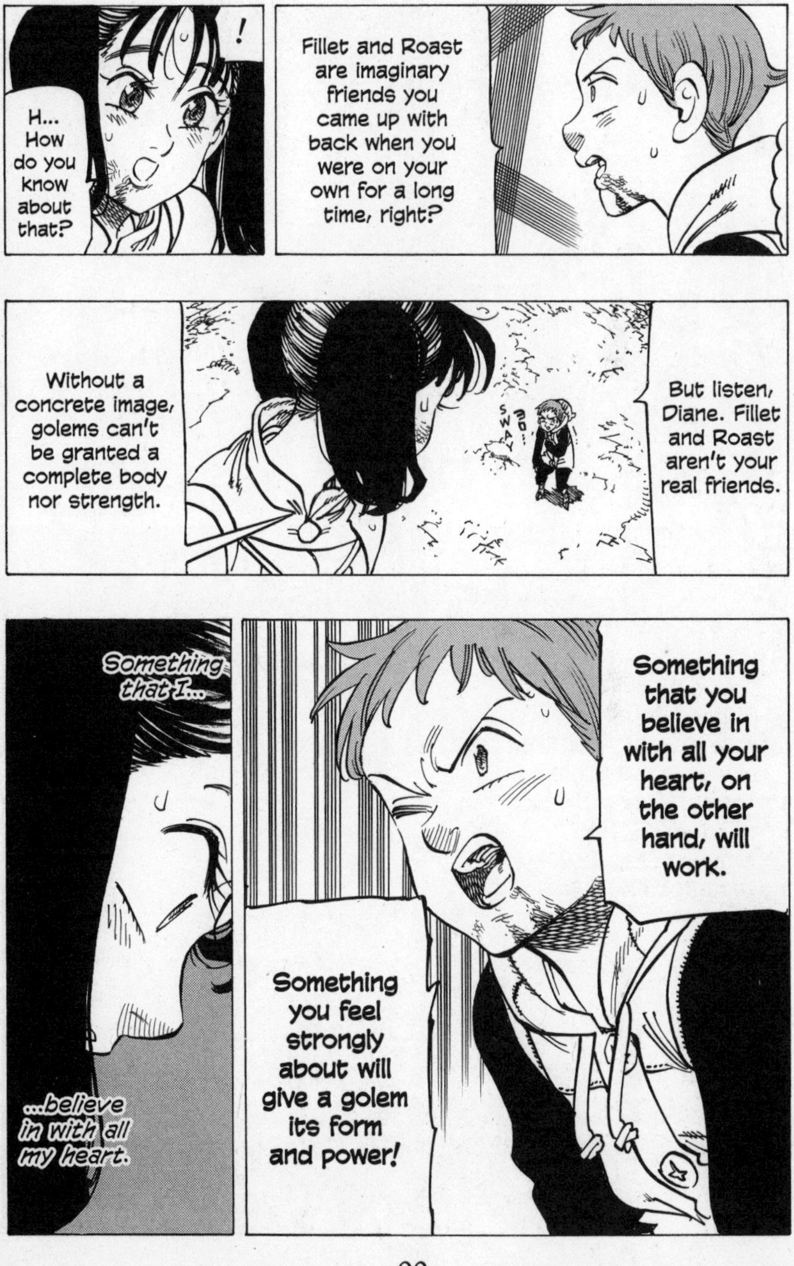
Fillet and Roast are imaginary friends you came up with back when you were on your own for a long time, right?
!
H... How do you know about that?
But listen, Diane. Fillet and Roast aren't your real friends.
SWAY
Without a concrete image, golems can't be granted a complete body nor strength.
Something that you believe in with all your heart, on the other hand, will work.
Something you feel strongly about will give a golem its form and power!
Something that I...
...believe in with all my heart.

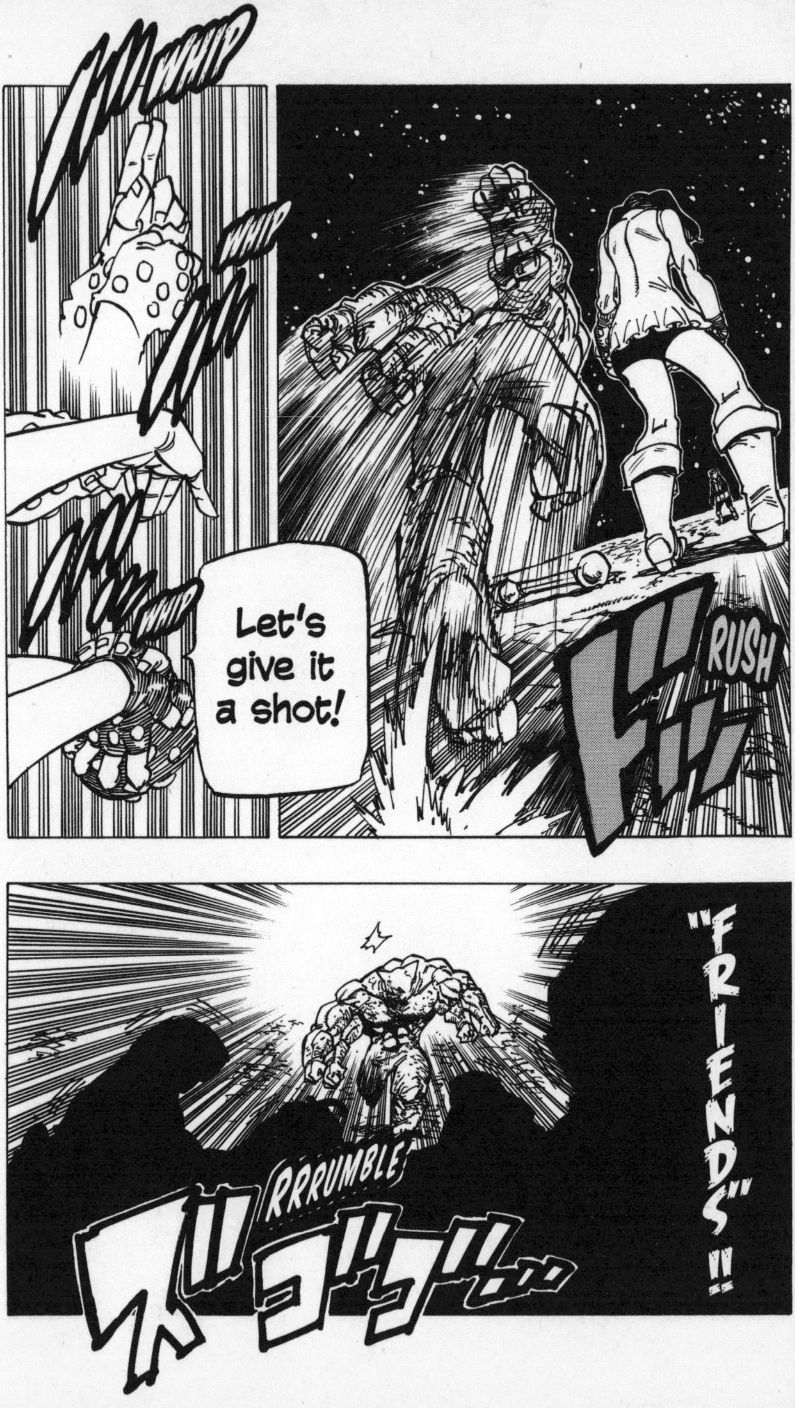
RUSH
WHIP
WHIP
WHIP
Let's give it a shot!
"FRIENDS"!!
RRRUMBLE

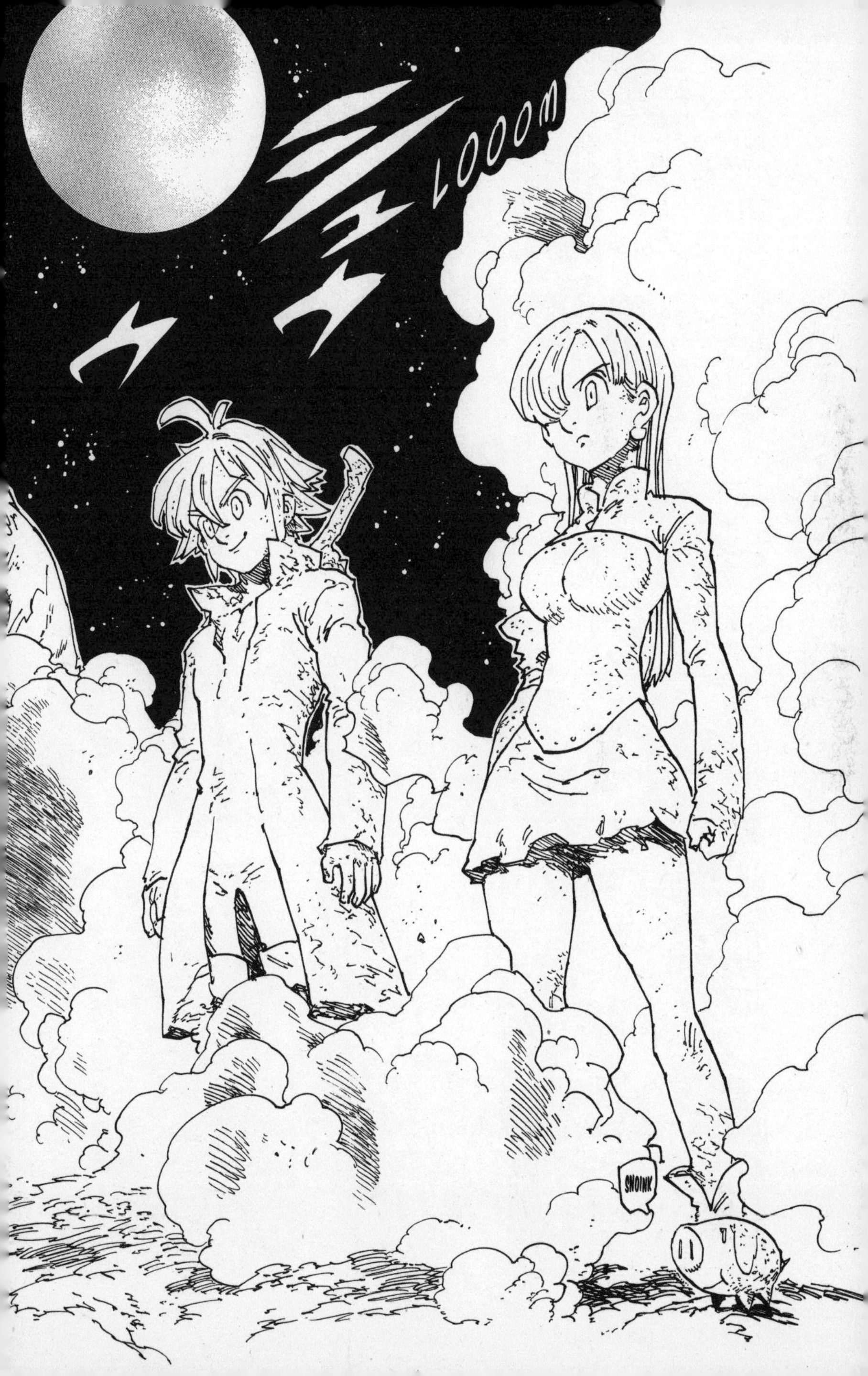
LOOOM
SNOINK

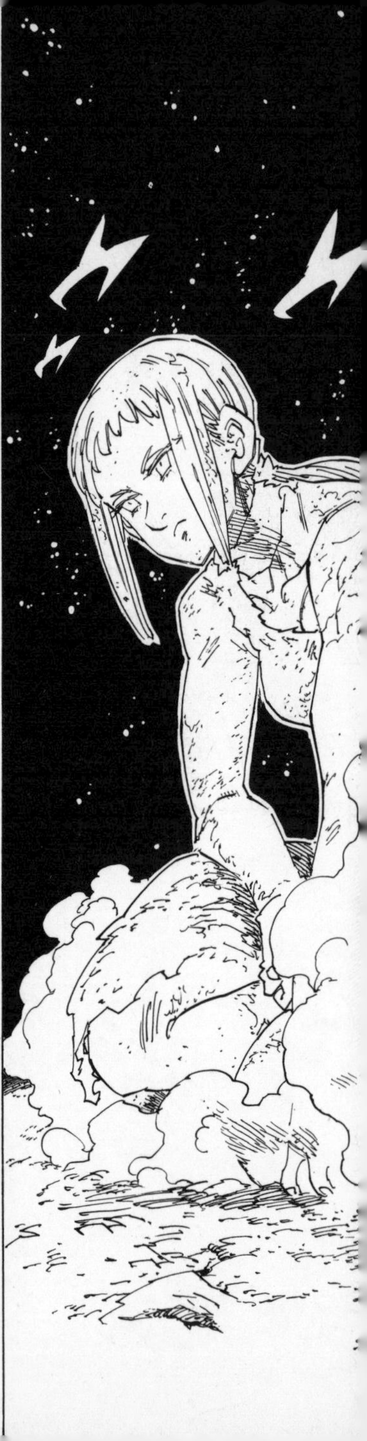

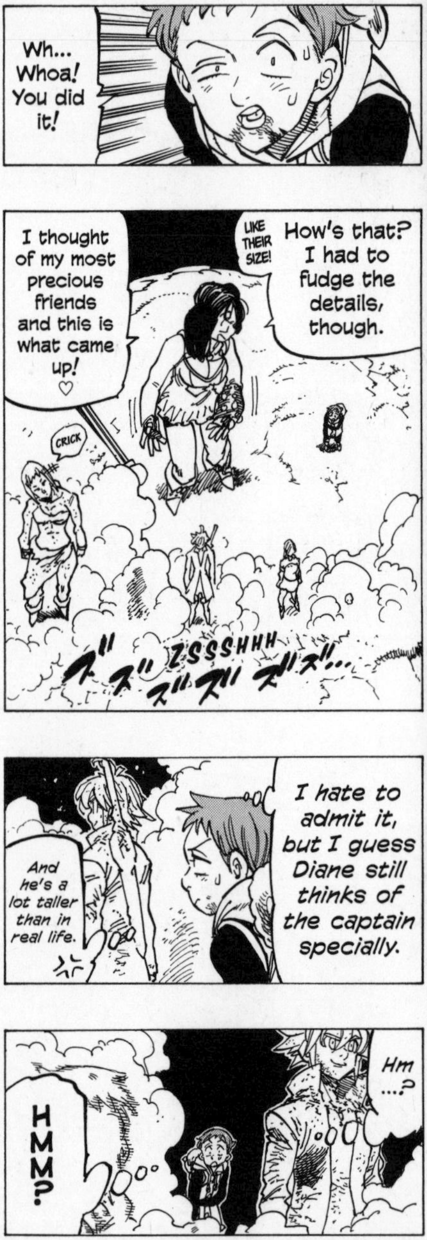

Wh... Whoa! You did it!
How's that? I had to fudge the details, though.
LIKE THEIR SIZE!
I thought of my most precious friends and this is what came up! ♡
CRICK
ZSSSHHH
I hate to admit it, but I guess Diane still thinks of the captain specially.
And he's a lot taller than in real life.
Hm ...?
HMM?

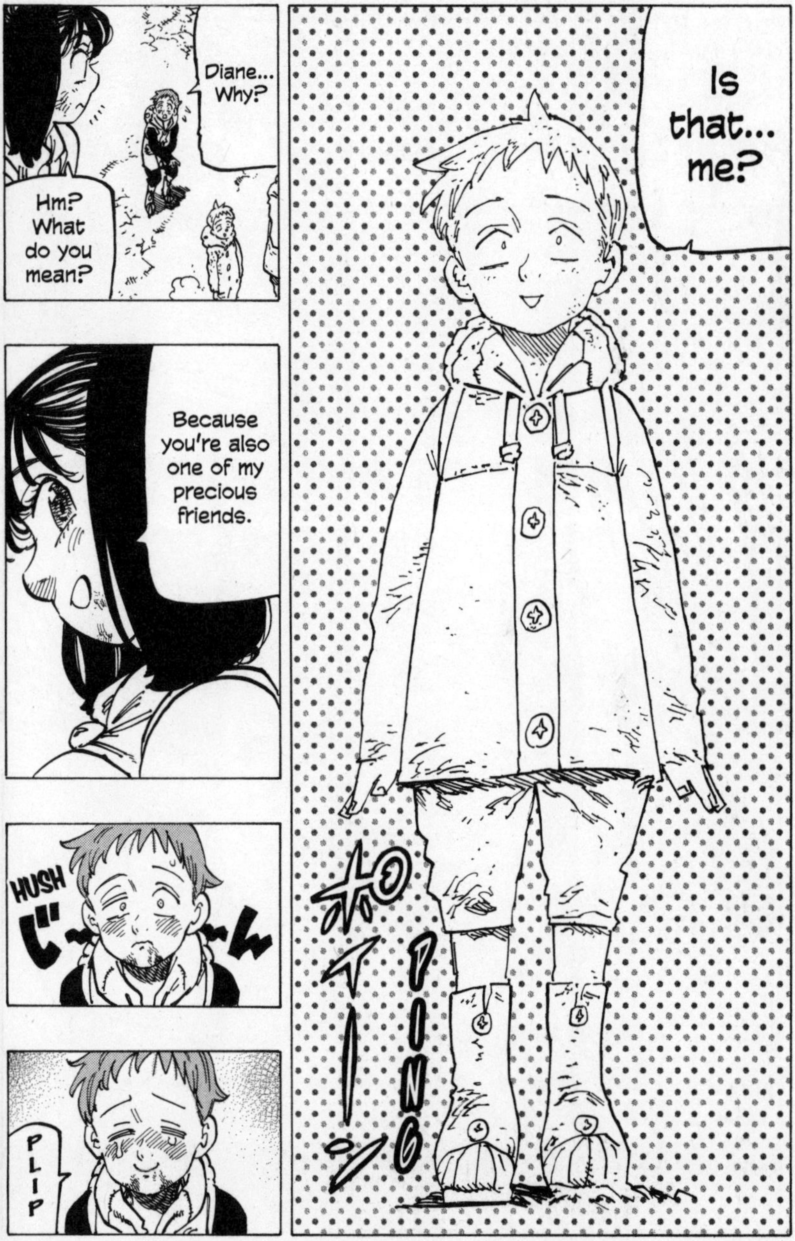
Is that... me?
PING
Diane... Why?
Hm? What do you mean?
Because you're also one of my precious friends.
HUSH
PLIP

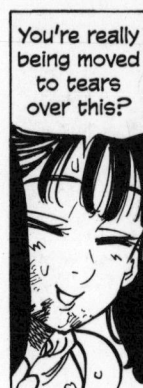

I'm...glad I'm alive.
He looks really weak, but...I'm still super... happy.
You're really being moved to tears over this?
LUNGE
BAM
STRAIIIIN
Ooh!
Eliza-beth is amazing!

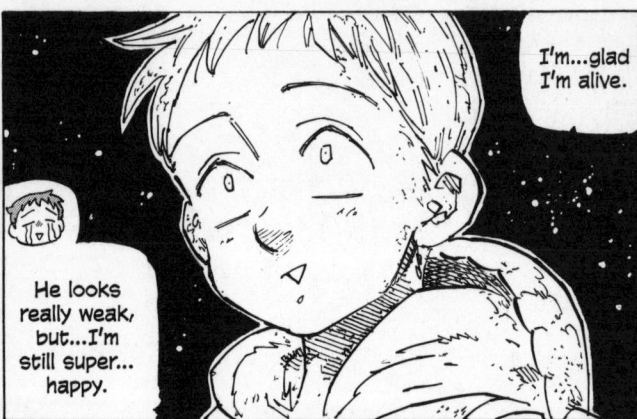

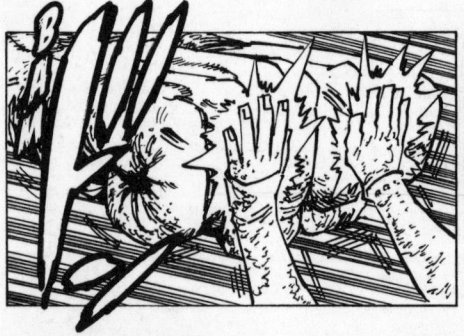

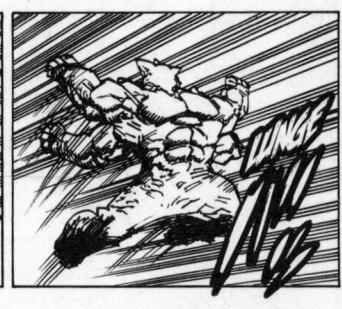

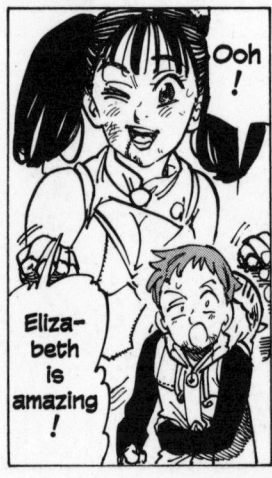

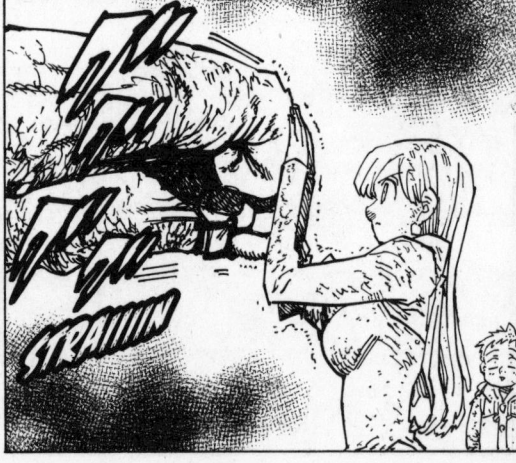

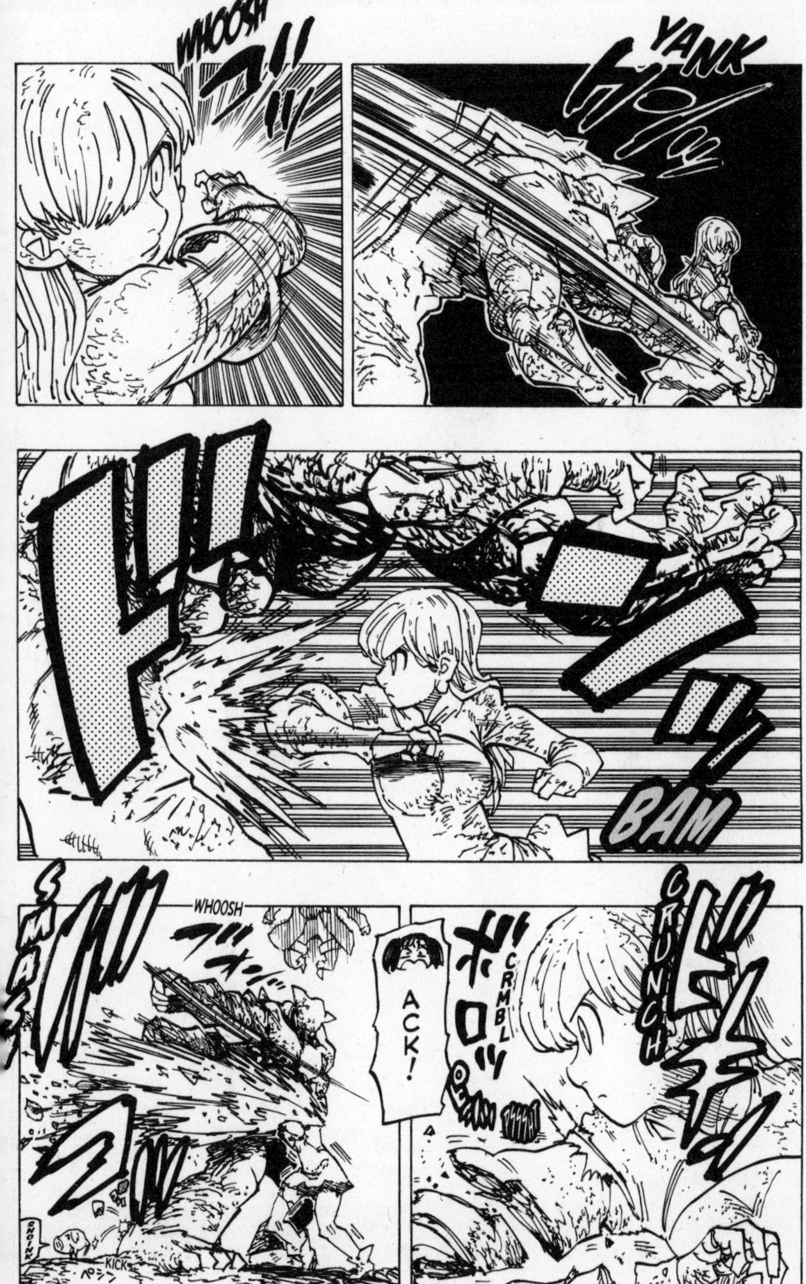
YANK
WHOOSH
BAM
CRUNCH
CRMBL
ACK!
WHOOSH
SMAS
SNOINK
KICK
ペシン

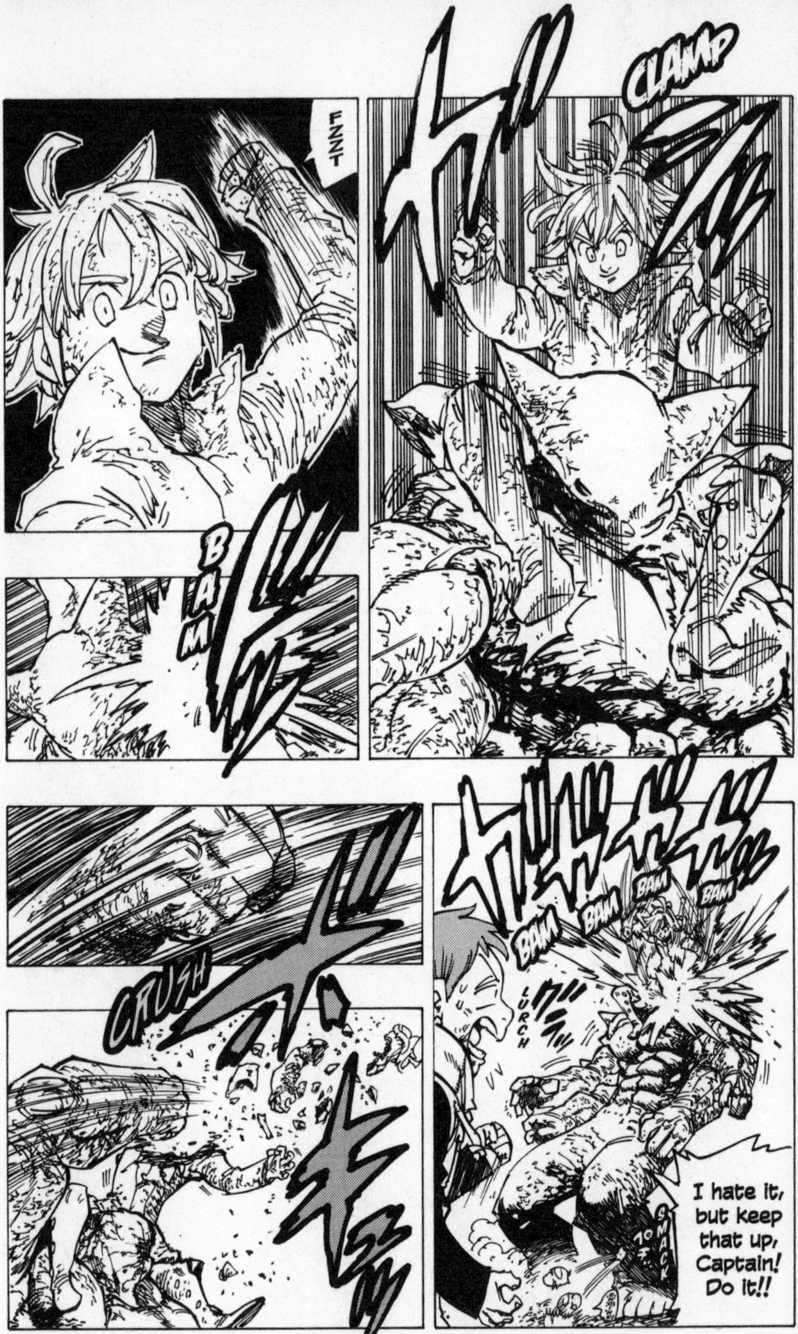
CLAMP
FZZT
BAM
BAM
BAM
BAM
BAM
LURCH
SMACK
I hate it, but keep that up, Captain! Do it!!
CRUSH

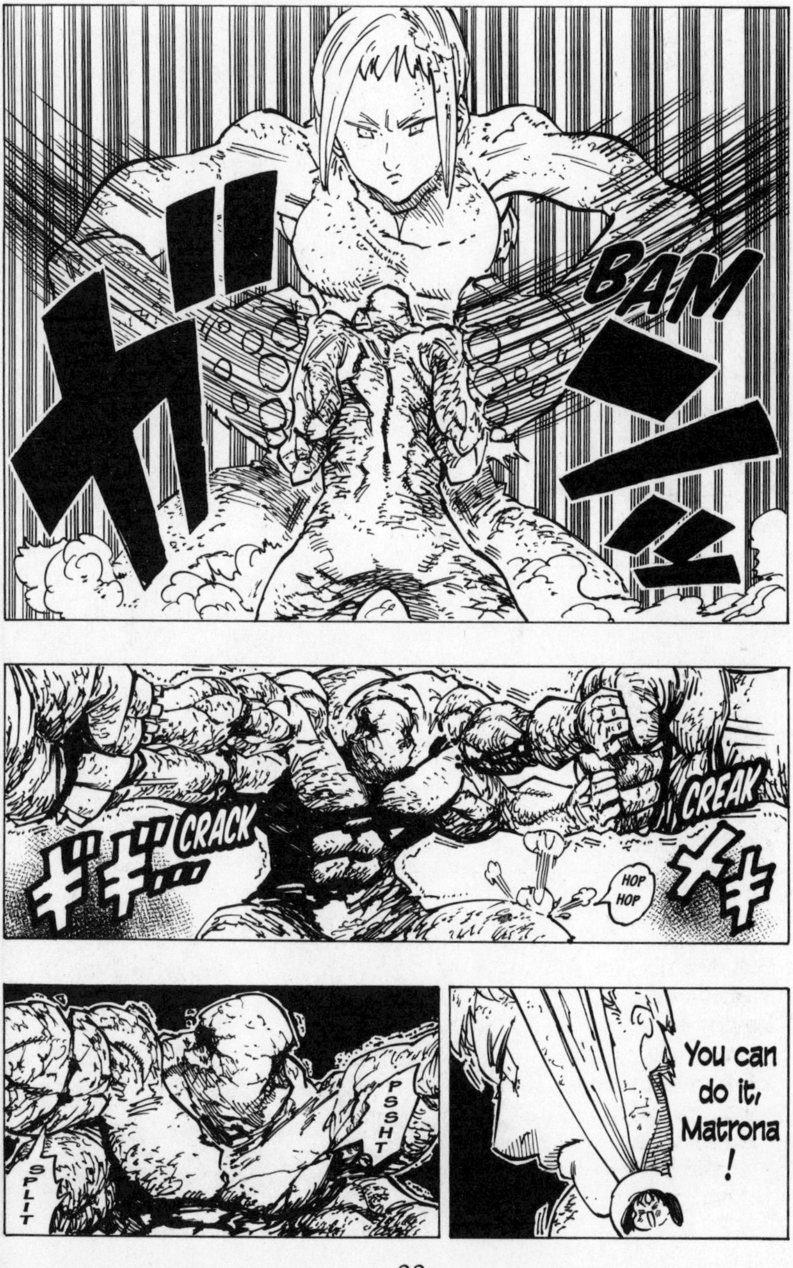
BAM
CREAK
HOP HOP
CRACK
You can do it, Matrona!
PSSHT
SPLIT

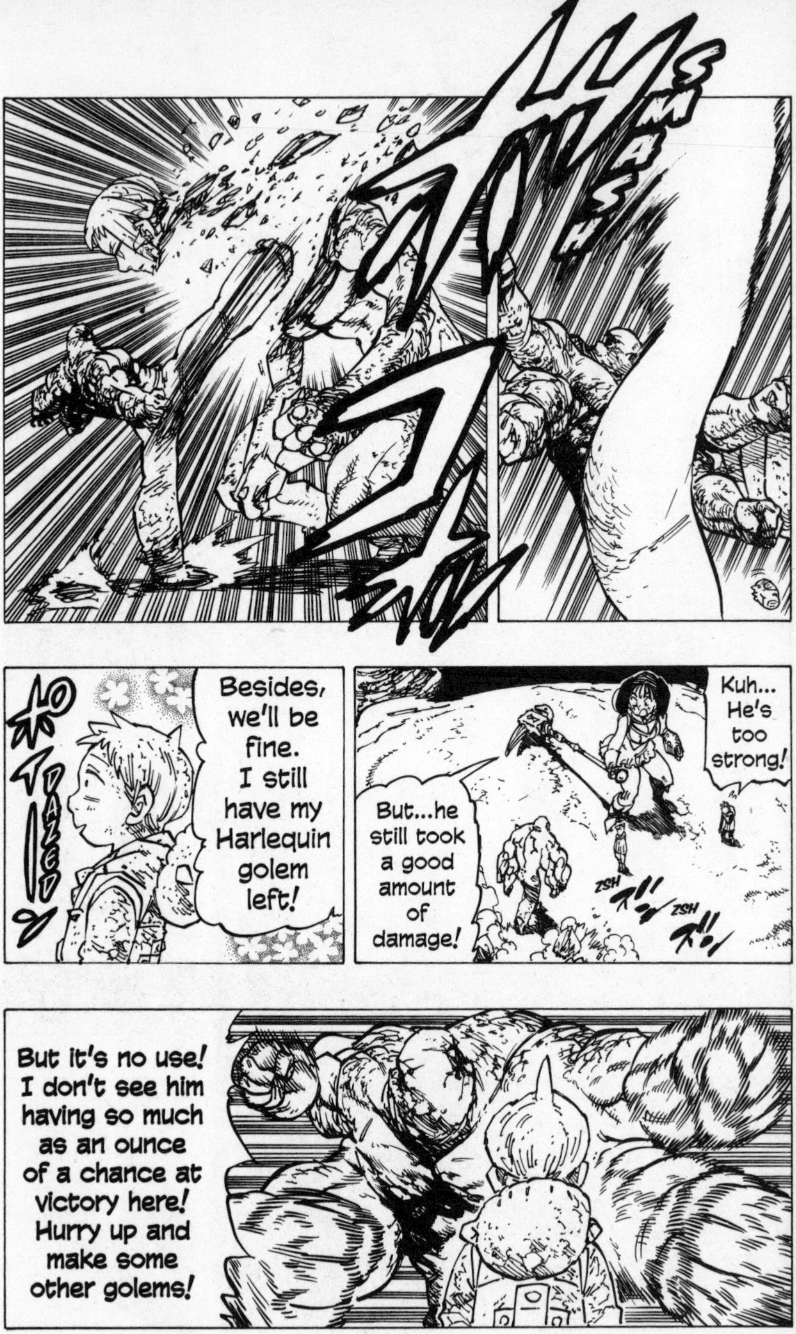
SMASH
Kuh... He's too strong!
But...he still took a good amount of damage!
ZSH
ZSH
Besides, we'll be fine. I still have my Harlequin golem left!
DAZED
But it's no use! I don't see him having so much as an ounce of a chance at victory here! Hurry up and make some other golems!

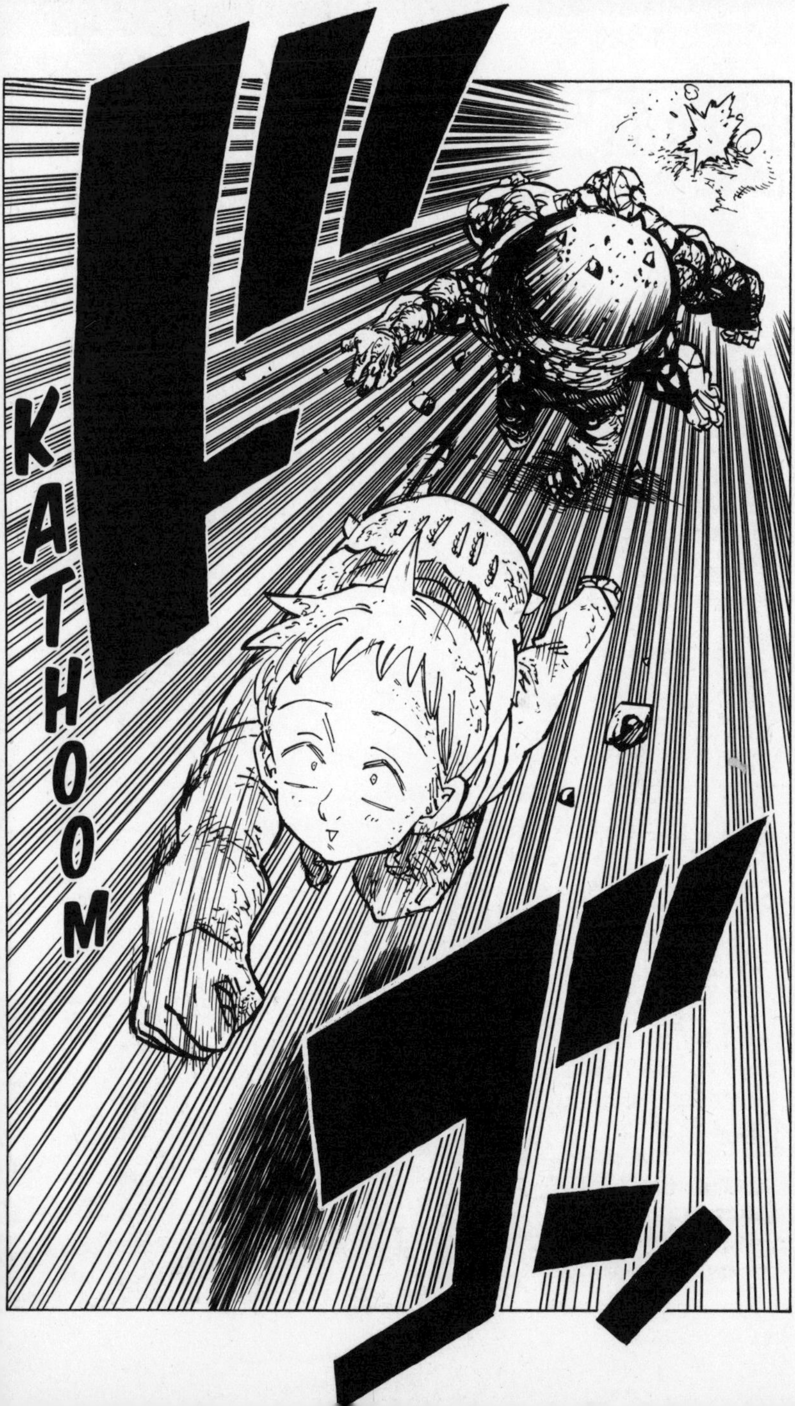
KATHOOM

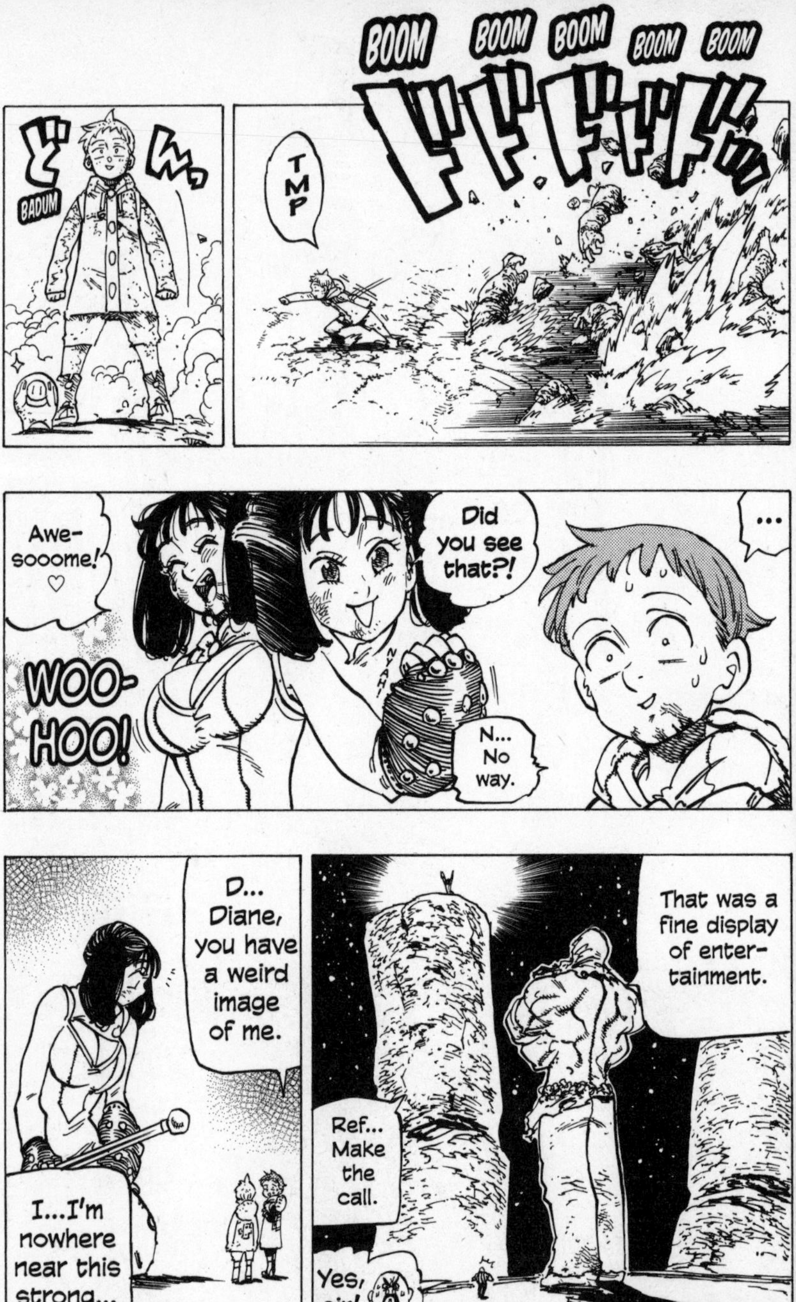
BOOM BOOM BOOM BOOM BOOM
TMP
BADUM
...
Did you see that?!
NYAH!
N... No way.
Awe-sooome! ♡
WOO-HOO!
That was a fine display of enter-tainment.
Ref... Make the call.
Yes, sir!
D... Diane, you have a weird image of me.
I...I'm nowhere near this strong...

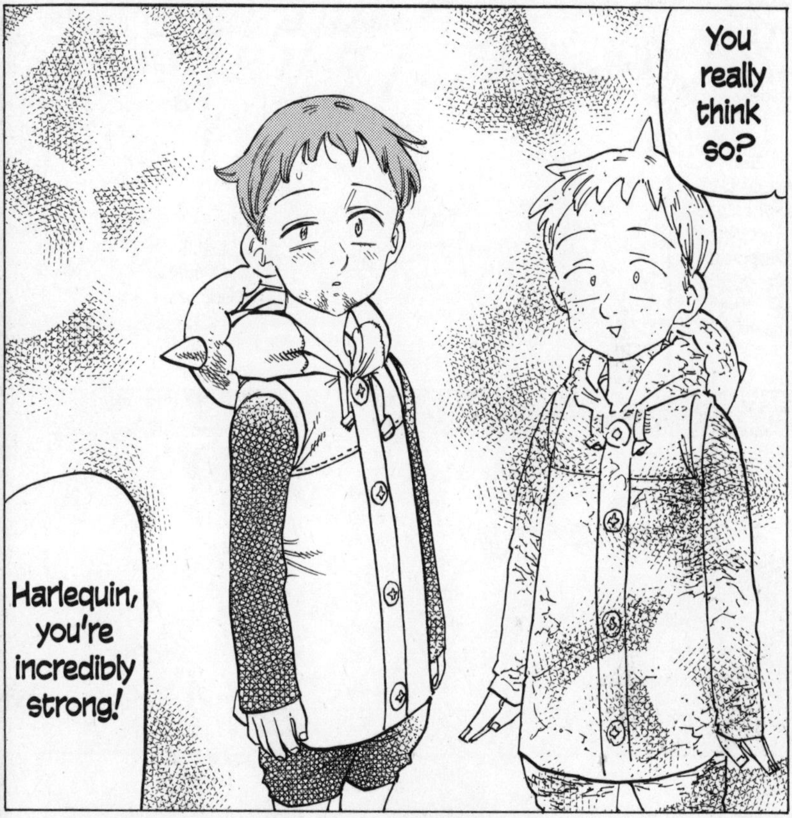
You really think so?
Harlequin, you're incredibly strong!

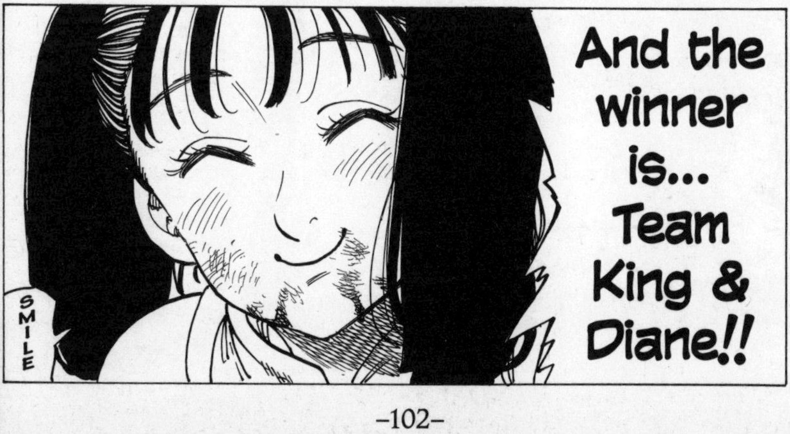
And the winner is... Team King & Diane!!
SMILE

Bonus Story - Adventures of the Knighthood of Scraps Disposal (1)

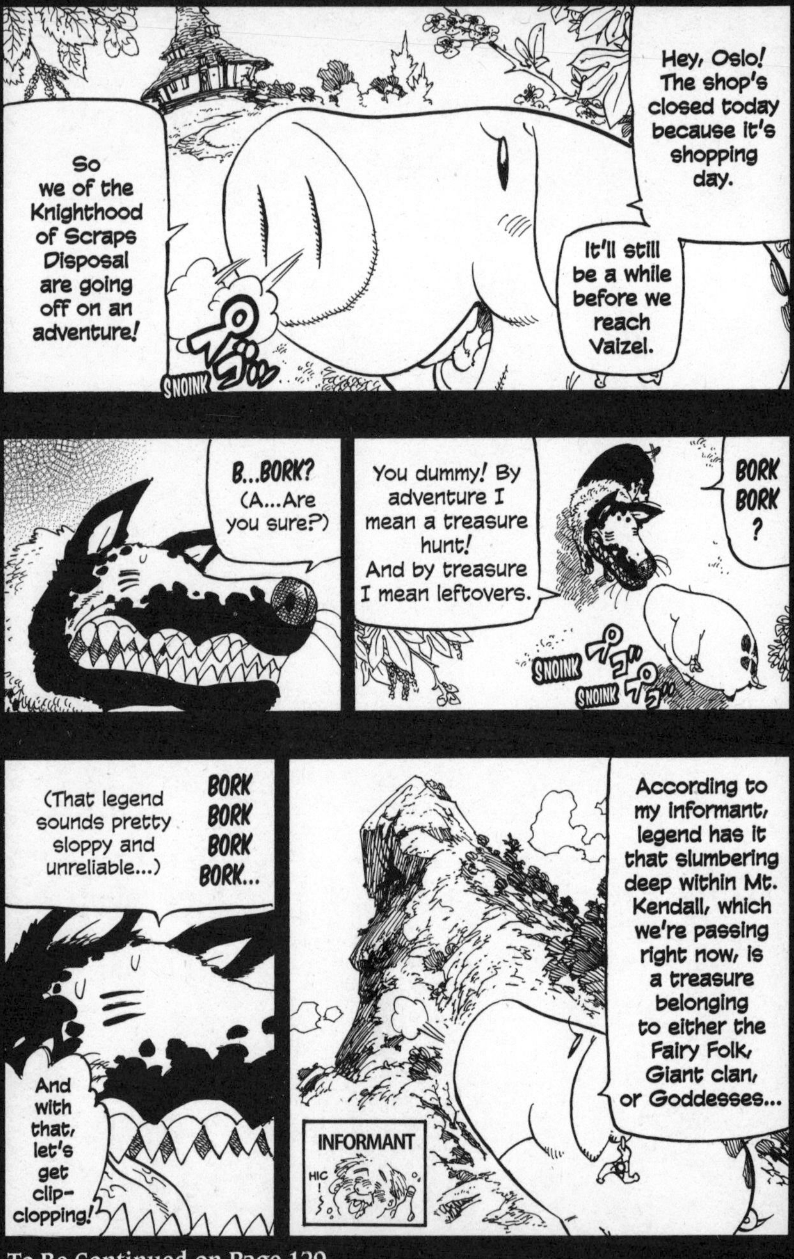
Hey, Oslo! The shop's closed today because it's shopping day.
It'll still be a while before we reach Vaizel.
So we of the Knighthood of Scraps Disposal are going off on an adventure!
SNOINK
BORK BORK ?
You dummy! By adventure I mean a treasure hunt! And by treasure I mean leftovers.
SNOINK
SNOINK
B...BORK? (A...Are you sure?)
According to my informant, legend has it that slumbering deep within Mt. Kendall, which we're passing right now, is a treasure belonging to either the Fairy Folk, Giant clan, or Goddesses...
INFORMANT
HIC
BORK BORK BORK BORK...
(That legend sounds pretty sloppy and unreliable...)
And with that, let's get clip-clopping!

To Be Continued on Page 129

Chapter 168 - Plan to Annihilate The Ten Commandments

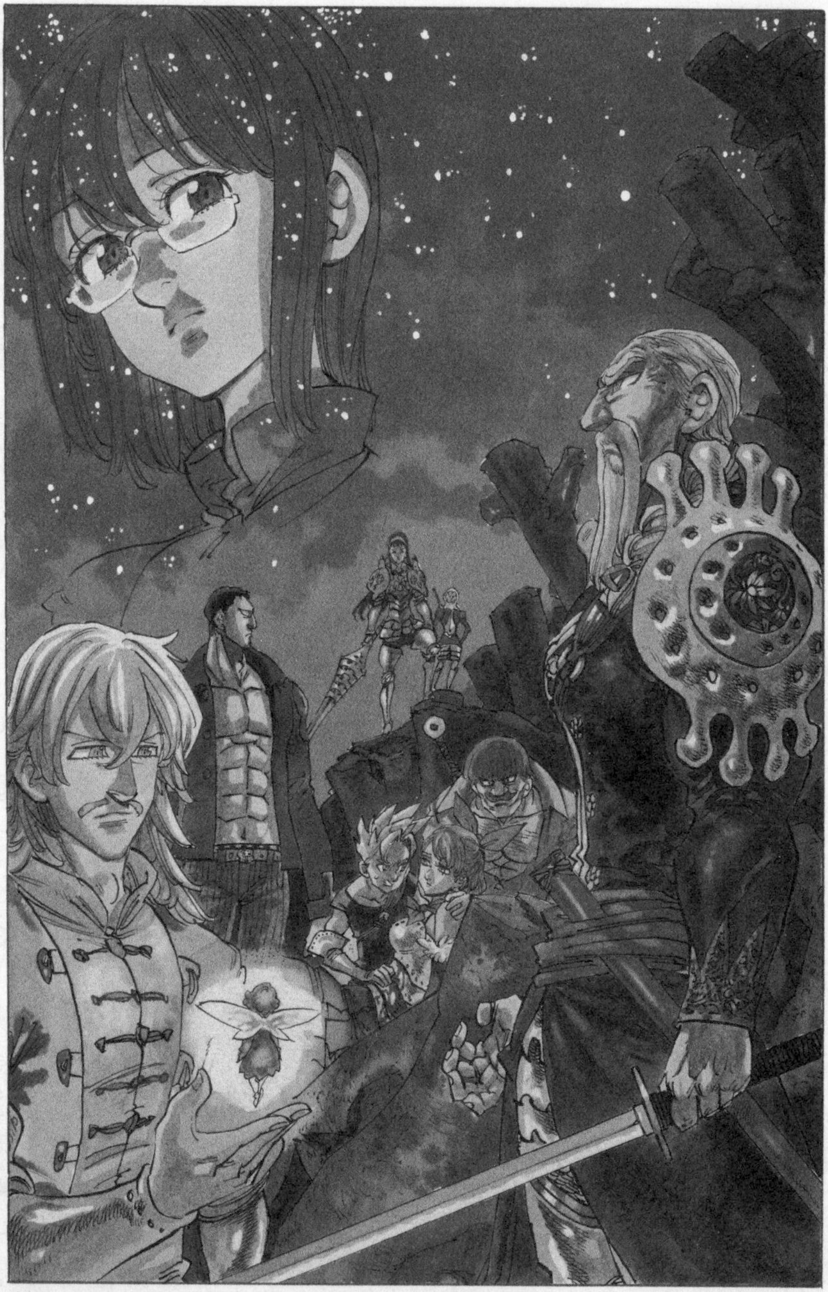

A SHORT TIME BEFORE...IN THE REMOTE REGION OF ZELDON.

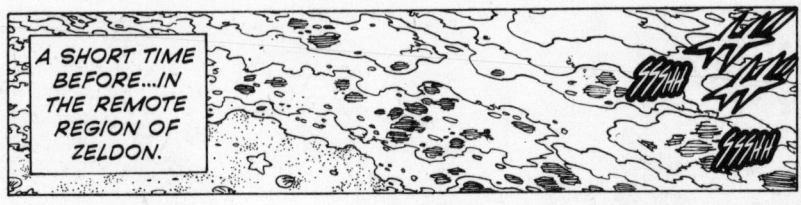

Looks like it must've been one terrific shock-wave... What a mess.

That aside, the familiar feeling of this lingering magic power bothers me.

It's Chief Holy Knight Dreyfus!

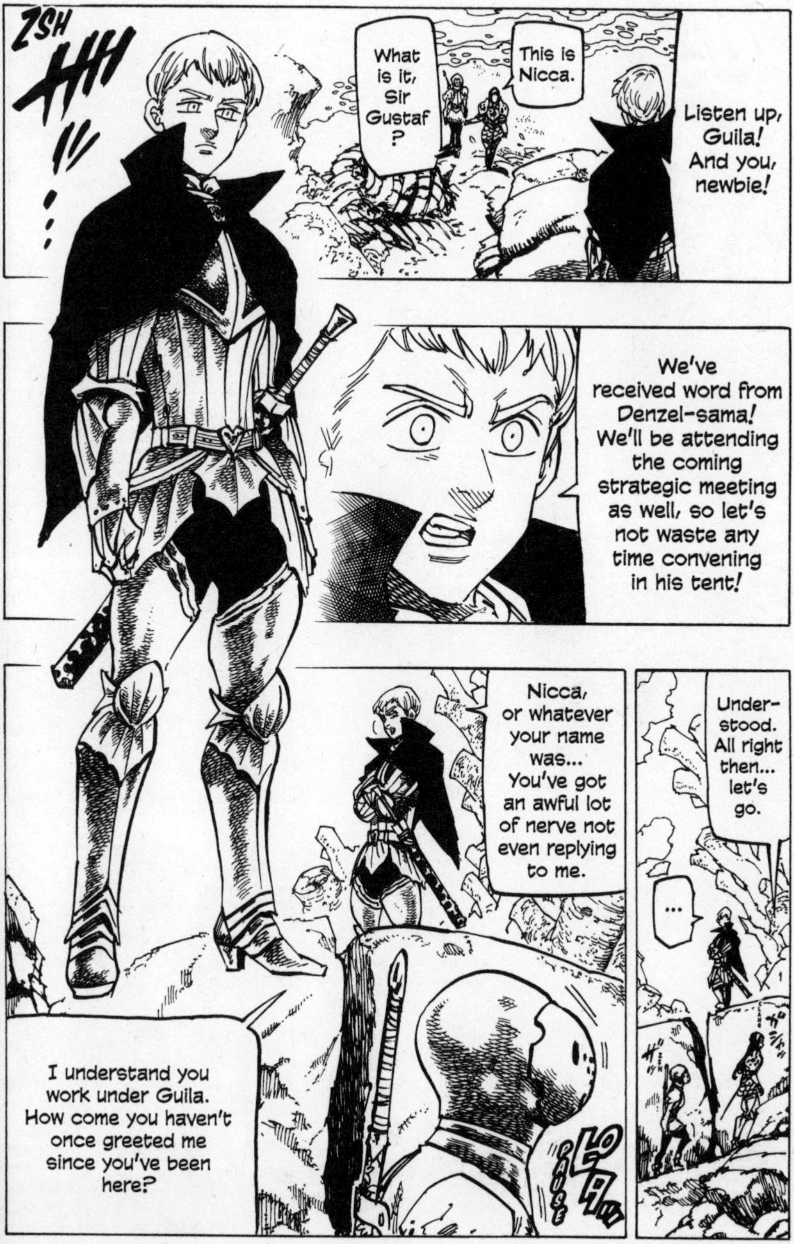

Listen up, Guila! And you, newbie!
This is Nicca.
What is it, Sir Gustaf?
We've received word from Denzel-sama! We'll be attending the coming strategic meeting as well, so let's not waste any time convening in his tent!
Under-stood. All right then... let's go.
...
Nicca, or whatever your name was... You've got an awful lot of nerve not even replying to me.
I understand you work under Guila. How come you haven't once greeted me since you've been here?
PAUSE
ZSHHH!!...

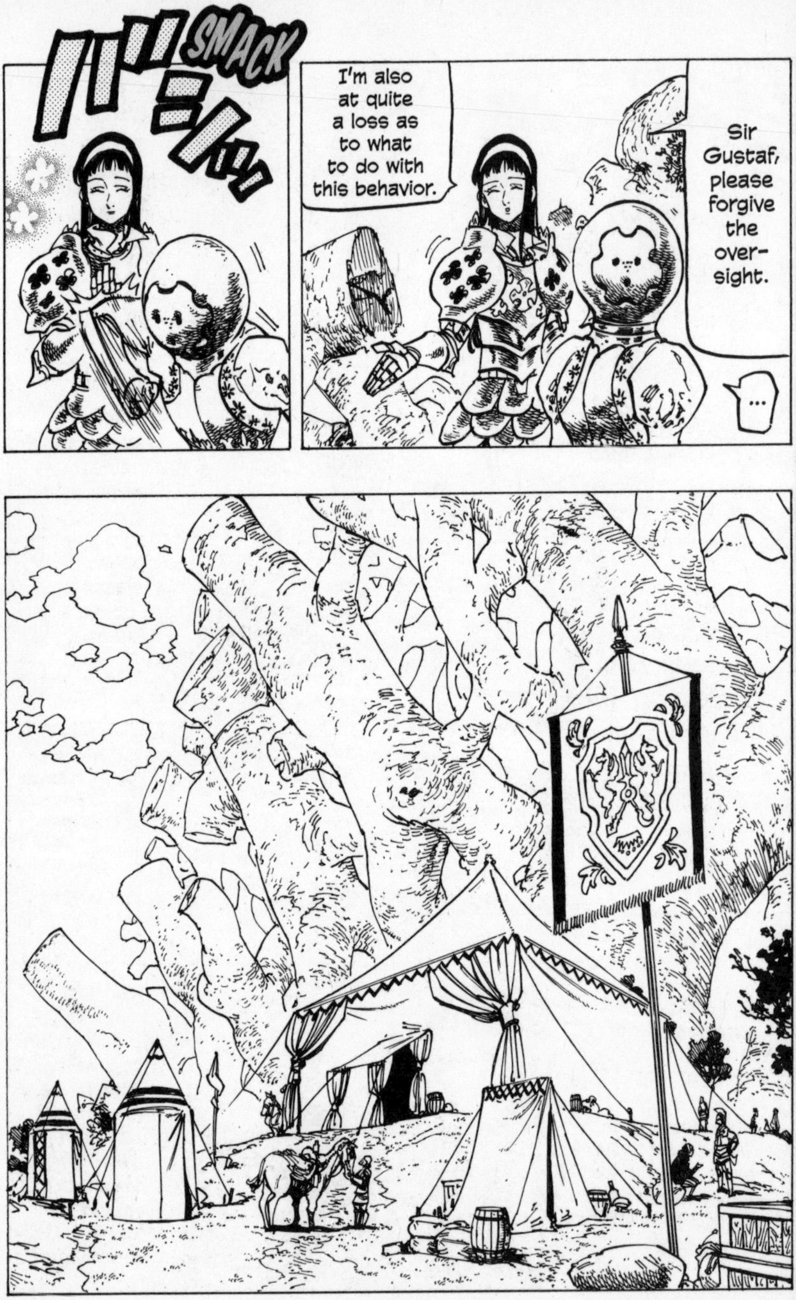
Sir Gustaf, please forgive the over-sight.
I'm also at quite a loss as to what to do with this behavior.
...
SMACK

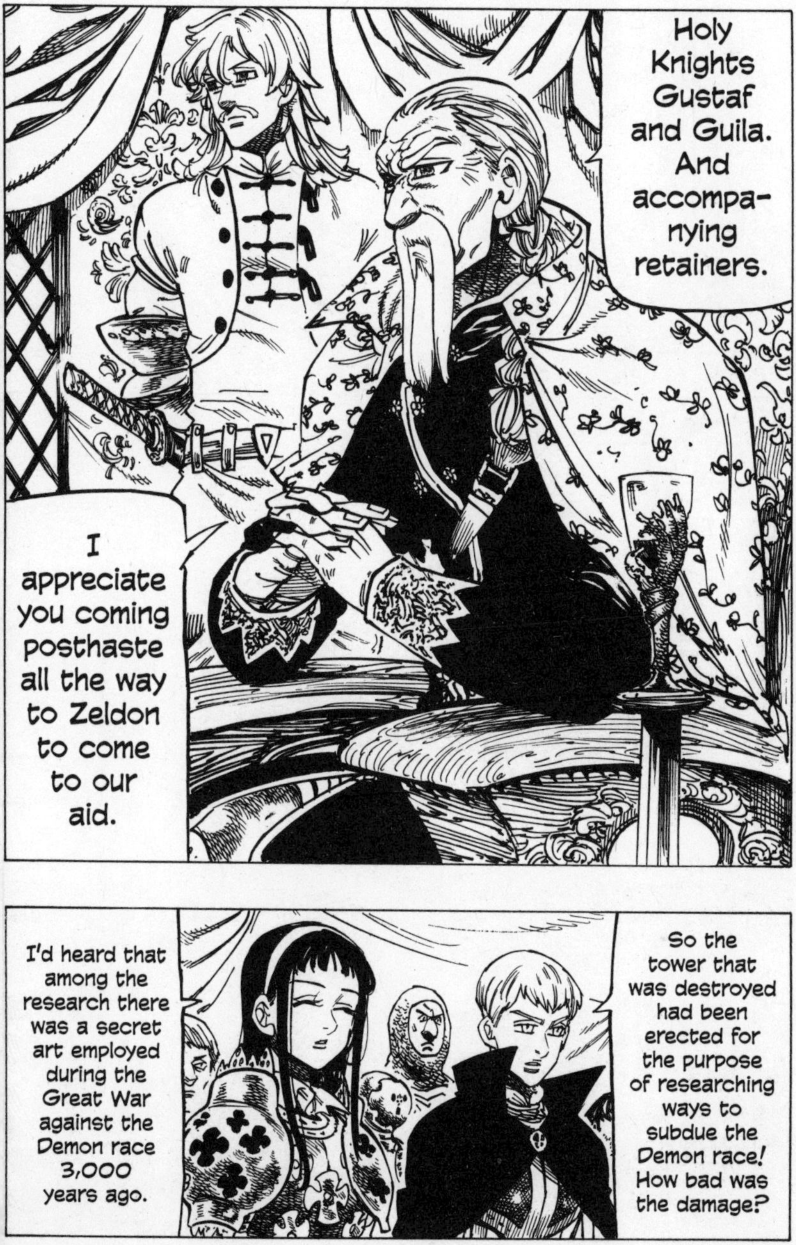
Holy Knights Gustaf and Guila. And accompa-nying retainers.
I appreciate you coming posthaste all the way to Zeldon to come to our aid.
So the tower that was destroyed had been erected for the purpose of researching ways to subdue the Demon race! How bad was the damage?
I'd heard that among the research there was a secret art employed during the Great War against the Demon race 3,000 years ago.

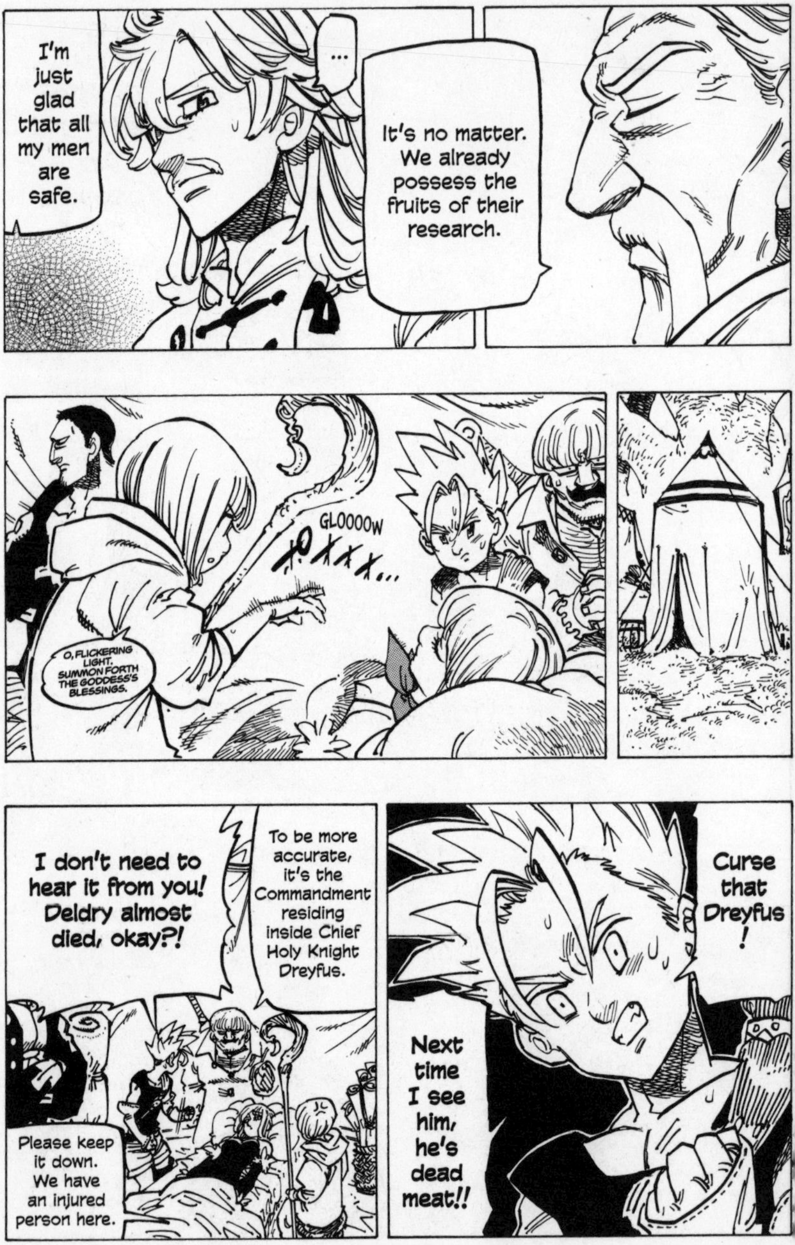
...
It's no matter. We already possess the fruits of their research.
I'm just glad that all my men are safe.
GLOOOOW
O, FLICKERING LIGHT. SUMMON FORTH THE GODDESS'S BLESSINGS.
Curse that Dreyfus!
Next time I see him, he's dead meat!!
To be more accurate, it's the Commandment residing inside Chief Holy Knight Dreyfus.
I don't need to hear it from you! Deldry almost died, okay?!
Please keep it down. We have an injured person here.

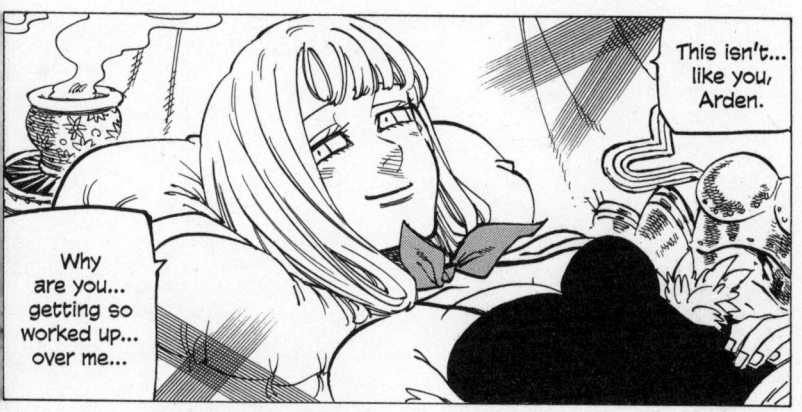

This isn't... like you, Arden.
Why are you... getting so worked up... over me...
TURN
...Shut it.
Oh, brother. I can't believe the bunch of you fell for an impostor.
You could've all died!
CREAK
My apologies!
BOW
Shit... I'm sorry.
If it weren't for your "Boost" spell, we'd all be mincemeat by now.
Thank you, Dogedo.

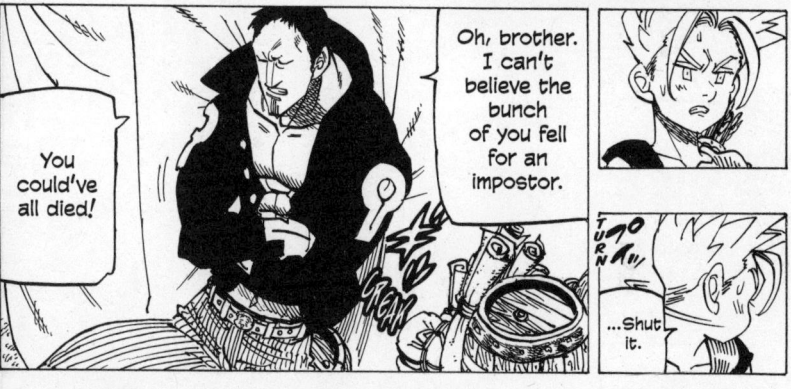

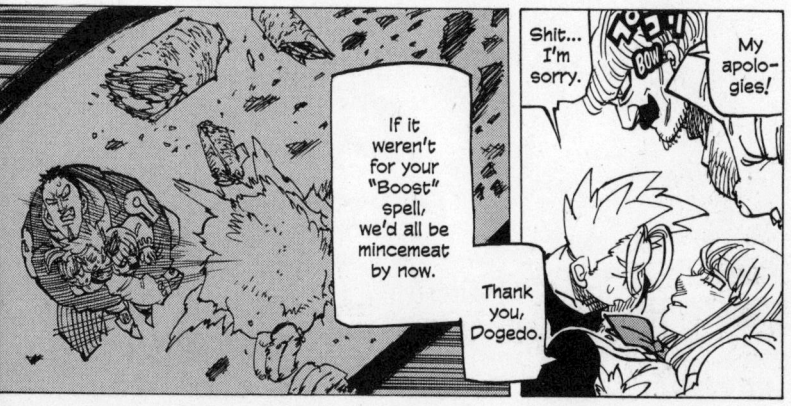

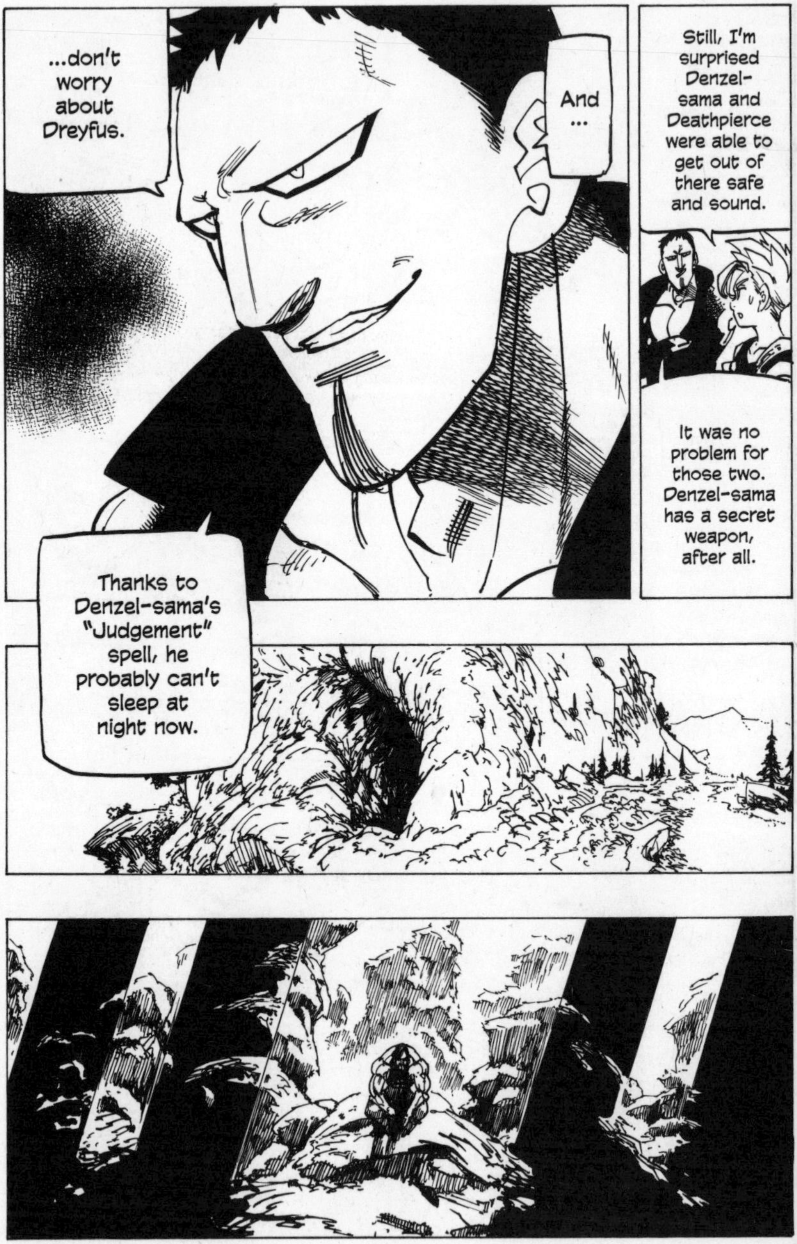
Still, I'm surprised Denzel-sama and Deathpierce were able to get out of there safe and sound.
It was no problem for those two. Denzel-sama has a secret weapon, after all.
And ...
...don't worry about Dreyfus.
Thanks to Denzel-sama's "Judgement" spell, he probably can't sleep at night now.

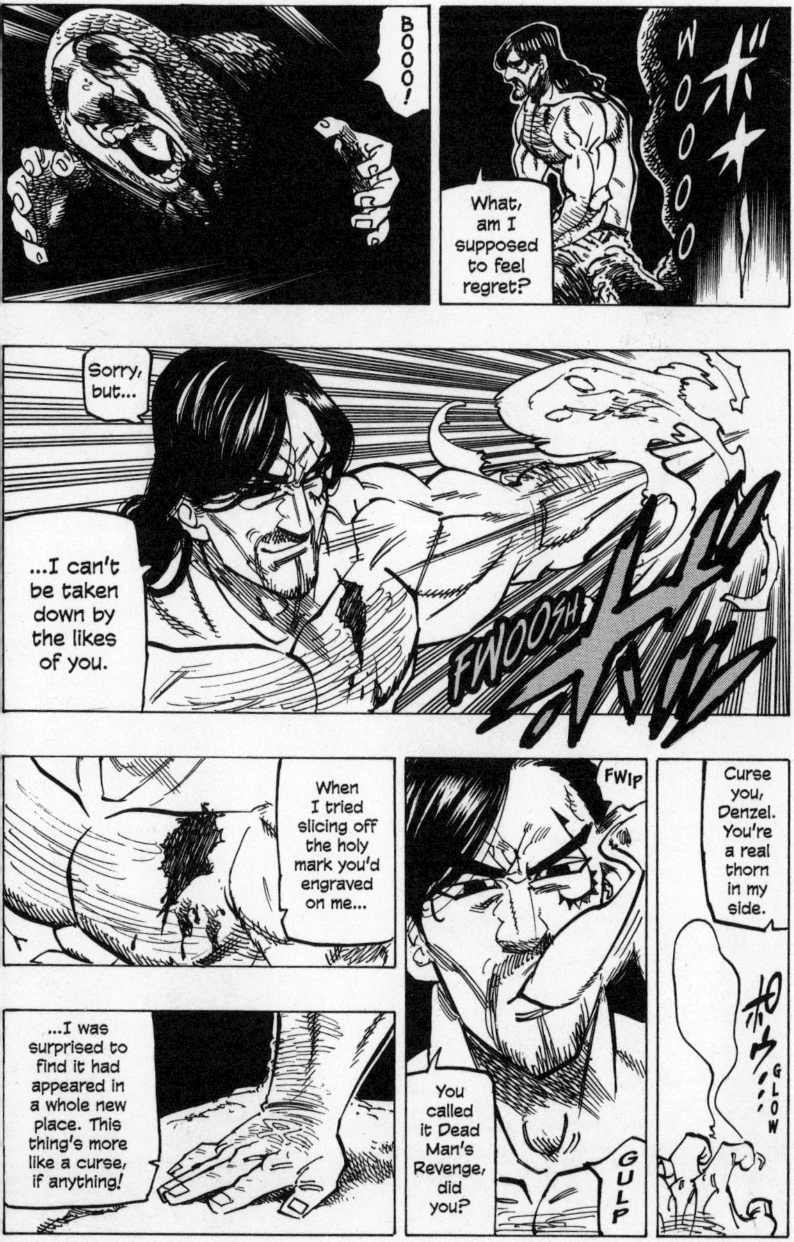
WOOOOO
What, am I supposed to feel regret?
BOOO!
Sorry, but...
FWOOSH
...I can't be taken down by the likes of you.
Curse you, Denzel. You're a real thorn in my side.
GLOW
FWIP
You called it Dead Man's Revenge, did you?
GULP
When I tried slicing off the holy mark you'd engraved on me...
...I was surprised to find it had appeared in a whole new place. This thing's more like a curse, if anything!

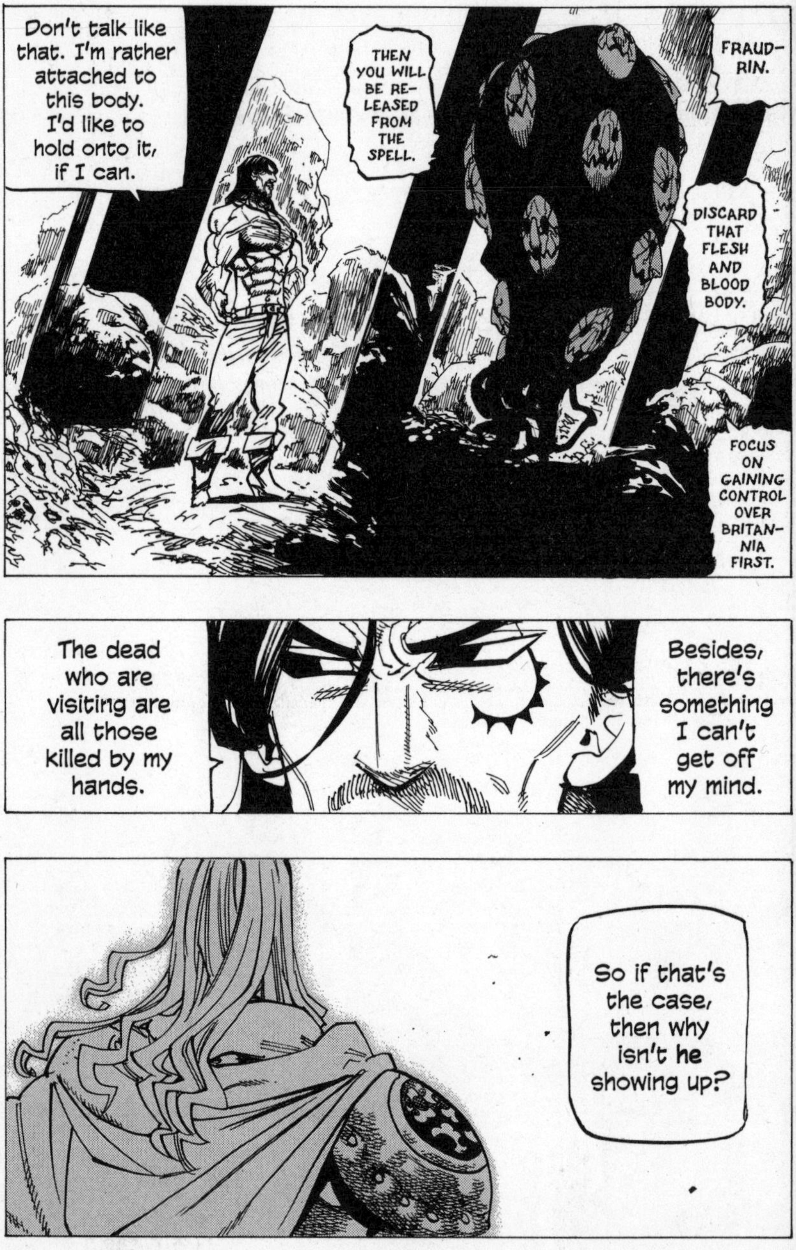
FRAUD-RIN.
DISCARD THAT FLESH AND BLOOD BODY.
FOCUS ON GAINING CONTROL OVER BRITAN-NIA FIRST.
THEN YOU WILL BE RE-LEASED FROM THE SPELL.
Don't talk like that. I'm rather attached to this body. I'd like to hold onto it, if I can.
Besides, there's something I can't get off my mind.
The dead who are visiting are all those killed by my hands.
So if that's the case, then why isn't he showing up?

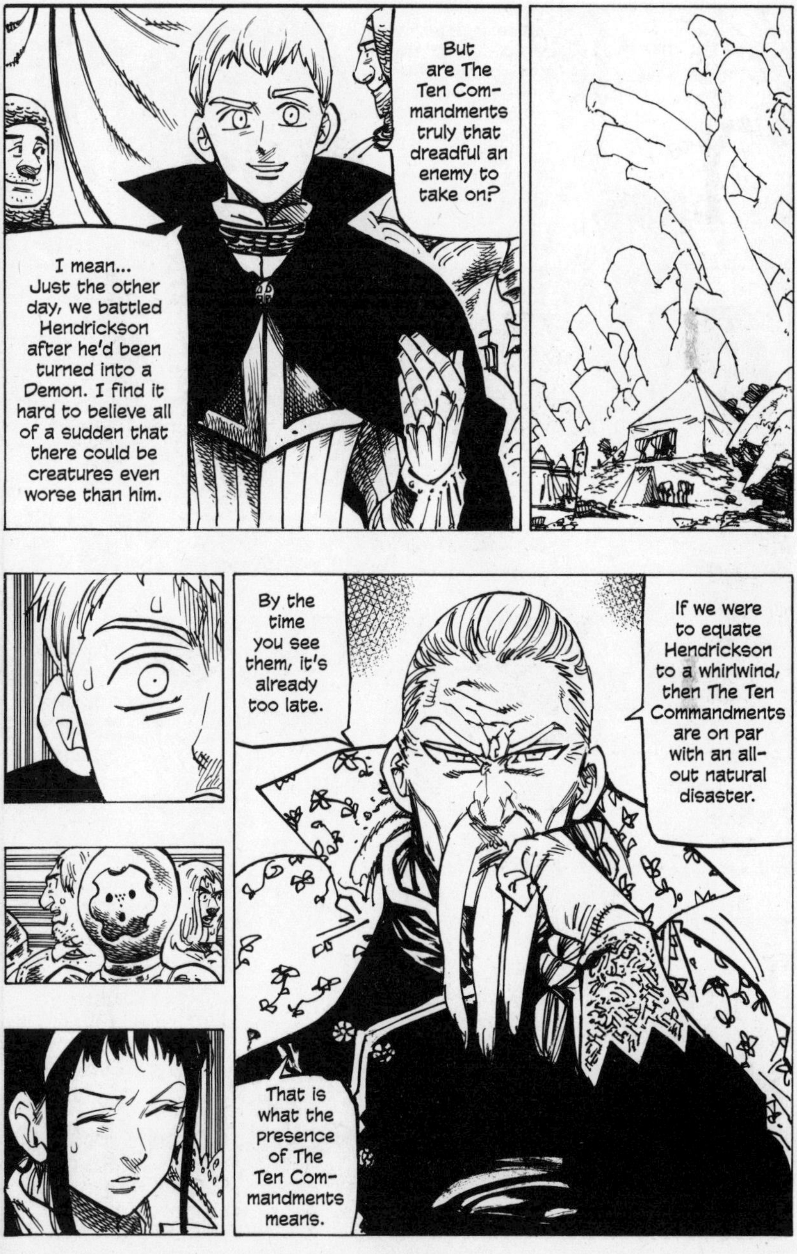
But are The Ten Commandments truly that dreadful an enemy to take on?
I mean... Just the other day, we battled Hendrickson after he'd been turned into a Demon. I find it hard to believe all of a sudden that there could be creatures even worse than him.
If we were to equate Hendrickson to a whirlwind, then The Ten Commandments are on par with an all-out natural disaster.
By the time you see them, it's already too late.
That is what the presence of The Ten Commandments means.

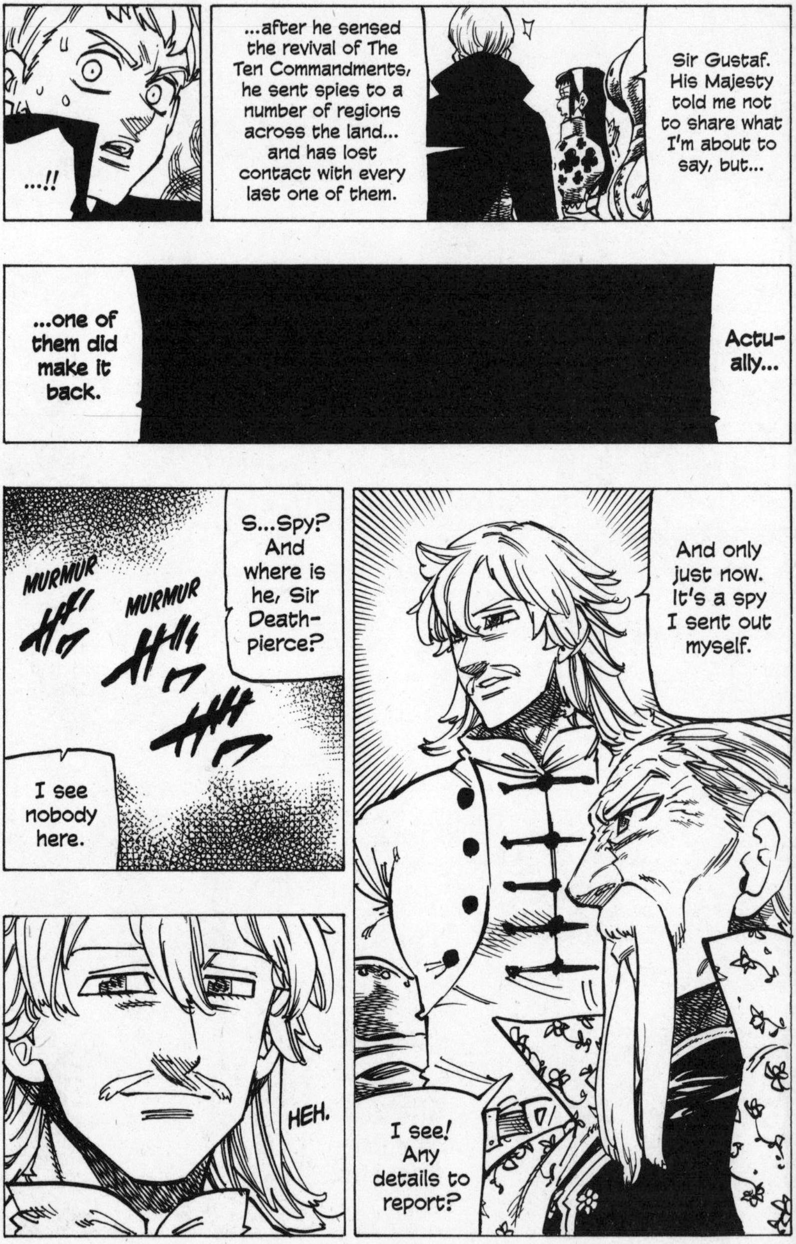
Sir Gustaf. His Majesty told me not to share what I'm about to say, but...
...after he sensed the revival of The Ten Commandments, he sent spies to a number of regions across the land... and has lost contact with every last one of them.
...!!
Actu-ally...
...one of them did make it back.
And only just now. It's a spy I sent out myself.
I see! Any details to report?
S...Spy? And where is he, Sir Death-pierce?
MURMUR
MURMUR
I see nobody here.
HEH.

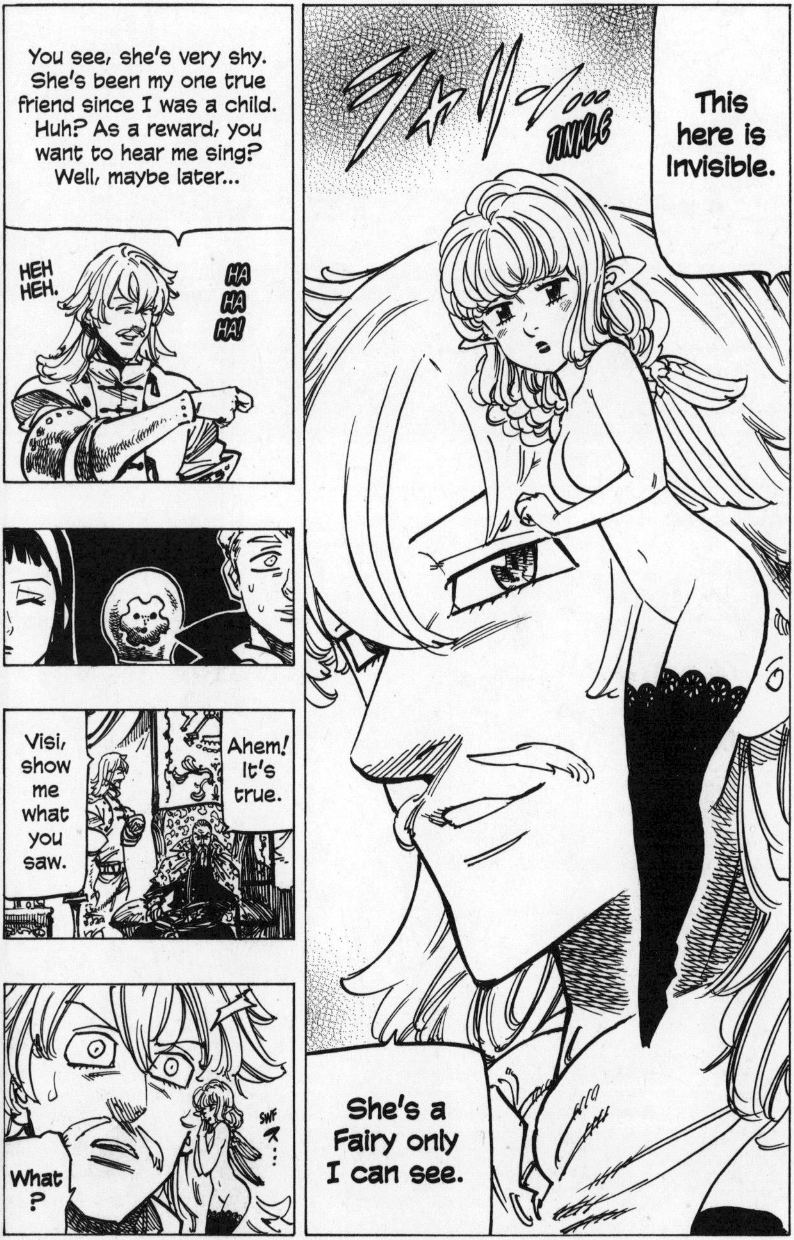
TINKLE
This here is Invisible.
She's a Fairy only I can see.
You see, she's very shy. She's been my one true friend since I was a child. Huh? As a reward, you want to hear me sing? Well, maybe later...
HA HA HA!
HEH HEH.
Ahem! It's true.
Visi, show me what you saw.
SWF
What?

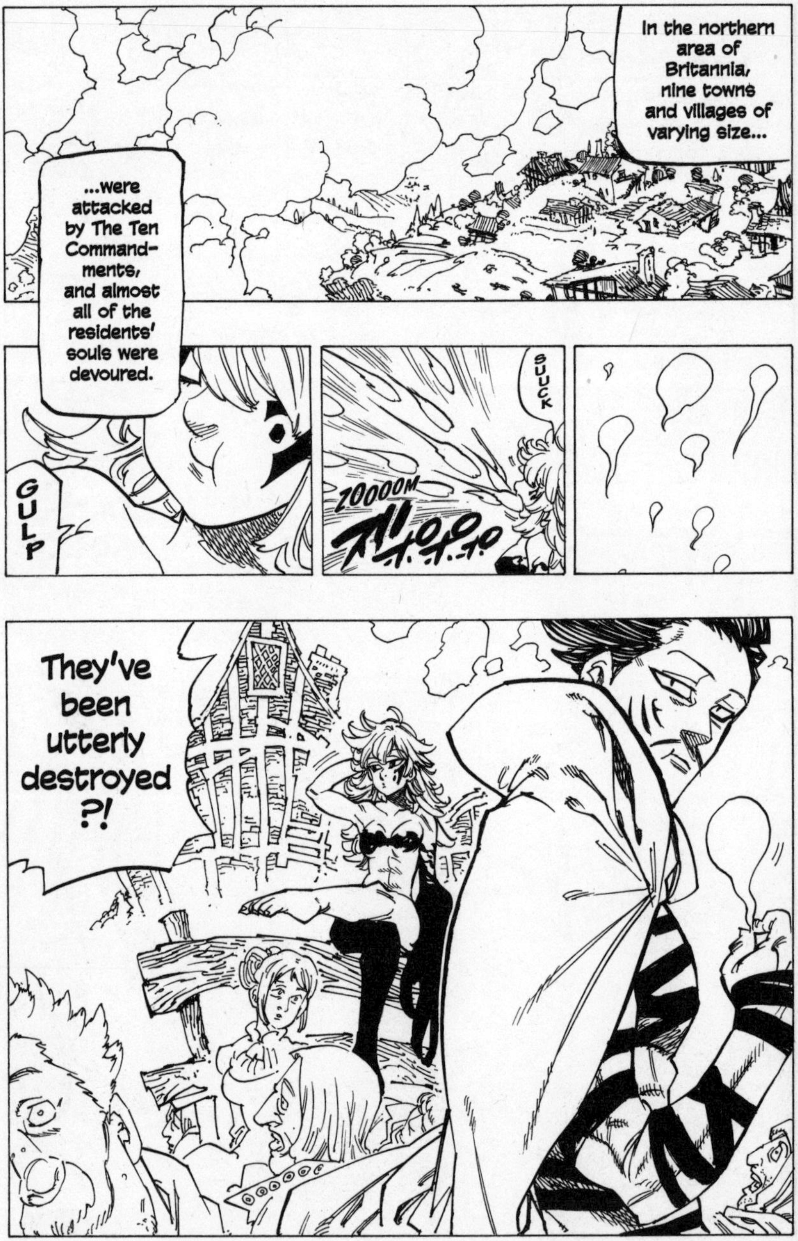
In the northern area of Britannia, nine towns and villages of varying size...
...were attacked by The Ten Command-ments, and almost all of the residents' souls were devoured.
SUUCK
ZOOOOM
GULP
They've been utterly destroyed?!

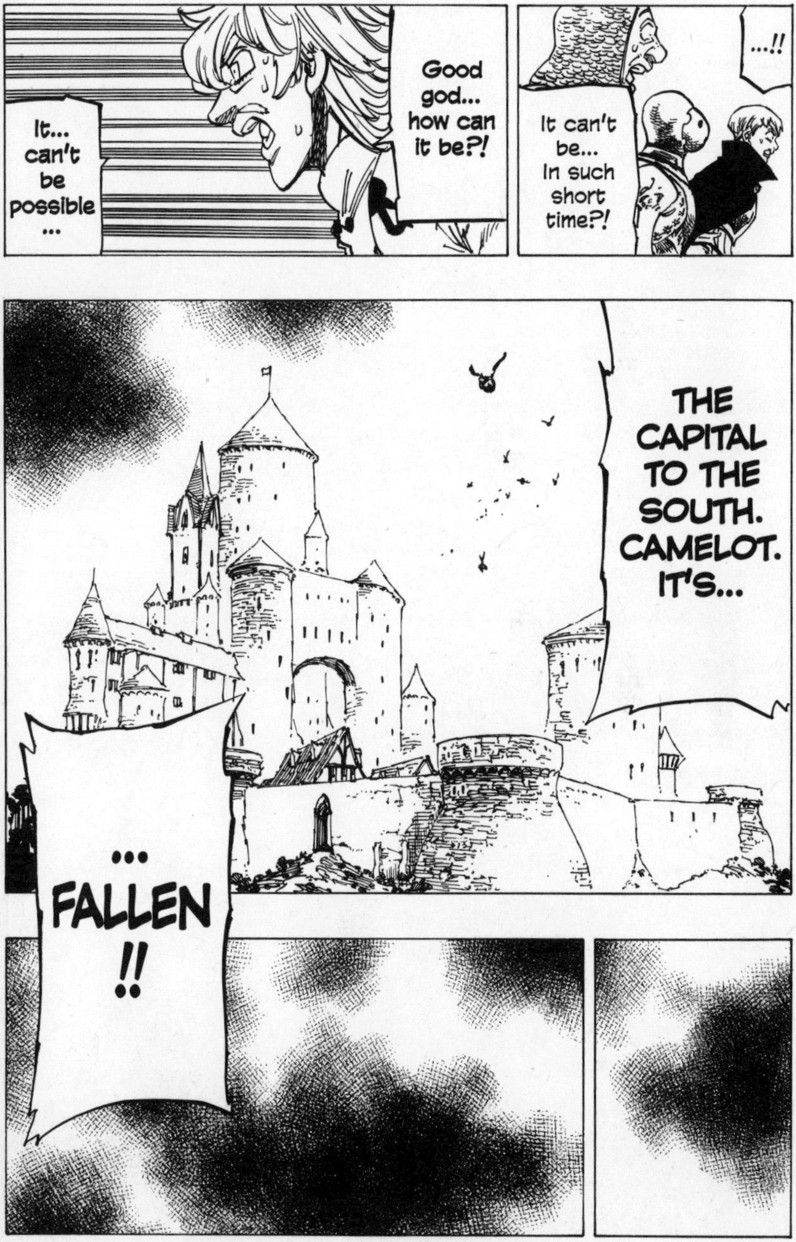
...!!
It can't be... In such short time?!
Good god... how can it be?!
It... can't be possible ...
THE CAPITAL TO THE SOUTH. CAMELOT. IT'S...
... FALLEN !!

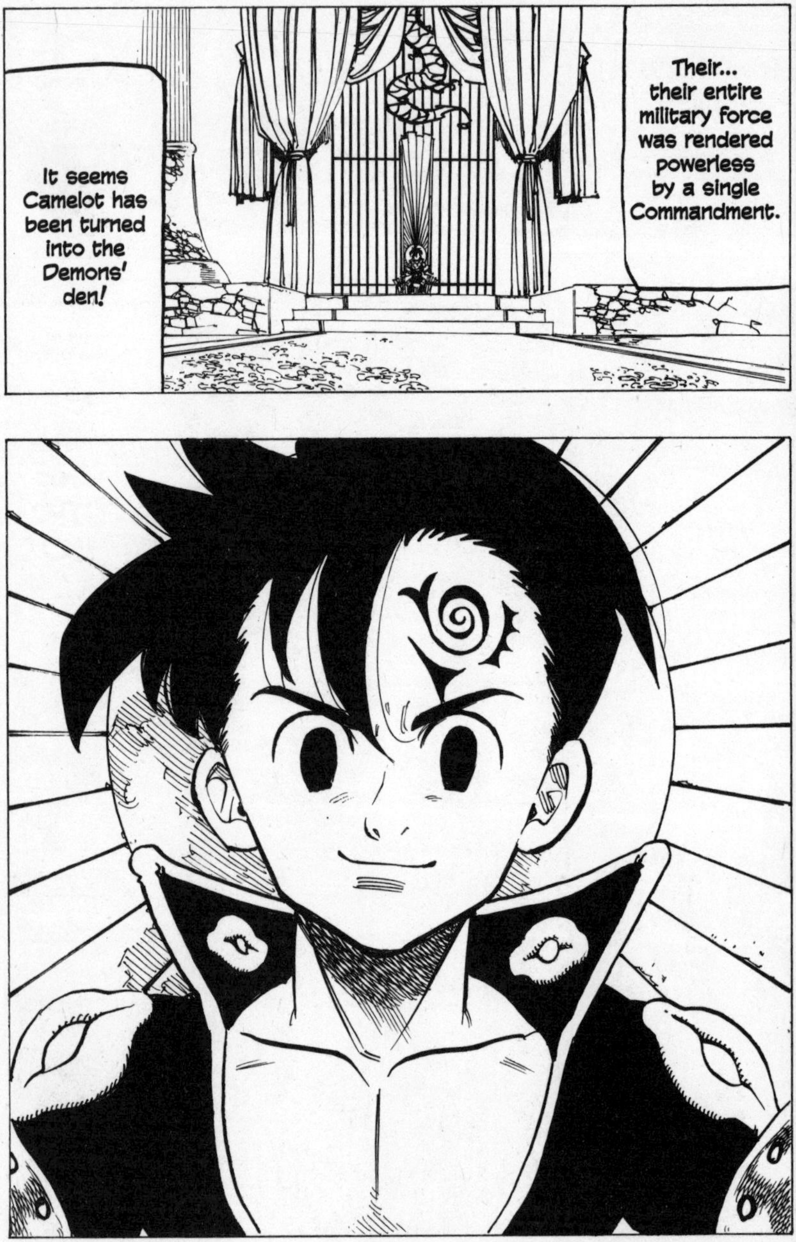
Their... their entire military force was rendered powerless by a single Commandment.
It seems Camelot has been turned into the Demons' den!

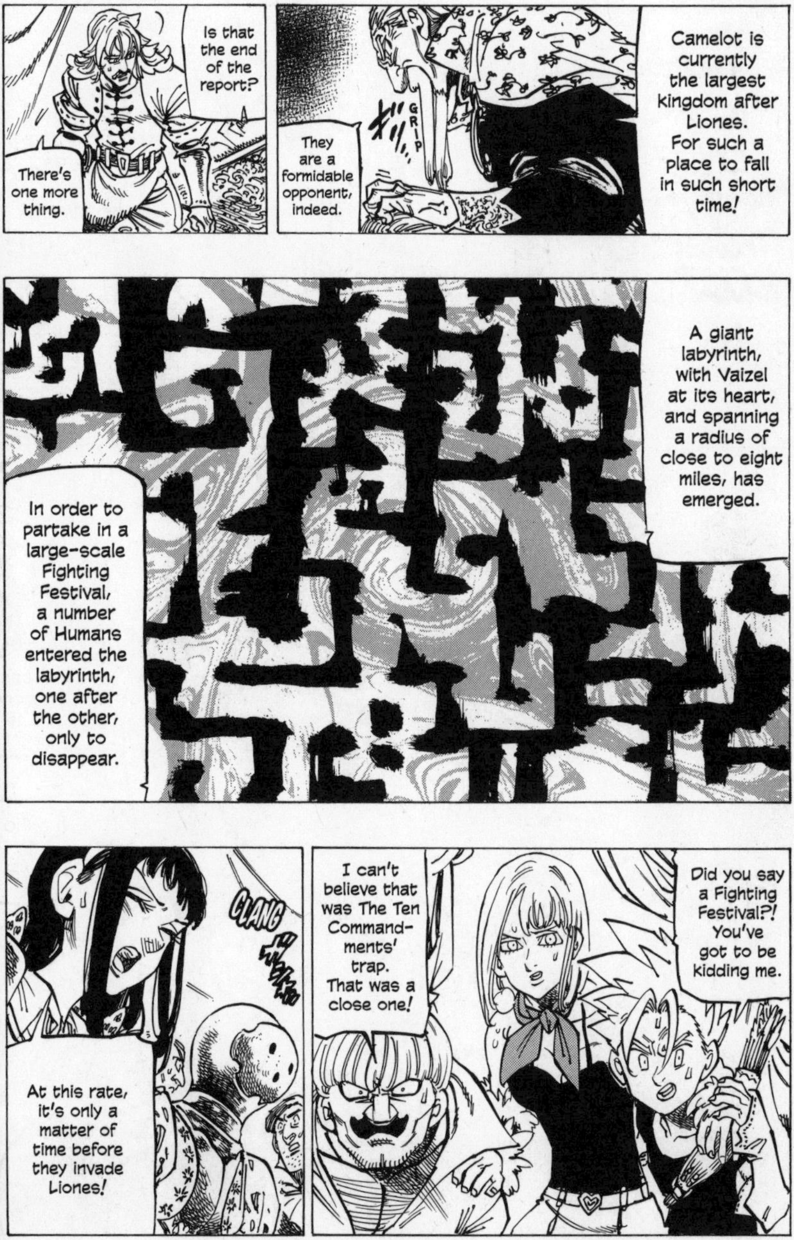
Camelot is currently the largest kingdom after Liones. For such a place to fall in such short time!
GRIP
They are a formidable opponent, indeed.
Is that the end of the report?
There's one more thing.
A giant labyrinth, with Vaizel at its heart, and spanning a radius of close to eight miles, has emerged.
In order to partake in a large-scale Fighting Festival, a number of Humans entered the labyrinth, one after the other, only to disappear.
Did you say a Fighting Festival?! You've got to be kidding me.
I can't believe that was The Ten Command-ments' trap. That was a close one!
CLANG
At this rate, it's only a matter of time before they invade Liones!

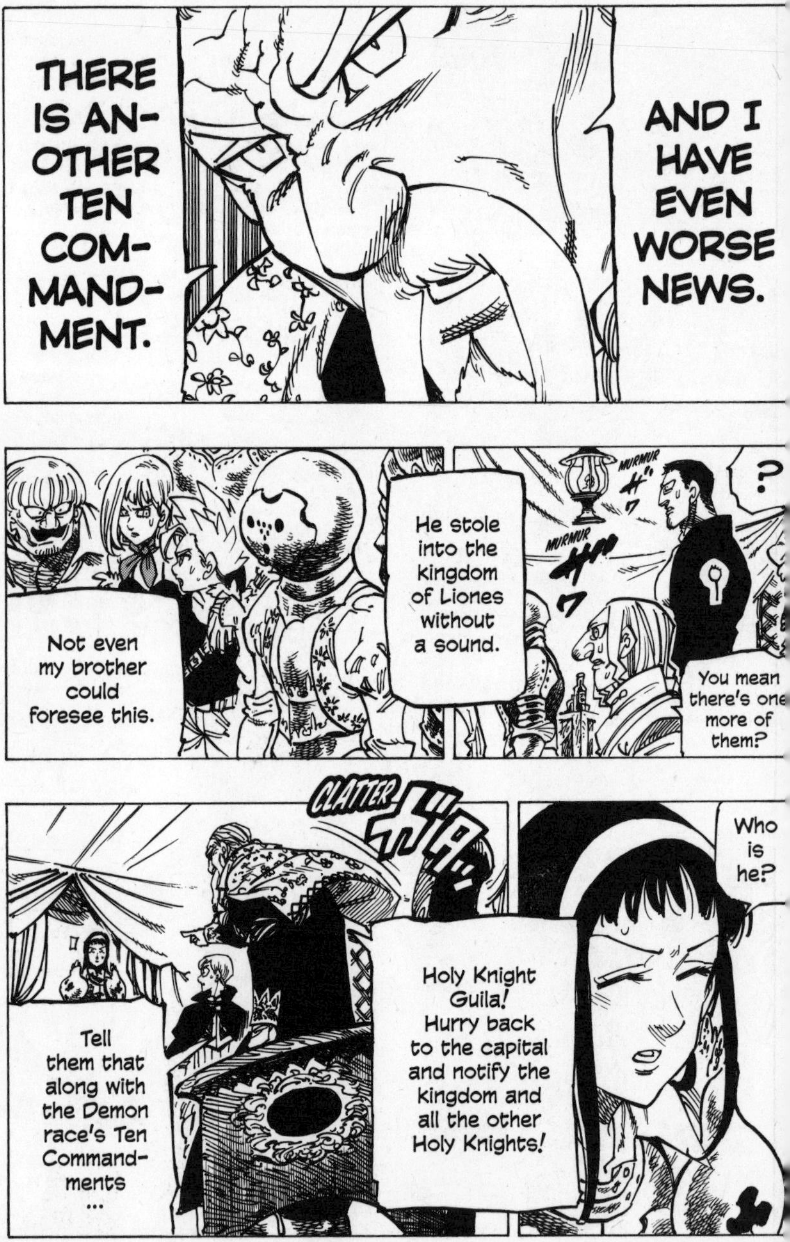
AND I HAVE EVEN WORSE NEWS.
THERE IS ANOTHER TEN COMMANDMENT.
?
MURMUR
MURMUR
You mean there's one more of them?
He stole into the kingdom of Liones without a sound.
Not even my brother could foresee this.
Who is he?
CLATTER
Holy Knight Guila! Hurry back to the capital and notify the kingdom and all the other Holy Knights!
Tell them that along with the Demon race's Ten Commandments ...

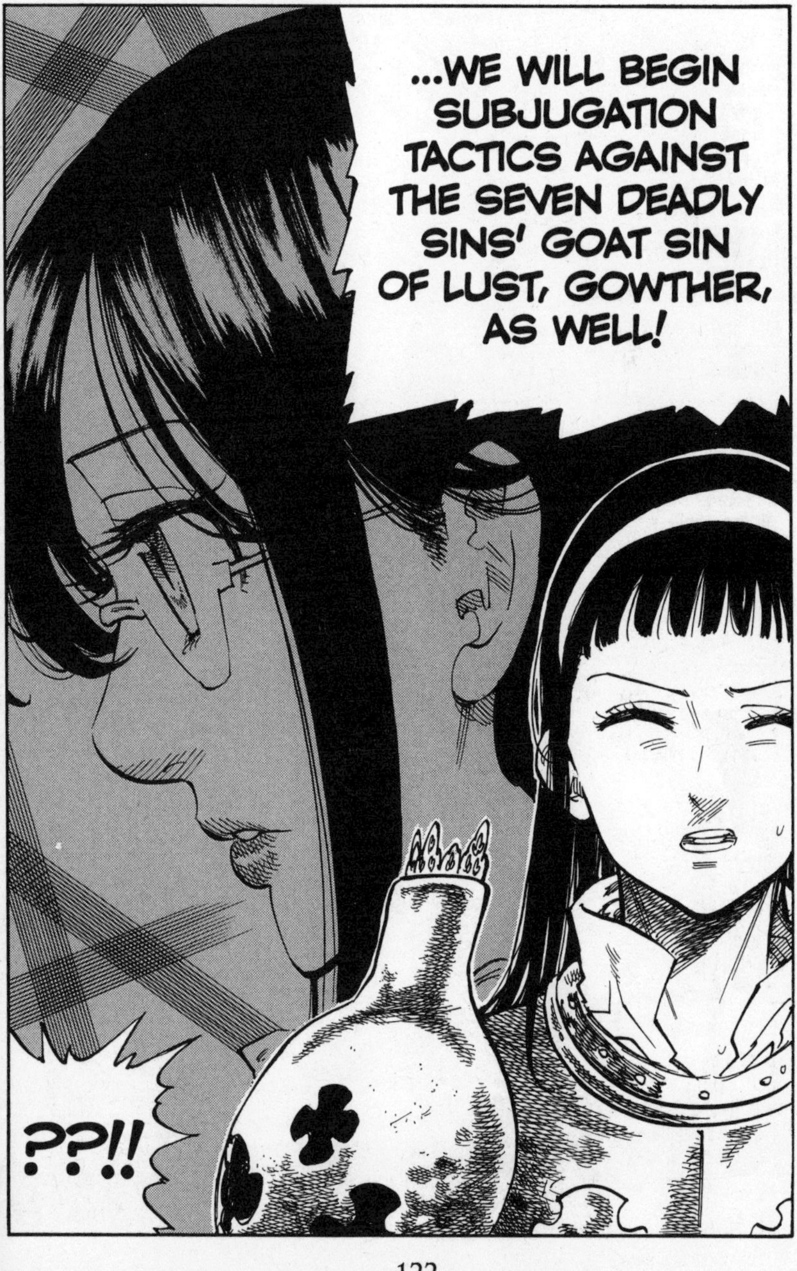
...WE WILL BEGIN SUBJUGATION TACTICS AGAINST THE SEVEN DEADLY SINS' GOAT SIN OF LUST, GOWTHER, AS WELL!
??!!

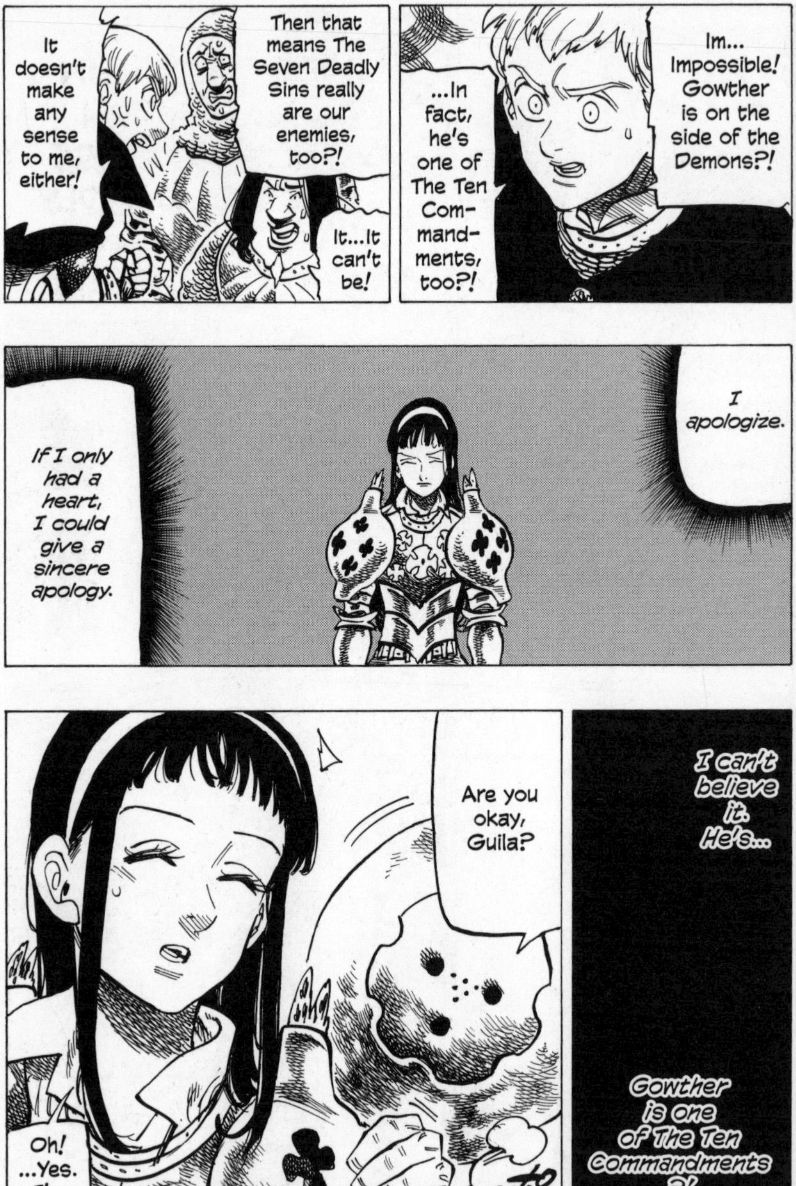
Im... Impossible! Gowther is on the side of the Demons?!
...In fact, he's one of The Ten Commandments, too?!
Then that means The Seven Deadly Sins really are our enemies, too?!
It doesn't make any sense to me, either!
It...It can't be!
I apologize.
If I only had a heart, I could give a sincere apology.
I can't believe it. He's...
Gowther is one of The Ten Commandments?!
Are you okay, Guila?
Oh! ...Yes. I'm fine.

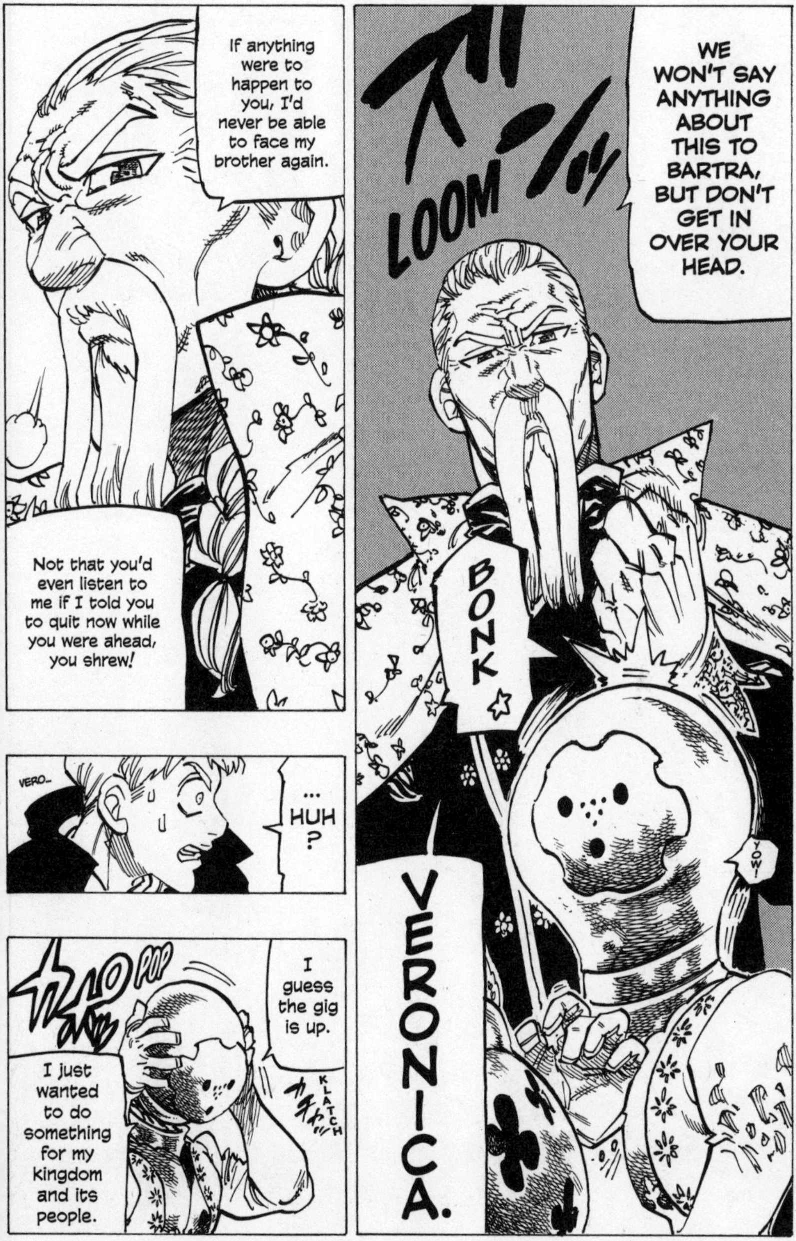
WE WON'T SAY ANYTHING ABOUT THIS TO BARTRA, BUT DON'T GET IN OVER YOUR HEAD.
LOOM
BONK
YOW!
VERONICA.
If anything were to happen to you, I'd never be able to face my brother again.
Not that you'd even listen to me if I told you to quit now while you were ahead, you shrew!
... HUH ?
VERO...
I guess the gig is up.
POP
I just wanted to do something for my kingdom and its people.
KLATCH

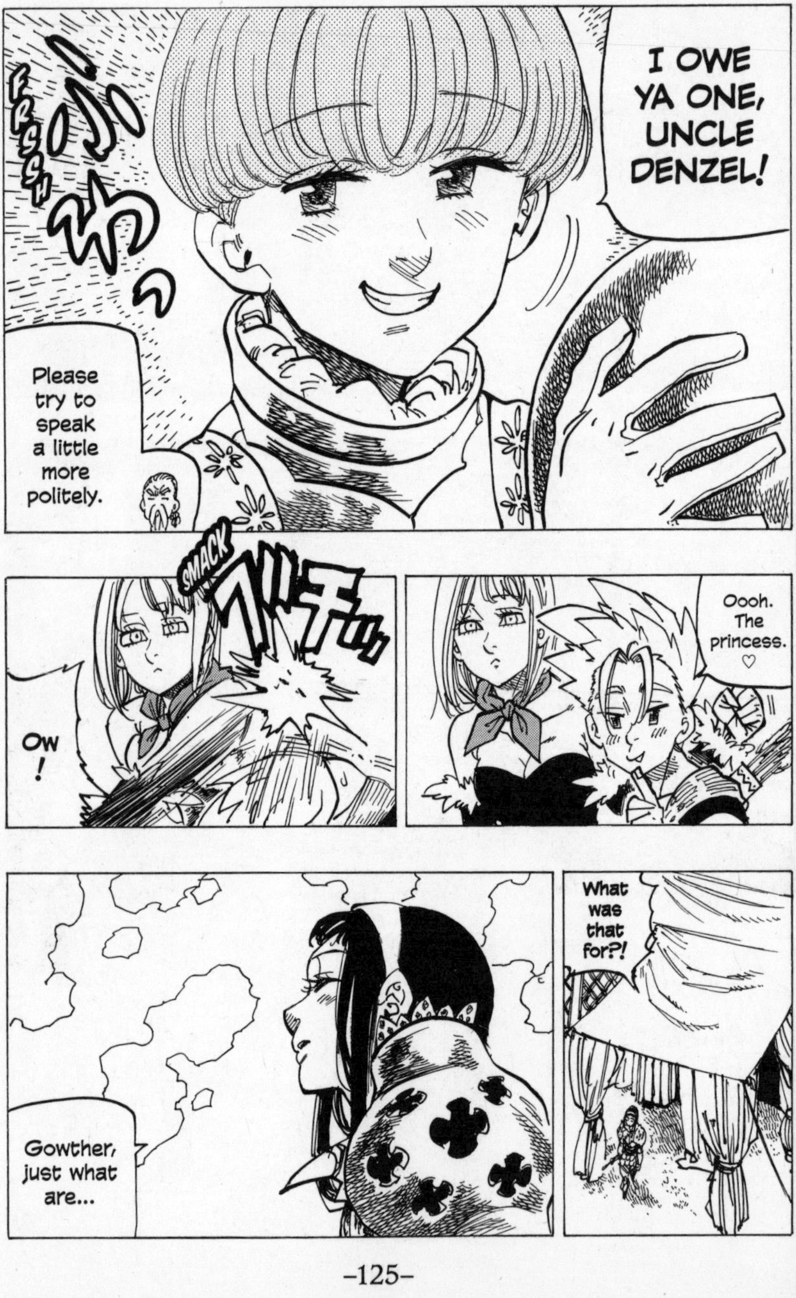
I OWE YA ONE, UNCLE DENZEL!
FRSSH
Please try to speak a little more politely.
Oooh. The princess. ♡
SMACK
Ow!
What was that for?!
Gowther, just what are...

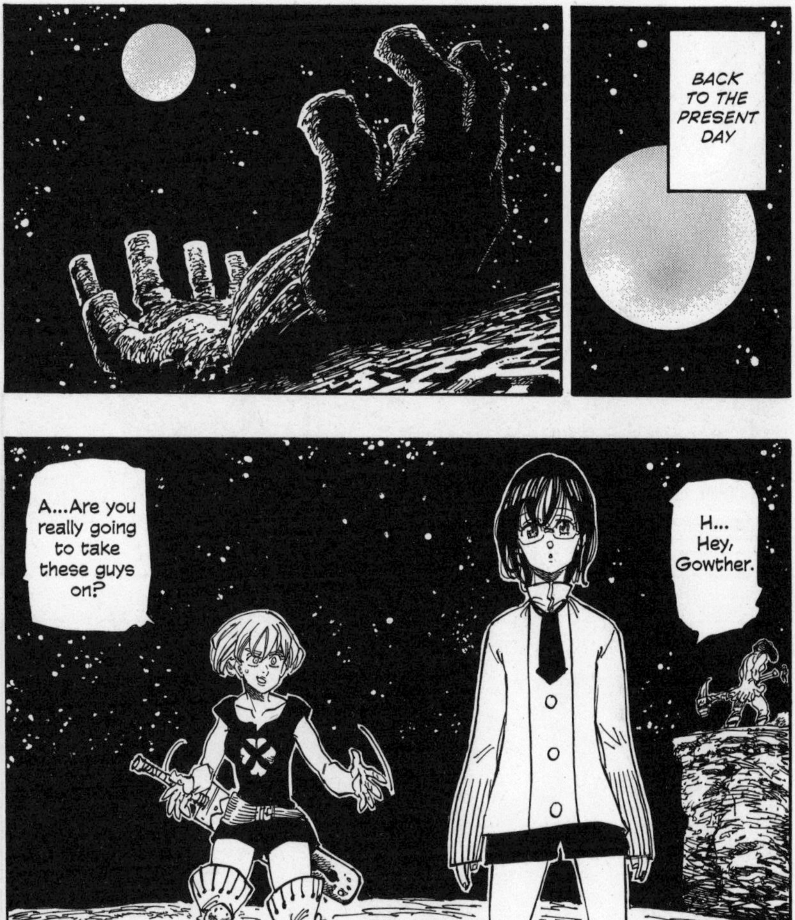
BACK TO THE PRESENT DAY
H... Hey, Gowther.
A...Are you really going to take these guys on?
THOSE ARE THE RULES OF THE FIGHTING FESTIVAL.

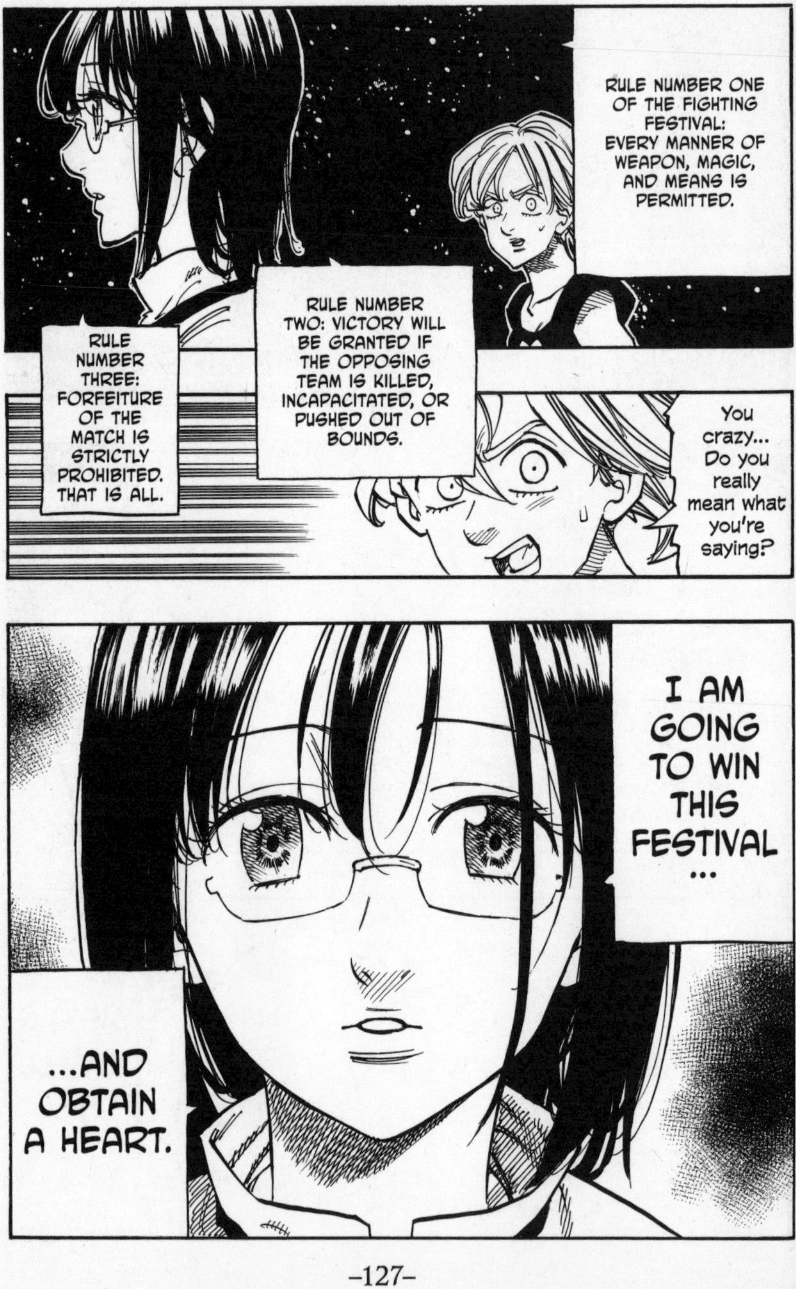
RULE NUMBER ONE OF THE FIGHTING FESTIVAL: EVERY MANNER OF WEAPON, MAGIC, AND MEANS IS PERMITTED.
RULE NUMBER TWO: VICTORY WILL BE GRANTED IF THE OPPOSING TEAM IS KILLED, INCAPACITATED, OR PUSHED OUT OF BOUNDS.
RULE NUMBER THREE: FORFEITURE OF THE MATCH IS STRICTLY PROHIBITED. THAT IS ALL.
You crazy... Do you really mean what you're saying?
I AM GOING TO WIN THIS FESTIVAL ...
...AND OBTAIN A HEART.

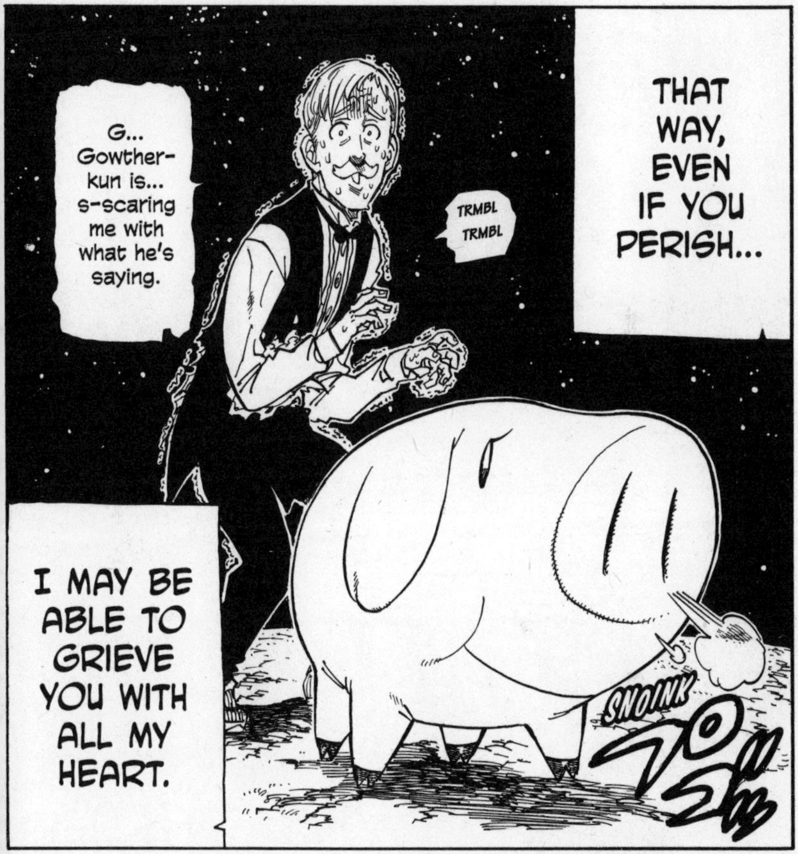
THAT WAY, EVEN IF YOU PERISH...
TRMBL TRMBL
G... Gowther-kun is... s-scaring me with what he's saying.
I MAY BE ABLE TO GRIEVE YOU WITH ALL MY HEART.
SNOINK

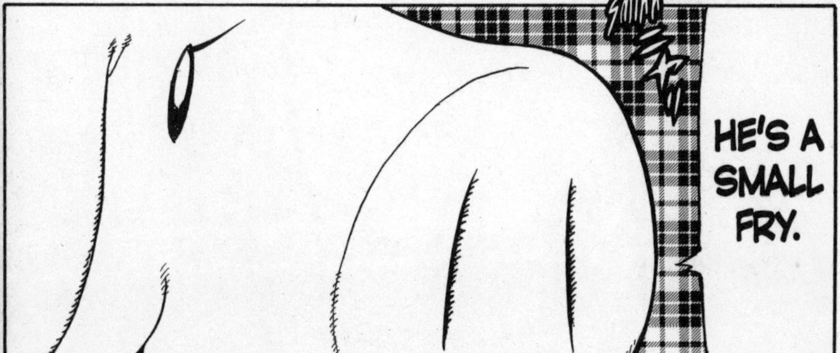
SMIRK
HE'S A SMALL FRY.

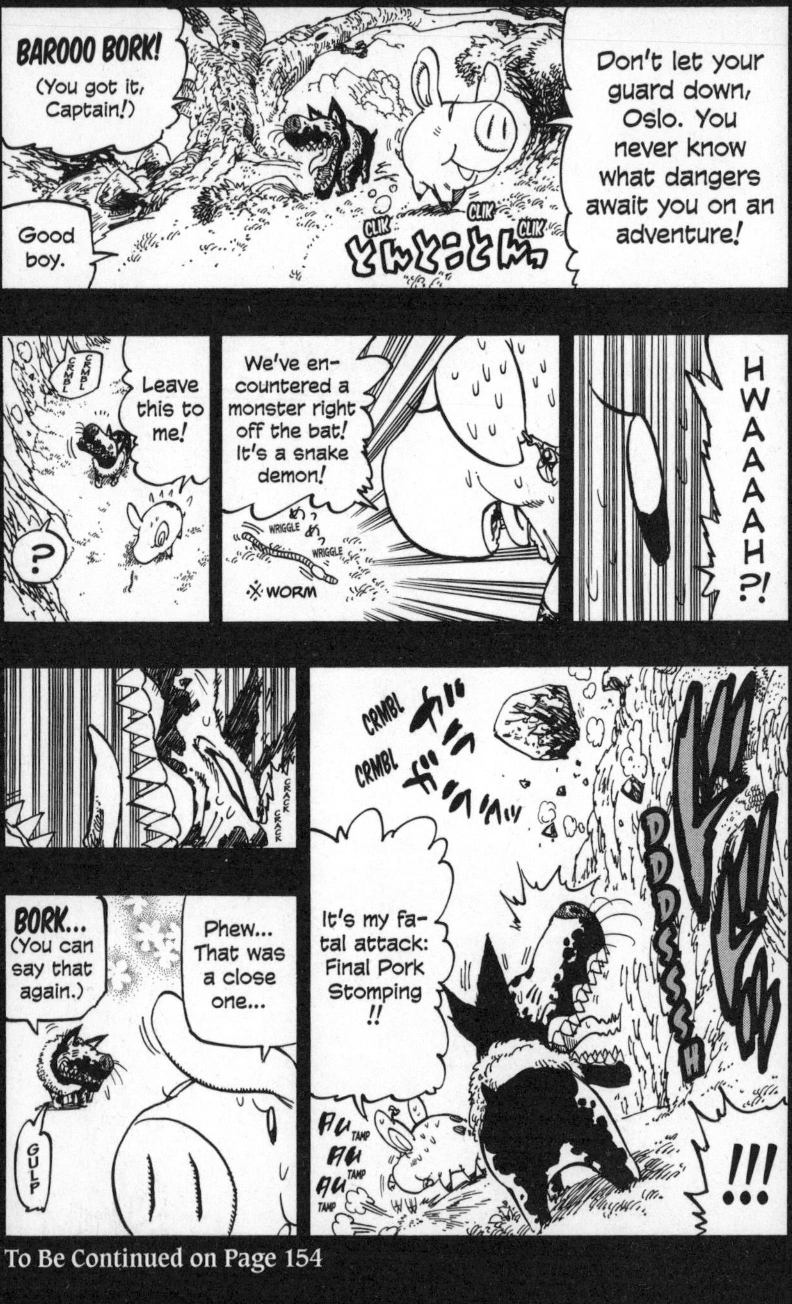
Don't let your guard down, Oslo. You never know what dangers await you on an adventure!
CLIK CLIK CLIK
BAROOO BORK! (You got it, Captain!)
Good boy.
HWAAAAAH?!
We've en-countered a monster right off the bat! It's a snake demon!
WRIGGLE WRIGGLE
※WORM
Leave this to me!
CRMBL CRMBL
?
CRMBL CRMBL
DDDSSSH
It's my fa-tal attack: Final Pork Stomping !!
TAMP TAMP TAMP
!!!
CRACK CRACK
Phew... That was a close one...
BORK... (You can say that again.)
GULP

To Be Continued on Page 154

Chapter 169 - The Legendary Weakest Holy Knight

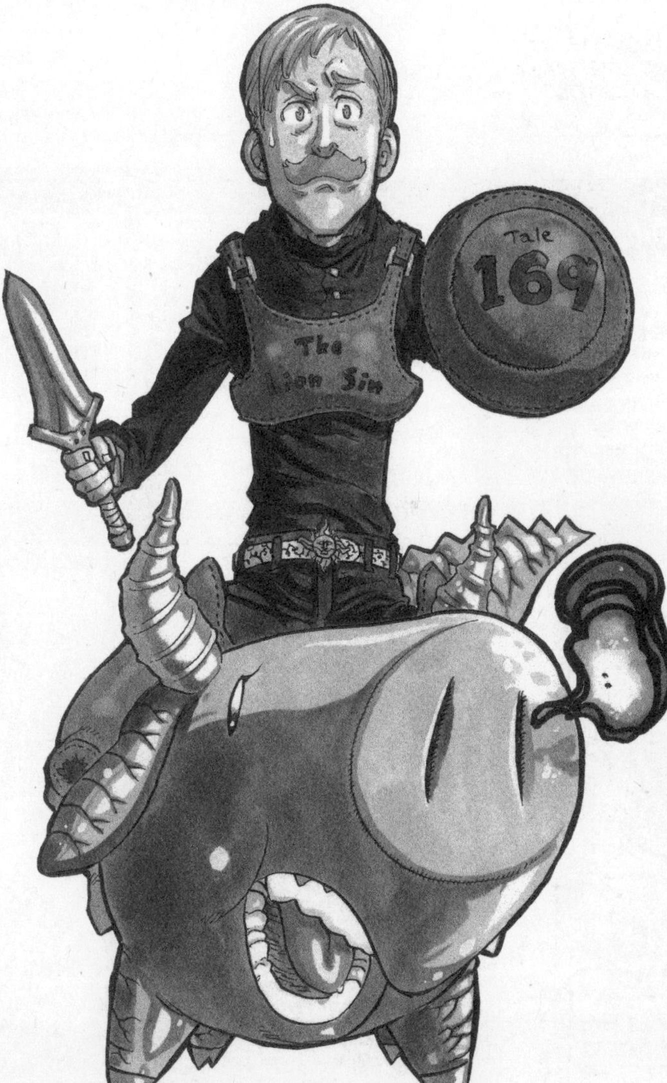
Tale
169
The
Lion Sin

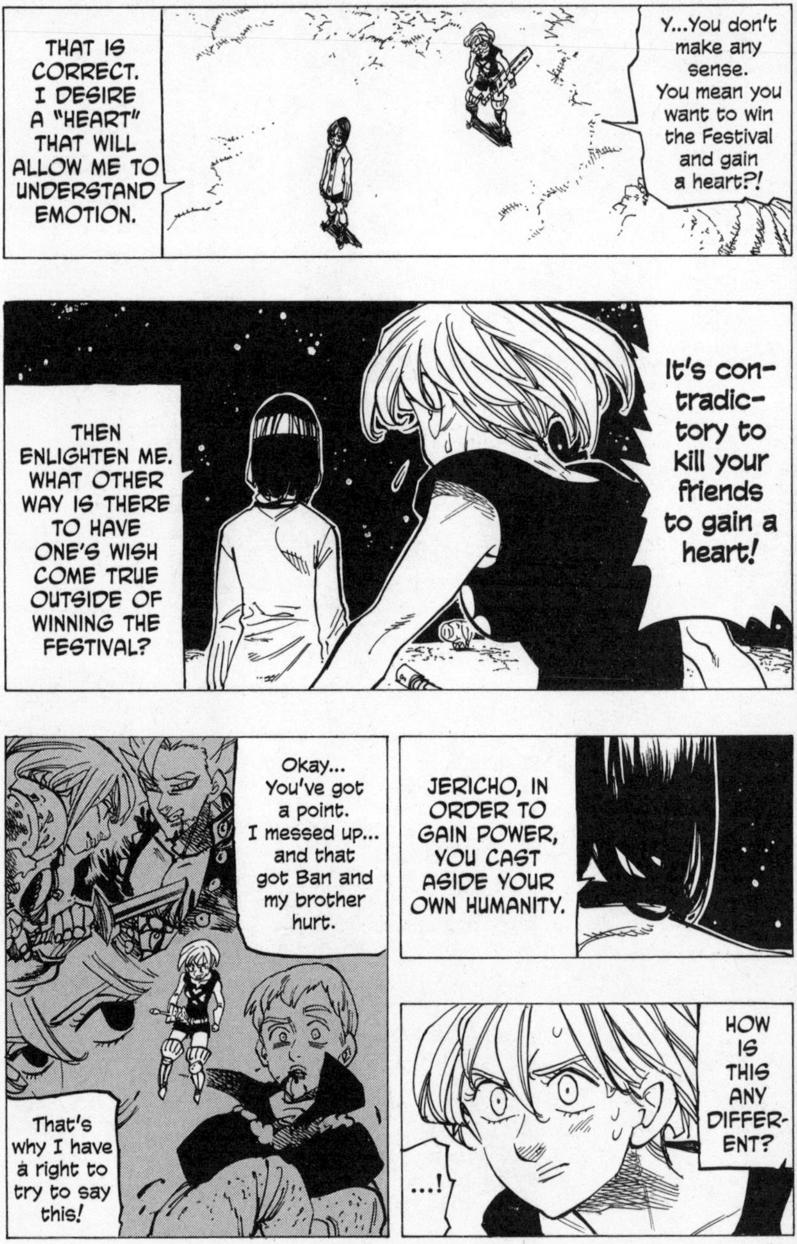
Y...You don't make any sense. You mean you want to win the Festival and gain a heart?!
THAT IS CORRECT. I DESIRE A "HEART" THAT WILL ALLOW ME TO UNDERSTAND EMOTION.
It's contradictory to kill your friends to gain a heart!
THEN ENLIGHTEN ME. WHAT OTHER WAY IS THERE TO HAVE ONE'S WISH COME TRUE OUTSIDE OF WINNING THE FESTIVAL?
JERICHO, IN ORDER TO GAIN POWER, YOU CAST ASIDE YOUR OWN HUMANITY.
HOW IS THIS ANY DIFFERENT?
...!
Okay... You've got a point. I messed up... and that got Ban and my brother hurt.
That's why I have a right to try to say this!

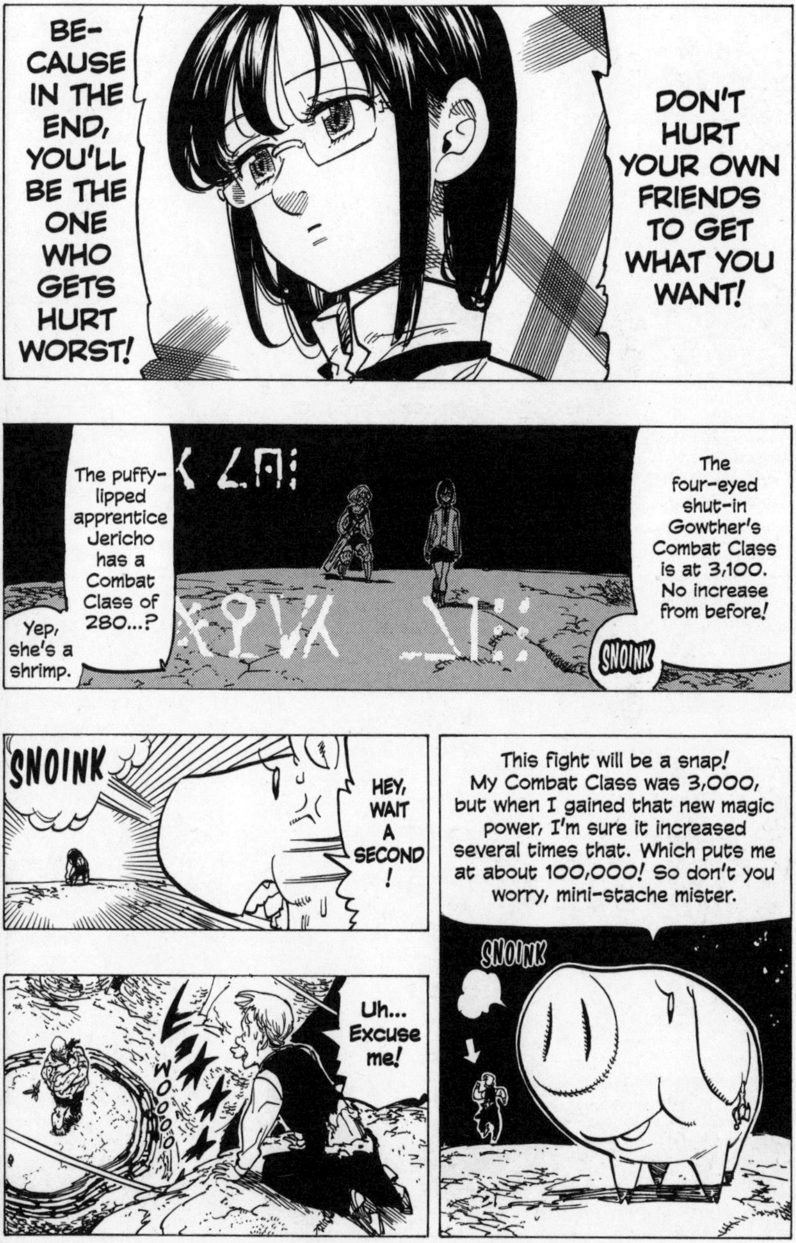
DON'T HURT YOUR OWN FRIENDS TO GET WHAT YOU WANT!
BE-CAUSE IN THE END, YOU'LL BE THE ONE WHO GETS HURT WORST!
The four-eyed shut-in Gowther's Combat Class is at 3,100. No increase from before!
SNOINK
The puffy-lipped apprentice Jericho has a Combat Class of 280...?
Yep, she's a shrimp.
This fight will be a snap! My Combat Class was 3,000, but when I gained that new magic power, I'm sure it increased several times that. Which puts me at about 100,000! So don't you worry, mini-stache mister.
SNOINK
HEY, WAIT A SECOND!
SNOINK
Uh... Excuse me!

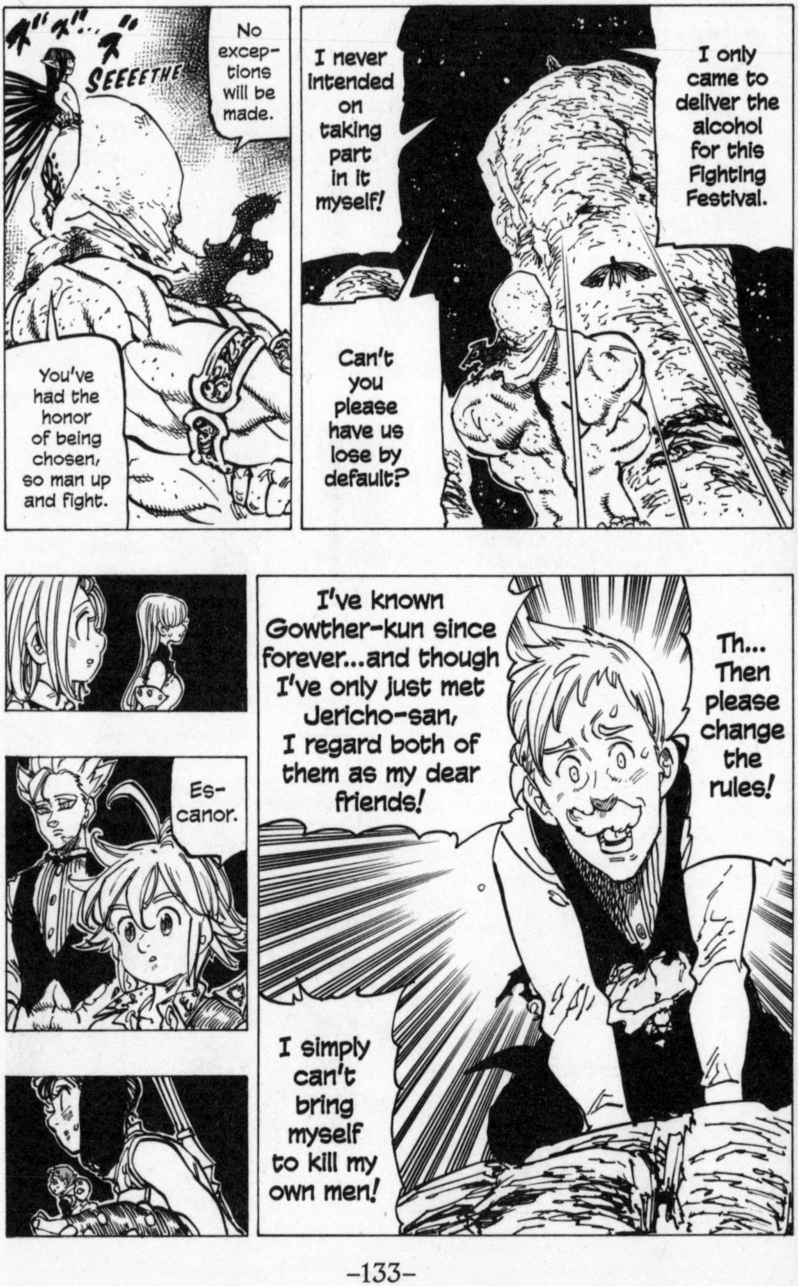
I only came to deliver the alcohol for this Fighting Festival.
I never intended on taking part in it myself!
Can't you please have us lose by default?
SEEEETHE
No exceptions will be made.
You've had the honor of being chosen, so man up and fight.
Th... Then please change the rules!
I've known Gowther-kun since forever...and though I've only just met Jericho-san, I regard both of them as my dear friends!
I simply can't bring myself to kill my own men!
Es-canor.

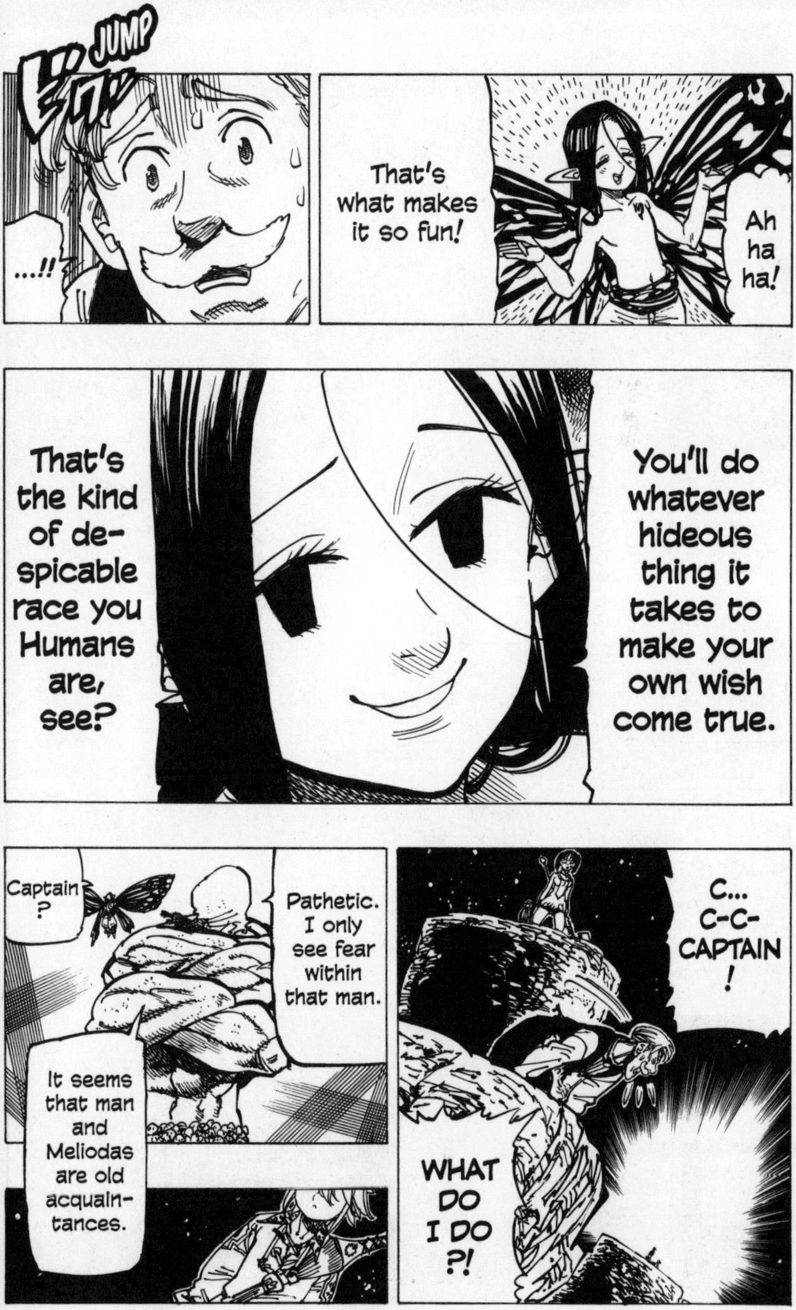
Ah ha ha!
That's what makes it so fun!
JUMP
...!!
You'll do whatever hideous thing it takes to make your own wish come true.
That's the kind of de-spicable race you Humans are, see?
C... C-C-CAPTAIN!
WHAT DO I DO?!
Pathetic. I only see fear within that man.
Captain?
It seems that man and Meliodas are old acquain-tances.

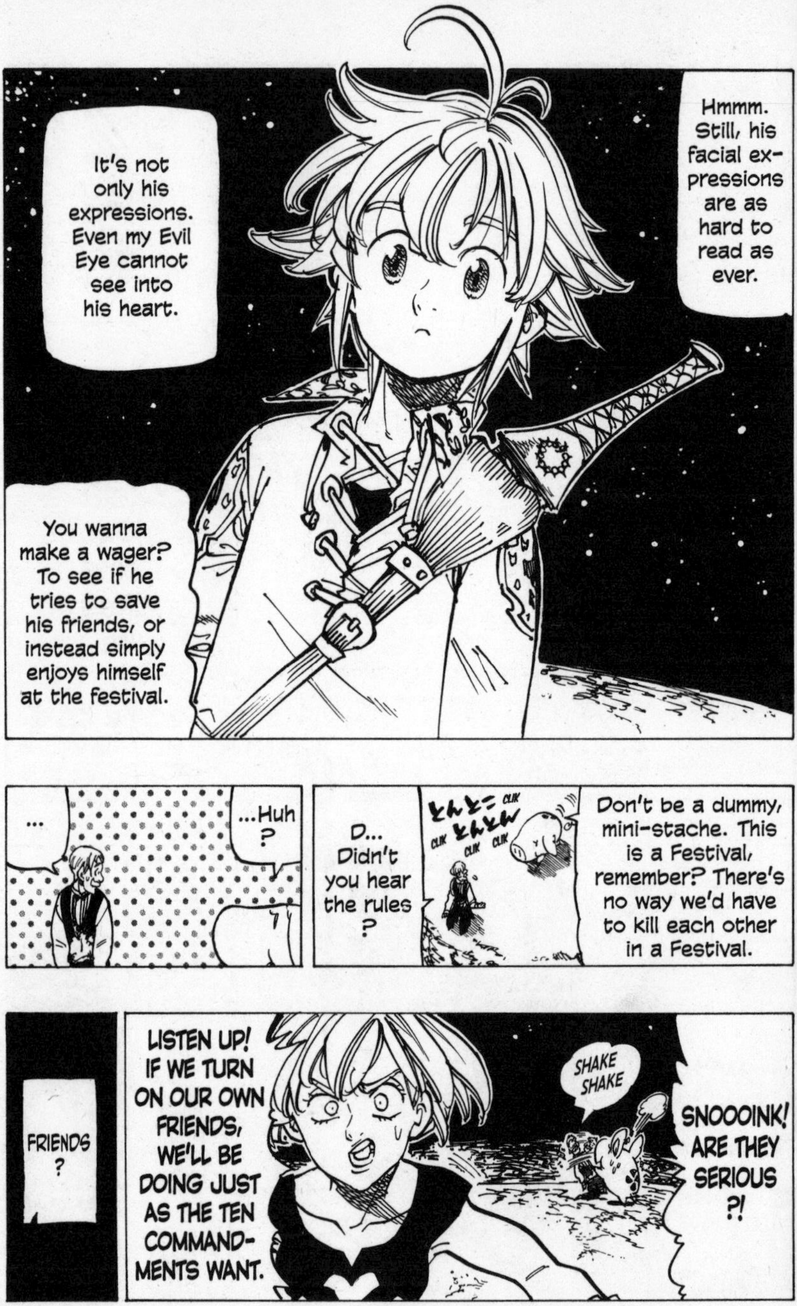
Hmmm. Still, his facial expressions are as hard to read as ever.
It's not only his expressions. Even my Evil Eye cannot see into his heart.
You wanna make a wager? To see if he tries to save his friends, or instead simply enjoys himself at the festival.
Don't be a dummy, mini-stache. This is a Festival, remember? There's no way we'd have to kill each other in a Festival.
CLIK
CLIK
CLIK
CLIK
D... Didn't you hear the rules?
...Huh?
...
SNOOOINK! ARE THEY SERIOUS?!
SHAKE SHAKE
LISTEN UP! IF WE TURN ON OUR OWN FRIENDS, WE'LL BE DOING JUST AS THE TEN COMMANDMENTS WANT.
FRIENDS?

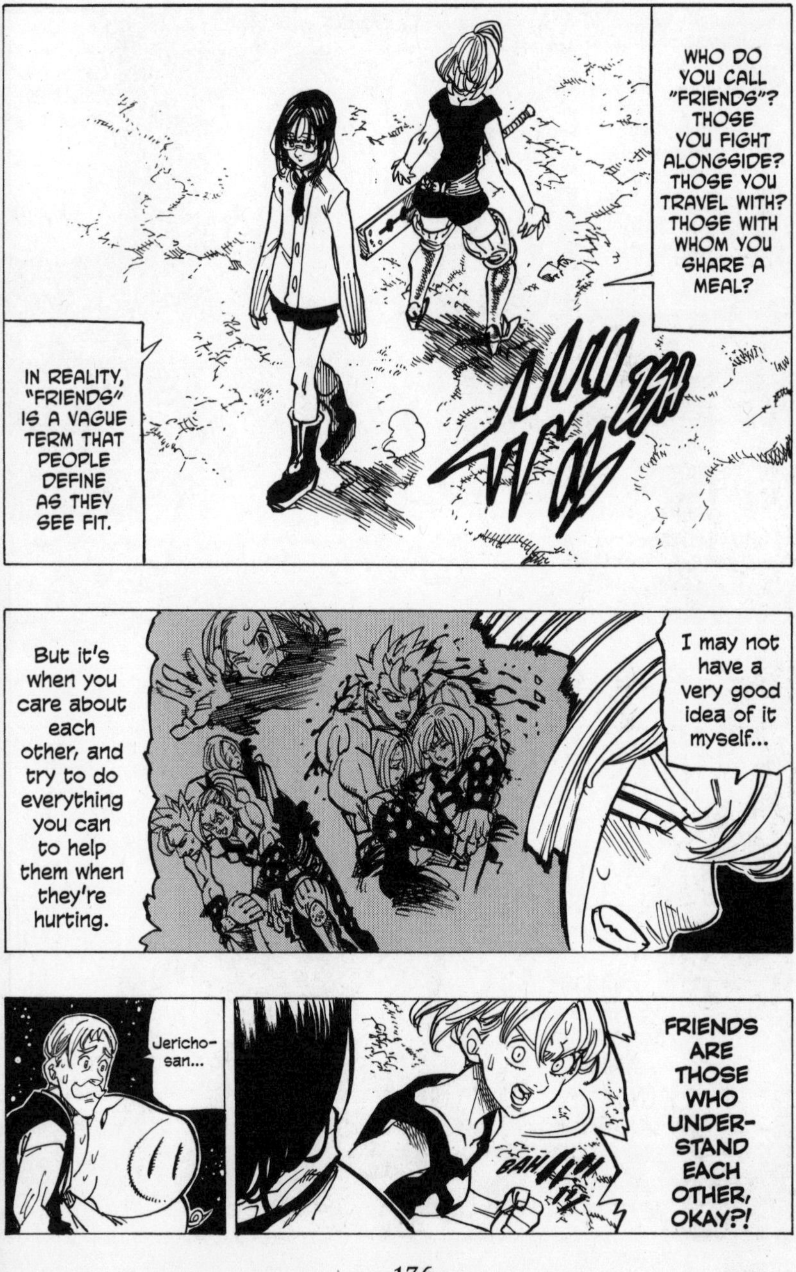
WHO DO YOU CALL "FRIENDS"? THOSE YOU FIGHT ALONGSIDE? THOSE YOU TRAVEL WITH? THOSE WITH WHOM YOU SHARE A MEAL?
IN REALITY, "FRIENDS" IS A VAGUE TERM THAT PEOPLE DEFINE AS THEY SEE FIT.
I may not have a very good idea of it myself...
But it's when you care about each other, and try to do everything you can to help them when they're hurting.
FRIENDS ARE THOSE WHO UNDER-STAND EACH OTHER, OKAY?!
Jericho-san...

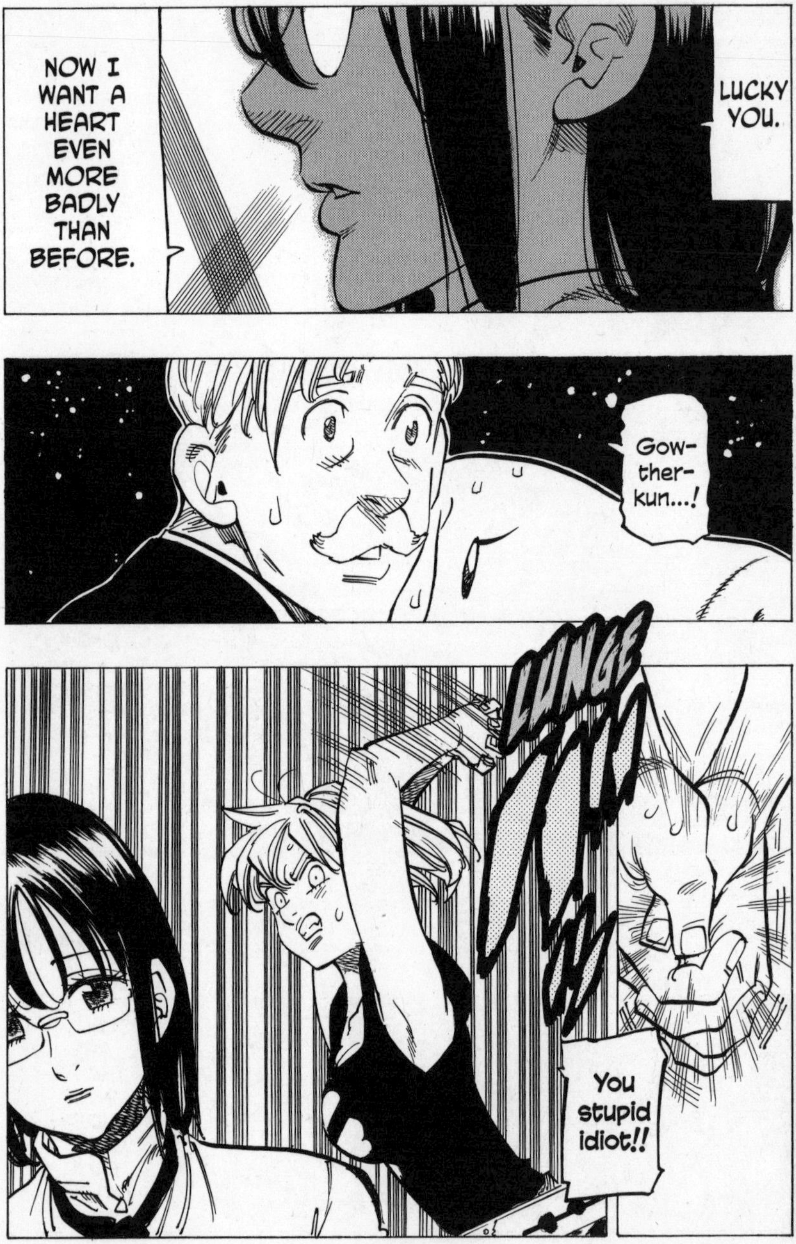
LUCKY YOU.
NOW I WANT A HEART EVEN MORE BADLY THAN BEFORE.
Gow-ther-kun...!
LUNGE
You stupid idiot!!

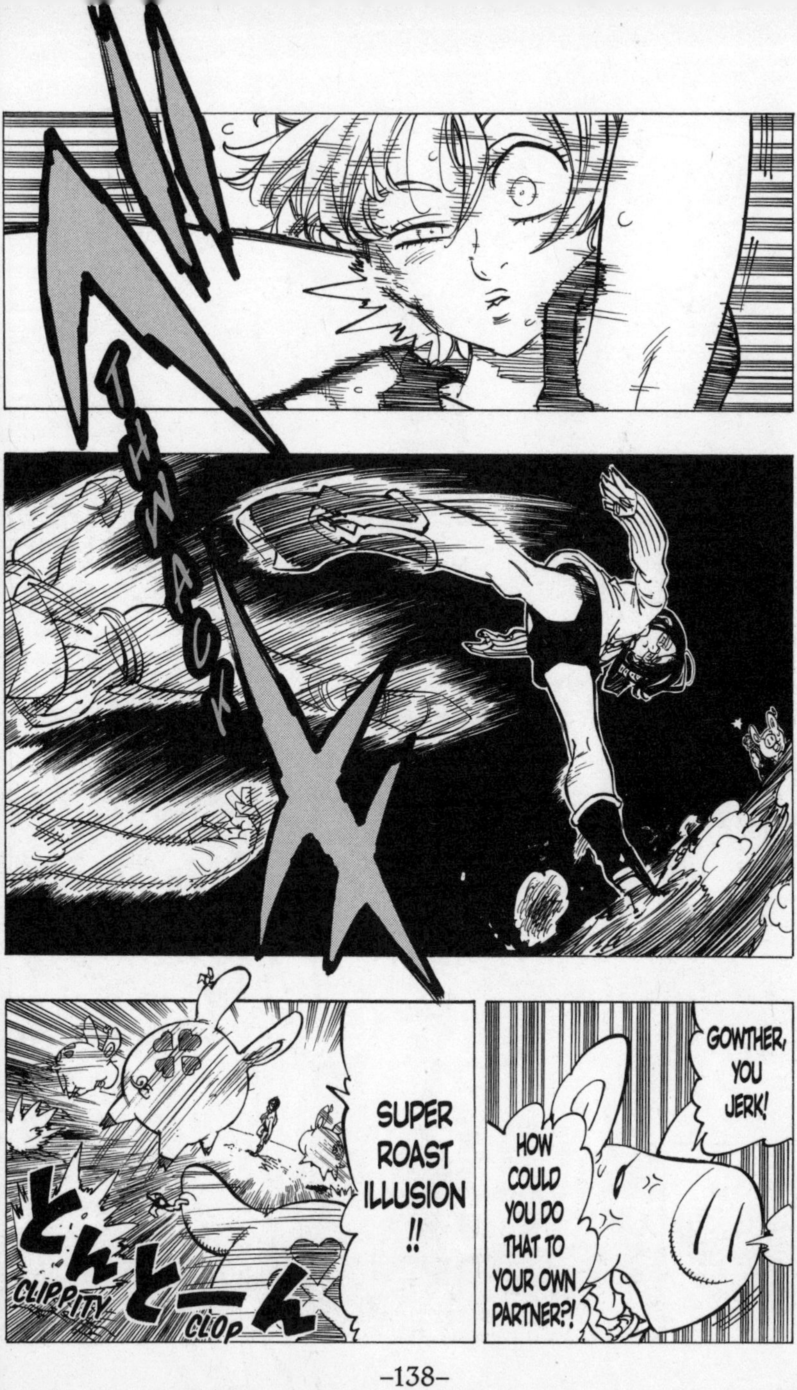
THWACK
GOWTHER, YOU JERK!
HOW COULD YOU DO THAT TO YOUR OWN PARTNER?!
SUPER ROAST ILLUSION !!
とんとーん
CLIPPITY CLOP

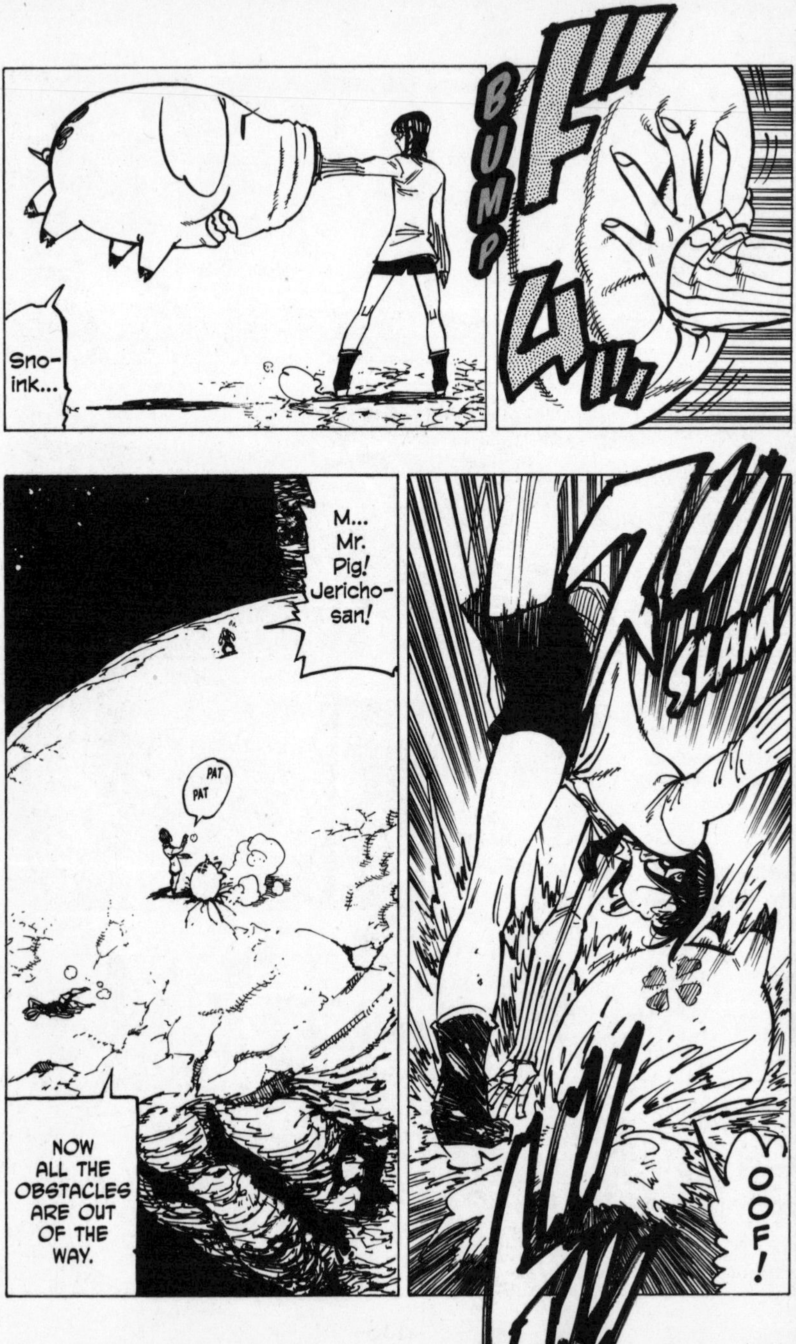
BUMP
Sno-ink...
SLAM
OOF!
M... Mr. Pig! Jericho-san!
PAT PAT
NOW ALL THE OBSTACLES ARE OUT OF THE WAY.

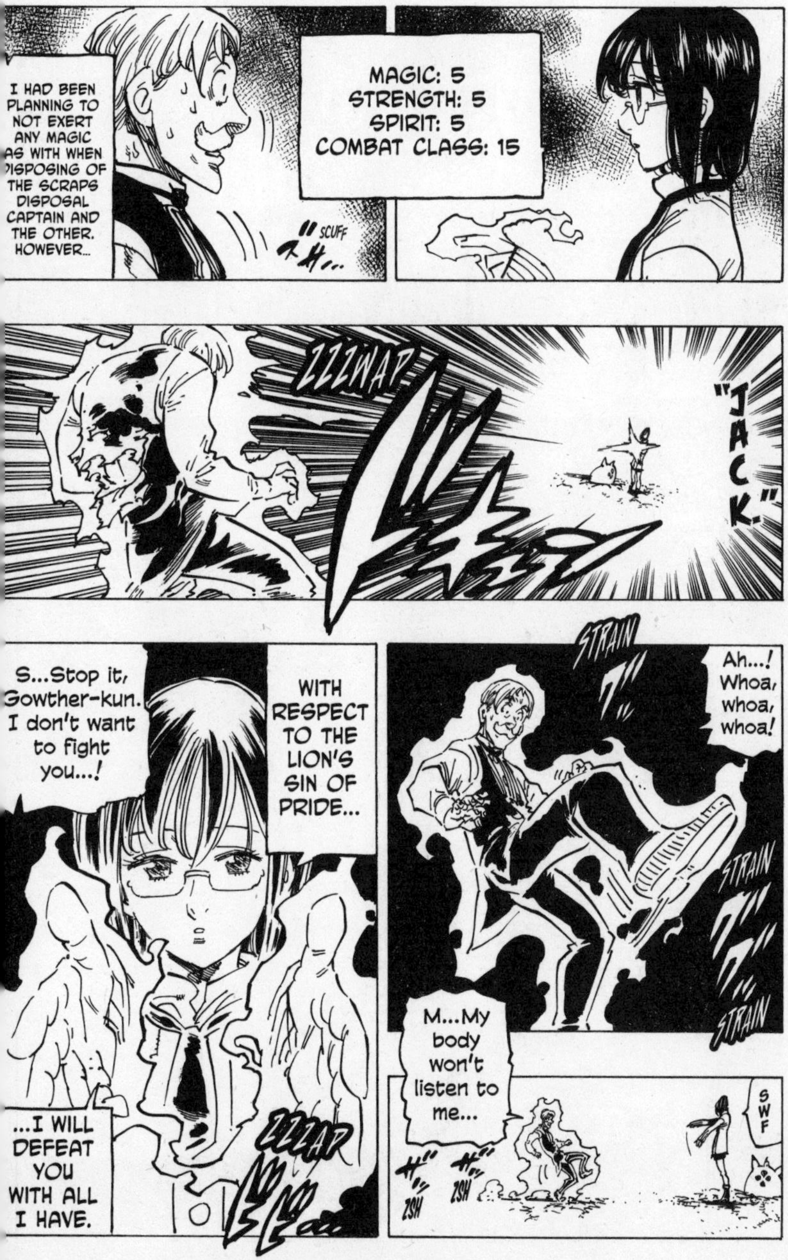
MAGIC: 5
STRENGTH: 5
SPIRIT: 5
COMBAT CLASS: 15
I HAD BEEN PLANNING TO NOT EXERT ANY MAGIC AS WITH WHEN DISPOSING OF THE SCRAPS DISPOSAL CAPTAIN AND THE OTHER. HOWEVER...
SCUFF
"JACK."
ZZZWAP
STRAIN
Ah...! Whoa, whoa, whoa!
STRAIN
STRAIN
SWF
M...My body won't listen to me...
ZSH
ZSH
WITH RESPECT TO THE LION'S SIN OF PRIDE...
S...Stop it, Gowther-kun. I don't want to fight you...!
...I WILL DEFEAT YOU WITH ALL I HAVE.
ZZZAP

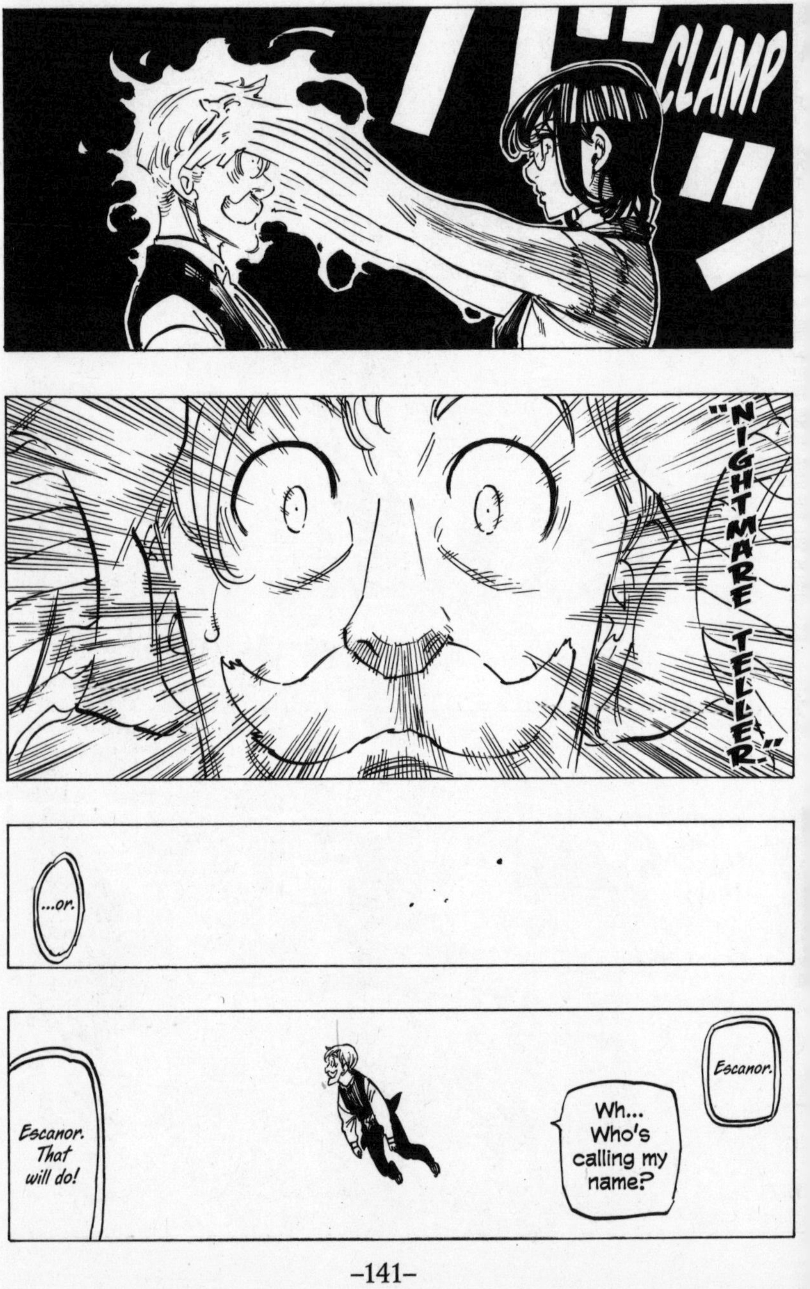
CLAMP
"NIGHTMARE TELLER."
...or.
Escanor.
Wh... Who's calling my name?
Escanor. That will do!

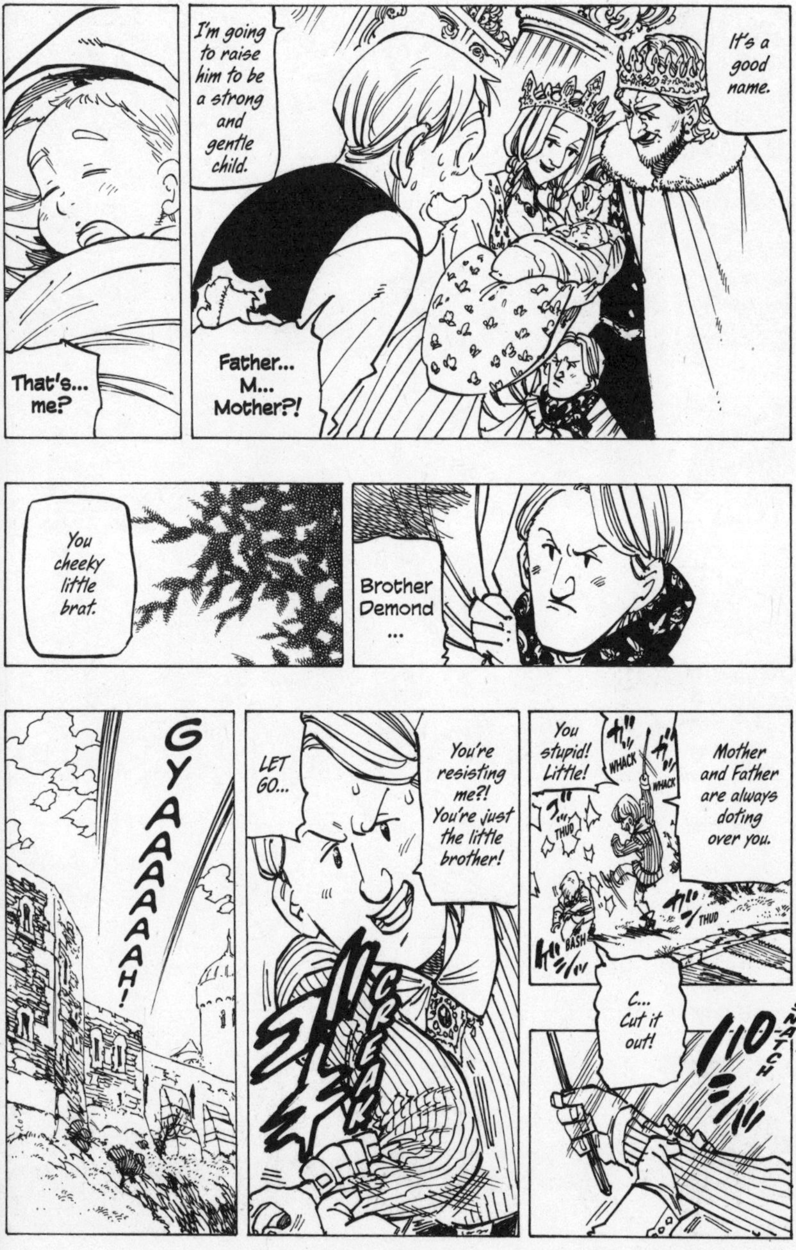
It's a good name.
I'm going to raise him to be a strong and gentle child.
Father... M... Mother?!
That's... me?
Brother Demond ...
You cheeky little brat.
Mother and Father are always doting over you.
You stupid! Little!
WHACK
WHACK
THUD
THUD
BASH
C... Cut it out!
SNATCH
You're resisting me?! You're just the little brother!
LET GO...
CREAK
GYAAAAAAAH!

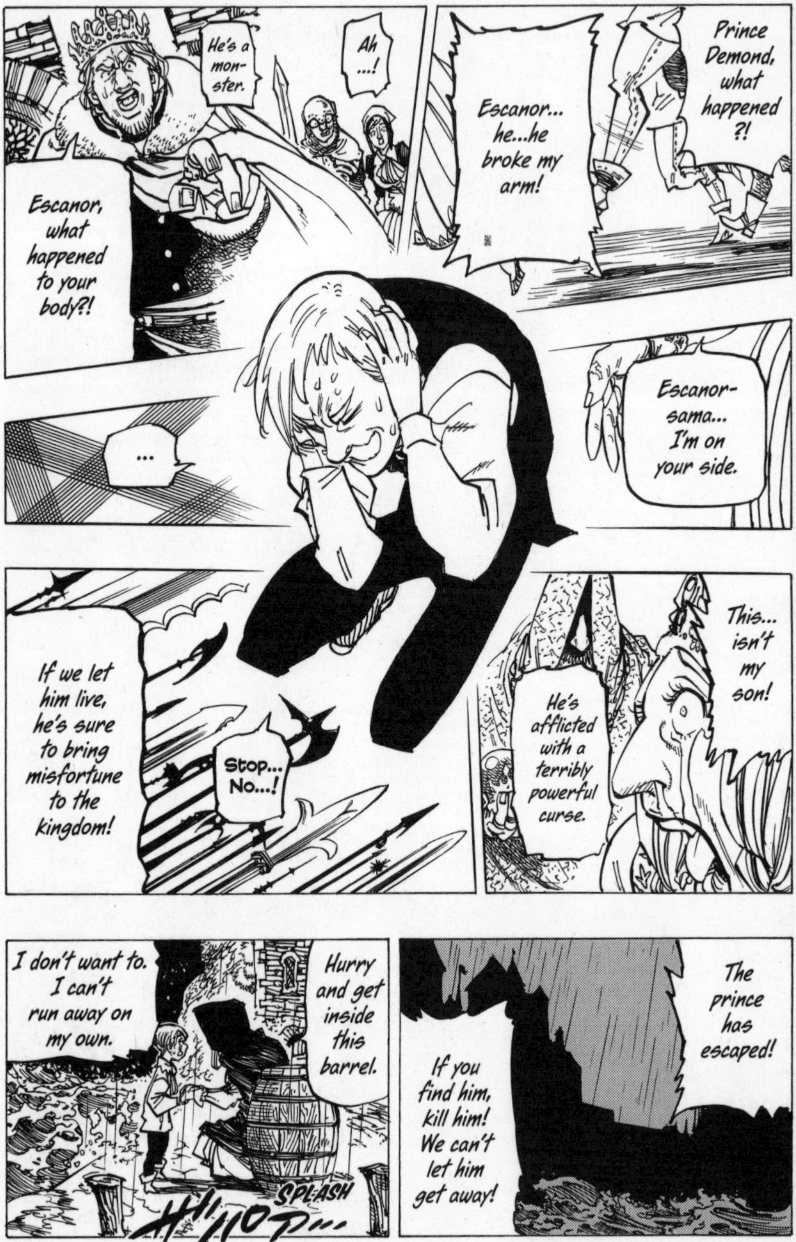

Prince Demond, what happened?!
Escanor... he...he broke my arm!
Ah ...!
He's a monster.
Escanor, what happened to your body?!
Escanor-sama... I'm on your side.
...
This... isn't my son!
He's afflicted with a terribly powerful curse.
If we let him live, he's sure to bring misfortune to the kingdom!
Stop... No...!
The prince has escaped!
If you find him, kill him! We can't let him get away!
Hurry and get inside this barrel.
I don't want to. I can't run away on my own.
SPLASH

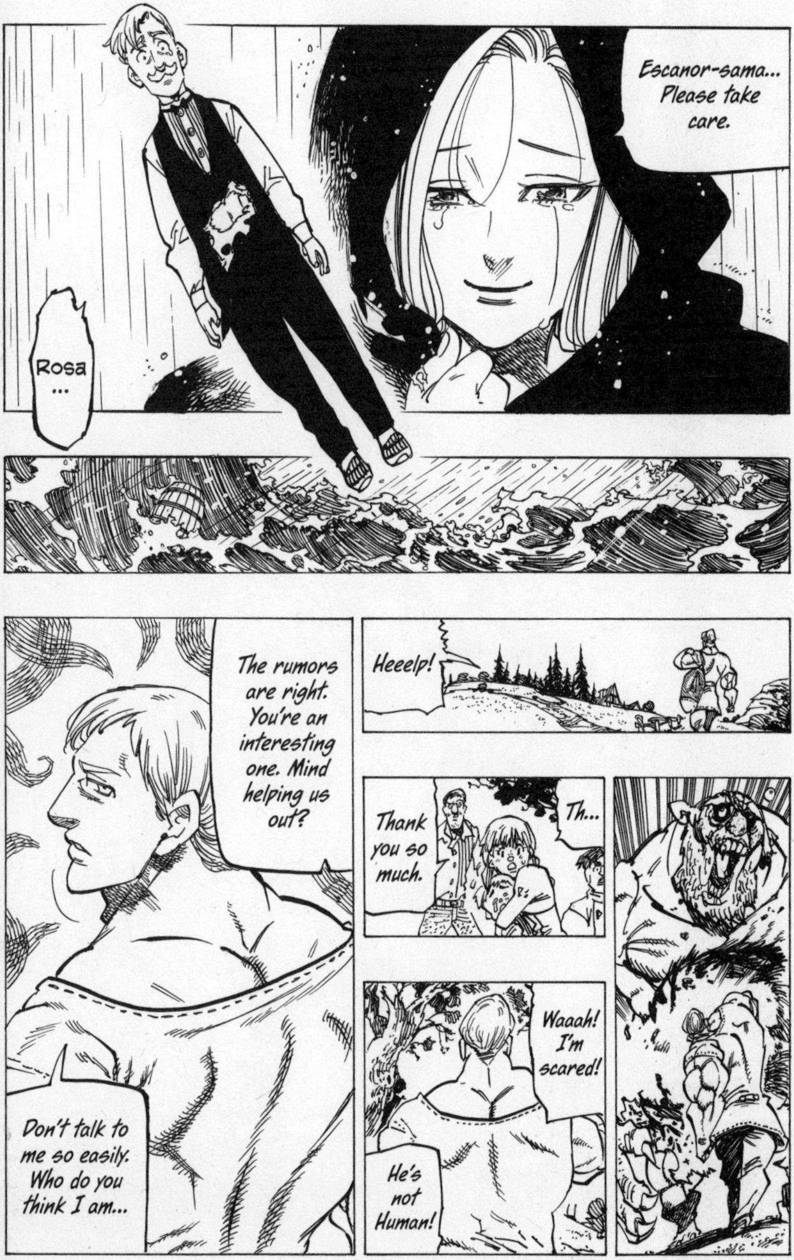

Escanor-sama... Please take care.
Rosa ...
Heeelp!
Th...
Thank you so much.
Waaah! I'm scared!
He's not Human!
The rumors are right. You're an interesting one. Mind helping us out?
Don't talk to me so easily. Who do you think I am...

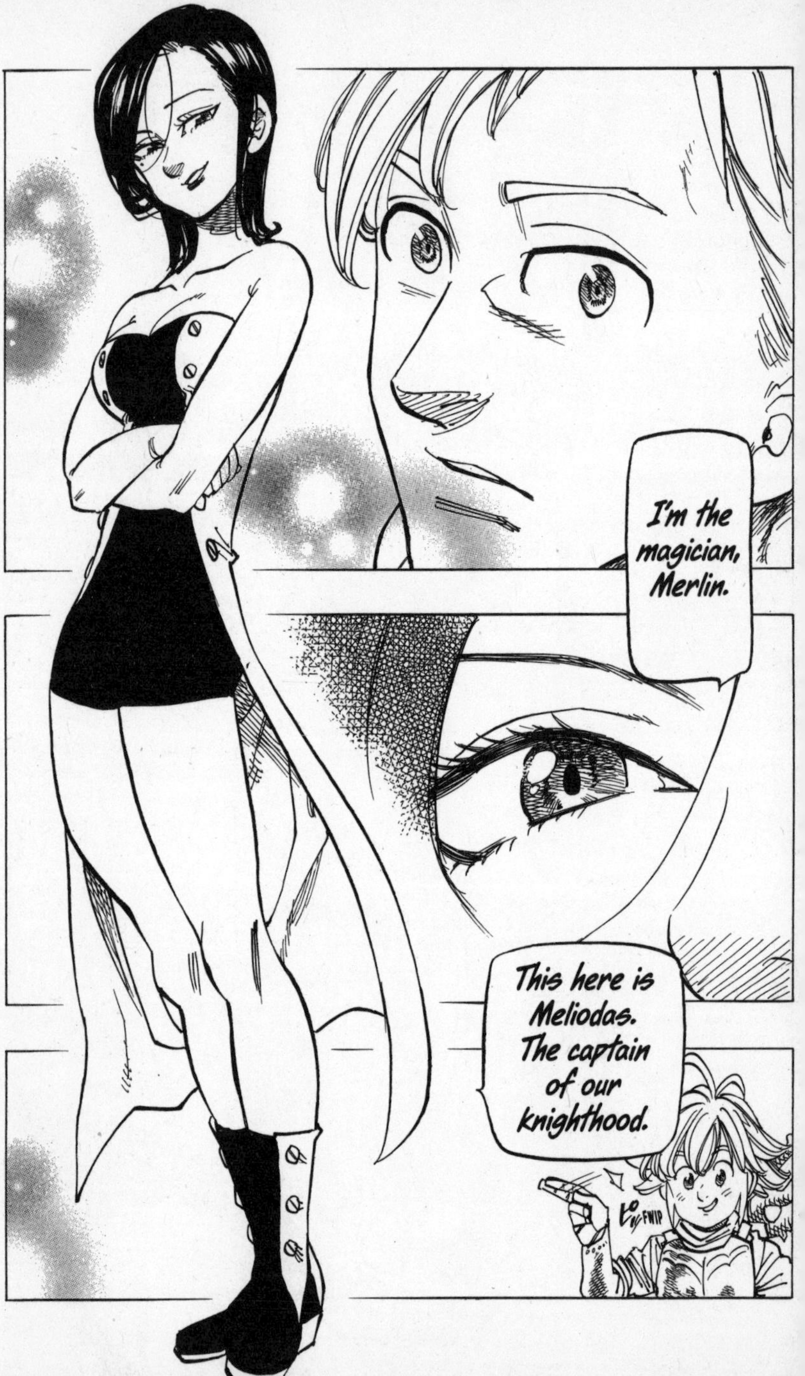
I'm the magician, Merlin.
This here is Meliodas. The captain of our knighthood.
FWIP

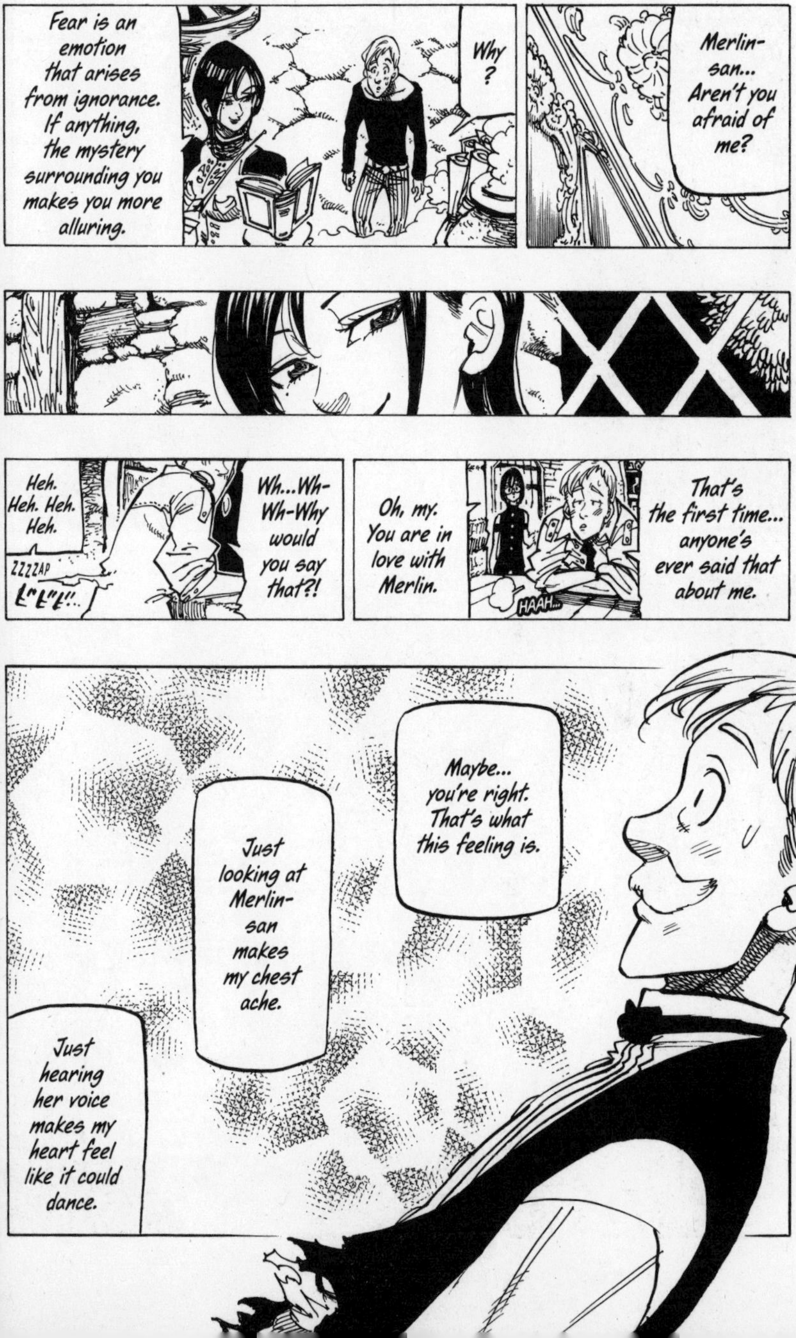
Merlin-san... Aren't you afraid of me?
Why?
Fear is an emotion that arises from ignorance. If anything, the mystery surrounding you makes you more alluring.
That's the first time... anyone's ever said that about me.
HAAH...
Oh, my. You are in love with Merlin.
Wh...Wh-Wh-Why would you say that?!
Heh. Heh. Heh. Heh.
ZZZZAP
Maybe... you're right. That's what this feeling is.
Just looking at Merlin-san makes my chest ache.
Just hearing her voice makes my heart feel like it could dance.

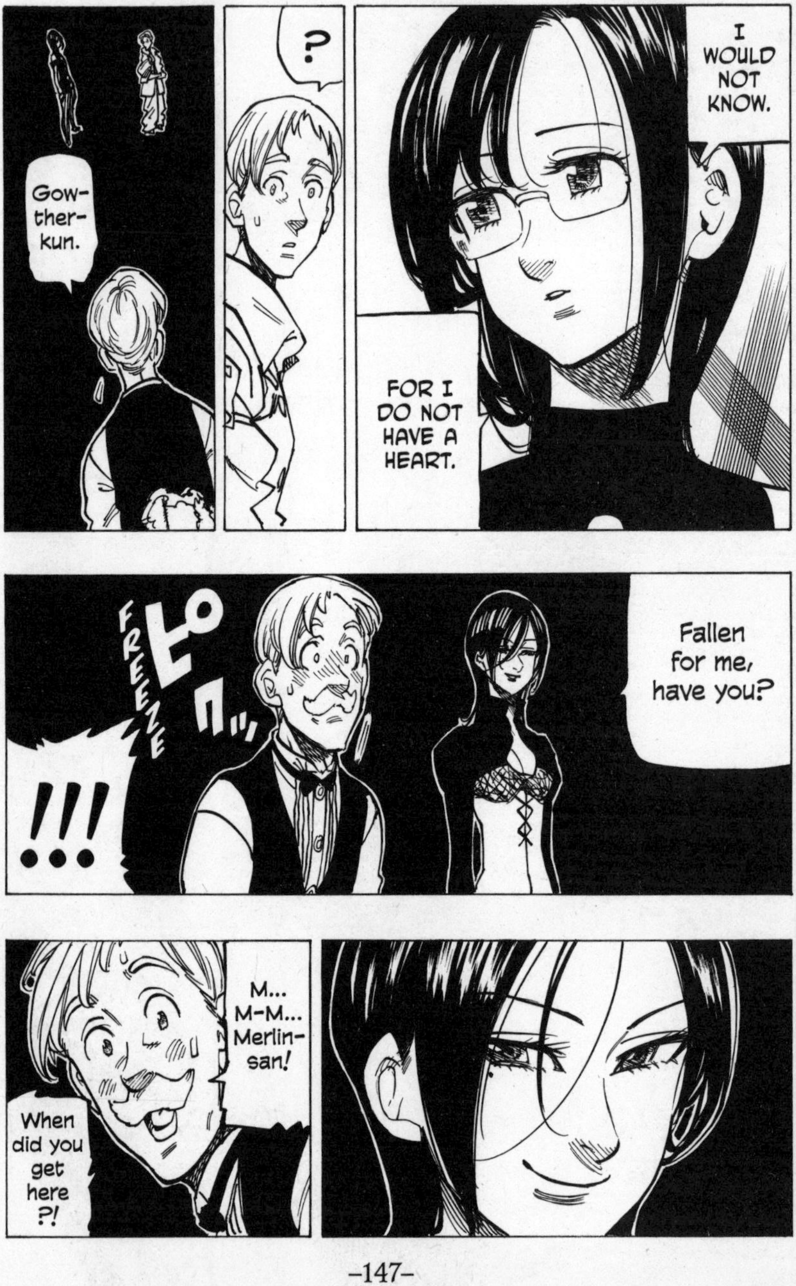
I WOULD NOT KNOW.
FOR I DO NOT HAVE A HEART.
?
Gow-ther-kun.
Fallen for me, have you?
FREEZE
!!!
M... M-M... Merlin-san!
When did you get here ?!

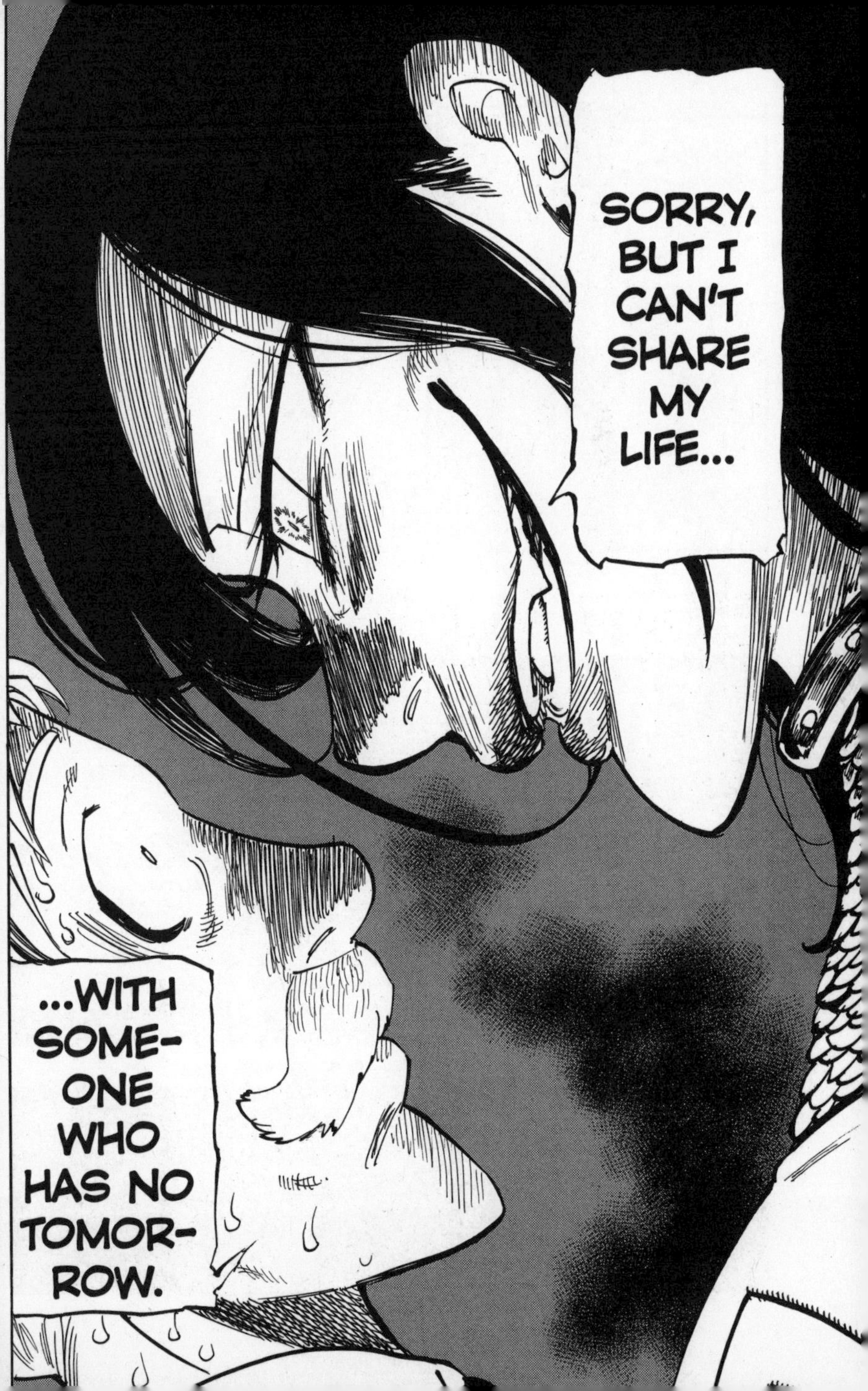
SORRY, BUT I CAN'T SHARE MY LIFE...
...WITH SOME-ONE WHO HAS NO TOMOR-ROW.

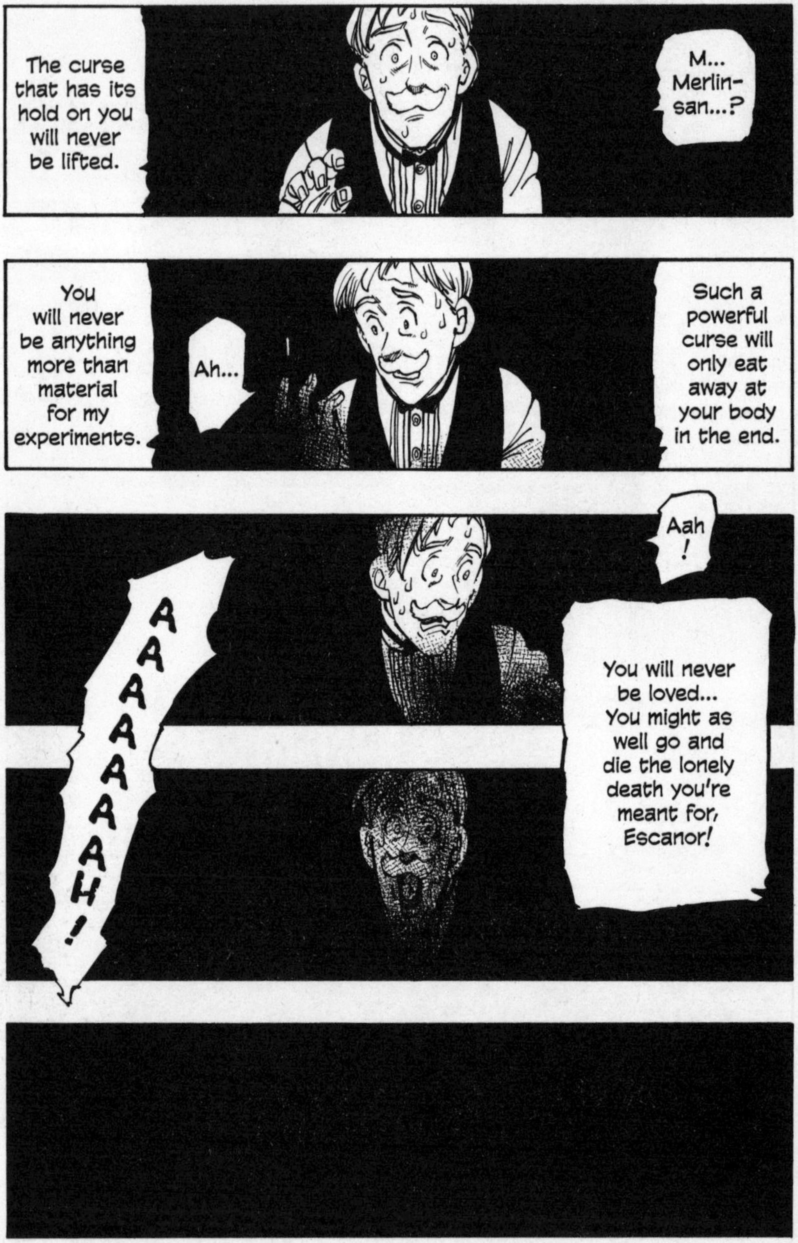
M... Merlin-san...?
The curse that has its hold on you will never be lifted.
Such a powerful curse will only eat away at your body in the end.
Ah...
You will never be anything more than material for my experiments.
Aah!
You will never be loved... You might as well go and die the lonely death you're meant for, Escanor!
AAAAAAAH!

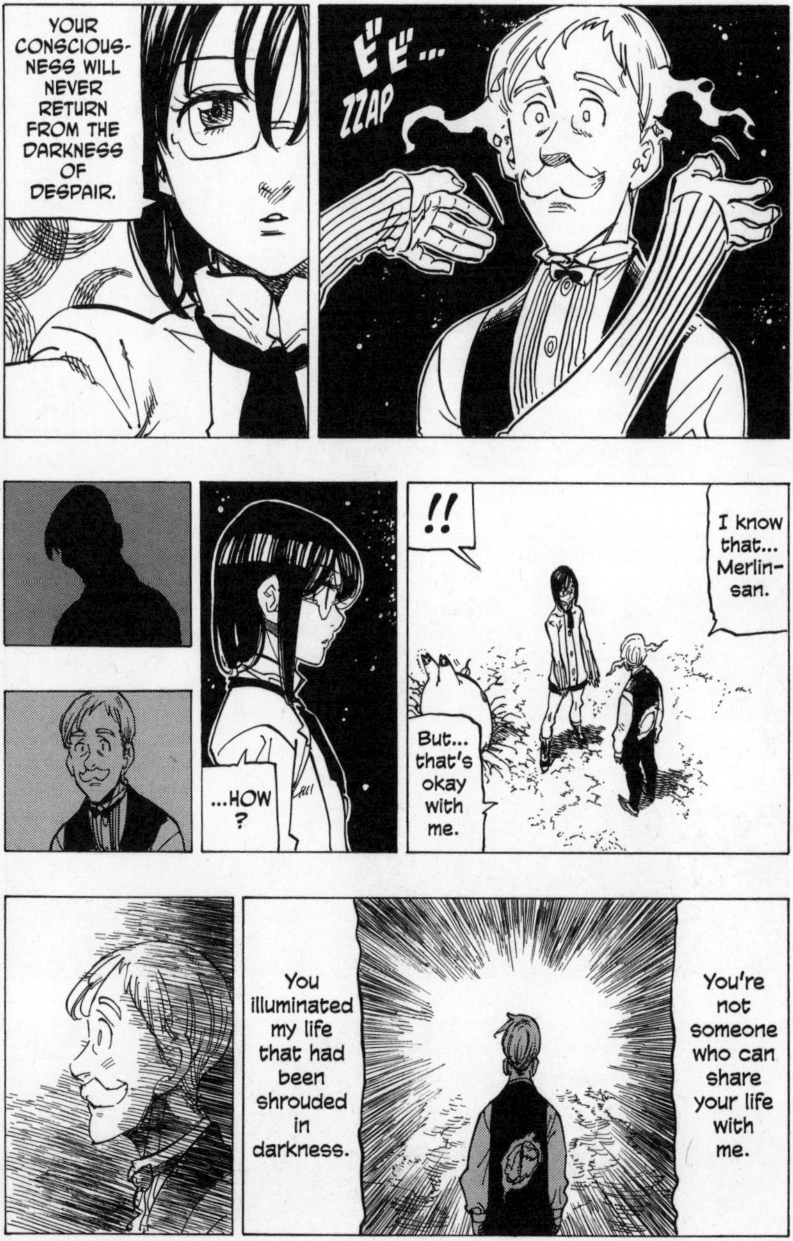
ビビ…
ZZAP
YOUR CONSCIOUSNESS WILL NEVER RETURN FROM THE DARKNESS OF DESPAIR.
I know that... Merlin-san.
!!
But... that's okay with me.
...HOW?
You're not someone who can share your life with me.
You illuminated my life that had been shrouded in darkness.

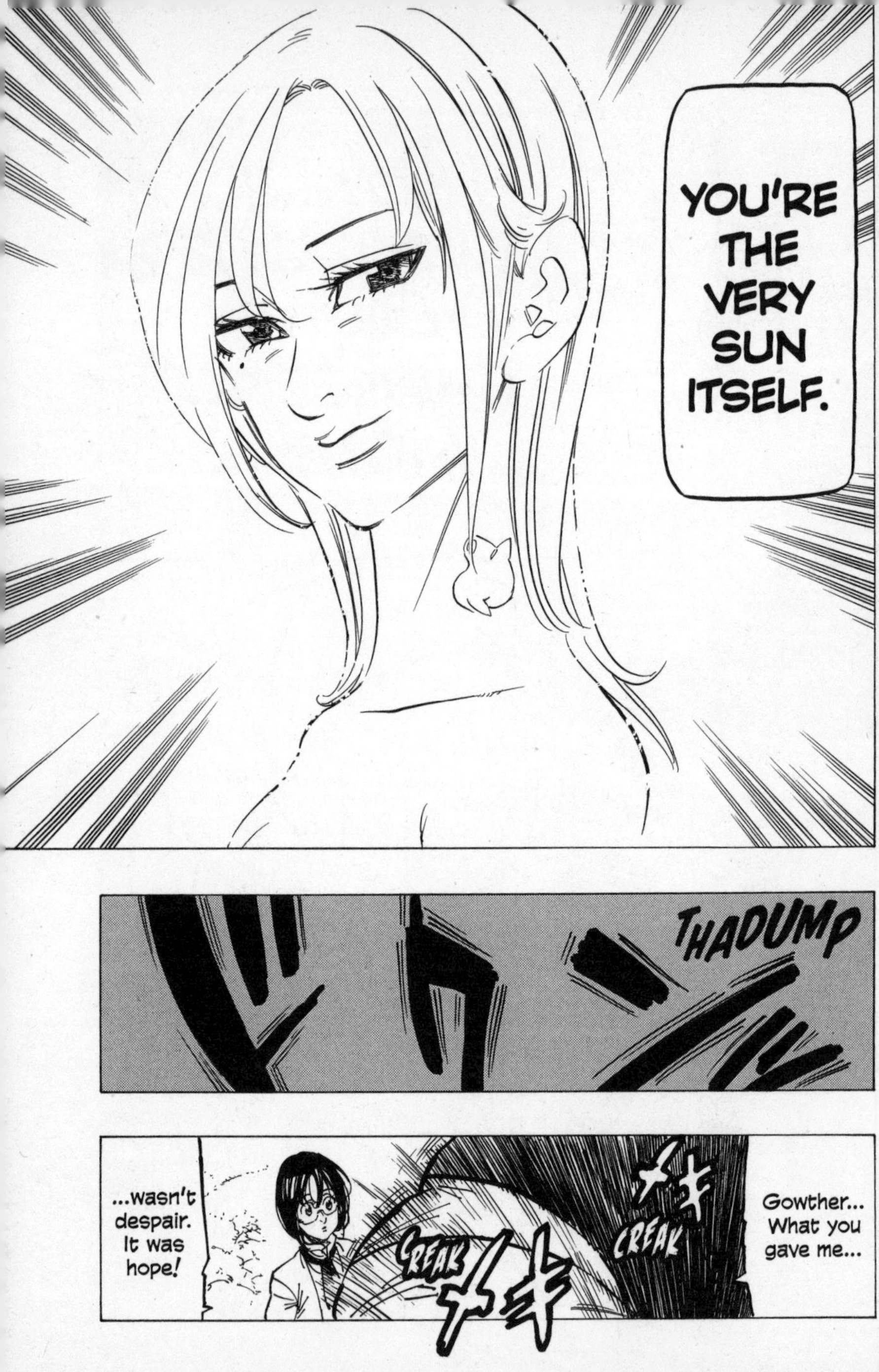
YOU'RE THE VERY SUN ITSELF.
THADUMP
Gowther... What you gave me...
CREAK
CREAK
...wasn't despair. It was hope!

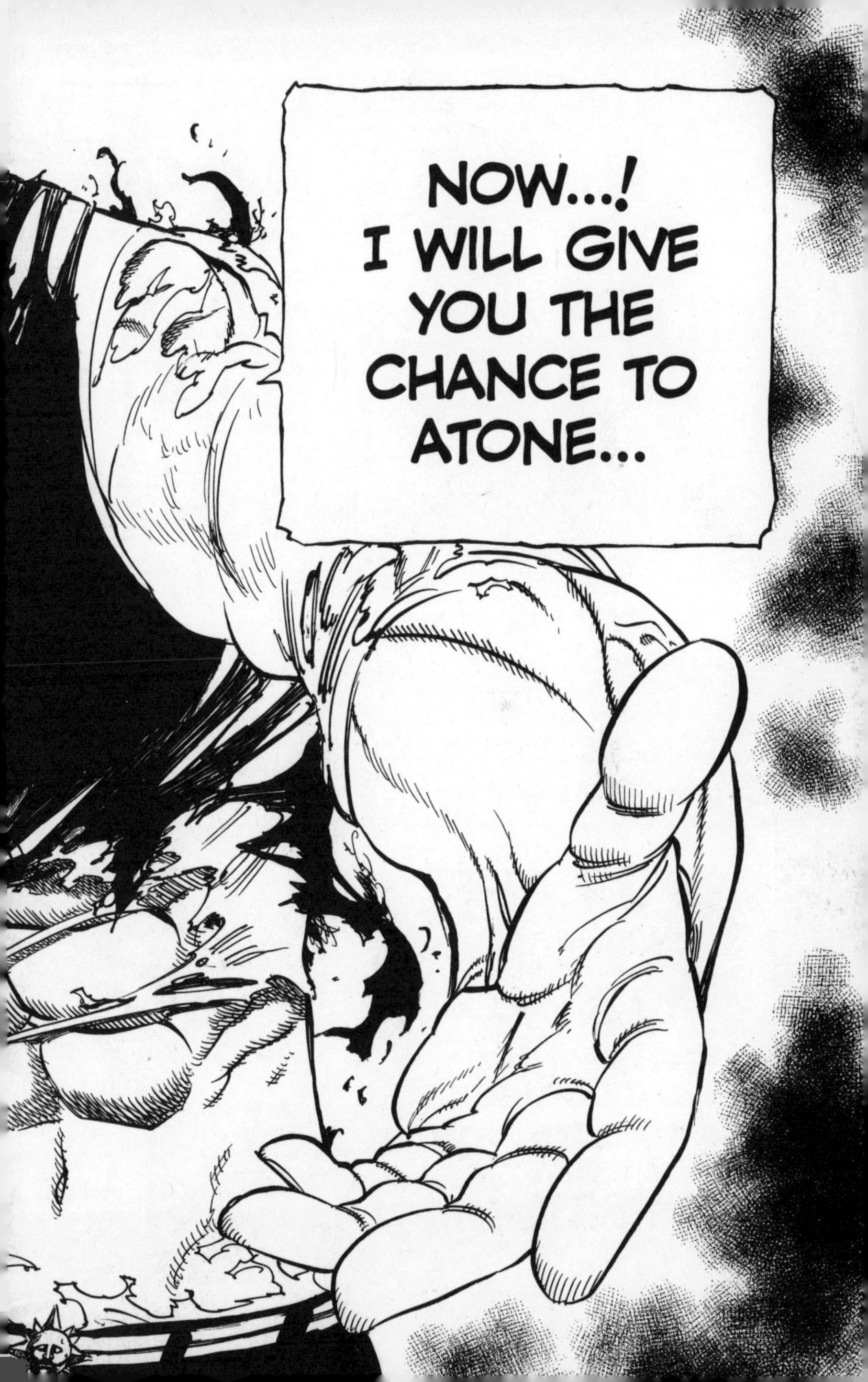
NOW...! I WILL GIVE YOU THE CHANCE TO ATONE...

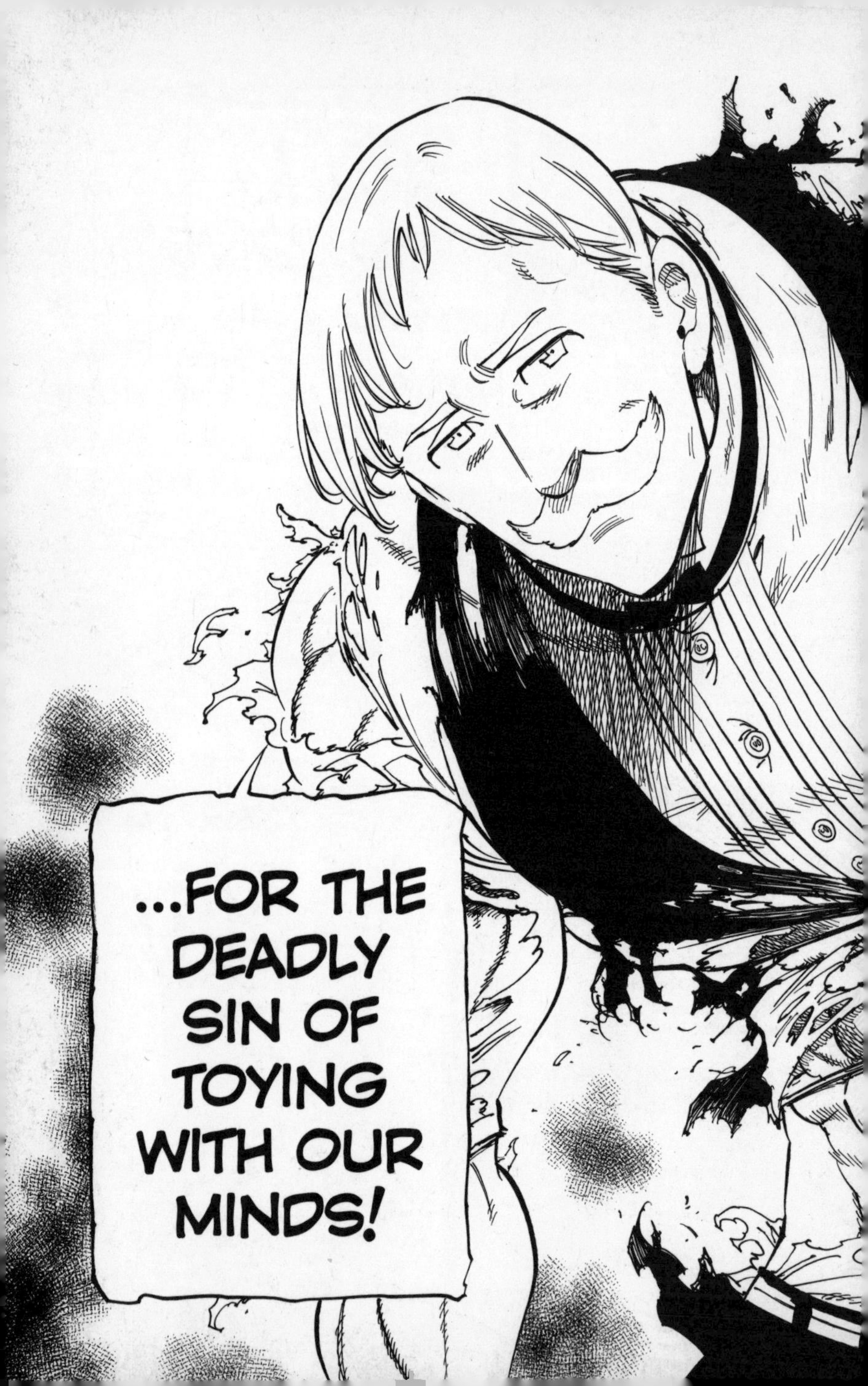
...FOR THE DEADLY SIN OF TOYING WITH OUR MINDS!

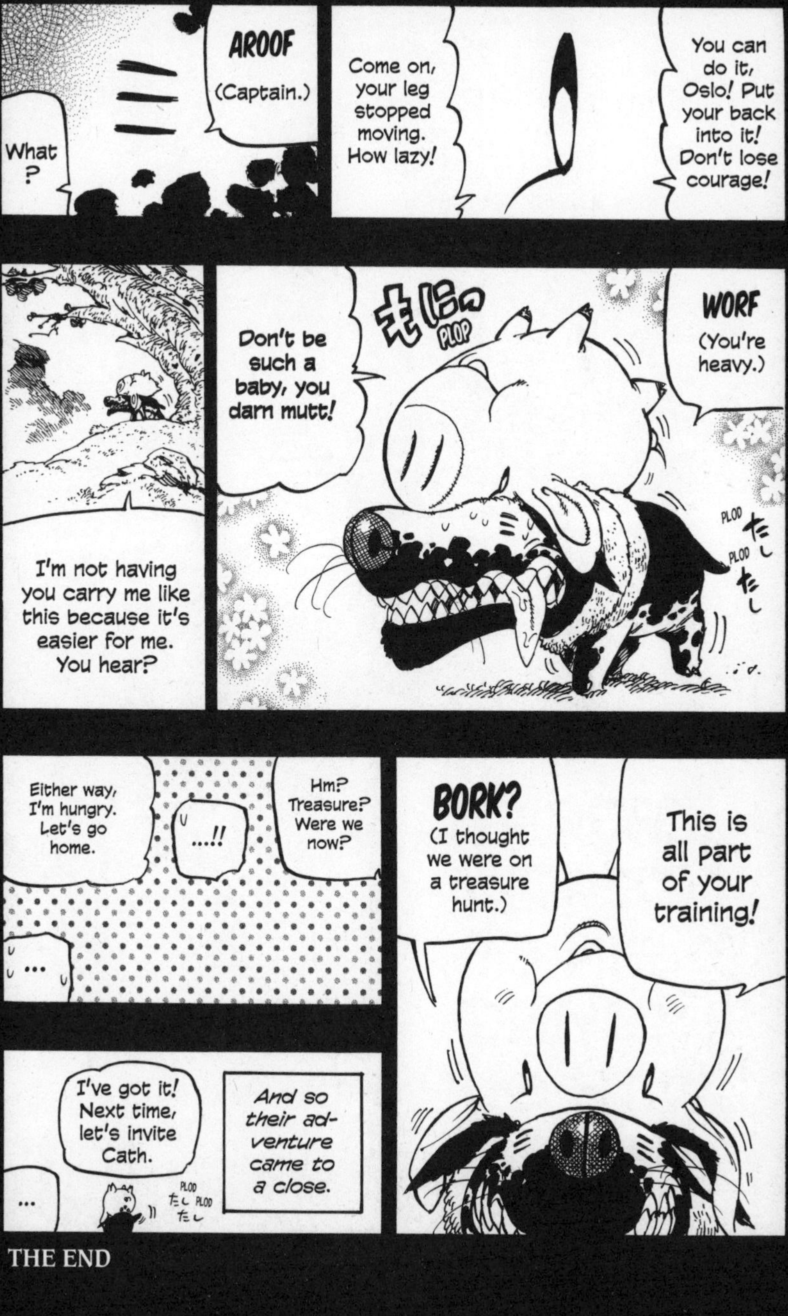
You can do it, Oslo! Put your back into it! Don't lose courage!
Come on, your leg stopped moving. How lazy!
AROOF
(Captain.)
What?
WORF
(You're heavy.)
PLOP
Don't be such a baby, you darn mutt!
PLOD
PLOD
I'm not having you carry me like this because it's easier for me. You hear?
This is all part of your training!
BORK?
(I thought we were on a treasure hunt.)
Hm? Treasure? Were we now?
...!!
Either way, I'm hungry. Let's go home.
...
And so their adventure came to a close.
I've got it! Next time, let's invite Cath.
PLOD
PLOD
...

THE END

Chapter 170 - For Whom Does That Light Shine?

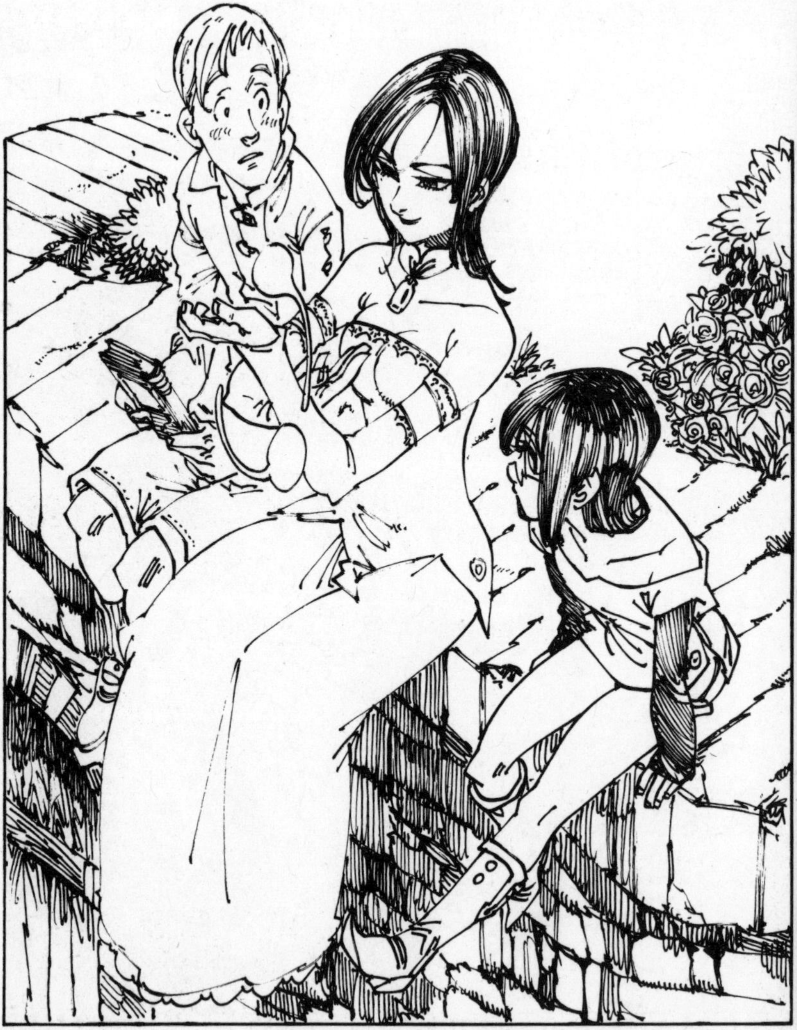

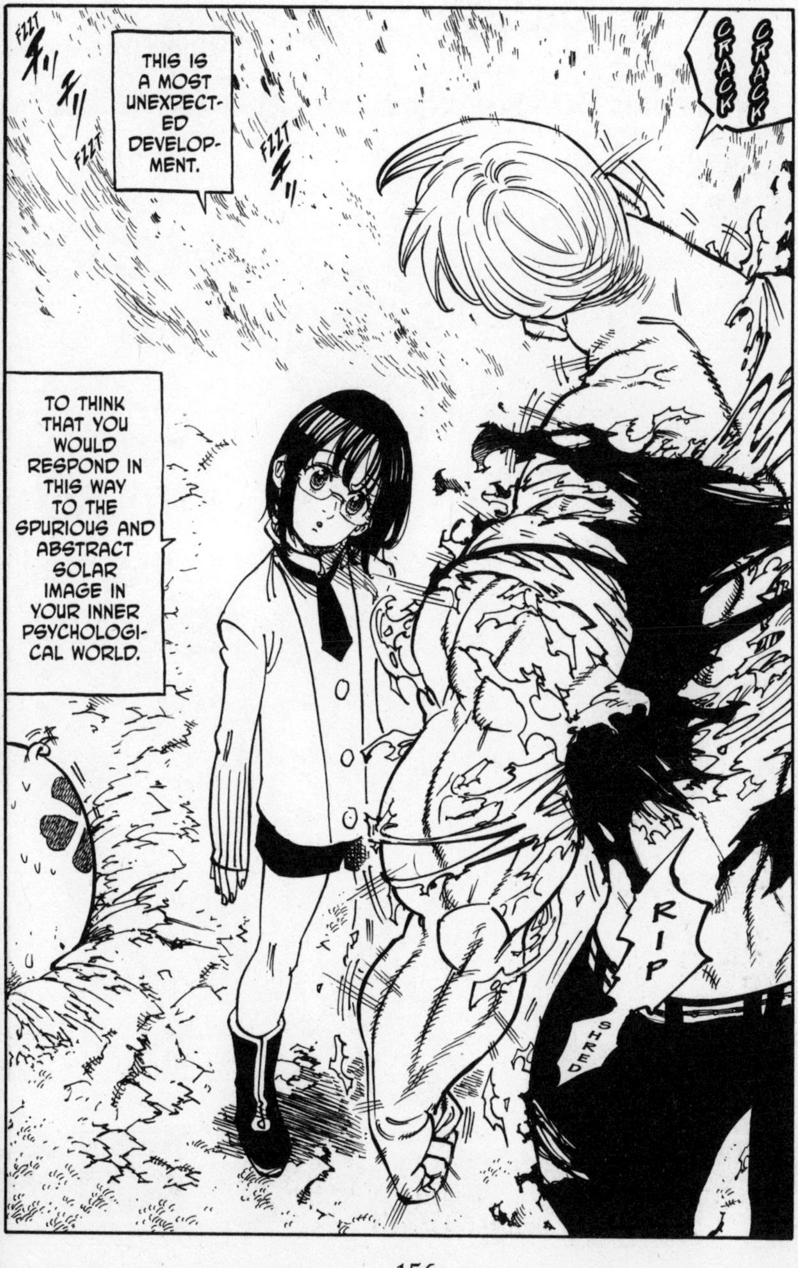
CRACK CRACK
FZZT
THIS IS A MOST UNEXPECTED DEVELOPMENT.
FZZT
FZZT
TO THINK THAT YOU WOULD RESPOND IN THIS WAY TO THE SPURIOUS AND ABSTRACT SOLAR IMAGE IN YOUR INNER PSYCHOLOGICAL WORLD.
RIP
SHRED

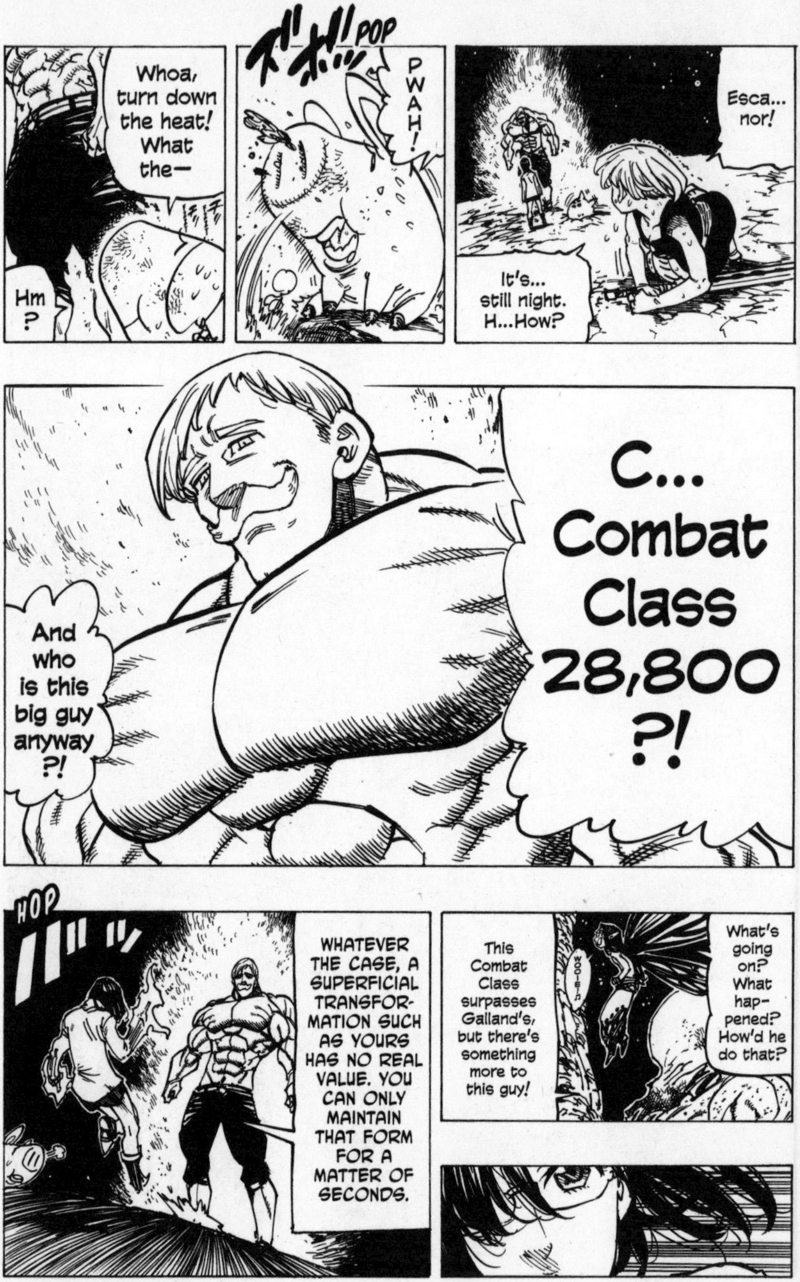

Esca... nor!
It's... still night. H...How?
ズボッ!! POP
PWAH!
Whoa, turn down the heat! What the—
Hm?
C... Combat Class 28,800?!
And who is this big guy anyway?!
What's going on? What hap-pened? How'd he do that?
WOOIE!♫
This Combat Class surpasses Galland's, but there's something more to this guy!
HOP
WHATEVER THE CASE, A SUPERFICIAL TRANSFOR-MATION SUCH AS YOURS HAS NO REAL VALUE. YOU CAN ONLY MAINTAIN THAT FORM FOR A MATTER OF SECONDS.

FWIP

A FEW SECONDS IS ALL I NEED.

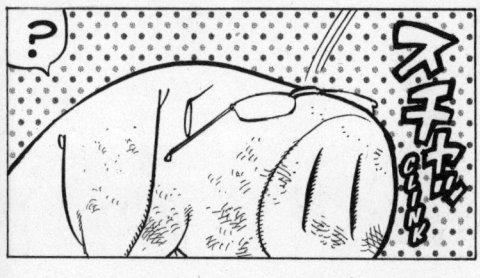

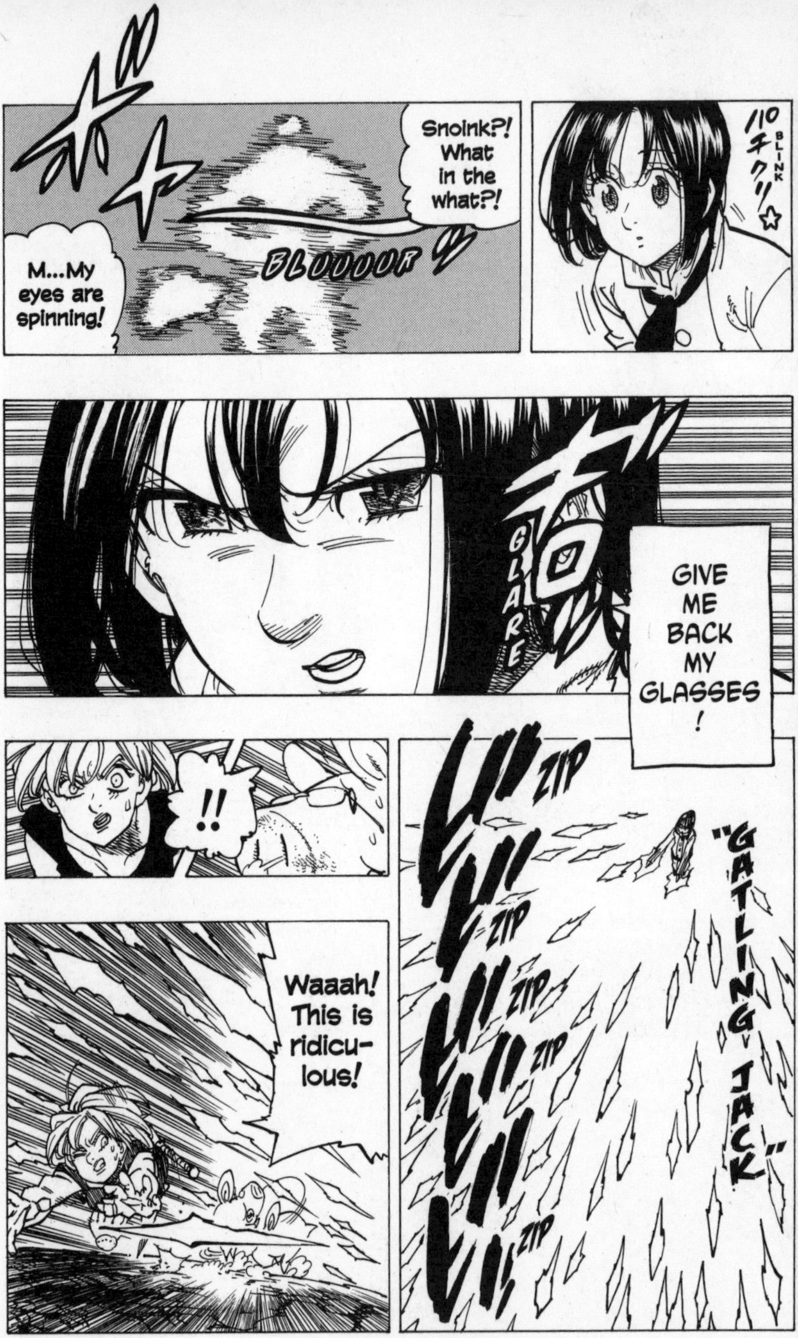

BLINK
Snoink?! What in the what?!
BLUUUUR
M...My eyes are spinning!
GLARE
GIVE ME BACK MY GLASSES!
ZIP
ZIP
ZIP
ZIP
ZIP
"GATLING JACK"
!!
Waaah! This is ridicu-lous!

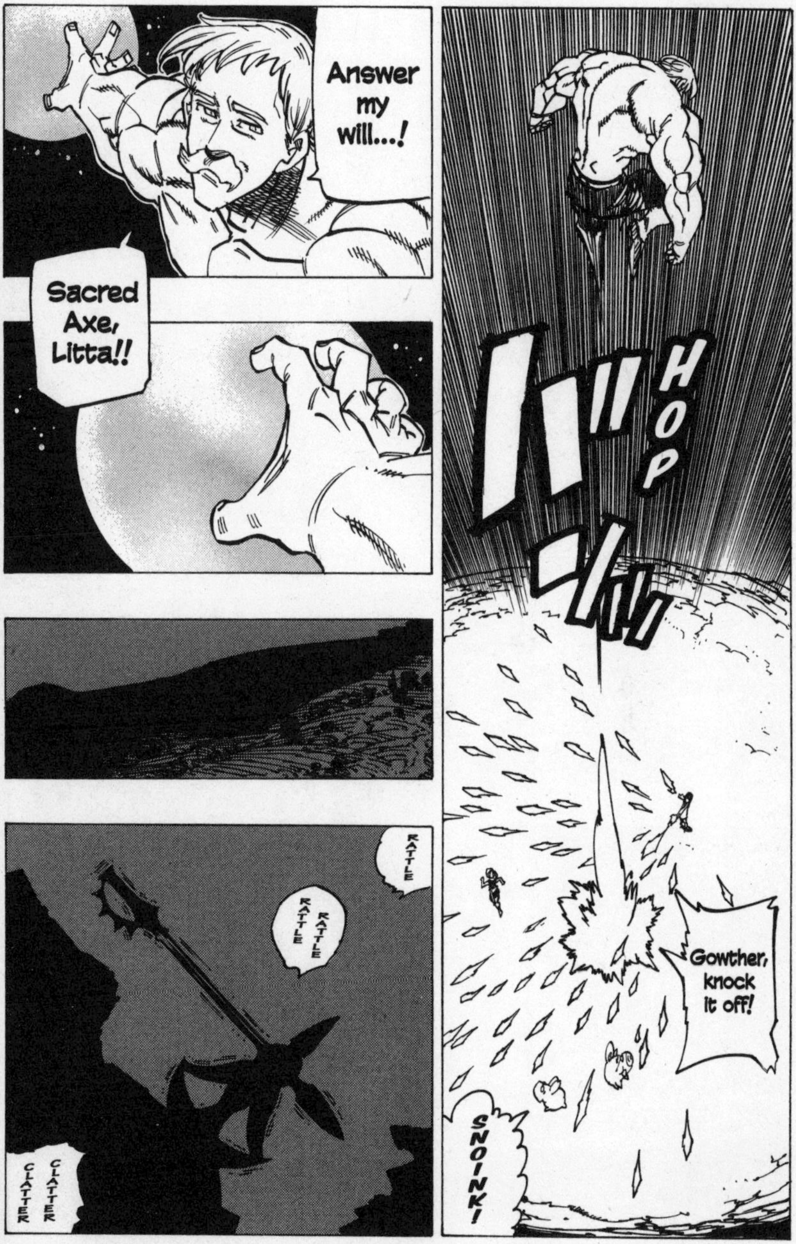
HOP
Gowther, knock it off!
SNOINK!
Answer my will...!
Sacred Axe, Litta!!
RATTLE
RATTLE RATTLE
CLATTER CLATTER

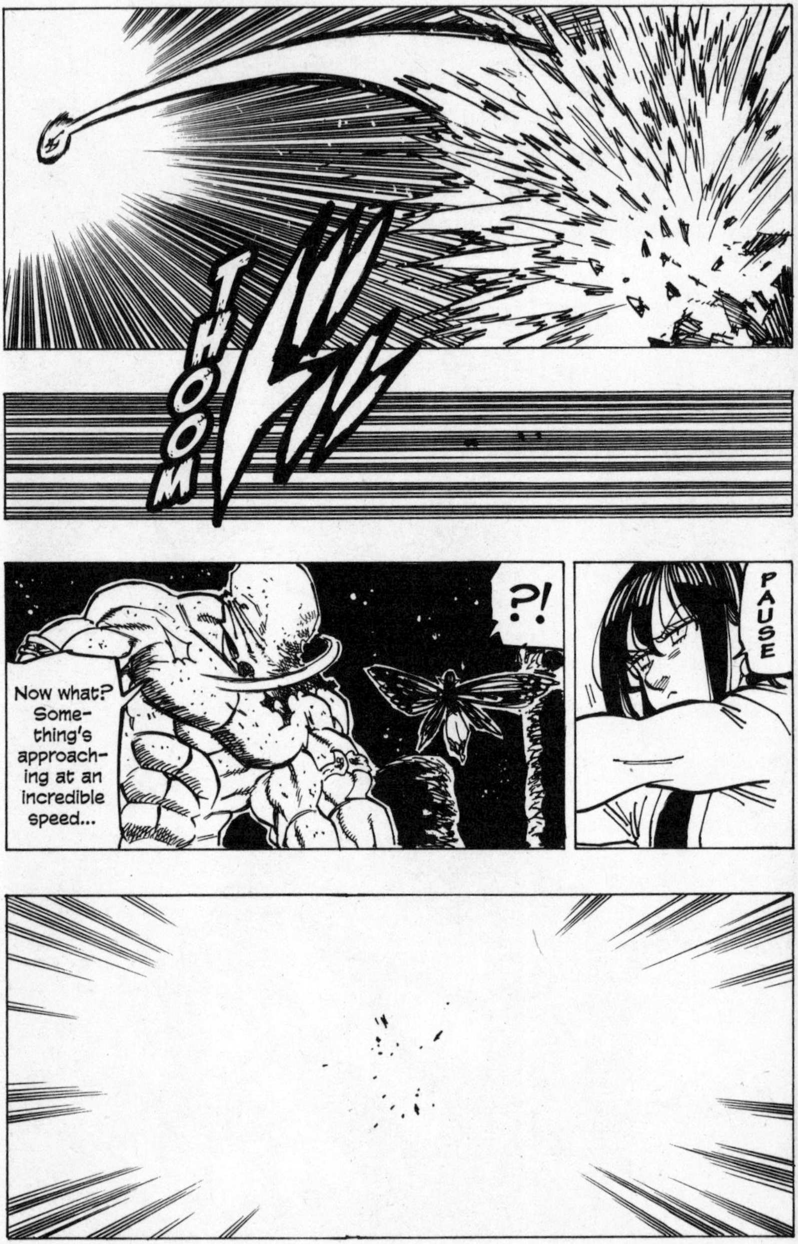
THOOM
PAUSE
?!
Now what? Something's approaching at an incredible speed...

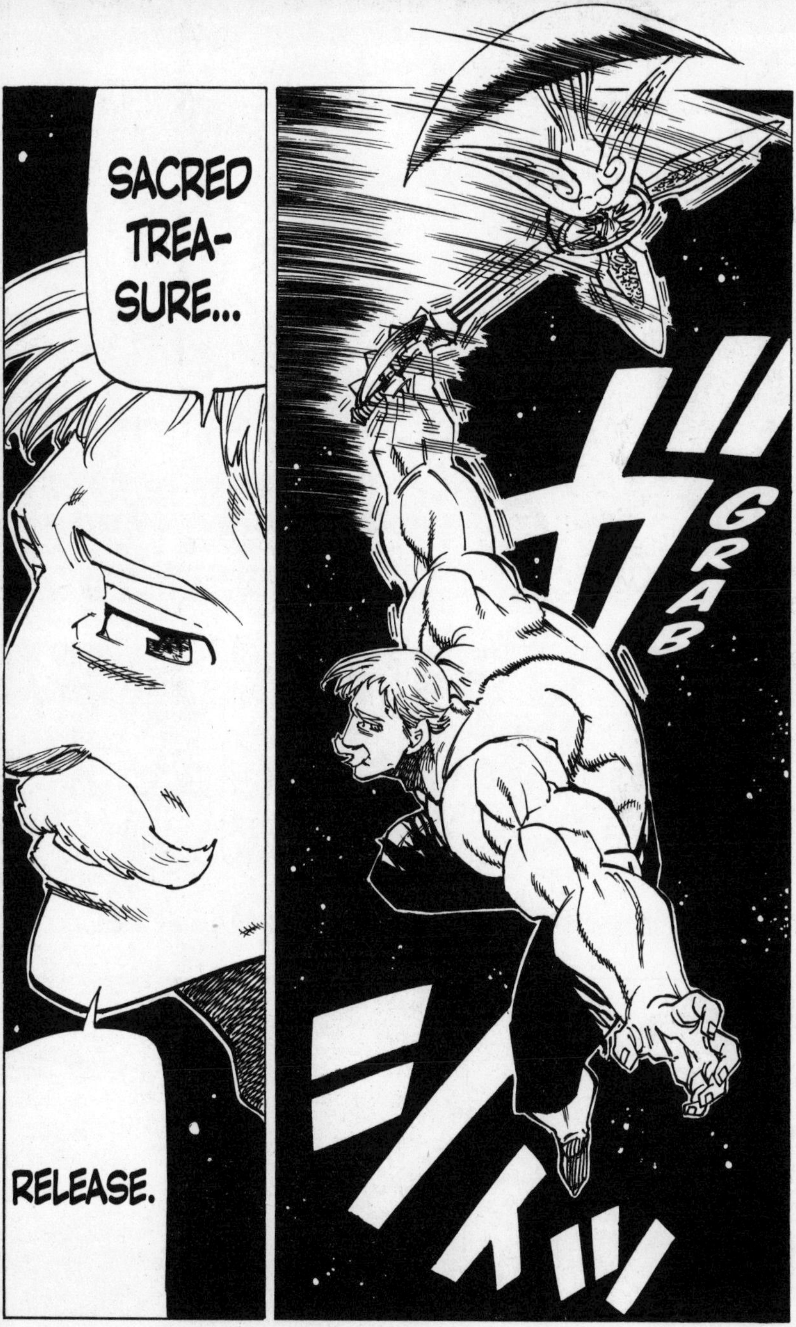
GRAB
SACRED TREA-SURE...
RELEASE.

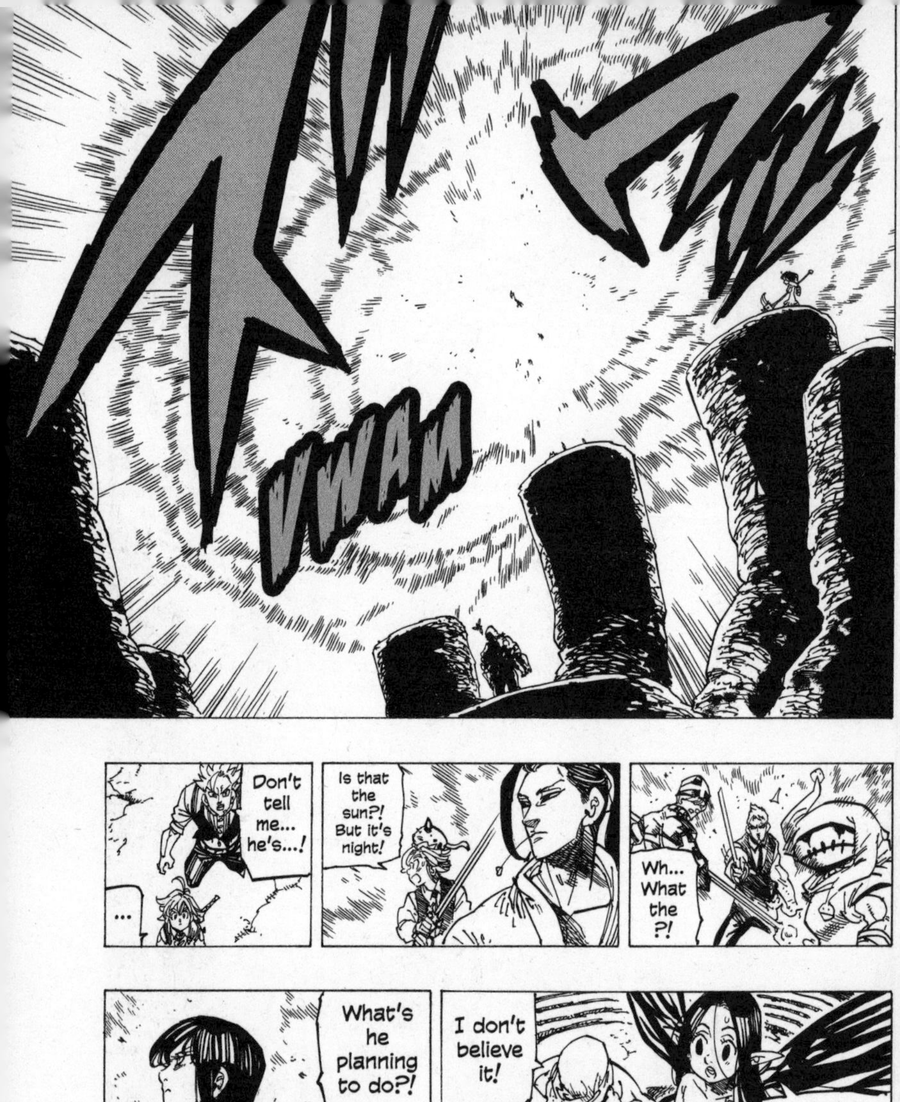
VWAM
Wh... What the ?!
Is that the sun?! But it's night!
Don't tell me... he's...!
...
I don't believe it!
Isn't this magic... on par with Estarossa's ?!
What's he planning to do?!
...

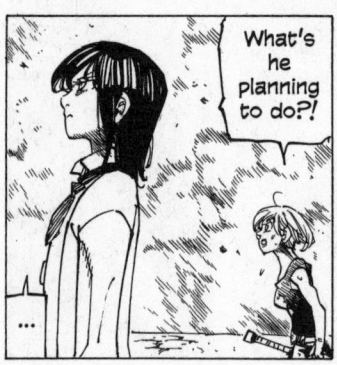

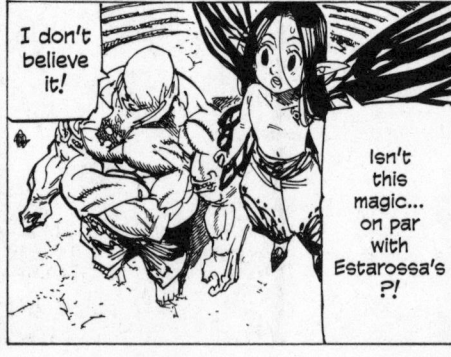

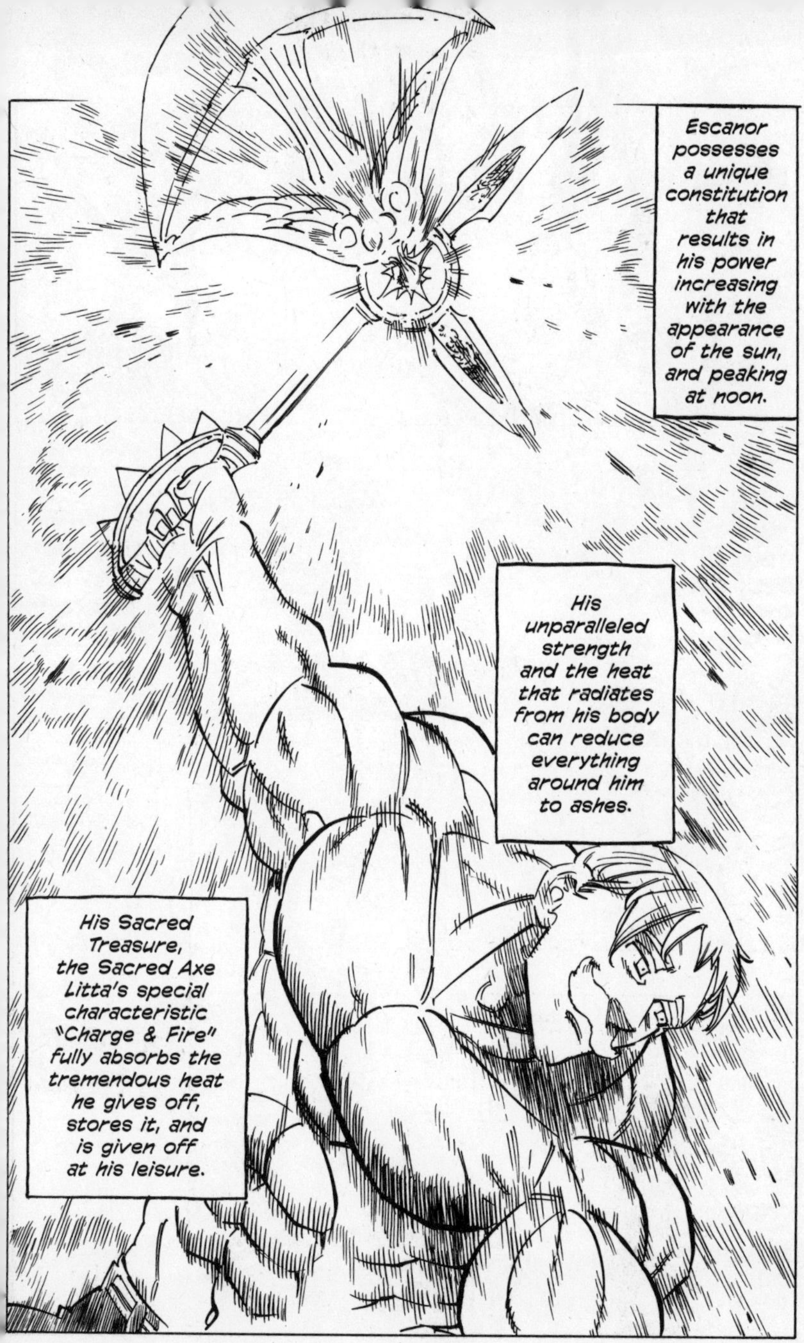
Escanor possesses a unique constitution that results in his power increasing with the appearance of the sun, and peaking at noon.
His unparalleled strength and the heat that radiates from his body can reduce everything around him to ashes.
His Sacred Treasure, the Sacred Axe Litta's special characteristic "Charge & Fire" fully absorbs the tremendous heat he gives off, stores it, and is given off at his leisure.

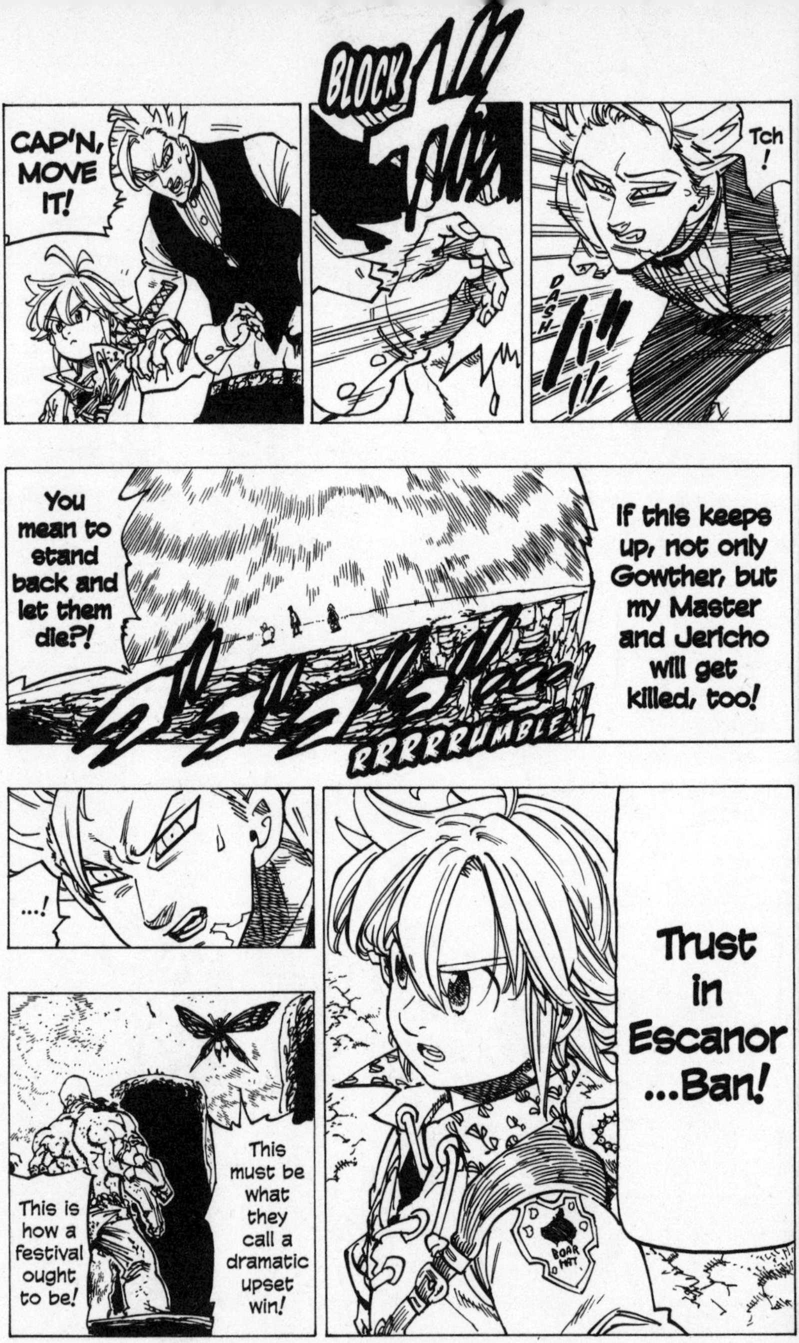
Tch!
DASH
BLOCK
CAP'N, MOVE IT!
If this keeps up, not only Gowther, but my Master and Jericho will get killed, too!
You mean to stand back and let them die?!
RRRRRUMBLE
Trust in Escanor ...Ban!
...!
This must be what they call a dramatic upset win!
This is how a festival ought to be!

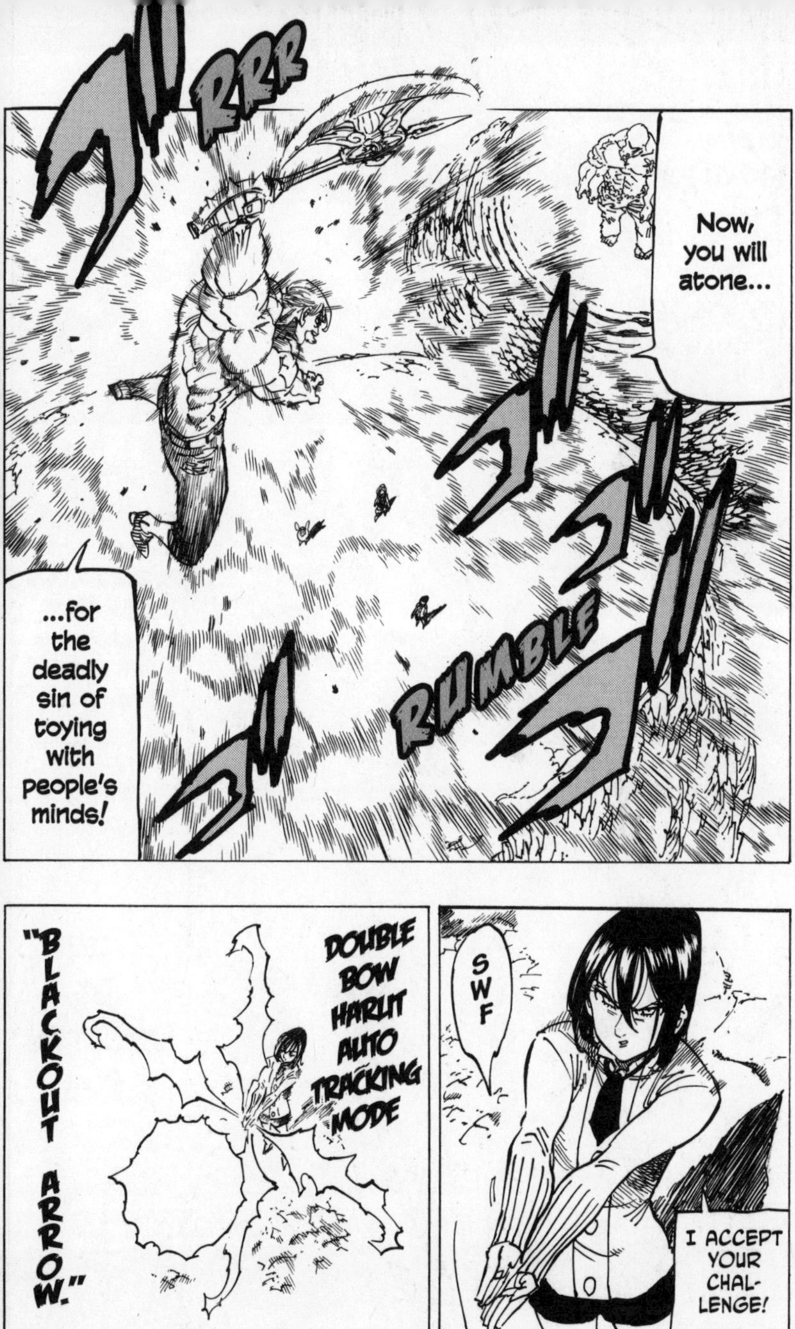

Now, you will atone...
RRR
RUMBLE
...for the deadly sin of toying with people's minds!
SWF
I ACCEPT YOUR CHAL-LENGE!
DOUBLE BOW HARLIT AUTO TRACKING MODE
"BLACKOUT ARROW."

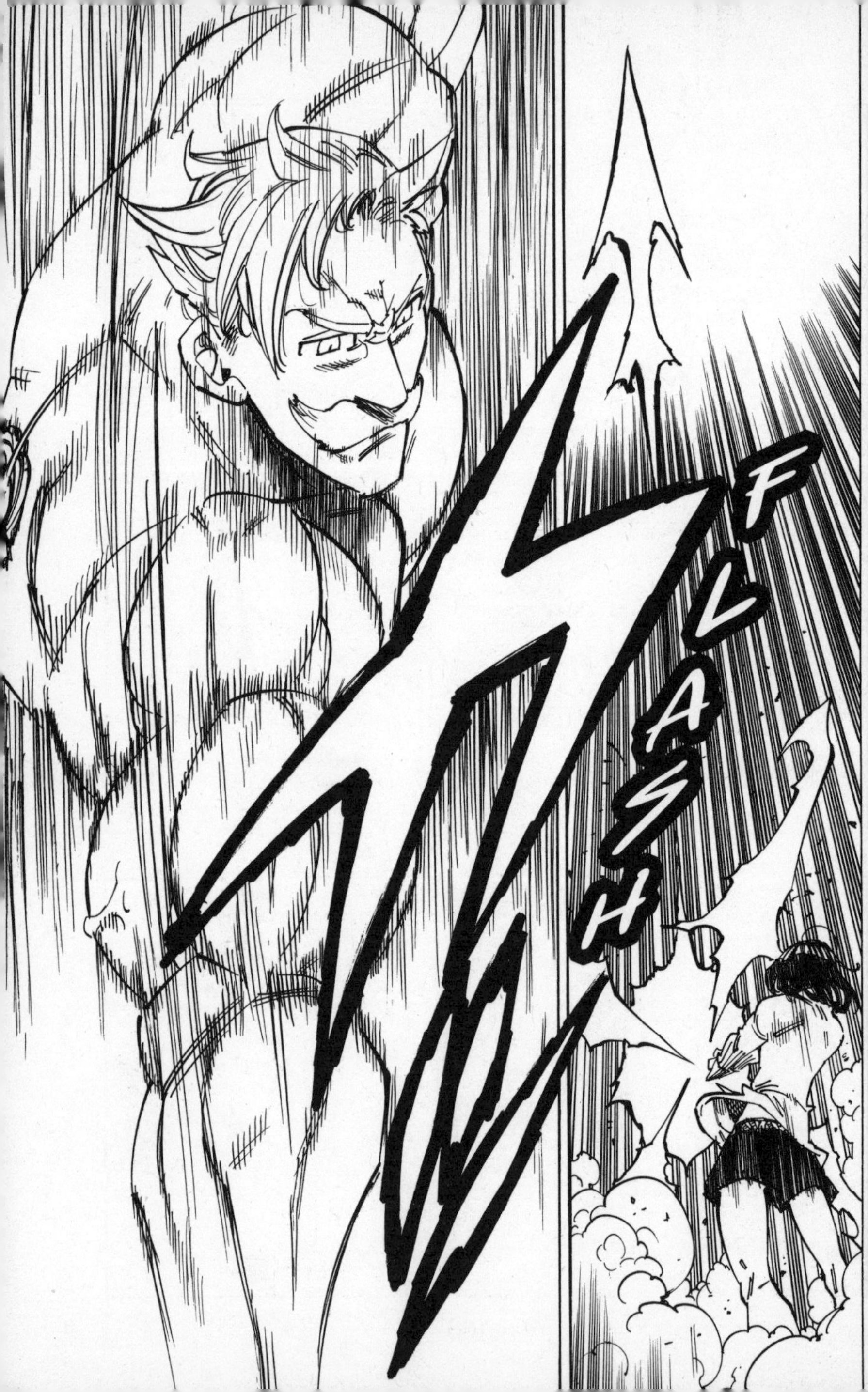
FLASH

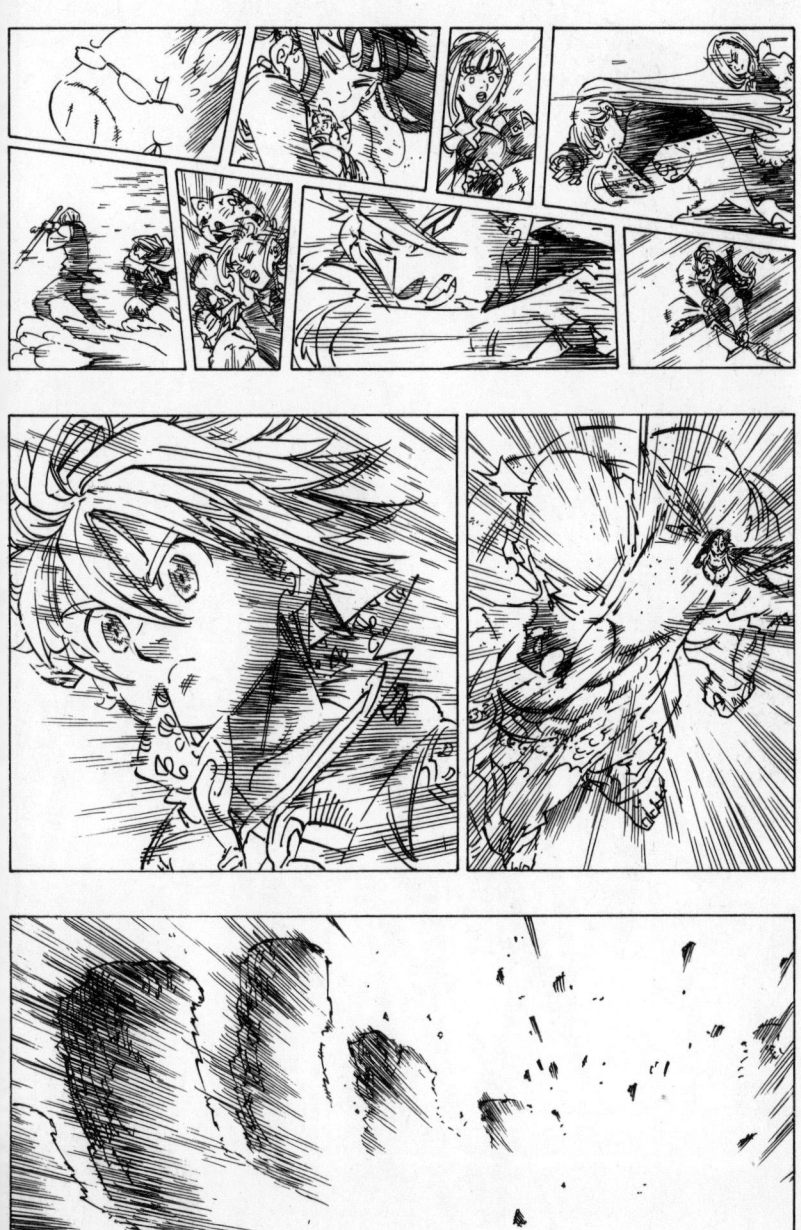

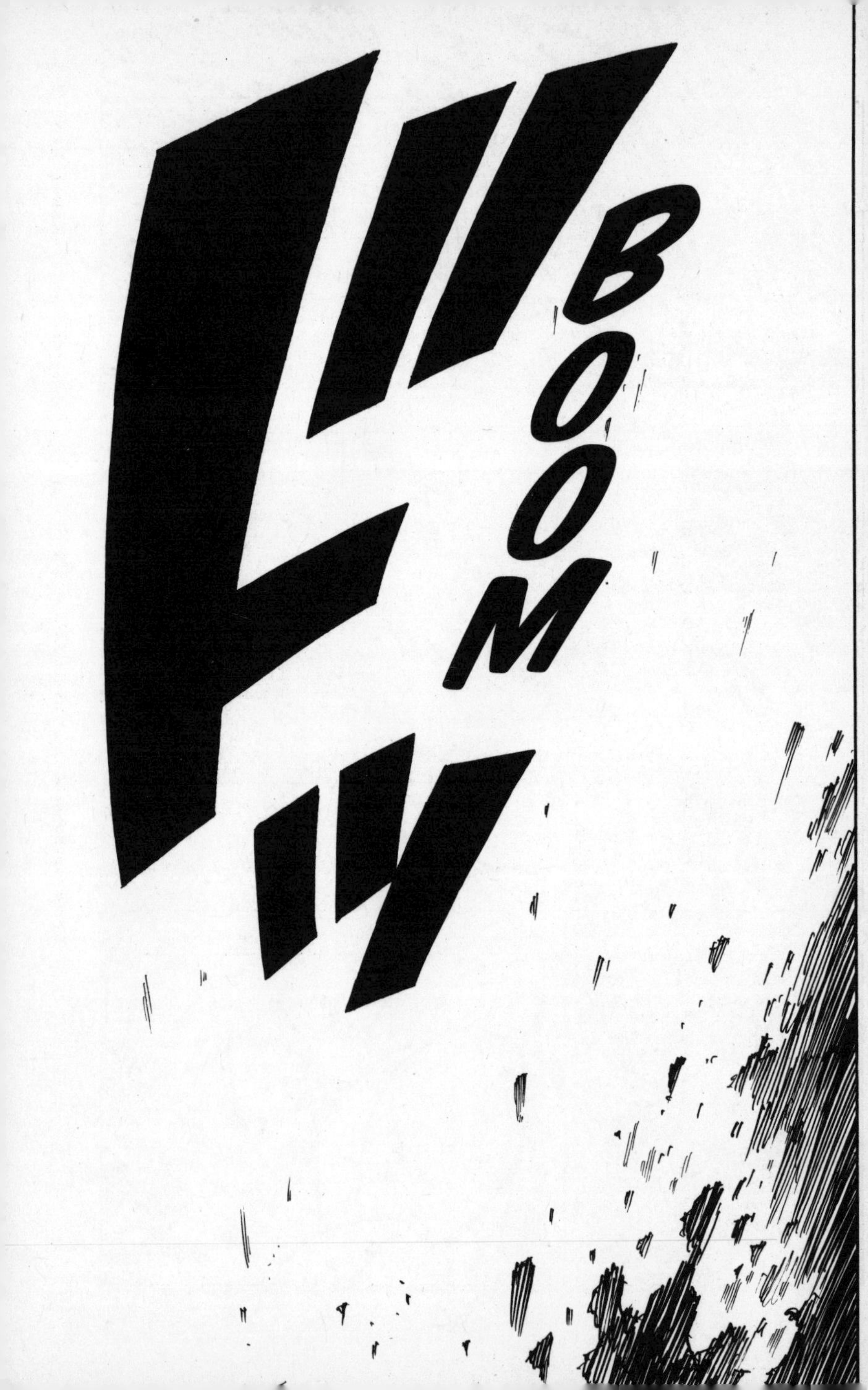
BOOM!!

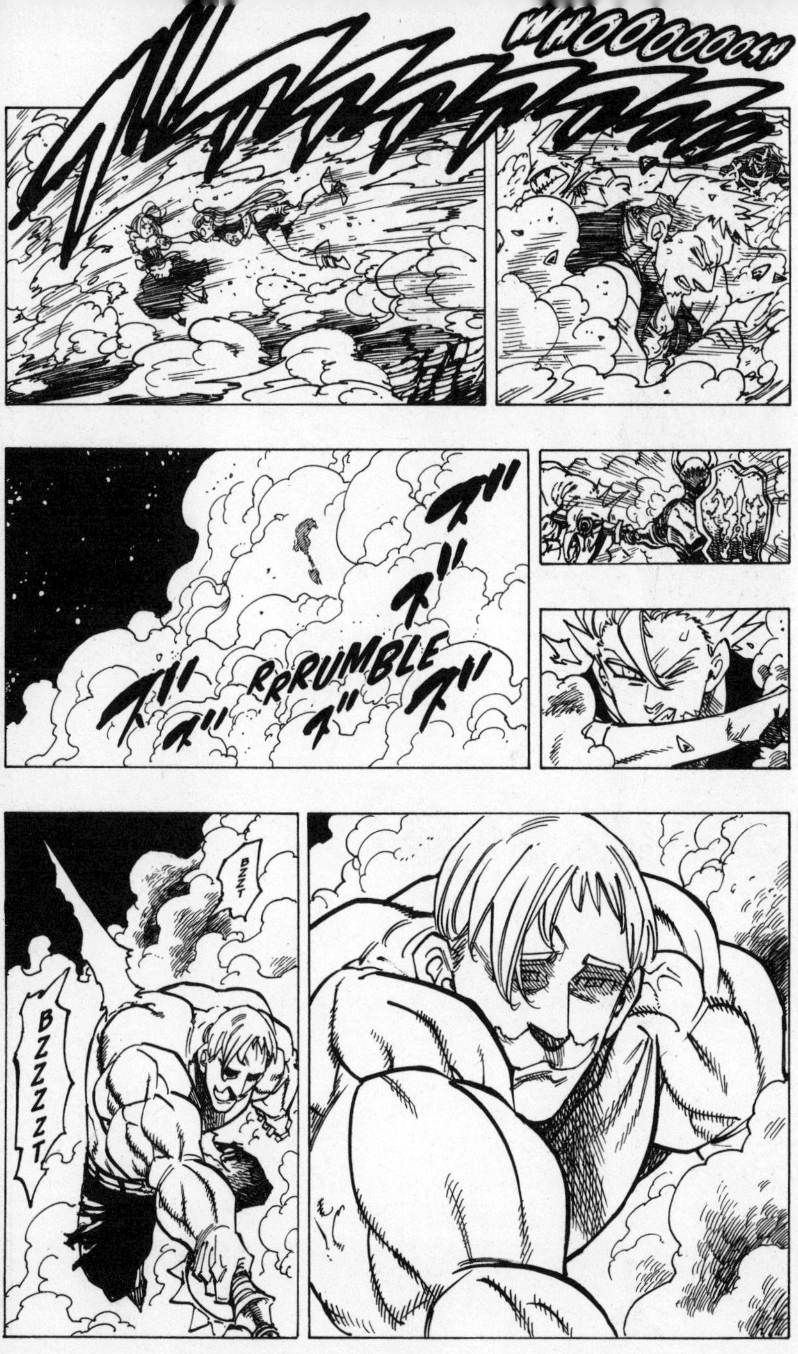
WHOOOOOOSH
RRRUMBLE
BZZZT
BZZZZZT

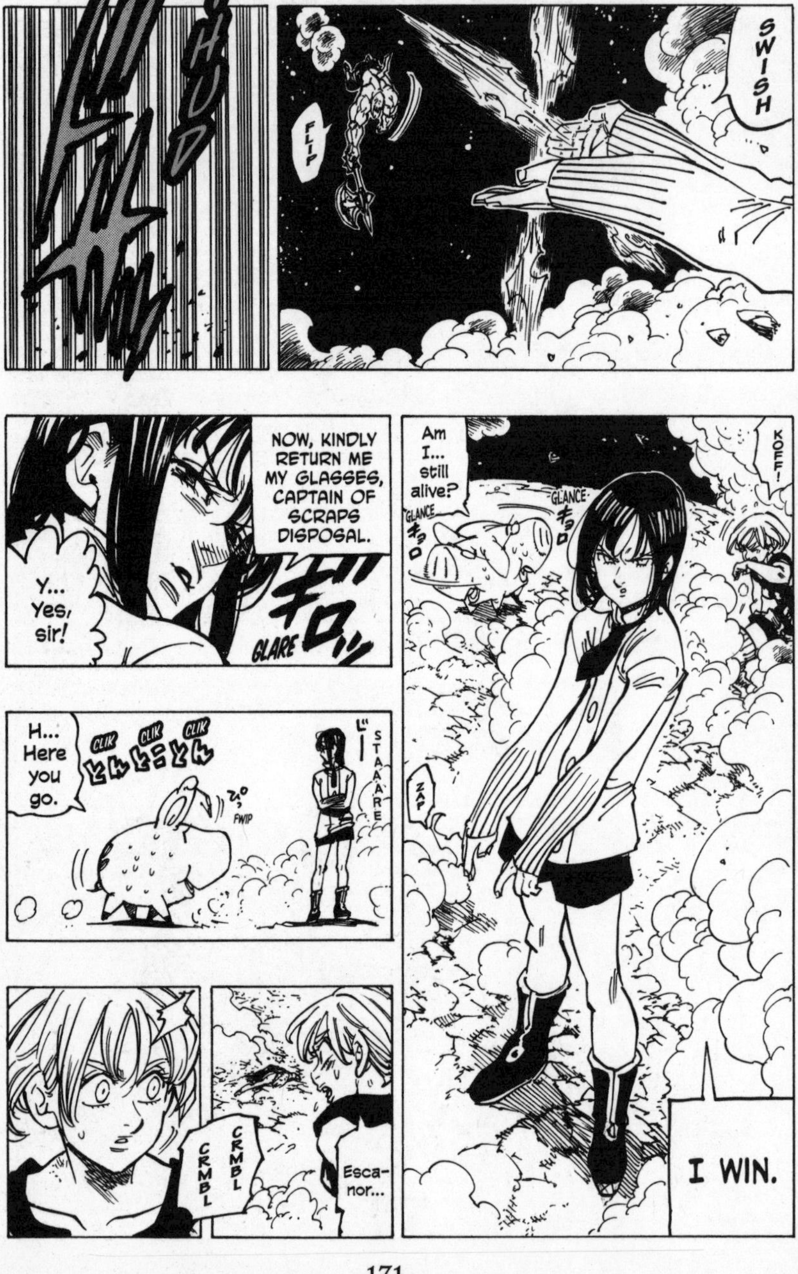

SWISH
FLIP
THUD
Am I... still alive?
GLANCE
GLANCE
KOFF!
ZAP
I WIN.
NOW, KINDLY RETURN ME MY GLASSES, CAPTAIN OF SCRAPS DISPOSAL.
Y... Yes, sir!
GLARE
STAAARE
CLIK CLIK CLIK
H... Here you go.
FWIP
CRMBL CRMBL
Escanor...

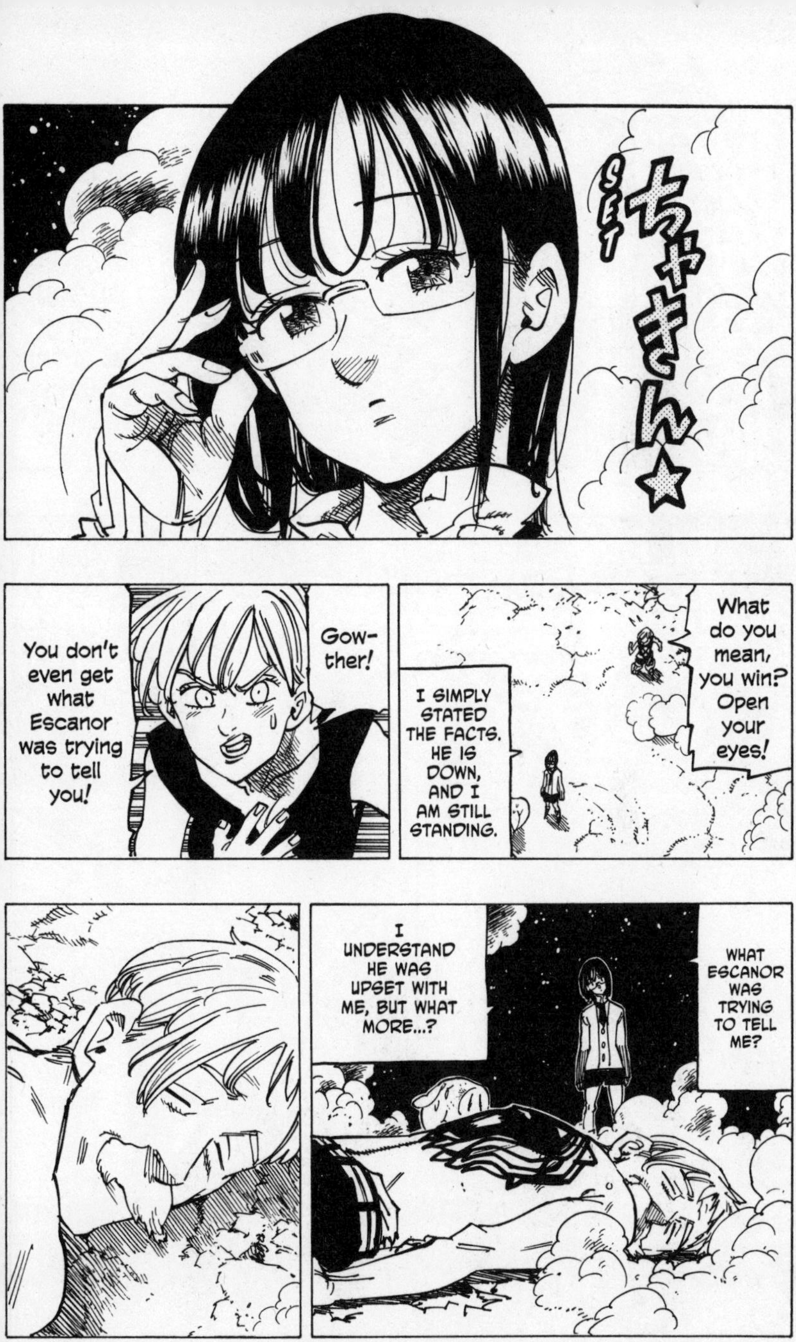

ちゃきん☆
SET
What do you mean, you win? Open your eyes!
I SIMPLY STATED THE FACTS. HE IS DOWN, AND I AM STILL STANDING.
Gow-ther!
You don't even get what Escanor was trying to tell you!
WHAT ESCANOR WAS TRYING TO TELL ME?
I UNDERSTAND HE WAS UPSET WITH ME, BUT WHAT MORE...?

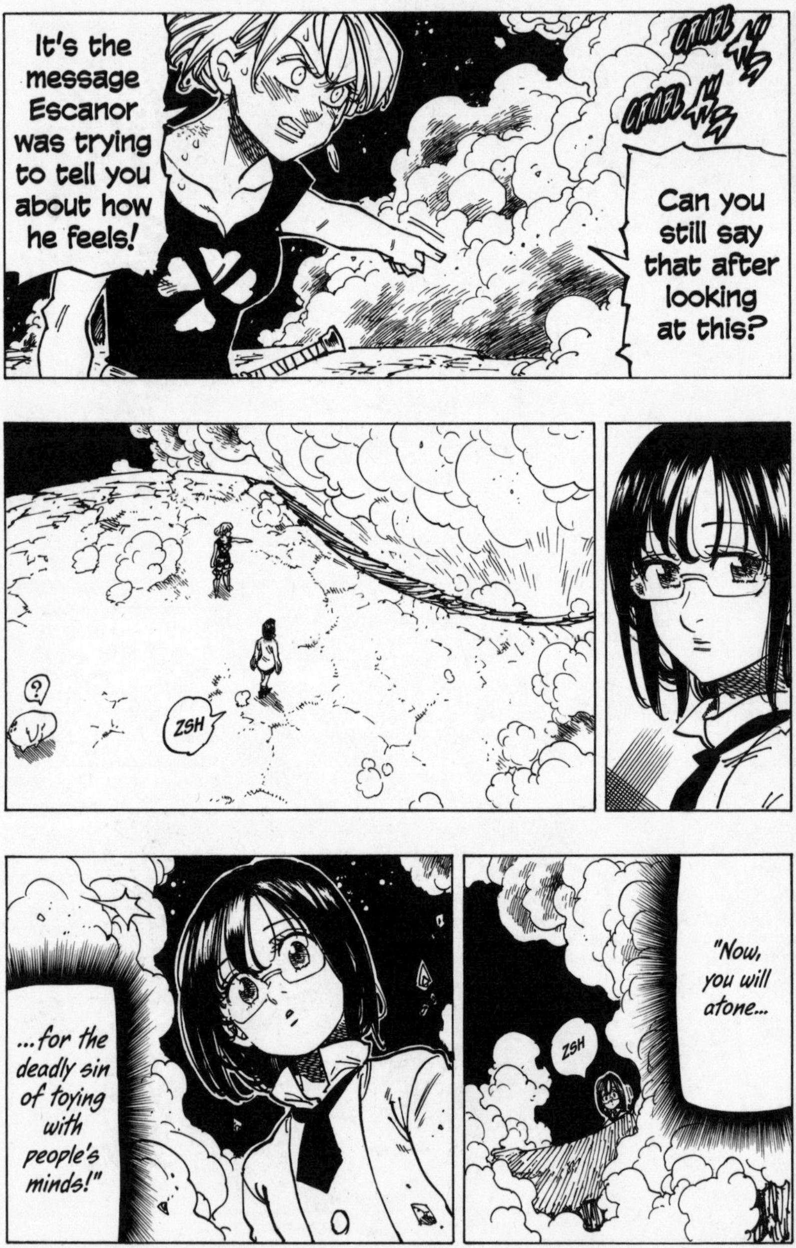
CRMBL
CRMBL
It's the message Escanor was trying to tell you about how he feels!
Can you still say that after looking at this?
?
ZSH
"Now, you will atone...
ZSH
...for the deadly sin of toying with people's minds!"

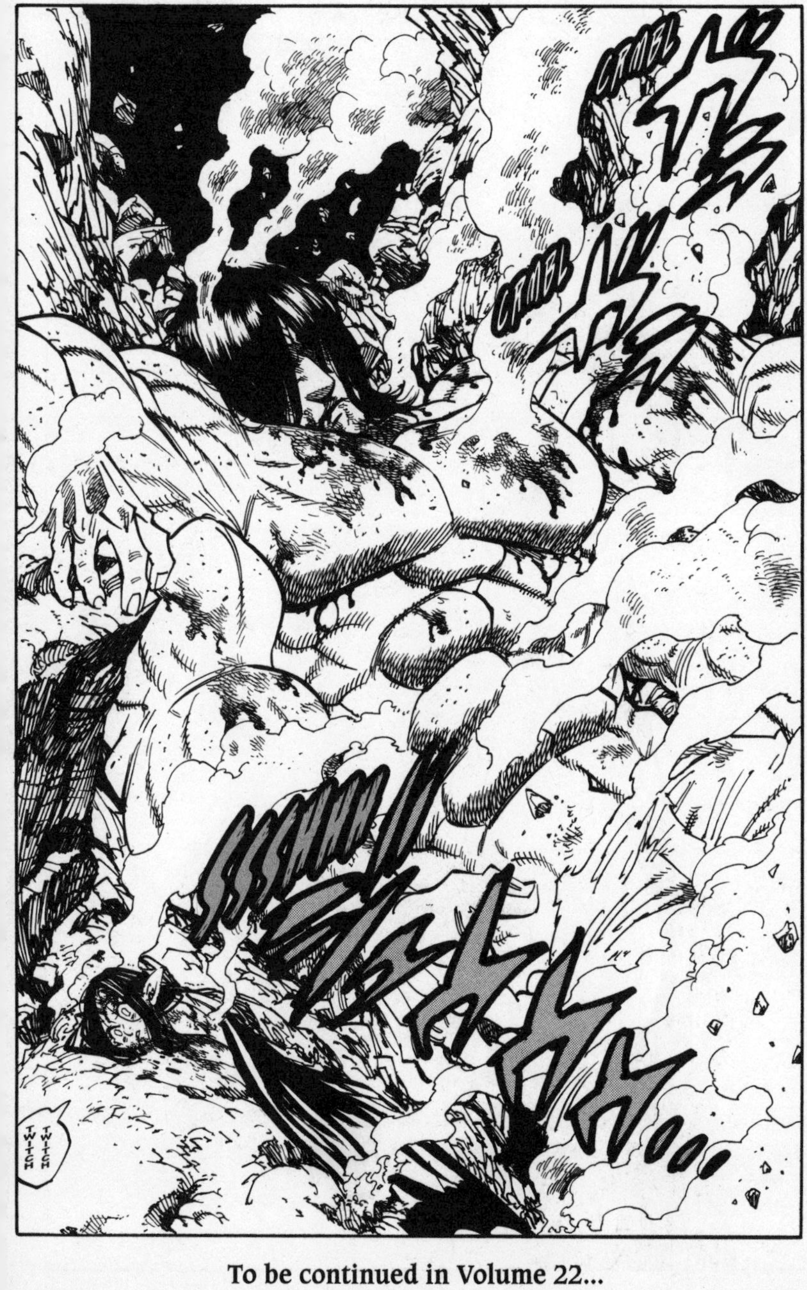
CRMBL
CRMBL
TWITCH TWITCH

To be continued in Volume 22...

Bonus Story - Naked Heart

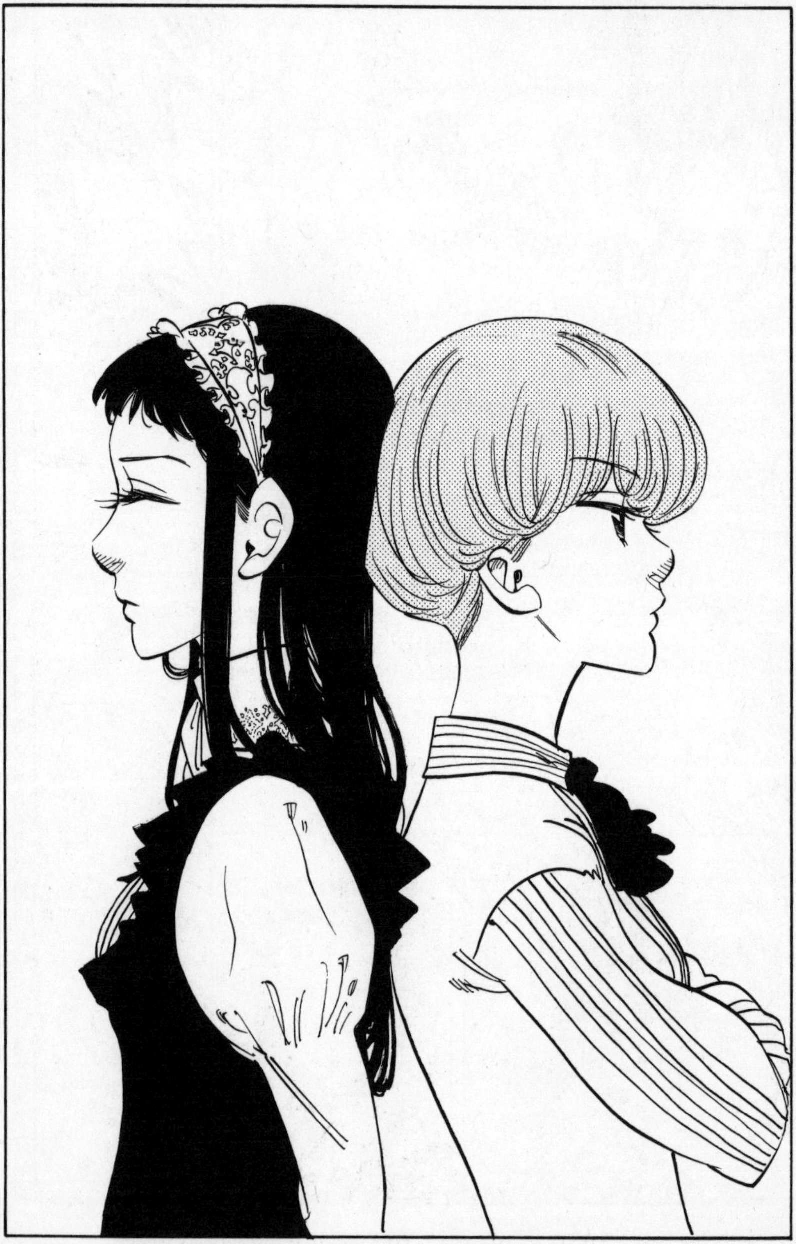

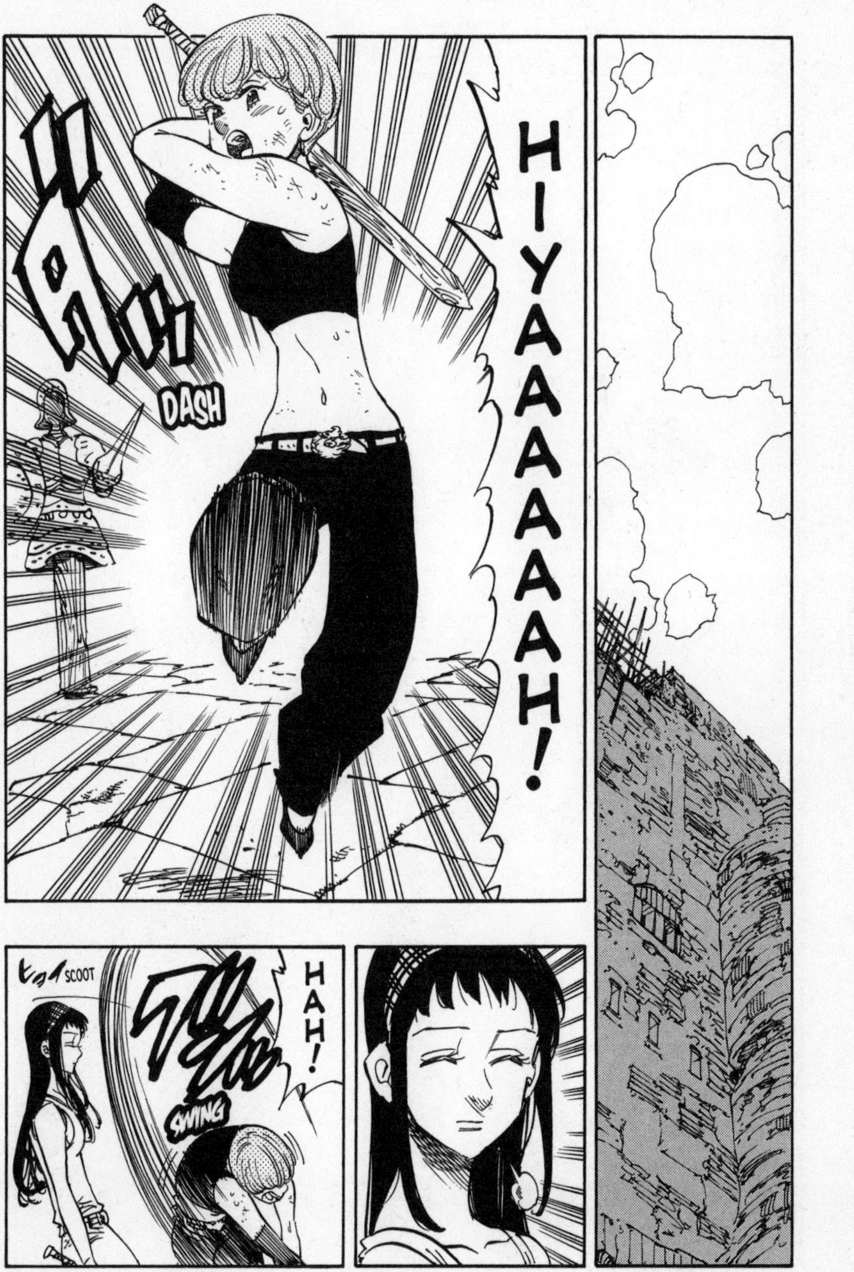
HIYAAAAAAH!
DASH
HAH!
SWING
ヒョイ SCOOT

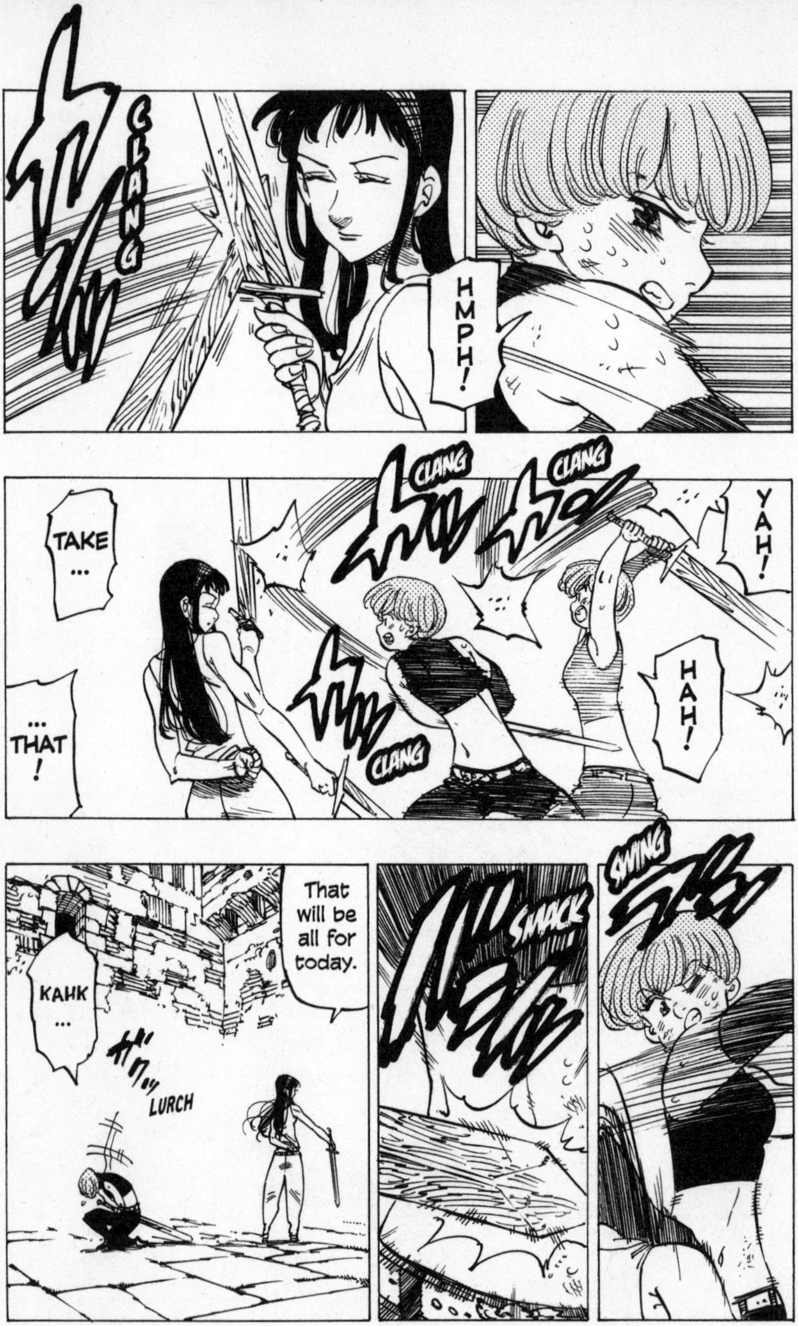
HMPH!
CLANG
YAH!
CLANG
CLANG
HAH!
TAKE ...
CLANG
... THAT!
SWING
SMACK
That will be all for today.
KAHK ...
LURCH

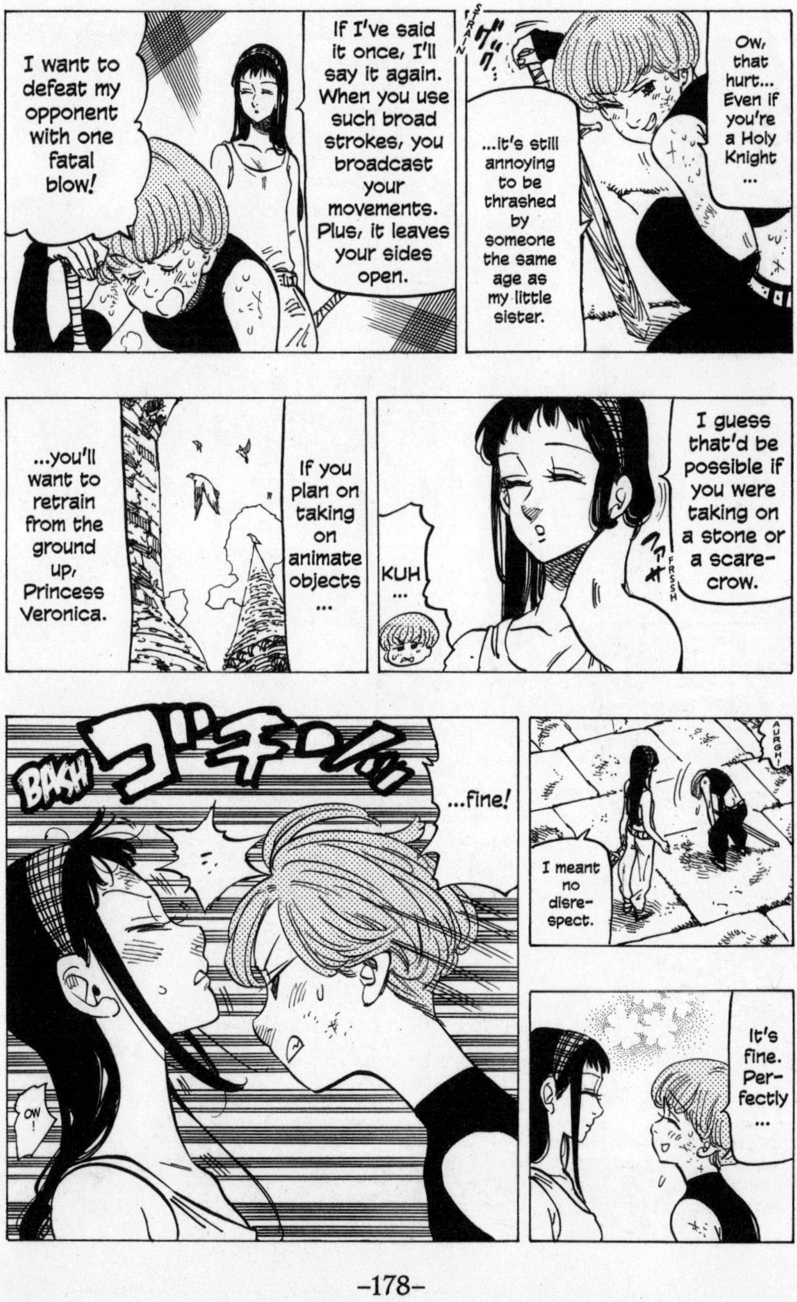
STRAIN
Ow, that hurt... Even if you're a Holy Knight ...
...it's still annoying to be thrashed by someone the same age as my little sister.
If I've said it once, I'll say it again. When you use such broad strokes, you broadcast your movements. Plus, it leaves your sides open.
I want to defeat my opponent with one fatal blow!
I guess that'd be possible if you were taking on a stone or a scare-crow.
FRSSH
KUH ...
If you plan on taking on animate objects ...
...you'll want to retrain from the ground up, Princess Veronica.
AURGH!
I meant no disre-spect.
It's fine. Per-fectly ...
...fine!
BASH
OW!

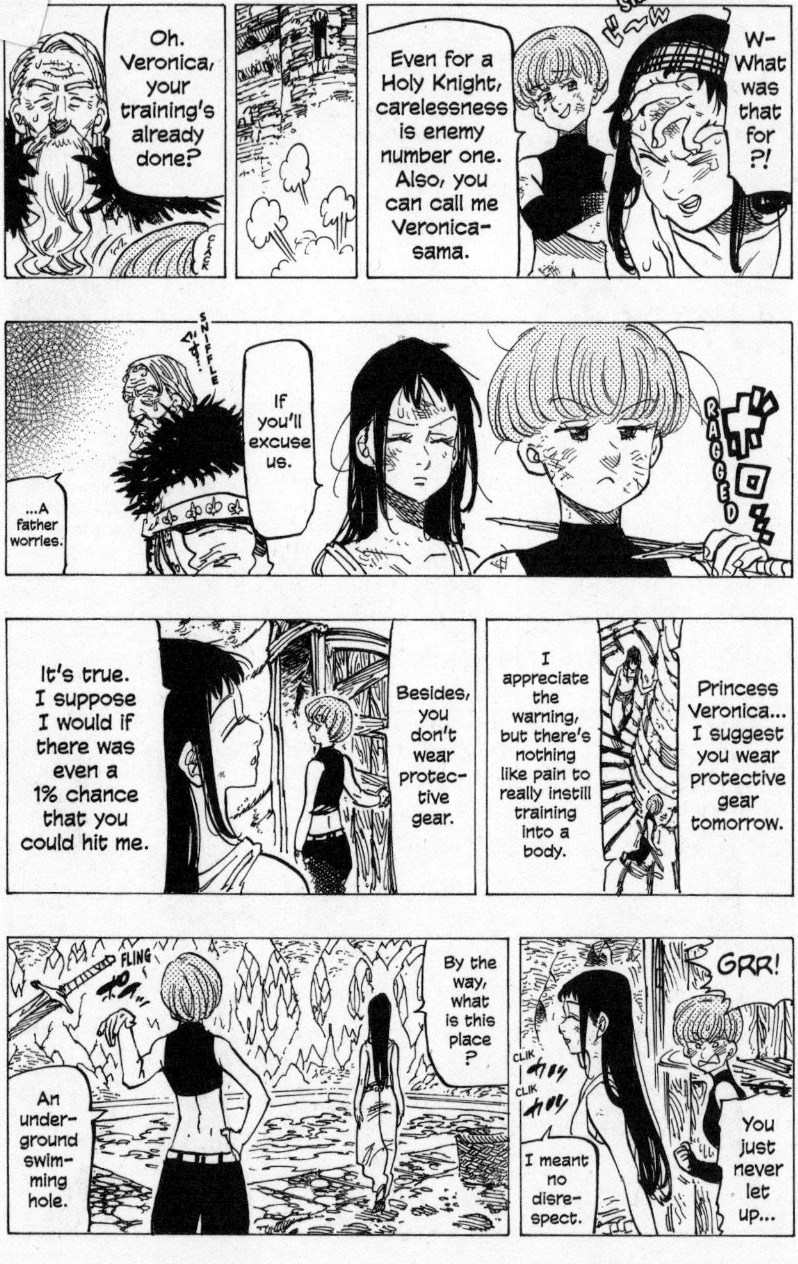
W- What was that for ?!
STING
Even for a Holy Knight, carelessness is enemy number one. Also, you can call me Veronica-sama.
Oh. Veronica, your training's already done?
CLACK
RAGGED
SNIFFLE
If you'll excuse us.
...A father worries.
Princess Veronica... I suggest you wear protective gear tomorrow.
I appreciate the warning, but there's nothing like pain to really instill training into a body.
Besides, you don't wear protec-tive gear.
It's true. I suppose I would if there was even a 1% chance that you could hit me.
GRR!
You just never let up...
CLIK
CLIK
I meant no disre-spect.
By the way, what is this place ?
FLING
An under-ground swim-ming hole.

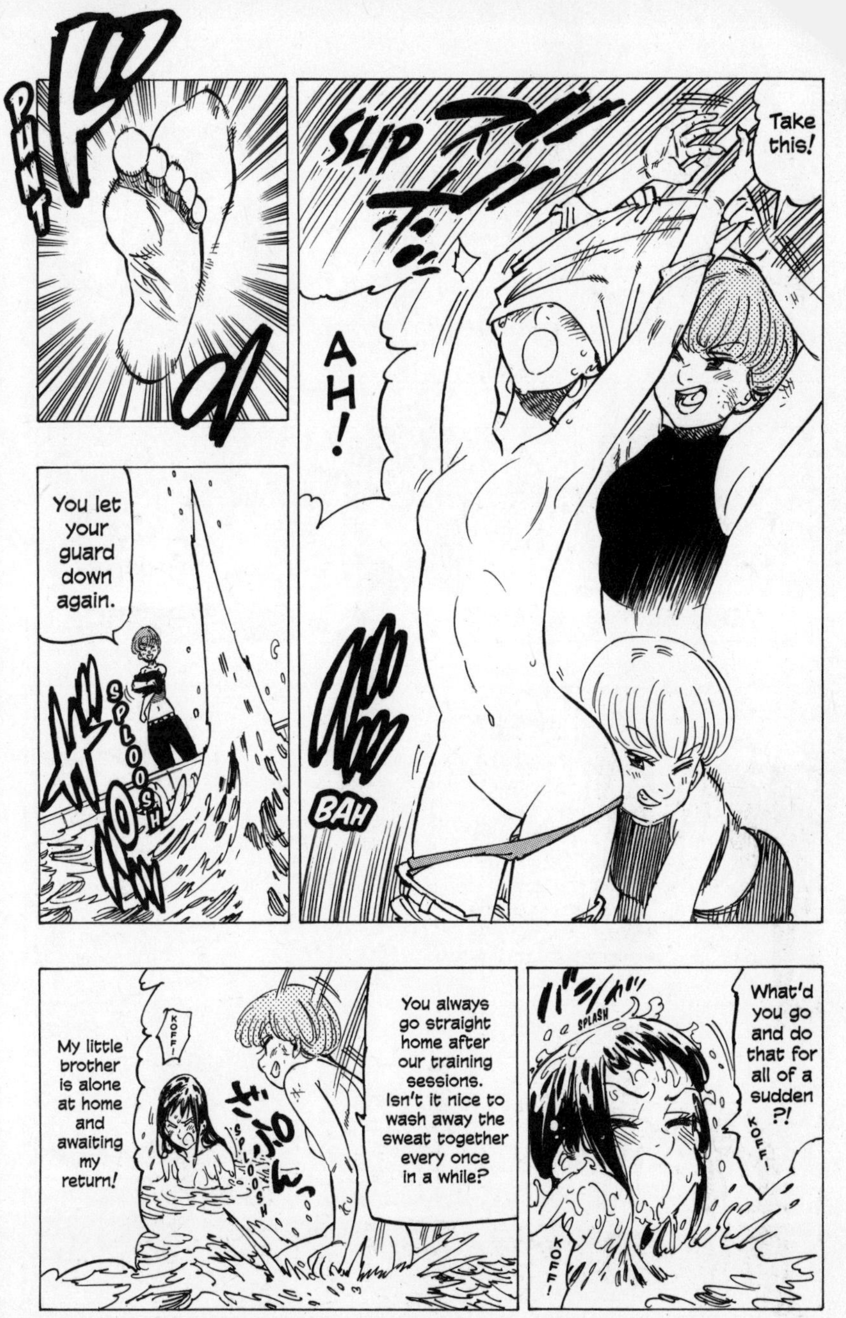

Take this!
SLIP
AH!
BAH
PUNT
You let your guard down again.
SPLOOSH
What'd you go and do that for all of a sudden?!
SPLASH
KOFF!
KOFF!
You always go straight home after our training sessions. Isn't it nice to wash away the sweat together every once in a while?
My little brother is alone at home and awaiting my return!
KOFF!
SPLOOSH

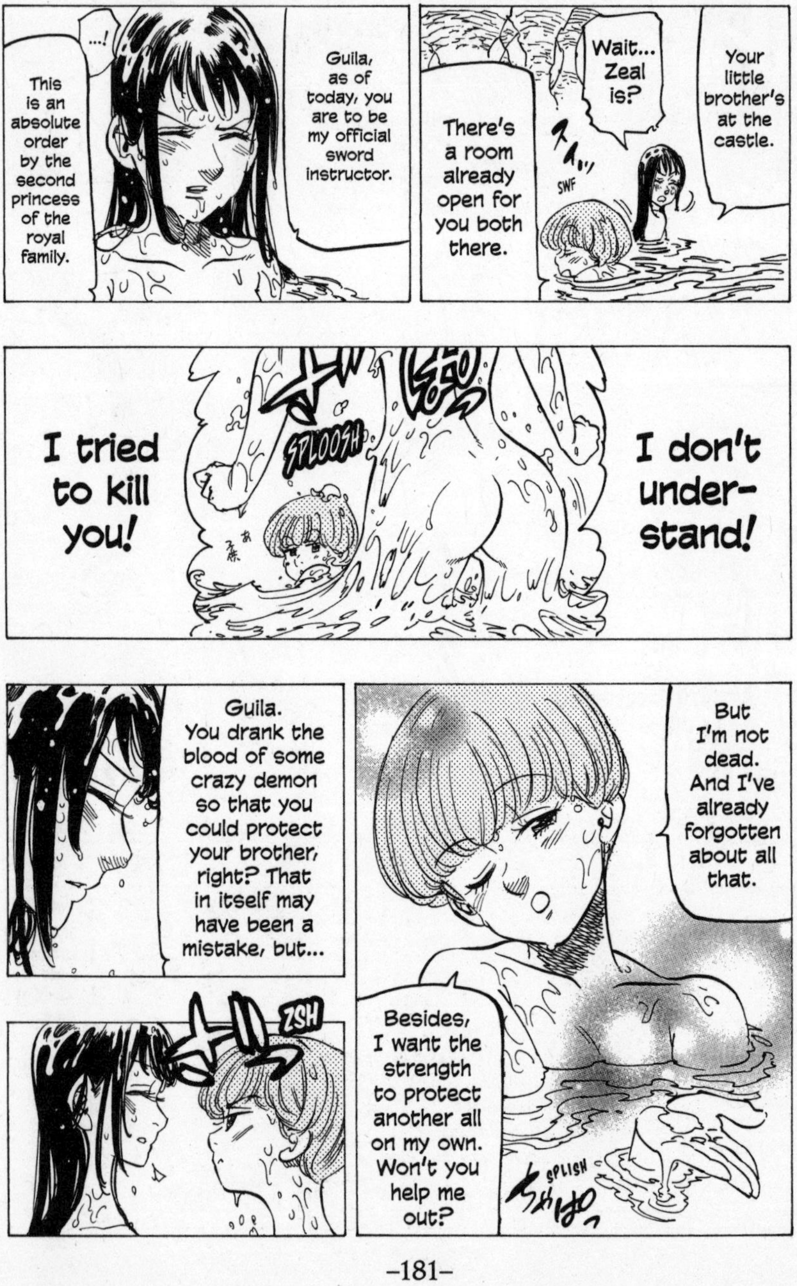
Your little brother's at the castle.
Wait... Zeal is?
SWF
There's a room already open for you both there.
Guila, as of today, you are to be my official sword instructor.
...!
This is an absolute order by the second princess of the royal family.
I don't under-stand!
SPLOOSH
I tried to kill you!
But I'm not dead. And I've already forgotten about all that.
Besides, I want the strength to protect another all on my own. Won't you help me out?
SPLISH
Guila. You drank the blood of some crazy demon so that you could protect your brother, right? That in itself may have been a mistake, but...
ZSH

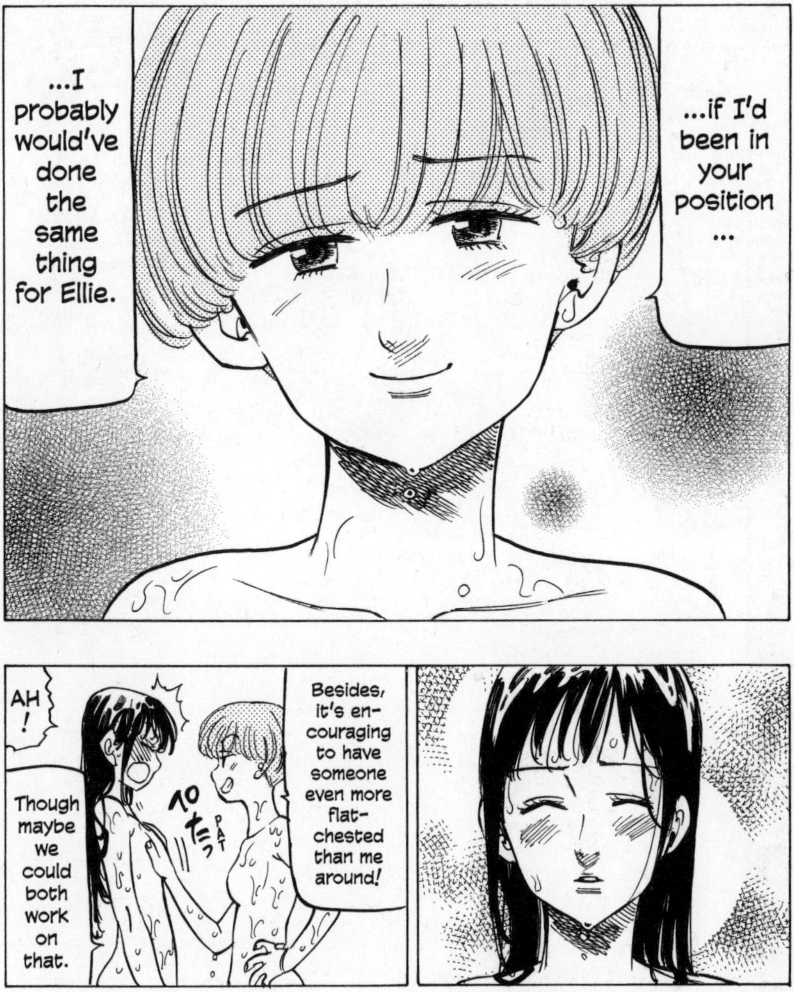
...if I'd been in your position ...
...I probably would've done the same thing for Ellie.
Besides, it's en-couraging to have someone even more flat-chested than me around!
AH!
PAT
Though maybe we could both work on that.
V... Veronica-sama!
BASH
Ow! Need I remind you I'm older than you?! Show some respect!
I will do no such thing!

THE END

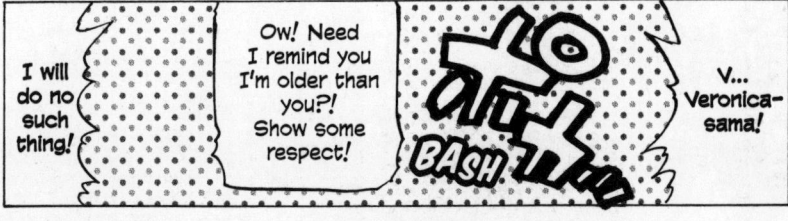

"THE DRAWING KNIGHTHOOD" SPACE

Be sure to include your name and location with your submission!!

M = H = E = D = B = K = G = MER = Es = EL = J =

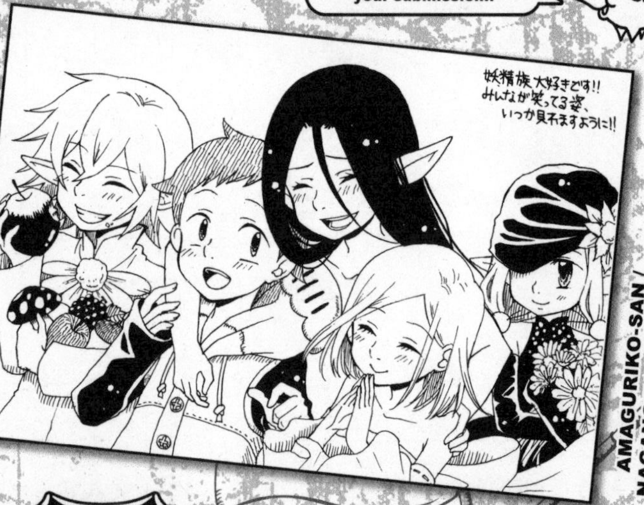
妖精族大好きです!!
みんなが笑ってる姿、
いつか見れますように!!

AMAGURIKO-SAN / NAGANO PREFECTURE

SPECIAL PRIZE

とく しょう

"Rumor has it that there are way too many unfortunate members of the Fairy Folk."

"...I want to be happy!! (sob)"

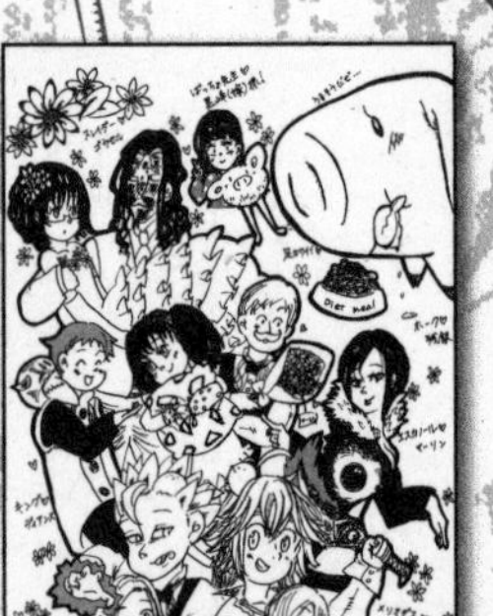

HENTAI ANGEL-SAN / KANAGAWA PREFECTURE

Es "It'd make me so glad if everyone could be happy."

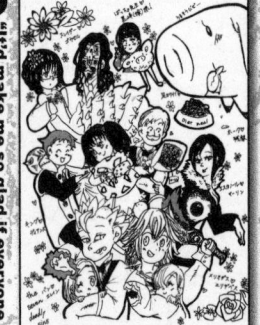

H "But there's two sets of strange couples missing."

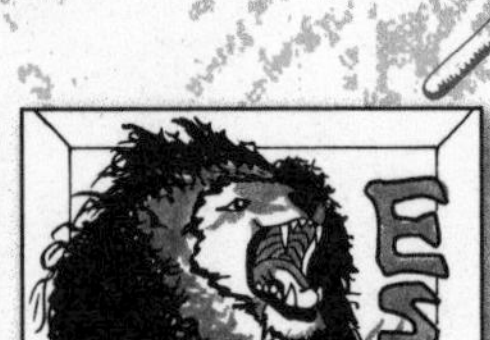
ESCANO

IYO BROTHERS-SAN / GUNMA PREFECTURE

E "There's something so elegant about Escanor-sama."

M "Hmmm. You're right... It's like he's the prince of some country."

SUMIKA MATSUBAYASHI-SAN / YAMANASHI PREFECTURE

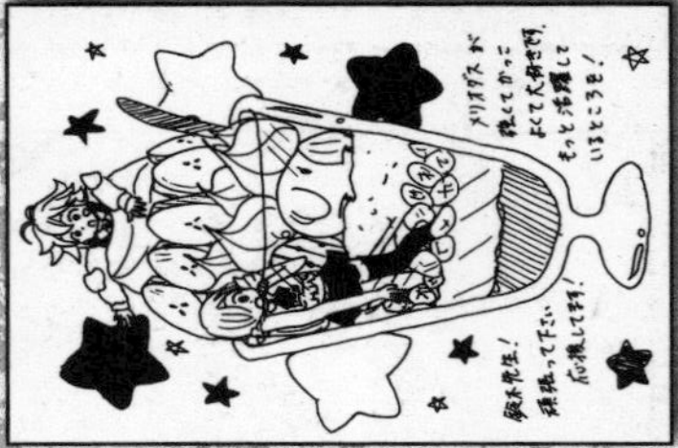
鈴木先生! 頑張って下さい 応援してます!
メリオダスが強くてかっこよくて大好きです。もっと活躍しているところを!

(M) "I'm going to lick off all the whipped cream that's stuck to you, Elizabeth!"

(E) "O...Okay! (blushing)"

LEONYA-SAN / NIIGATA PREFECTURE

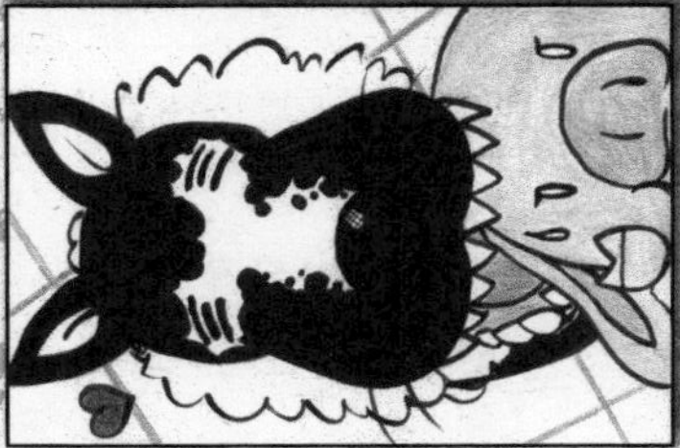

(H) "Ow! Ow! Knock it off, Oslo! You better not be mistaking me for a quick snack!"

(O) "Aroo arf! (Maybe just a little.)"

SHINICHIRO YUKIMARU / OSAKA

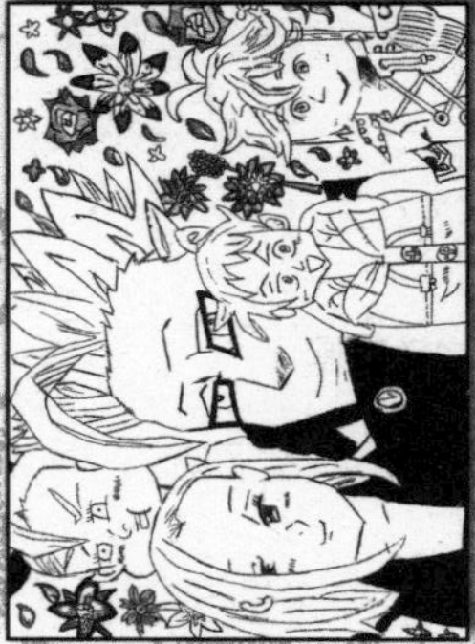

(M) "Well, well! Ban-san, you're quite the ladykiller."

(K) "Ban! If you make Elaine cry, then next time you'll get off with a lot worse than being turned to stone!"

MII-SAN / IWATE PREFECTURE

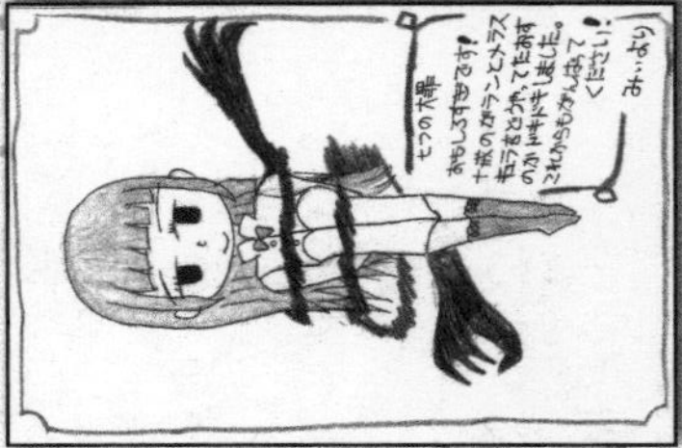

(H) "Though she looks cute, that girl's baaad news deep down!"

(B) "I hate girls like her the most." ♫

(J) "...Do you think she's really dead?"

NOZOMI KUSHIMOTO-SAN / SHIMANE PREFECTURE

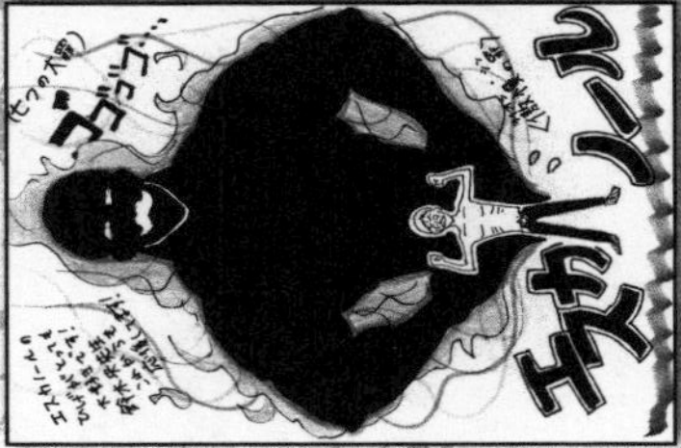
エスカノール

(K) "That mustache looks pretty good on you."

(Es) "Th...Thank you very much! (But I'd much prefer it if Merlin-san told me that.)"

GYOGYO-SAN / AOMORI PREFECTURE

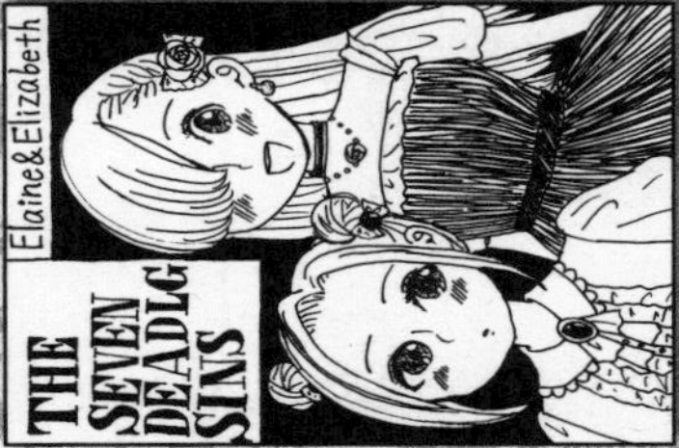
THE SEVEN DEADLG SINS
Elaine&Elizabeth

(El) "I feel like we'd get along! Let's take our time to get to know each other next time, okay?"

(E) "Yes! I'd love that!"

(D) "Hey! Let me join in, too!"

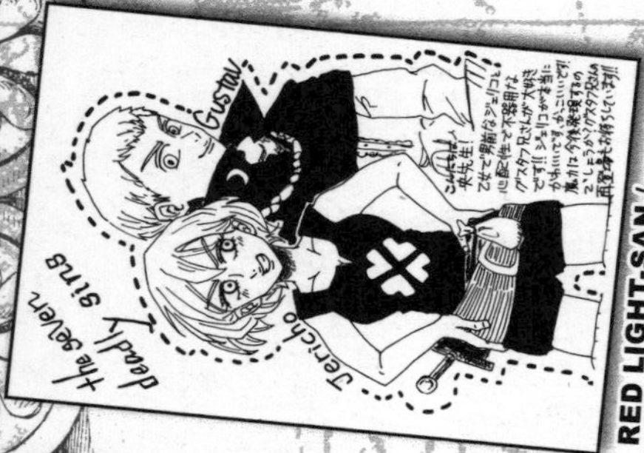
the seven deadly sins
Gustav
Jericho

RED LIGHT-SAN / MIE PREFECTURE

"These two siblings look the same but aren't anything alike! Unlike Elaine and I, who are two peas in a pod."

"Actually, you two don't share a single thing in common." ♫

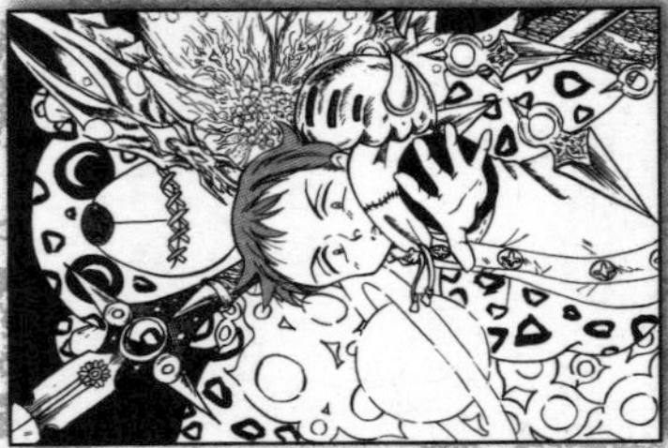

RADDO-SAN / KANAGAWA PREFECTURE

K "I've got to train hard so that I can call upon Chastiefol's powers easily."

EL "Don't give up, Brother!"

SAE TANABE-SAN / OKAYAMA PREFECTURE

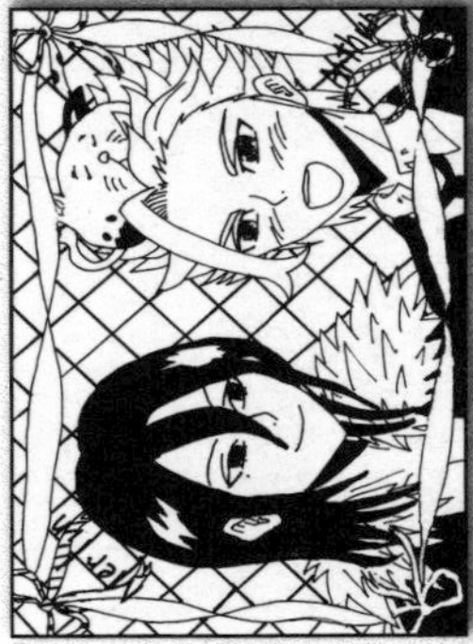

H "Merlin's always getting these big shots to fall for her."

M "But you can never tell what's on her mind."

AYA-SAN / EHIME PREFECTURE

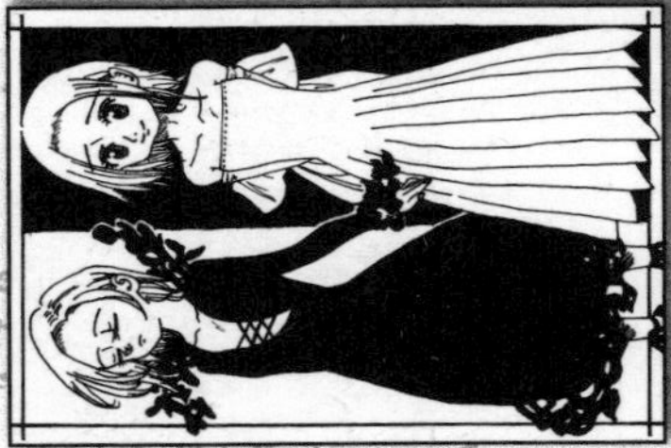

B "Whether black or white, Elaine is still Elaine." ♫

EL "Ban... I'm so happy!"

K "Ha ha... I-Isn't that nice?"

JUNYA TSUKAMOTO / IBARAKI PREFECTURE

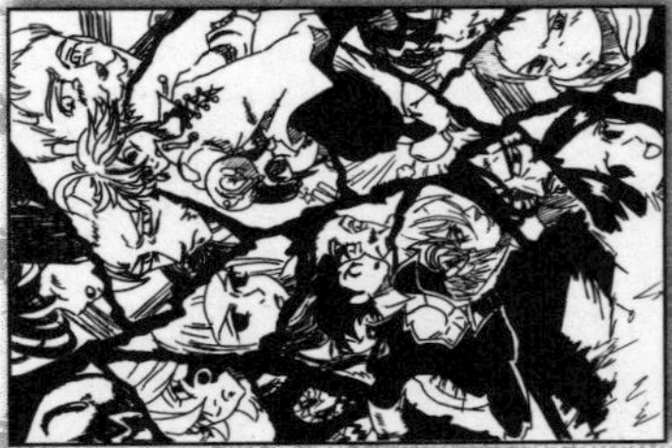

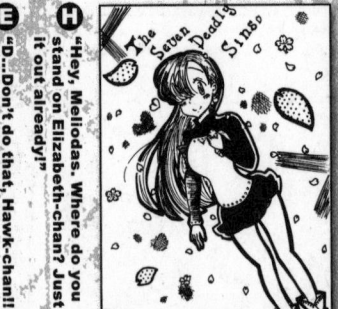

H "In Japanese, they're *Jikkai* but in English their name is 'The Ten Commandments!'"

D "Wow, that's kinda cool sounding!

MIHO HINATA-SAN / IWATE PREFECTURE

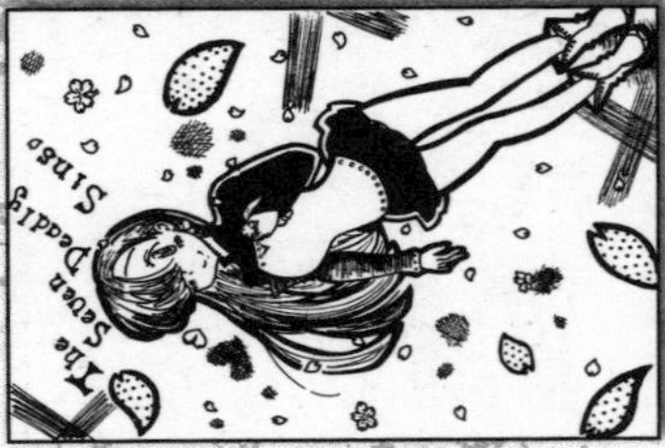
The Seven Deadly Sins

H "Hey, Meliodas. Where do you stand on Elizabeth-chan? Just spit it out already!"

E "D...Don't do that, Hawk-chan!! (blushing)"

メリオダス
ゼルドリス
エリザベス
リズ

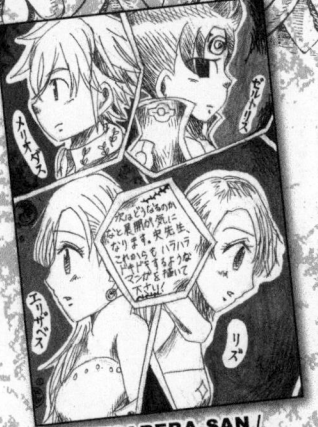

BETSARERA-SAN / SAITAMA PREFECTURE

"I really do wonder what went down in the captain's past... On one hand, I want to try asking him, on the other hand, I'm afraid to ask..."

じぇりコ
LOVE!
はう。

YEN-SAN / TOKYO

EI "Jericho's so adorable. You understand why I worry about her, don't you?"

K "Sorry. I don't."

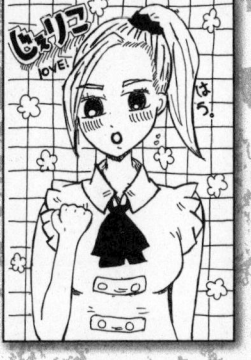

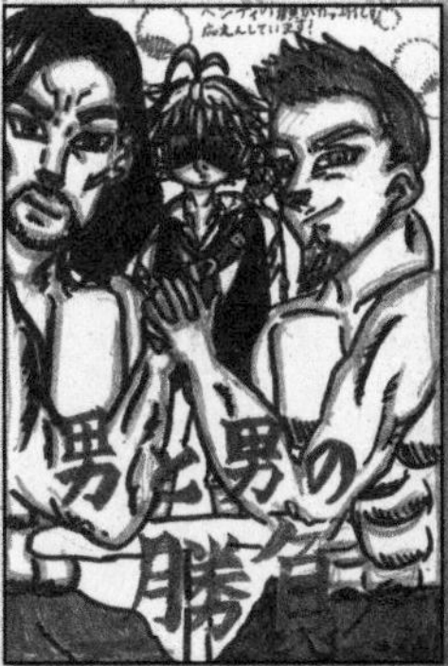

CHEESECAKE-SAN / SAITAMA PREFECTURE

M "Sorry, guys... But could you take your topless arm wrestling outside?"

HEN "Wh...Why?"

ホーク大すき♡

LEMON-SAN / TOKYO

H "I want a Sacred Treasure, too! Something that'd make me suuuuper strong, suuuuper cool, and would bring me tooooons of leftovers."

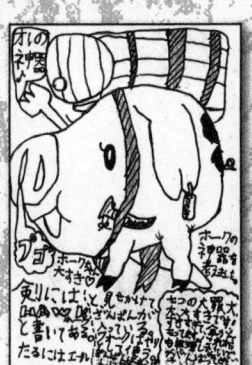

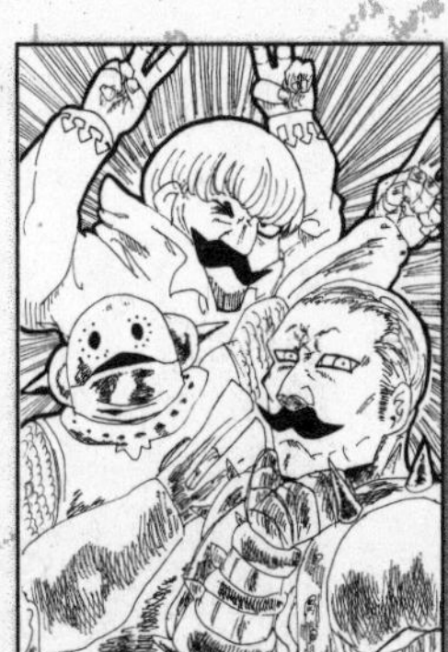

HINA-SAN / TOTTORI PREFECTURE

M "There's something about this clan... It's like they're way too closely related, you know?"

K "They're the frightful...Clan of Hunks!"

ALL "...Huh?"

E "They're like a grandpa and his grandchild."

M "You're not altogether wrong. Gloxinia does have a pretty young face, and Galland is the old-timer of The Ten Commandments."

〈十戒〉大好きッス!
いつも…
七つの大罪…

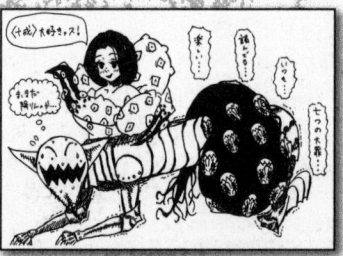

OCEAN-SAN / YAMAGUCHI PREFECTURE

FISH-SAN / HOKKAIDO

M "We're all going on an ogre extermination!"

K "The ogre...is s-so cute.♥"

H "That blasted pheasant turned sides lickety-split!"

FISH-SAN / HOKKAIDO

M "Looking at this reminded me! Aren't pet-friendly pubs all the rage?"

H "Snoink! I'm no pet!!"

SAYAKA MAESUMI-SAN / NAGANO PREFECTURE

NEW
BOAR HAT

E "Is this Hawk's Mama's reopening after being remodeled? She's adorable!"

H "This version makes it look the rooms are even more spacious up to the very top."

MINOHO YOKAWA-SAN / TOKYO

鈴木央先生
いつも見ています
これからもがんばってください!!

G "I did some investigating, and it seems that this cat is by no means an ordinary cat."

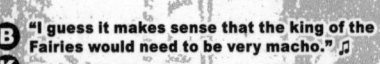

H "Uh, I think anybody can tell that just by looking."

TESHIO-SAN / MIYAGI PREFECTURE

H "Well, my Combat Class has already exceeded his."

G "The fact that you can say that with a straight face is most impressive, Captain of Scraps Disposal."

B "I guess it makes sense that the king of the Fairies would need to be very macho." ♫

K "Hmm? Apparently the second king was pretty macho, though."

The seven deadly sins
Fairy King
Harlequin

NARIMI INDE-SAN / IBARAKI PREFECTURE

ELIZABETH

ASUKA SUGIYAMA-SAN / YAMAGATA PREFECTURE

M "I'll be thinking up your next outfit, so look forward to it!"

HARUNA TANAKA-SAN / EHIME PREFECTURE

E "Heh heh... I will!"

B "Come on, just 'fess up already." ♫

K "Why am I being blamed as the culprit?"

D "Say it! Say it! ♥"

K "Okay! I did it!!"

SPICA-SAN / TOKYO

D "Yaaay! ♥ Matrona!!"

H "Looking at you now, you really do come off as childish, Diane."

B "She's a downright brat. Utterly and completely." ♫

M "I'm curious about what Arthur's magic is and Cath who lives on his head. Oh, well... Arthur doesn't seem all that concerned about himself."

HYDRANGE-SAN / NIIGATA PREFECTURE

HARUKA MINAMIKO-SAN / KAGOSHIMA PREFECTURE

E "When Hawk-chan's around, it's like we're in a field of flowers!"

H "You're the only one who ever puts it like that, Elizabeth-chan. (sob)"

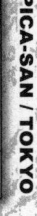

YUKIONNA-SAN / FUKUSHIMA PREFECTURE

E "Here you go, Diane! This floral hair decoration's for you."

D "Then I'll make a flower crown for you!"

MER "I'm surprised how deft they can be."

EGBERT II-SAN / CHIBA PREFECTURE

おっぱいを揉ませてくれ。
『七つの大罪』楽しませてもらっています。先生の絵はとても魅力的です。メリオダスの真顔で変なことするのが個人的に気に入っています。これからも応援しています!!

K "Only the captain would (could) say this..."

Es "Maybe that's why he's the Captain of The Seven Deadly Sins."

CAPTAIN OF THE "BAN-ELA SHIP"-SAN / OKAYAMA PREFECTURE

Happy Birthday
しばし休戦..

M "Here! Have a piece of Ban's birthday cake!"

B "Come on, Master, don't eat it ahead of us!"

MANAKA MAEKAWA-SAN / NARA PREFECTURE

"Look at this masterpiece! It looks like a rubber stamp!"

"Besides you, Hawk, the rest must've been quite an undertaking!"

Now Accepting Applicants for the Drawing Knighthood!

- Draw your picture on a postcard, or paper no larger than a postcard, and send it in!
- Don't forget to write your name and location on the back of your picture!
- You can include comments or not. And colored illustrations will still only be displayed in B&W!
- The Drawing Knights whose pictures are particularly noteworthy and run in the print edition will be gifted with a signed, specially-made pencil board!
- And the best overall will be granted the special prize of a signed shikishi!!

Send to:

The Seven Deadly Sins Drawing Knighthood

c/o Kodansha Comics 451 Park Ave. South, 7th floor,

New York, NY 10016

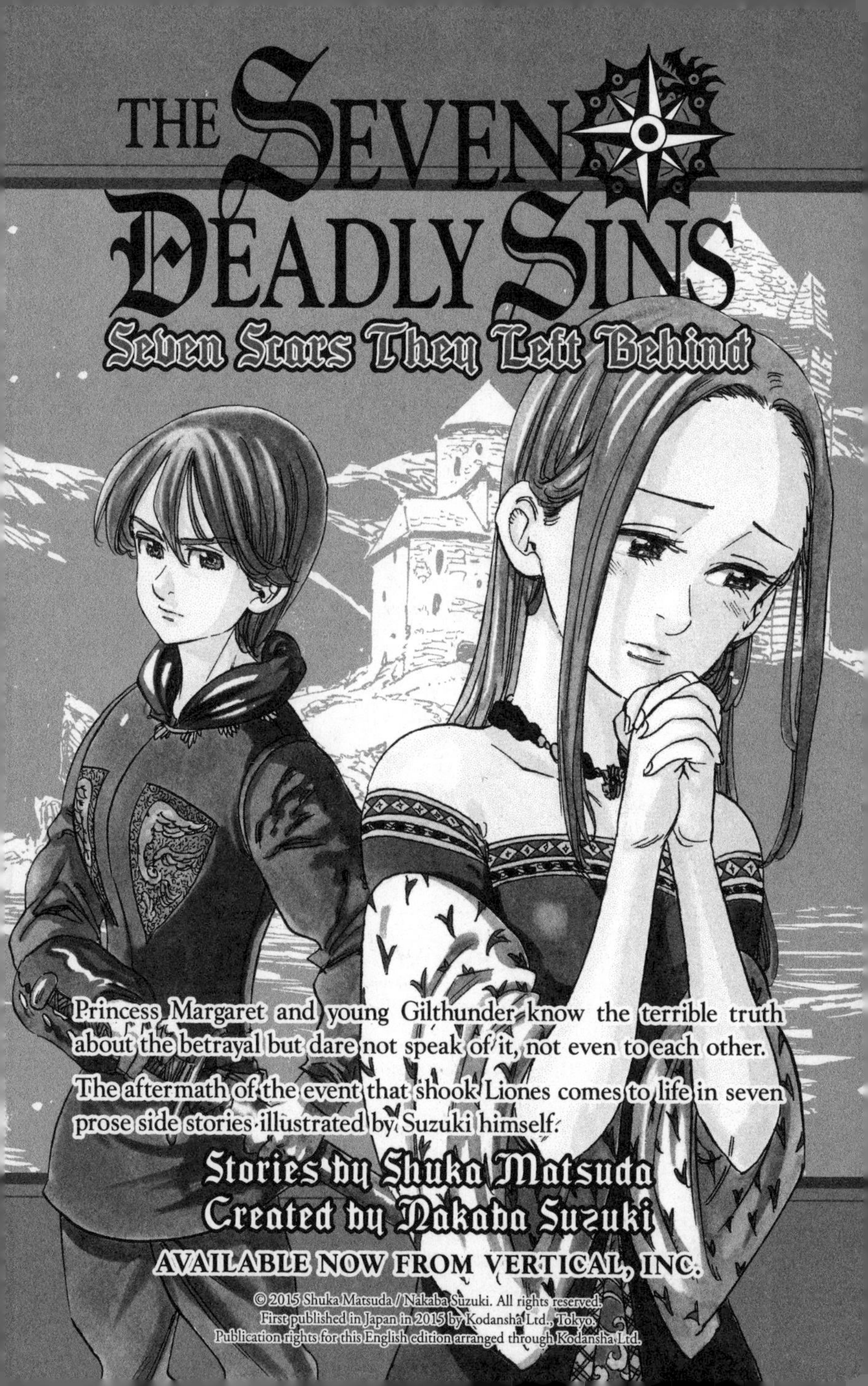
THE SEVEN DEADLY SINS
Seven Scars They Left Behind
Princess Margaret and young Gilthunder know the terrible truth about the betrayal but dare not speak of it, not even to each other.
The aftermath of the event that shook Liones comes to life in seven prose side stories illustrated by Suzuki himself.
Stories by Shuka Matsuda
Created by Nakaba Suzuki
AVAILABLE NOW FROM VERTICAL, INC.
© 2015 Shuka Matsuda / Nakaba Suzuki. All rights reserved.
First published in Japan in 2015 by Kodansha Ltd., Tokyo.
Publication rights for this English edition arranged through Kodansha Ltd.

KC
KODANS
COMICS

FIRESOLDIER
8
TOKYO
CO2

A new series from the creator of *Soul Eater*, the megahit manga and anime seen on Toonami!

"Fun and lively... a great start!"
-Adventures in Poor Taste

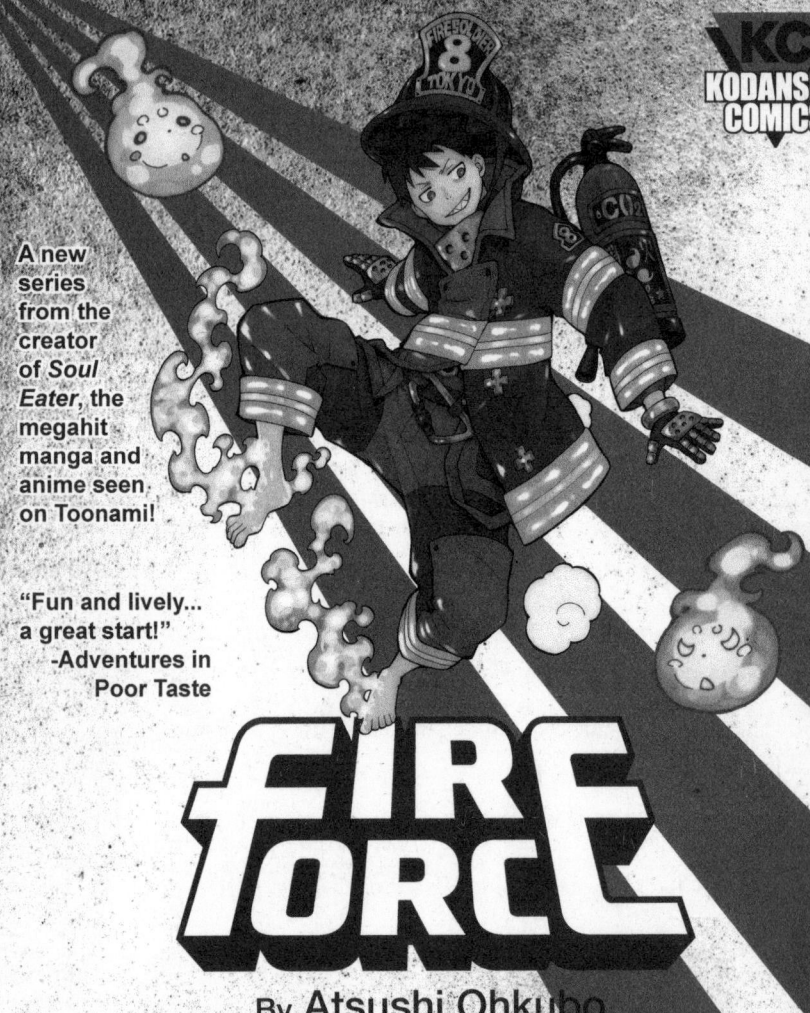

FIRE FORCE

By Atsushi Ohkubo

The city of Tokyo is plagued by a deadly phenomenon: spontaneo human combustion! Luckily, a special team is there to quench t inferno: The Fire Force! The fire soldiers at Special Fire Cathedra are about to get a unique addition. Enter Shinra, a boy who possess the power to run at the speed of a rocket, leaving behind the famo "devil's footprints" (and destroying his shoes in the proces Can Shinra and his colleagues discover the source of this stran epidemic before the city burns to ashes?

The Seven Deadly Sins volume 21 is a work of fiction. Names, characters, places, and incidents are the products of the author's imagination or are used fictitiously. Any resemblance to actual events, locales, or persons, living or dead, is entirely coincidental.

A Kodansha Comics Trade Paperback Original.

Published in the United States by Kodansha Comics, an imprint of Kodansha USA Publishing, LLC, New York.

Publication rights for this English edition arranged through Kodansha Ltd., Tokyo.

First published in Japan in 2016 by Kodansha Ltd., Tokyo.

ISBN 978-1-63236-442-5

Printed in the United States of America.

www.kodanshacomics.com

9 8 7 6 5 4 3 2 1

Translation: Christine Dashiell
Lettering: James Dashiell
Editing: Lauren Scanlan
Kodansha Comics edition cover design: Phil Balsman